WAR AND SURVIVAL IN SUDAN'S FRONTIERLANDS

War and Survival in Sudan's Frontierlands

Voices from the Blue Nile

WENDY JAMES

OXFORD
UNIVERSITY PRESS

OXFORD

UNIVERSITY PRESS

Great Clarendon Street, Oxford OX2 6DP

Oxford University Press is a department of the University of Oxford.
It furthers the University's objective of excellence in research, scholarship,
and education by publishing worldwide in

Oxford New York

Auckland Cape Town Dar es Salaam Hong Kong Karachi
Kuala Lumpur Madrid Melbourne MexicoCity Nairobi
New Delhi Shanghai Taipei Toronto

With offices in

Argentina Austria Brazil Chile Czech Republic France Greece
Guatemala Hungary Italy Japan Poland Portugal Singapore
South Korea Switzerland Thailand Turkey Ukraine Vietnam

Oxford is a registered trade mark of Oxford University Press
in the UK and in certain other countries

Published in the United States
by Oxford University Press Inc., New York

British Library Cataloguing in Publication Data

Data available

Library of Congress Cataloging in Publication Data

Data available

Typeset by SPI Publisher Services Ltd, Pondicherry, India
Printed in Great Britain
on acid-free paper by
Biddles Ltd., King's Lynn Norfolk

ISBN 978–0–19–929867–9

1 3 5 7 9 10 8 6 4 2

For Douglas

Map 1. The Sudan: provinces, main towns, and CPA boundary

Preface
The People, the Place,
and the Making of this Book

In the course of our lifetimes, the Sudan has become a byword for conflict and suffering, for vulnerable human beings caught between ambitious rebels and intransigent governments. Siblings, parents and children, and wider communities who used to live together are now separated, even set at odds against each other. By 2006 the Darfur war had become known across the globe, provoking almost everyone to have an opinion, from American accusations of genocide to Al Qaeda's threats to join in if UN peacekeepers showed up there. The preceding decades of civil war are much less well known, and have never been so publicly championed or criticized. Moreover, the 'first' and 'second' Sudanese civil wars, as they are known, are often located firmly 'in the south', or described as 'the southern problem'. In fact these struggles, especially the second, 1983–2005, involved large sections of the Sudanese people from all regions. There was convincing political support and military success by the Sudan People's Liberation Movement/Sudan People's Liberation Army (SPLM/SPLA) in some localities of the 'northern' as well as 'southern' provinces. The earlier wars inside the Sudan have, moreover, all impinged on several neighbouring countries, as we now see happening in the far west as Khartoum's military projects extend from Darfur into Chad. It is not always understood how intimately the events of the war in Darfur, though usually treated as something separate, in fact arose directly from the same structural tensions as the wars which originated in the south in the mid-1950s; and how the twenty-first-century techniques of insurgency and especially counter-insurgency in Darfur have their prototypes in the earlier struggles.

The sheer technology of war has intensified, of course, and the pace of events has been speeded up through key players' access to the new electronic communications. But as this study shows, all the elements of the Darfur situation which developed from 2003 were foreshadowed—not just in the core military and strategic southern arenas of Upper Nile, Jonglei, and Bahr el Ghazal provinces—but also in the 'marginal' areas transitional between north and south, such as the Nuba Hills, or adjacent to neighbouring countries, such as the Blue Nile region in relation to Eritrea and Ethiopia. Here, in the frontierlands of the old core of the Sudanese state, we find settled farming communities with distinct languages and cultural traditions. Many of them are now Muslims, long accustomed to using Arabic as a lingua franca, and managing in a more or less successful way to live with seasonal nomadic pastoral groups, both 'Arab' and of West African provenance. But partly because of their long engagement with the central state-forming core of the Sudanese state, here—as now in Darfur too—we find a terrible transformation effected by modern civil war.

The scenario seems familiar from contemporary media reports. Small parties of armed opposition appear in remote regions; this brings down the heavy wrath of the national armed forces, plus the co-opting of nomadic herders and other local men as militia. The local farming communities have their crops and houses burned, and are obliged to flee. The rebel groups may promise them liberation and a return to their homeland, but repeated reverses in the fortunes of the front-line battle over many years, intensified by the presence of an 'active' international frontier, mean that a generation and more are born in exile and if they do return home it will be to a rather different place. International interests take sides and through selective relief support can complicate the war itself. The humanitarian industry has to maintain a politically neutral stance, though inevitably through distributing goods it becomes part of the conflict and has to negotiate its way with assorted sovereign governments and rebel groups. Aid reports, along with those of many academics, focus on material issues of needs for shelter, food, and medicine for civilians, while seeming impotent to deal with the political or military conditions that have produced the crisis in the first place. They do try, these days, to incorporate some account of the 'voices of the people' in such reports, though this is actually very difficult to do in the middle of a crisis, especially when the 'beneficiaries' have learned to appear uninvolved in the politics around them. My contribution here addresses this issue head on.

This book investigates the experience of people caught up in events that led up to the wholesale sacking of villages in the southern part of the northern Sudanese province of Blue Nile in 1987, and what has happened since to their sense of a shared life across the major forced separations of a very changed world. The focus is on the people known in the academic literature, and increasingly in the wider world of humanitarian and Sudanese political reportage, as 'Uduk'. Calling themselves the '*kwanim pa* or 'we home people', the Uduk are just one 'traditional' community of north-east Africa who have been battered and divided through the civil wars and international upheavals of the last two generations. My book on one level is a concentrated story of this 'one group' but their experience resonates with that of many dozens, even hundreds, of similar cases in north-east Africa, most particularly the indigenous minorities in the hilly peripheries of the northern Sudan and across its frontiers into Ethiopia. This study is a sequel to my earlier volumes, '*Kwanim Pa: The Making of the Uduk People. An Ethnographic Study of Survival in the Sudan–Ethiopian Borderlands* (1979) and *The Listening Ebony: Moral Knowledge, Religion and Power amongst the Uduk of Sudan* (1988). The world described in those books was destroyed, in the physical sense, along with the continuing loss of many human lives, when the Sudanese civil war engulfed the 'homeland' described there. The villages were mostly burned to the ground in 1987, the crops and animals destroyed or looted, and the surviving people had to flee.

This book is not a conventional ethnography, in the expected style of a cultural account linked to some framework of 'dramatic unity' in place and time, or what in anthropology we have called 'the ethnographic present'. To the extent that it is an analysis of cultural tradition it could not have been imagined when I first went to the southern Blue Nile in 1965. No one could have forecast, then, the extraordinary story of multiple upheavals that were to visit that region. This book does present in outline the political events, and the circumstances of displacement and change which are on the surface the most important things that have shaped the lives of all Uduk communities since the flight of 1987, and in this respect it is a kind of 'history' rather than social or cultural anthropology. But at the same time I have attempted to tell the story of these changes and events through the words, and experiences, of the people themselves. This does not mean that I have presented a merely local view, or the story of what has happened to a relatively closed social world. In my first book I pointed to key memories of late nineteenth-century disturbances in the region and how they shaped the 'present' social world of the 1960s. By here taking the theme of history a little further back, to the fairly violent processes of state formation on the southern fringes of the Sudanese state over a couple of centuries, I show how communities on such a frontier are not merely changed *in situ* but how their people have been and still are co-opted into the body of the predatory state itself. Some are drawn in, and others are left out; but this is not a final or permanent severing of ties or cultural 'belonging'. Values and practices change both among those who are absorbed into the political and civil society of the core state, and among those who are excluded, or who flee the state. While it is true both in the past and present of the Uduk community that social and cultural activities among the latter seem to flourish by drawing on a deep archive of ideas and memories and artistic skills, today this is happening among those newly drawn together in the refugee context alongside an appetite for 'modern' education and religious identity. It is even more true today than it was in the nineteenth century that links and exchanges are maintained between the separated members of a community like this one poised on a frontier, though the 'politics' of the time can keep them apart for long periods.

These dimensions of the life of refugees over the changing shapes of political space and time are not easily recognized in studies focused on the displaced as such. It is only by chance that I have been able to see and investigate these aspects of the longer-term social history of the Uduk, through having had the opportunity to live with them and learn something of their language and ideas some time before disaster struck. The factual material in this book is based on a series of fairly short field trips, mostly in the context of emergency humanitarian aid over the last twenty years, but my interpretations have been informed by the earlier fieldwork. While this particular story has to be very 'local' in its specific detail, it is presented as only one example of what must be a set of general processes affecting what were formerly fairly coherent and continuing rural communities who find themselves transformed into frontier societies.

My first contact with some of the displaced was in 1988 in Khartoum. To these, however, the majority had been lost sight of, as they had disappeared over the frontier to 'communist' Ethiopia. This turned out to be no safe haven, however, as the Cold War came to an end and the

Mengistu regime started to crumble. Nor could there be a return home, given the escalation in the Sudanese war prompted by the Islamist coup of Omer el Beshir in 1989. These twin events precipitated an extraordinary saga of zigzag flight for the refugees as they had no choice but to move further and further southwards from their Blue Nile home. Over the five years from 1987 to 1992 the core population of the *'kwanim pa* crossed one way or another over the international frontier five times. It was not until 2006 that an official repatriation programme was initiated. I have had opportunities to visit 'the Uduk in exile' at different points along the way and over the years, specifically Nasir in the southern Sudan (1991), Karmi (1992, 1993) and Bonga (1994, 2000) in Ethiopia, and in the USA (2002, 2006). I have also seen individuals on occasion in Kenya (1989, 1995, 2003, 2005) and once in the UK. These visits are listed, along with relevant regional events and political changes, in the Appendix. I am much indebted to regular contact with a network of Sudanese friends and acquaintance, from both northern and southern areas of the country, and with academic colleagues from all over the world engaged with Sudanese and Ethiopian affairs.

The book opens with a sketch of how the major movements of political change in the global arena over the last century and a half transformed the nature of the world for 'remote' peoples indigenous to the region I call the Blue Nile Borderlands. This encompasses the north-western hilly country of the Ethiopian plateau drained by the Blue Nile and its tributaries, together with the adjacent escarpments, extending ridges, and outlying hills which fall into the Sudanese plains. This region had, and to some extent still has, a geographical, historical, and cultural coherence but it has been divided politically and its people fragmented by the processes of imperial and post-imperial history. Competition between the newly 'modern' nations of the Sudan and Ethiopia and, more recently, controversies over Eritrea and the new north/south division in the Sudan, have sharpened up issues relating to borders and have profoundly affected conditions of life and death among the communities located on either side of them. Whereas, at one time, what these might have had in common were aspects of cultural tradition and practice, today they have been thrown together by events and could be said to share a set of similar historical experiences.

I indicate, in particular, how the making of the central section of the modern boundary between the Sudan and Ethiopia in the early twentieth century created special 'frontier' places where people were drawn together in new ways, and whose subsequent history was very much at the mercy of border politics. I also point to the way in which an increasingly sharp sense of difference between the northern and the southern Sudan during the Condominium period led to a new internal frontier zone, and therefore new strategic frontier places. Looked at from the centre of the Sudanese state, the town of Kurmuk has always been a frontier post guarding the border with Ethiopia; and from the time of the Second World War onwards its twin town across the small ravine that marks the border has been of strategic significance also to the Ethiopian state. From Khartoum's perspective, the village of Chali, where a station of the Sudan Interior Mission (SIM) was set up in 1938, has always been on the very threshold of 'the south', and was irrelevant to the concerns of Ethiopia until very recently. While the frontier character of these places was established long before the time of Sudanese independence, their significance has intensified in the post-imperial era of rising nationalism, international and global economic competition, and the pressures exerted by religious and regional movements. Here I can only summarize some of the ways in which these processes, emanating from the world's centres of power and influence, have impinged directly on our region since the time of the Sudan's independence in 1956, and on the Ethiopian side especially since the overthrow of the imperial Ethiopian regime in 1974. These major events created the conditions in which peoples of the region found themselves catapulted together into new kinds of modernity among the world's 'marginalized'.

One of the increasingly strident claims from the world's marginalized has been for 'self-determination', for the right of 'self-evidently' distinct groups of people to have control over the way they live, including at least some political control over their immediate home area and its resources. What are these groups, though, and what are the boundaries between them, especially the territorial boundaries which have in the end to be drawn on the ground? How small can such a group be without foundering among the competing claims of larger projects? How tiny can be an armed project for the liberation of the homeland? Can the relative independence that a remote group might have enjoyed ever be regained after it has struggled for a new kind of 'liberty' against a modernizing state?

A day in late 1986 illustrates this problem in an iconic way. A small band of young men are trudging through the African bush loaded with supplies, slung with Kalashnikovs, and carrying rocket-propelled grenades on their shoulders. They have completed their training nearby, and are intent on liberating their own district from the current government, locally represented by one small garrison. Unfortunately their approach is reported by a pro-government militia, and the guerrilla band is routed. The regime has meanwhile been recruiting young men from the very same region into its armed forces as part of national policy to strengthen the state. Some of these are among the forces who undertake massive counter-insurgency measures over the next few months, destroying any civilian support base. Villagers scatter into the bush, where those who do not die of hunger and thirst are escorted to a place of safety by their own youngsters now in the rebel movement. The final 'settlement' some decades later scarcely meets the ideals of self-determination or liberation in an imagined new democracy that had motivated the first generation of fighters.

The place was Chali in the Kurmuk district of the Blue Nile Province of the northern Sudan; the footsoldiers approaching their own homeland in late 1986 were the home lads, the *ucim pa* (literally 'children of the home' or 'Uduk youngsters') who had been trained just over the border in Ethiopia and now constituted the Arrow Battalion of the SPLA. The story of their adventure, their fate, and the continuing consequences is told in the three main parts of this book, along with a number of different perspectives on the memory of that time when a peaceful backwater became a war zone. Though a generation has now passed, what happened that day seems, to surviving relatives in exile and now separated by hundreds or even thousands of miles, only the day before yesterday. The memory of the intervening years has almost been suspended among those who talk about that fateful set of events, and hang on to the fiction that one day things will return to rights. In fact, the intervening twenty years have seen all kinds of transformations which cannot be undone; the status quo will never return. That day in 1986, initially one of hope and a degree of honour and glory, had consequences which in retrospect one could construe as a historical tragedy for the people involved. And for many others—including, in a marginal way, myself—the events of that day have led to a set of dilemmas almost impossible to resolve. That stab at self-determination, by guerrillas who happened to belong to a minority group 'transitional' between the north and south of Sudan, has led to further ambiguities of 'identity' and further obstacles to the re-establishment of peaceful community life 'back home'. Sudan's Comprehensive Peace Agreement signed on 9 January 2005 between the regime of Omer el Beshir and the SPLM has inevitably created new compromises on the ground, especially in the southern Blue Nile where the salience of boundaries is now more marked than before.

The three chapters of Part I below set out the way that international pressures and projects of the states in the region led to the series of battles for Kurmuk and for Chali that have shaped lives there since 1986. The chapters in Part II follow the treks of the displaced southwards from the Blue Nile. They are heavy with a sense of *déjà vu* for those who have read my first ethnography; here is a rerun of the 'survival story' of the *'kwanim pa,* as far as possible through their own words, and in their own idiom, inevitably reflecting those stories I heard in the 1960s of their remembered flights and displacements of the previous century, in response to the violent depredations of the then expanding Sudanese and Ethiopian states. Those earlier stories reflected a strong motive towards survival especially in the 1890s, and the same is true of the stories now told of the 1990s. Through relying as far as possible on the words of the people themselves, I hope to help combat those stereotypes of passivity and helpless victimhood which are so common in western media reports and in fact also in the reports of humanitarian agencies in Africa's war zones. In the face of the locally violent outcome of the projects and targets of the powerful, as detailed in Part I, there is indeed real suffering and tragedy. But here I try to emphasize also the agency and active roles of the 'vernacular' social world, across the boundaries and oppositions of the formal political spaces—and the 'regathering of the clans' from time to time as it were.

Twenty years after the destruction of their villages, a visitor would find much familiar in the initial appearance of everyday life among the *'kwanim pa* in the refugee settlements in Ethiopia; neat, clean huts framed by a few well-kept stands of maize; the language apparently flourishing, the music, song, and social world generally very recognizable. A photo of a family outside their home here might suggest that little was wrong. Even without the underpinning securities of a citizen's rights in land and resources, surprisingly, the non-material aspects of their world may have 'survived' in some surprisingly creative ways. The final part of the book concentrates on some of these themes, many of which were set out in my earlier books, and suggests how powerfully a network of overlapping memory and practice can thrive through the life of a vernacular language, recreating old patterns even in the most 'modern' circumstances. Here I focus on the ways displaced people thrown together are able, or at least are trying, to turn their experiences into 'art', into fun with language, dramatic narratives, provocative enactments, witty songs, resurgent dances, and music. These activities and expressions are not a matter of simple 'survival', or 'coping', or even 'healing'—in the bland language of the humanitarian agencies. Some of the results of deeply impassioned modes of understanding the truth of one's situation in the world are more complex than this, less obviously palliative, less 'well behaved'. The cultural imagination can even inform decisions over political and violent action.

This work is offered as a contribution to historical anthropology, spanning the years from the resurgence of civil war in the Sudan in 1983, the year when the SPLA was founded, up to the year of the Comprehensive Peace Agreement between the Sudan government and the SPLA of January 2005. Within that period, I attempt to sketch the pattern of military events and engagements as they affected the southern Blue Nile up to about 1997, but not beyond. Details of what is going on currently in a war zone are often hidden from a fieldworker anyway, and the story can only be put together from later memories and reflections. The later chapters focusing on the remaking of social relations and the re-creation of cultural life focus mainly on the period from 1994–2000, when I had chances to spend time in the refugee scheme at Bonga. Memory, events, and expectations for the future are all linked, and in an ongoing social history there is no clear beginning and no convenient ending. For this reason I provide an introduction which draws attention to the formation of characteristically 'frontier' social patterns in the past, especially those of the eastern frontierlands of the Sudan in the nineteenth century which foreshadow the present.

This book does not attempt to deal in detail with very recent events, and in particular recent military events. In so far as I draw on individual testimony from military actors, whether on the Sudan government side or from the SPLA, these are all persons who have long since retired from the fray. Enough time has passed, however, for us to see from their testimonies something of the way Sudan's 'second civil war' actually took root in the southern Blue Nile. Those former public figures whose voices I quote, such as Stephen Missa Dhunya, Sudan army brigadier (now retired), or Peter Kuma Luyin, the first Uduk officer in the SPLA (now retired), have all since entered into work concerned with peace negotiations and civilian development projects. I have made it clear when I occasionally use a pseudonym for an individual. To study relations between past and present in a war zone is problematic: the journalist or human rights investigator on the spot may hear many accounts, and be able to give a better overall snapshot of the political situation than I could, but how do their findings relate to memory, to ongoing processes, and to the unspoken? In the central chapters of this book I have distinguished between things I heard on the spot, or at least close to an event, and things I was told later, in some cases twenty years later. The advantage of a little distance in time, even a decade or two, helps justify the project of a historical anthropology. If left too late, the historian might find all living testimony has gone. The anthropologist with a collection of testimonies, recorded perhaps in notebooks but especially on tape over a long period of time, can try not only to trace connections herself between events and experiences over recent history, but also the changing ways the people themselves make these connections in memory.

I have been inspired by the researches of many colleagues who have studied the marginalized regions of north-east Africa. The closest geographically to my own work on the eastern Sudan border are those of Charles Jedrej and Akira Okazaki on the Ingessana (or Gamk) and Joachim Theis on the Koma. Jedrej has also contributed powerful historical analysis of the 'frontier' character of the southern periphery of the old Funj Kingdom of Sennar on the Blue Nile. On the Eritrean and Ethiopian sides of the Blue Nile Borderlands, from north to south relevant works would be those of Dominique Lussier on the Kunama, Berihun Mebratie Mekonnen and Wolde-Selassie Abbute Deboch on the Gumuz, Laura Hammond on resettled Amhara refugees in northern Ethiopia, Alessandro Triulzi on western Ethiopia, Eisei Kurimoto on the Anuak (or Anywaa), Dereje Feyissa on Gambela, and Christiane Falge on the Ethiopian Nuer. South of the Baro outstanding examples of work which resonates with the present study would include David Turton on the Mursi and Jon Abbink on the Suri. Comparable conditions on the southern frontiers of the Sudan have been illuminated by the work of Tim Allen and Mark Leopold, in particular. There are 'internal frontierlands' too, of which the Nuba Hills are a prime example, where Gerd Baumann, Leif Manger, and Justin Willis have explored the fragilities and strengths of 'traditional' forms, and African Rights has documented the impact of genocidal war. And it is perfectly evident, from recent work such as that of Anders Hastrup, that we are now obliged to see the whole population of the western Sudanese province of Darfur as transformed in very recent years into 'frontier' conditions by the Sudanese state in a comparable way. Here a key guide has been the work of Alex de Waal on Darfur, from his original anthropological research in the early 1980s up to the present times—the time span of a crisis for anthropology itself, as so many of us have had to turn ourselves into amateur historians, political journalists, humanitarian aid workers, and occasionally activists. Revolution has touched the remotest villages, as Don Donham has shown for Maale in southern Ethiopia and Jenny Hammond has shown for Tigray in the north. Valuable general guides to current affairs in troubled parts of the world would include Alex de Waal's *Famine Crimes*, Jok Madut Jok's *War and Slavery in Sudan*, Mark Duffield's *Global Governance and the New Wars*, David Keen's *Conflict and Collusion in Sierra Leone* and *The Benefits of Famine*, and Paul Richards's *No Peace, No War*. Deborah Scroggins has shown in an exemplary way how hard-nosed political journalism can be presented through the art of the storyteller, and I owe a great deal to her encouragement and her achievements. All those working in, or writing about, frontier conditions are indebted to the pioneering collection edited by Brian Ferguson and Neil Whitehead, *War in the Tribal Zone*, and to the recent sophisticated set of essays in Thomas Wilson and Hastings Donnan's volume *Border Identities*. Detailed references to the work of many of these are made in the text below, and all may be found in the Bibliography.

The present book has grown out of collaborative work over many years, both with friends and informants 'in the field' and with friends, family, and colleagues 'back home'. The lines between field and home have in fact become rather blurred. Anthropologists and historians of Africa based in the West spend more and more time on field visits and consultancies, while the majority of individuals and families from the 'remote' villages where I stayed in the 1960s have been displaced internationally for the last twenty years—in some cases to

North America, where I have been able to catch up with a few. My long-standing debts will be evident, that is to all those whom I first knew from those original days, people whose words help tell the story in this book, in particular William Danga Ledko and Martha Nasim Ahmed, and I would like to express my deepest appreciation to them all. Those who acted as key assistants on various visits to the refugee sites, and on whom I was extremely dependent at times, include Enoch Cornelius and the late David Musa. Contacts with Hawus Yakub and others in Nairobi, renewed long-distance conversations with Emmanuel Mola Jajal in Yemen, and news from old friends in Khartoum have helped me keep in touch over the distances. I have recently been given vital help in polishing translations and updating information through the generosity of Davis Sukut Burapa, James Shama Pulale, Mathias Shadrach Dhunya and his wife Malhasan, Martin Ebet BuBa, Titus Solomon Gathe, Taib Awad Chito, Sabanaya Moses Kengi, and their friends and families during a stay in the United States. When contact with the displaced people from the southern Blue Nile was at its most difficult, I benefited from friendly exchanges with Don Stilwell of the SIM. In recent years Barbara Harper, herself returned energetically to work with the Uduk when most people would be thinking of retirement, has been extremely generous with her supportive welcome on my own visits to Bonga, her memories, and provocative conversations. I would also like to express my appreciation to Alistair and Patta Scott-Villiers, their field colleagues, and officials of Operation Lifeline Sudan in 1991; and to the Ethiopian Administration for Refugee and Returnee Affairs, as well as to Makonnen Tesfaye, of the UNHCR in Ethiopia, and Jan-Gerrit van Uffelen of ZOA Refugee Care, and their colleagues for allowing me to work at different times between 1992 and 2000 as a partner in their programmes of practical assistance to the displaced from the southern Blue Nile. More recently, Fiona Leggat, Jody Henderson, and Agnes Schaafsma have provided me with updates on the repatriation of refugees from Gambela region to the Sudan, while Chris Crowder of the SIM has filled me in on various developments back 'home' in the Kurmuk district.

A number of long-standing colleagues have provided me with crucially important insights in the course of this book's evolution, and here I can only mention a few: Abdel Ghaffar Mohammed Ahmed, Janice Boddy, Sharon Hutchinson, JoAnn McGregor, Julia Powles, Terence Ranger, John Ryle, David Turton, and Richard Vokes. I received invaluable help with final detailed comments and corrections to this text from Judith Aston, Naseem Badiey, Carol Berger, Eva Gillies, Barbara Harper, Don Stilwell, and Alex de Waal. I am grateful to Sheila Atton for her skill in drawing the maps. At every stage, and in every way, my husband Douglas H. Johnson has been a pillar of support.

In 1993 I had the revealing experience of helping make a documentary film in Karmi transit camp, with Granada TV's Disappearing World series. I learned new ways of thinking about visual experience and performance, and ways of 'doing ethnography' which captured these things, through working with Bruce MacDonald, our director, and our researcher Sarah Errington, who had made several films in north-east Africa herself. Entitled *Orphans of Passage*, our film provides, together with the whole corpus of footage made at that time, a parallel story in images and sound to that of this book. I have not quoted here from the recordings of interviews made for that film project, for two reasons. The first is to allow that material to stand on its own merits; and second and most significant is that the interviews recorded as part of that project were prompted by what I already knew had happened to the people. Many of the filmed conversations went over ground I had already covered in my own audio tapes on earlier visits. With the exception of a very few songs recorded by Granada, and where these occur they are acknowledged, all the quotations here are from my own personal tapes, mostly audio conversations but a few video from the later visits. Except where indicated, they are translated from the Uduk language.

The audio-visual dimension does add great depth to written historical ethnography, and I have learned a great deal from Alan Macfarlane's advice and recent collaboration with Judith Aston, a specialist in multimedia design at the University of the West of England. She and I have compiled a selection of illustrative material to accompany this book. This can be viewed at **www.voicesfromthebluenile.org**. Most of the songs quoted in this book will be found there, along with the various kinds of instrumental music and dance referred to, and a good number of interviews and conversations to add emotional tone and a sense of the character and personalities of people quoted here.

Oxford
January 2007   W. J.

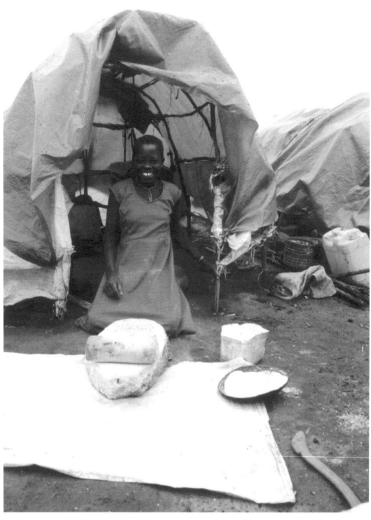

Frontispiece. Pake, William Danga's wife, in their shelter in Nor Deng, July 1991. Pake has carried a block of concrete and some wood from a bombed building in Nasir to shape into a grindstone and hand grinder

Contents

List of Maps, Thumbnail Sketches, and Figures

Maps

Thumbnail Sketches

Figures

Photographs by the author unless otherwise indicated.

Note on Texts and Translations

Quoted interviews and songs in this book are mostly close translations from recordings made in Uduk, in the vernacular called *'twam pa* or 'the home language', unless otherwise indicated. A few were in Arabic or English. Help with translation is acknowledged above, but I take responsibility for the English versions. Recordings were nearly all on audio tape, but a note is made in the few instances where it was on video tape. The conversational form of these interviews is indicated by including a number of questions asked by myself or by others (where indicated) in italics.

The system of transliteration for Uduk follows that originally created by the Sudan Interior Mission and used in their mimeographed *Uduk–English Dictionary* produced at Chali-el-Fil, 1956, reissued as Linguistic Monograph Series No. 4 of the Sudan Research Unit of the University of Khartoum in 1970, under the attributed authorship of Mary S. Beam and A. Elizabeth Cridland. An apostrophe before a consonant indicates implosion (for b and d) or explosion (for c, k, p, t, th); an oblique indicates a glottal stop; underlining indicates aspiration. The phoneme η represents the sound in the middle and at the end of English words such as 'singing' or 'longing'. To make for easier reading, these diacritics and special characters are omitted from proper names. There is an important set of tonal contrasts, indicated in the *Dictionary* but omitted from written texts.

By convention, the word *pa* meaning a home or lived-in village often precedes a place name, and sometimes as in Pam Be may have become part and parcel of the name. Where this has not happened, 'pa' is printed in italics and as in a number of other cases may end with a euphonic *m*, *n*, *ng*, *ny*, or *i* according to the word following. In the Uduk language context, the name of Chali as a place is always *pany* Jale, but to make the text more accessible, in most cases I have translated this as Chali. Many place names in the vicinity which are mentioned in this book but do not occur on the maps here may be found on the maps in my earlier books (*'Kwanim Pa*, 6, 9, 21, 26, 29; *The Listening Ebony*, 20).

Particular problems for translation in the present context are the terms *uci* or *ucim pa*, which could mean 'children' or 'our children' in a domestic setting or 'Uduk children' in a larger one. These terms often crop up in the setting of war and soldiery, but do not necessarily mean 'child soldiers' in the modern international sense of under-age fighters. I have translated it sometimes as 'our boys' or 'those lads' (or youngsters, chaps, fellows) meaning soldiers in the sense of 'our boys on the front', but I have also tried to match those uses where it means specifically the Uduk soldiers among them, whether in the army or in the SPLA guerrilla forces. These could well be quite young teenagers, but not regarded locally as too young to fight or marry.

Arabic words appear quite frequently in spoken Uduk, and occasionally examples of English ones. Where these are particularly significant they have been indicated. Vernacular speakers usually refer to their own people as '*kwanim pa*, and to capture the insider's perspective I have often left this untranslated but at other times felt it easier on the reader to use the term Uduk. Where a vernacular speaker is deliberately using the latter, as if quoting what outsiders call them, I use quotation marks in the translation, thus: 'Uduk'.

Background on the place of Uduk in the context of linguistic history, its conservatism with respect to consonantal phonemes, and its key place in the formation of the Nilo-Saharan family of languages is provided in Christopher Ehret's *A Historical-Comparative Reconstruction of Nilo-Saharan* (Cologne: Rüdiger Köppe Verlag, 2001). Others who have worked on the language include Robin Thelwall and Lionel Bender (see Bibliography for examples of their work).

Personal names such as David or Moses often take on their Arabic form in local conversation, i.e. Dawud or Musa. I have attempted to be consistent with respect to individuals.

Religious and spiritual terminology present particular difficulties for the translator. There are detailed discussions of the way that Uduk terms were modified for the purposes of Bible translation and Christian teaching in *The Listening Ebony*. Here I should simply note that I use *arum* for a generalized concept of life-force; Arum for a vague and non-specific concept of divinity above; and Arumgimis, following the usage of the Sudan Interior Mission, for the God of the Bible ('that *arum* which is in the sky').

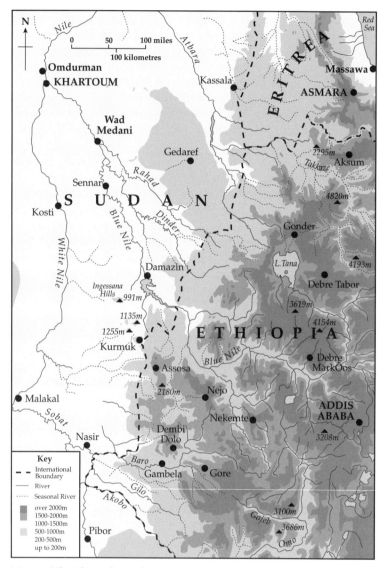

Map 2. The Blue Nile Borderlands

Historical Introduction
The Blue Nile Borderlands

Reality is to be found in the flux itself...everything is what it has become.

(R. G. Collingwood[1])

More than half a century has now passed since the independence of the Sudan in 1956, and more than three decades since the overthrow of imperial rule in Ethiopia in 1976. In these years the question of minority distinctiveness within large and sometimes fragile nations has loomed larger than it did during imperial or colonial times. In 'the old days' various terms were used by central elites of the old states which blanketed fringe communities together under more or less exclusionary names. The most glaring example was the old Ethiopian *shangalla* meaning something like the American term 'nigger' (banned in the reforms of 1974), and in the case of the Sudan it was (and still is) common to hear the use of '*abid* (slave peoples) or *zurga* (blacks) or regionally inclusive blanket terms such as 'Nuba'. In the case of the Blue Nile, there is an old term, 'Hameg' or Hamaj, applied to people living on the southern fringes of the former Kingdom of Sennar, and another, 'Burun', used of a range of peoples in the foothills and valleys west of the Ethiopian escarpment. Within these blanketed socio-political categories were dozens, if not hundreds, of local indigenous language communities with a strong sense of self as against a variety of neighbours, and increasingly so in concert against the state and its elites. 'The Uduk' are an example of such a small local community who used to have a very low 'visibility' on the national or international scene, blanketed by their

---

[1] R. G. Collingwood, *The Principles of History: And Other Writings in Philosophy of History*, ed. W. H. Dray and W. J. van der Dussen (Oxford: Clarendon Press, 1999), 178.

northern neighbours as 'Burun', becoming publicly known as a distinct-ive linguistic group only to twentieth-century administrators or mis-sionaries—the Sudan Interior Mission (SIM, now retitled Serving in Mission) was given permission to start work in the northern regions of Upper Nile Province, which then included the Uduk area, in 1938.

In Sudan's colonial era local identities did begin to emerge and be acknowledged through the policies of Native Administration, but the momentum of national politics now tends to sweep people up into blanket categories such as 'northerners' or 'southerners', Africans or Arabs, 'Nilotics' or 'Equatorians', regardless of local complexity. Inter-national aid agencies, journalists, mission organizations, and no doubt anthropologists, have sought on the other hand to recognize particular minority status or 'ethnic identities' caught up in the maelstrom, and perhaps to exaggerate their diversity in proportion as their suffering increases and their misfortunes reach the headlines. Writers, artists, activists, and even bloggers from the 'remoter' communities are, how-ever, now making both their individual voices and their collective circumstances heard—especially from the refugee camps and the inter-national diaspora, where people are gathered together and interacting in newly intensive ways.

AN OLD REGION NOW DIVIDED

There are good reasons for recognizing the long-term coherence of the region of the hills and valleys of the upper Blue Nile basin and its adjacent lowlands to the west—the region I label here the Blue Nile Borderlands (Map 2). Archaeological studies have recently proposed a strongly connected set of practices in relation to material culture, over a span of perhaps 4,000 years.[2] Traceable linguistic continuities are even longer than this, the Uduk language itself for example having its roots in the earliest forms of proto-Nilo-Saharan.[3] There is a remarkable set of analogous and overlapping social forms and cultural activities among the groups now perceived as separate minorities on either side

---

[2] Victor Fernandez, 'Four thousand years in the Blue Nile: paths to inequality and ways of resistance', *Complutum*, 14 (2003), 409–25.

[3] Christopher Ehret, *A Historical-Comparative Reconstruction of Nilo-Saharan* (Cologne: Rüdiger Köppe Verlag, 2001).

of the international border, whose world has been transformed over two centuries or so. The inequalities introduced by trade and political centralization were once fairly mild, and of an interpersonal kind; for example, in both the old kingdoms of Sennar and of the Ethiopian highlands, outsiders and outlying communities could be brought into relationship with the central elite through intermarriage and material exchange, and 'categories' of belonging, even that of 'Funj', 'Arab', or 'Amhara', were a matter of relative social position and genealogy. The modern era, with its larger-scale operations, capital investment, and industrial technology, has hardened such terms and associated the concept of the nation-state with a *kind of people* different from these outsiders. Older forms of status distinction have tended to become racial stereotypes, now challenged by liberal ideas which seek diversity and individuality in the fringes. But has the 'post-modern' tendency to find diversity everywhere come to cloud our vision?

There is a common assumption that wars in weak or failing states, or post-imperial conditions, tend to be between 'ethnic' or religious groups as such. Together with this goes an easy acceptance of the rhetoric of everybody's rights to self-determination, along with the symbolism of nationalism applied at a more local level—flag-waving and so on as a way of claiming territory, resources, or political representation. It is sometimes thought that drawing boundaries between such groups will solve the problem and produce peace. The countries of north-east Africa are a case in point. Ethiopia since 1991 has designed its constitution to recognize the rights of all ethnic groups and base its forms of local government upon this recognition.[4] However, the struggle on the ground is not always best understood as between ethnic or religious groups, and drawing boundaries can produce as much conflict and misery as it solves, as my story in this book will illustrate. The conflicts which global modernity seems to provoke do not stem simply from pre-existing rivalries, but are created to a large extent by the processes of expanding modernity itself. A focus not primarily on groups, but on places, and the emerging patterns taken by individual agency over time among the people who live in them, can provide more of an insight into

---

[4] Christopher Clapham, 'Controlling space in Ethiopia', in W. James et al. (eds.), *Remapping Ethiopia* (Oxford: James Currey, 2002). David Turton (ed.), *Ethnic Federalism: The Ethiopian Experience in Comparative Perspective* (Oxford James Currey, 2006).

the divisive impacts of recent world-political processes. And a focus on places within regions 'made marginal' by world events can illustrate particularly well the way these processes fuel the momentum of armed conflict, between and within nations.

An older generation of 'Sudanist' scholarship, not to mention the more extreme case of 'Ethiopianist' studies, focused on the national level, of high culture, central institutions, and historical continuities, or, in the case of anthropology, on relatively timeless cultural portraits of remote rural groups. But the ground has shifted under the older style of scholarly studies in these countries. Both historians and social scientists seek out happenings on the ground, events affecting both remote and central places, and actors of a kind who rarely used to appear in the nation's archives. Frontiers are no longer assumed of marginal interest, simply on account of their distance, by definition, from the nation's core.[5] Ethnographic studies in the remoter areas of modern countries can no longer be dismissed as marginal to serious scholarship, and indeed ethnographers themselves are seeking to place their work within, rather than outside, national history. My own earlier writings on the Uduk aimed to do this in a general way, though I have pushed the point much more explicitly in my work on Ethiopia.[6]

Marginality is of course relative. There are marginal places and peoples everywhere. But the political emergence of the marginalized has a clear history in both the countries we are considering. In many such cases we see the emergence, or even re-emergence, of the salience of regions which earlier saw their own integrity, and sometimes even prosperity, destroyed by the imperial carve-up, as modern states imposed themselves. Post-colonial struggles are not necessarily a product of their own times alone. In the Sudanese case, they are the latest in what is fundamentally a historically continuing project, by those who control the central core of the state, economy, and political structures, to extend this control to the frontierlands: whether south, east, west, or even far north. This state, whose roots as a political formation of the central Nile

    [5] Thomas M. Wilson and Hastings Donnan (eds.), *Border Identities: Nation and State at International Frontiers* (Cambridge: Cambridge University Press, 1998).
    [6] For example, 'Lifelines: exchange marriage among the Gumuz', in D. L. Donham and Wendy James (eds.), *The Southern Marches of Imperial Ethiopia: Essays in Social Anthropology and History* (Cambridge: Cambridge University Press, 1986; reissued in paperback with new preface, Oxford: James Currey, 2002).

valley are older than often recognized—arguably going back at least 2,000 years to the Kingdom of Meroe or its successors in medieval Nubia or the Funj Kingdom of Sennar—has always sought to co-opt or engage frontier peoples on its own terms. The processes of drawing in formerly 'independent' communities have never been totally benign, but with the first imperial conquest of the Funj Kingdom by the Ottoman Empire in 1821 they became harsh and exploitative. The period of 'Turco-Egyptian' rule (1821–85) was extinguished by the rise of Sudanese Mahdism and the establishment of an independent regime in its name (1885–98). There followed the 'Reconquest' of the Sudan by Britain and Egypt. The regime of the Anglo-Egyptian Condominium, sometimes today loosely referred to as the British colonial period, lasted up to Sudanese independence in 1956. Western imperial control thus lasted only a little over half a century, but built on a longer Sudanese experience of imperialism. Now a further half-century has passed, much of which has been taken up with armed resistance from the periphery to successive efforts to build a united Sudanese nation-state. Modern imperial Ethiopia (1896–1975) lasted a little longer than the British were in the Sudan (1898–1956) but it was then engulfed by an intense traumatic and violent post-imperial political struggle resulting in a period of central state socialism patronized by the Soviet Union. This was succeeded only in 1991 by a form of people's democracy based on the devolution of power to local territorial groups. This was much welcomed at the time, though some of its inner contradictions have since become evident.

Since I first wrote on the relevance of historical perspectives to understanding the present of the Uduk and similar peoples, I have been able to draw together evidence that they were directly affected by the expansion of the Sudanese state at an earlier date than I had previously realized. In the 1960s, for example, I found differences of dialect, kinship principles and practices, and rituals as between the 'northern' Uduk of the Ahmar and Tombakh valleys and the 'southern' Uduk of the Yabus valley and hills beyond it, and assumed these arose from the fact that the northern groups had simply moved further away from the eastward expansion of the Nuer in the first part of the nineteenth century.[7] However, it now seems more likely that the northward movement was provoked mainly by the initial

---

[7] Wendy James, *'Kwanim Pa: The Making of the Uduk People. An Ethnographic Study of Survival in the Sudan–Ethiopian Borderlands* (Oxford: Clarendon Press, 1979).

slave-raiding campaigns of the new Turco-Egyptian regime up the White
Nile and into the Sobat valley in the 1820s and 1830s.[8] The Uduk have
early stories of fleeing from 'Dhamkin', which is a blanket term they apply
to Nuer and Dinka alike, and in this context could well apply to people
displaced by the early Turkish raids. The Uduk-speaking population,
along with others, was thus transformed into a 'frontier' society: a few
may have been directly captured as military slaves for the army, while
some moved far enough north to seek shelter and possibly employment
with the very outposts of the government which was conducting the raids.
Others may have fled into the hills south of the Yabus, to be as far away
from the disturbances as possible. Hence, there was a new separation
between those who had been drawn under the umbrella of the Turco-
Egyptian state and those who had retreated from it: a classic 'frontier'
theme.[9] This separation might even have had its seeds in the previous era of
the Kingdom of Sennar, when it is not unlikely that a few had been forcibly
or voluntarily drawn into the orbit of the state, especially into its trading
networks and armies, men who might have settled in retirement back in the
southern frontiers. This certainly was the broad history of the people of
Jebel Gule, formerly speaking a Koman language (and thus very close to
Uduk); they became the key seat of the 'Hamaj' who overthrew the Funj
rulers of Sennar in the late eighteenth century. The language had almost
become extinct even by the early twentieth century, having been replaced by
Arabic. It is beyond question that the Koman people of Gule and its
neighbourhood were thoroughly drawn into the workings of Sennar, and
it followed very naturally that Jebel Gule should become a key southern
outpost of the Turco-Egyptians when they arrived.

A 'PARADISE' AT RISK: SCHUVER'S TESTIMONY

We have a particularly observant traveller in the Dutch adventurer Juan
Maria Schuver.[10] Schuver attempted to pioneer a way up the Blue Nile,

---

[8] Richard Hill (ed.), *On the Frontiers of Islam: The Sudan under Turco-Egyptian Rule
1822–1845* (Oxford: Clarendon Press, 1970), esp. chs. 1 and 2.
[9] Brian Ferguson and Neil Whitehead (eds.), *War in the Tribal Zone: Expanding States
and Indigenous Warfare*, 2nd edn. (Santa Fe, N. Mex.: School of American Research, 2000).
[10] Juan Maria Schuver, *Juan Maria Schuver's Travels in North East Africa, 1880–83*,
ed. W. James, G. Baumann, and D. H. Johnson (London: The Hakluyt Society, 1996).

through the highlands and to the East African coast, in the early 1880s. But he became entangled in local politics. Jote Tullu of the western Oromo, who had already roped in a large number of Dinka followers from the plains (no doubt some who had fled the raiding mentioned above), tried to recruit Schuver as a mercenary in his attempt to fend off the Ethiopians of Shoa. The crumbling authority of the Turco-Egyptian government could not guarantee his passage anywhere, and unable to escape southwards from Jote's reach, he had to content himself with a hilltop view over the flooded plains of the Baro-Sobat valley.

As he first entered the hilly country of the upper Blue Nile in 1881, via the Turkish garrison town of Famaka, Schuver described how the old chief of Geissan led him to the summit of a mountain. Extending his arm towards the slopes formerly covered with dwellings, he cried 'with the accents of an accomplished tragedian': 'There you see what the Turks have done. My father, my mother, my brothers, all of them are dead or have been taken away as slaves; as for me, stranger, had I not the duty of looking after their graves, I should be there, far away in the southern mountains, where so many others have gone to seek back their lost freedom, where the Turk has never set foot.'[11] This vignette sadly prefigures the story of this book: because southward flight, death, and dispossession for the peoples of the Blue Nile Borderlands were to be played out again and again over the succeeding century and a half, right up to the present. Their co-optation too; Schuver himself engaged a 'Gambiel boy' called Abina from somewhere below western Oromo country, and this young man eventually accompanied him back to Khartoum, where he died. From the vocabulary Schuver recorded of his language Abina's mother tongue was Shyita, a Koman language very close to Uduk. From the geographical and other indications, his home area was somewhere a little north of what we know today as Kigille, on the upper Jokau tributary of the Baro-Sobat river, known in Ethiopia as the Garre (often pronounced 'Jikau').[12]

Schuver made a point of visiting as many as he could of the 'independent areas' just beyond the reach of Turco-Egyptian control. He did not make it to any village of the Uduk as such, though he marked without explanation a 'J. Uduk (*unbewohnt*)', that is, 'uninhabited', on his map in the Tombakh valley, from his observations westwards from

---

[11] Ibid. 26.   [12] Ibid. 334–40.

the escarpment. But he referred several times to the populations of hills west of the escarpment, and mentioned recent raids against them. He labelled these populations 'Bari', a usage which might well be derived from another ethnic term 'Barya', which was used until recent times of the Nera people of western Eritrea, both almost certainly stemming from the Amharic *baria*, 'slave'. Schuver's travelling companions regarded 'the Bari' as their enemies, however, and were afraid to go as far down the Yabus valley as Jebel Bisho, where the easternmost of the Bari had secluded themselves.[13] We do know that this mountain was— and still is—a favourite refuge of the *'kwanim pa*, and I am convinced many of them would have been there in Schuver's day. Where were the others, and why was there a hill called 'Jebel Uduk', some thirty miles to the north, 'uninhabited'? Had its people retreated southwards, or further north towards Gule for safety? This question is raised again below.

Schuver did make first-hand observations in the land of the Koma, speakers of another language closely related to Uduk. He found a guide in the person of Wad Bilal, a trader who originally came from Sennar, but who had made a home in a village called Inzing. On today's maps there is still a hilly peak called Inzing, but the settlement is known today as Assosa, and this place will figure in the chapters below. Schuver described Inzing as 'a very prosperous village as several slave-merchants live here', with extensive cultivations, and a number of active Islamic teachers. It was sufficiently powerful to have gone to war with its own local overlord in Gomasha, situated on the lower slopes of the escarpment below Inzing.[14] Before travelling with him to the Koma country, Wad Bilal described his trade in quite charming terms:

Before leaving home he had given me in all sincerity, the following information and instructions.... 'The commerce', he had continued, 'which we carry out from time to time in Koma country, consists of the exchange of salt, cloth and white beads which we bring to barter for the wild honey and the abandoned women or orphan children of the district... In each village they welcome us with demonstrations of joy; the news spreads from mouth to mouth that our friend Wad Bilal or our friend so-and-so has arrived with salt... The next day... they gather and one brings us a goat, one a skin or a gourd of honey

[13] Juan Maria Schuver, *Juan Maria Schuver's Travels in North East Africa, 1880–83*, ed. W. James, G. Baumann, and D. H. Johnson (London: The Hakluyt Society, 1996). Map opposite 52; pp. xc–xci, 60, 131, 133, 141, 143.

[14] Ibid. 108–9.

and the chief makes us a gift of some orphan or widow. It is only when we are specially looking for a pretty girl at the request of some Sheikh of the Berta, that we buy her formally for a price agreed with her parents.'[15]

Schuver was entranced on arriving in the country of the Koma, which he described as an idyllic republican paradise. He found there 'the easygoing happiness of primitive man', and waxed lyrical over the delightful climate, the superabundant vegetation of cereals, spices, and stimulants, and the truly republican liberty and general goodwill of the people.[16] However, he saw that this paradise was threatened, by trade in general and the slave trade in particular. He gives us a tongue-in-cheek portrait of the benevolent manner of the man he had been obliged to accept as a guide.

Wad Bilal offers the perfect type of the kind-hearted slave-dealer. While others have to drag away their living purchases in the forked pole and keep them in the slave-irons at their stations, this philanthropist possesses the knack of concili-ating the affections of his helots in an uncommon degree. I have seen him make friends with a recently acquired Dinka-boy in the following manner: 'Take this pot of beer' he said 'my brother and let us drink and be merry. For I have got a trusty servant now and you, my boy, ought to feel glad and rejoice: for you have found to-day not a master, but a father, a mother and a brother all in one ... The same evening the boy was walking about unfettered, more dreaming of the paradise awaiting him at Inzing than of running away. Next morning I overheard Wad-Bilal say to him, 'O my child, *be so kind as to* put these 20 salt-loaves on your back and come with me. Alas, I am too old and feeble to carry them.'[17]

Wad Bilal's base was already a substantial trading post. The geography here was, and is, particularly dramatic in itself, as Trémaux's sketch from the 1850s shows (Figure 1). The view here is from the escarpment near modern Assosa down towards the gold-bearing mountain of Dul (adja-cent to the mountain of Kurmuk, though no town of Kurmuk yet existed). Close to Dul, the somewhat rebellious outlying Sudanese chiefdom of Gomasha was flourishing by the 1880s, causing local conflicts that were later exacerbated by the making of the frontier itself. Schuver described the view from the escarpment thus: 'Fine views are obtained at Inzing into the forestclad deep ravines that plunge down into the White Nile basin. At sunset a young *muezzin*, clad in flowing, snow-white garments climbed the gigantic granite boulder that overlooks

---

[15] Ibid. 155.   [16] Ibid. 151.   [17] Ibid. 73–4.

Figure 1. View westwards from the hills of Dul near Kurmuk, Pierre Trémaux, *c.*1852

the whole scene. In a pure, far reaching voice he proclaimed the credo of Mecca to the heathen continent before him...'[18]

Schuver also visited Gomasha itself, already famous as a slave-trading station with the reputation of being well defended as a natural fortress, poised halfway down a spur from the escarpment. He was not permitted by the Sheikh, Mahmud Himmeidi, to descend to the gold washings at the foot of the famous mountain of Dul. However, he was offered (and refused) the present of a girl, one of the 'Gomasha beauties' he had noted with clear ringing voices, 'of whom it might be said *negra sed pulchra est*'.[19] What were these girls doing here? It is very likely they had been abducted from the nearby lowlands. This Sheikh Mahmud, who joined the Mahdist movement in 1882 when the Mahdi wrote to him

[18] Juan Maria Schuver, *Juan Maria Schuver's Travels in North East Africa, 1880–83*, ed. W. James, G. Baumann, and D. H. Johnson (London: The Hakluyt Society, 1996), 108–9.
[19] Ibid. 115; for non-Latin speakers, 'she is black but she is beautiful'.

personally, had two sons, Muhammed and Ibrahim. They attempted to retain power over the borderlands for themselves against the Mahdist state, and they continued slave raiding into the lowlands right up to the end of the century. Their activities were partly responsible for the way the border was drawn, separating the raided valleys and outlying hills from the raiders' posts higher up to the east. Muhammed Wad Mahmud was detained by the Abyssinians in 1900. Ibrahim, called Burhen by the Uduk, had a violent and cruel reputation among them, which I heard all about in the 1960s. By 1904, his particular mountain of Jerok having been, by design, deliberately included for security reasons on the Sudan side of the border, he was arrested by the British and hanged in Wad Medani.[20] The drawing of the boundary, based on a survey of 1901,[21] and the imposition of *pax Britannica* on the Sudan side meant that the raided homeland of the Uduk was separated from the control of Assosa and Gomasha, which were included in Ethiopia, and border posts were set up to control trade and illegal activity. The first southerly such post was located at Jebel Surkum in 1904, but this was moved to Jebel Kurmuk in 1910, in order to be right on the frontier. Here it provided some protection for a network of peaceful trading villages such as 'Jalei' on the Khor Tombakh—which later came to be pronounced and written in English as Chali. Neither of course had appeared on Gwynn's map of 1901, but the strategic importance of both Kurmuk and Chali was to increase by remarkable stages during the twentieth century. It is a historical irony that the first refugee camp established for the Uduk was at Tsore, a little below Assosa. Gomasha turns up in one of my eyewitness accounts of that time, a nearby village which the refugees found handy for shopping (Chapter 4).

OLD FRONTIER POLARITIES:
THE FARAGALLAH STORY

In the Bonga refugee scheme in 2000, I was unexpectedly offered a spontaneous and to me quite new account of 'where the *'kwanim pa* came from'. Dawud Kaya Lothdha, at that time possibly in his seventies,

---

[20] James, *'Kwanim Pa*, 48–51.
[21] C. W. Gwynn, 'Surveys on the proposed Sudan–Abyssinian frontier', *Geographical Journal*, 18/6 (1901), 562–73.

wanted to announce, with great confidence, that they were an enslaved people who came from the north, mentioning various historic places such as Meroe, Kush, Sobi (*sic*: possibly a reference to Soba), and Sennar. They had once been left at the riverbank in Omdurman for the crocodiles, but then rescued by white people who took them across in a boat. I did not take this story seriously at first and grilled Dawud about where he had heard it, maybe from a book, or from some teacher who had read a book about the ancient Sudan. He was adamant that this was not so, that he used to hear these stories from his grandfather, Faragallah, who he claimed had died in 1932. I knew the name 'Faragallah Abu Kura'' because it was marked as a village in the Tombakh valley on the old Sudan maps.[22] And Schuver's notes from talking to Abina in 1881, very interestingly, include 'Paragalla-Gambiel' as the name given by Oromo traders who used to visit the market of 'Kepiel', which we can identify as Pil, just north of Kigille.[23] 'Faragalla' as a place near Chali is also mentioned in the mid-twentieth century handbook of the southern Fung region,[24] but none of these occurrences has survived as a place name. They do however suggest that the places where the name occurs might well once have been tributary to a significant chief or administrator. I should mention here that the old Turkish frontier garrison of Famaka was replaced by Roseires as the main administrative centre further down the Blue Nile during the Condominium period. This town itself was eclipsed in due course by Damazin on the opposite bank at the railhead, as industry reached the area with the construction of the Rosieres Dam in the 1960s.

Dawud's account started as follows.

We people belong to a line [*wak*, 'matriline' or birth-group] of *ciŋkina/* [here with the strong meaning 'slaves', but also used in the sense of servant, orphan, or foundling] who came from Meroe. We came from Meroe, to a place called Kush. . . . We arrived in Omdurman as slaves, and then we crossed the river to Khartoum . . . and to a place called Sobi. . . . Then we set out again and met the Funj people at Medani. Then from Medani we arrived at Sennar, and it was just Funj all the way. We arrived at Singa and found people called Shilluk. We went

---

[22] Survey Office, Khartoum, Sudan 1:250,000 series, sheet 66 G 'Kurmuk', corrected 1940.

[23] *Schuver's Travels*, 335.

[24] 'Hanbook [*sic*]: Southern Fung District, Blue Nile Province', Roseires archives, 1959, 4. The older spelling 'Fung' is now replaced by 'Funj'.

on and reached Roseires. We found other people there, and it was there we
started killing rats. We had met the Bunyan [Bertha], and they said, 'Any rats
you find, give them to these people.' We are people who eat rats, all of us.

After some more circumstantial details, including a tale about how their
eating rats led to the place name Damazin, via the remarks of disap-
proving Bertha, I took him back to the story about his grandfather, and
he explained again with great emphasis:

We were *slaves of the Egyptians!* From Meroe. We are from Meroe. We went to a
place called Kush. In Kush we lived together with the Nuba. We joined them,
then we split from them, the Nuba, because of a quarrel over the head of a pig.
There were diviners [*ɲari/*] with the Nuba, and some of the Uduk were
diviners, and we fought over the head of pig in the diviners' place! Then we
split up! That's our story, maybe somebody might find it in a notebook [Arabic:
deftar] of the old days!

   The Dinka used to call that river Khartoum, and at that time, people were
taken across the river in a motorboat. The Dinka were taken over by motorboat,
and the Uduk were left in Omdurman for the crocodiles to eat. [Another voice]
In Omdurman?—Yes, Omdurman! The Nuba were left to follow the river up to
the Nuba Hills, to those places far away, Kadugli, Heiban, Abri. While the
group of Uduk were left there. Then some white people came and helped the
Uduk across the river, and they went to rest in a place called Sobi, just across
from Khartoum. They went from Sobi to Medani, and found the Funj, black
people . . . and from there to Sennar, and found the *makk* there, their chief
called the *makk*. We found our chief there, our own *makk,* in Sennar! We came
and found Shilluk in Singa, Singa Abdalla.[25]

Part of that town is still called Singa Abdalla, and Dawud reminded me
that he and I had once travelled through it together by Land-Rover. He
gave more details which I have since pondered in rereading the older
literature.

   The historical background in fact provides a substantial degree of
support for Dawud's basic account. He claimed that Faragallah had
been a tax collector for the Turks, before the Mahdiyya. We know that
the regional base for tax collection in the Turco-Egyptian era was Jebel
Gule, which had been an important outpost of the Kingdom of Sennar
and very soon after the Turkish conquest of 1821 was used as a base for
exploitative raiding southwards. There is physical and documentary

----

[25] Dawud Kaya Lothdha, 2 Sept. 2000 (video).

evidence to support the oral tradition of large thorn enclosures in the Ahmar valley, probably *zeriba*-style encampments set up in the mid-nineteenth century for the protection of trading and raiding parties and the population of captives and refugees they had secured.[26] Many from the raided regions were no doubt incorporated in the 1820s–1830s and onwards into the Turkish armies or government service. Faragallah or even his father before might well have been impressed into state service in this way. The Sheikh of Jebel Gule, however, was detained by the Khalifa during the later part of the Mahdist regime and imprisoned in Omdurman.[27] This would have left something of a governmental vacuum in the southern Funj region, which then suffered heavy raiding from the Ethiopian border sheikhs. Among the arch-figures of this time, regarded as chief of them all and much feared by the lowland villages, was Sheikh Khogali Hassan of Assosa. He became known simply as 'Kujul' to the Uduk and their neighbours, and is remembered to this day as having devastated the land and enslaved the people at the end of the nineteenth century. He was detained in 1898, though released later to live a relatively long and peaceful life.[28] When the victorious Anglo-Egyptian forces entered Omdurman in 1898, quite apart from taking 38,000 men of the Khalifa's army prisoner with their women and children,[29] they found over 2,000 persons formerly in Egyptian employ in Omdurman's own prisons. These included former soldiers and clerks

---

[26] The term *zeriba* can mean a thorn enclosure for cattle, but was extended to the fortified enclosure of the merchants who penetrated the southern Sudan in the nineteenth century, seeking valuables such as ivory and also, notoriously, slaves for the army. See Douglas H. Johnson, 'Recruitment and entrapment in private slave armies: the structure of the *zara'ib* in the Southern Sudan', in Elizabeth Savage (ed.), *The Human Commodity: Perspectives on the Trans-Saharan Slave Trade* (London: Frank Cass, 1992), 162–73.

[27] 'The Gezira district [of the Mahdist period] extends as far south as Gebel Idris, which mountain is of the Hamag tribe.... The hereditary Emir of the Hamag is Idris Ragab, who was detained in Omdurman by the Khalifa. After the capture of Omdurman, a dispute arose as to whom should be the legal governor of the Hamag tribe. Idris Ragab, having received the Aman, left Omdurman for Gebel Idris on 25th September 1898, and on reaching Gebel Idris found the Khalifa's Emir, Adlan Surur, in possession.' The 'Aman', meaning 'peace' but with the particular sense of 'amnesty', was extended by the Anglo-Egyptian government to former Mahdists. The case of Idris Ragab was referred to Cairo, where it was decided to recognize him. He later 'carried the Aman' to several dependent sheikhs, including at least one in what later became Ethiopia. *Sudan Intelligence Reports (SIR)*, 60 (May–Dec. 1898), 18–19.

[28] James, *'Kwanim Pa*, 37–46.

[29] 'Dervish Prisoners in Omdurman', *SIR* 60 (May–Dec., 1898), appendix 45: 76–8.

and family members among other categories. Over 550 of these, that is, more than a quarter, were from the province of Sennar and Fazoghli.[30] These men were freed and encouraged to return to their homes. Faragallah might well have been among these; but whether he had been or not, he was captured at about this time by the Ethiopian border sheikhs. We know that he was subsequently freed from Ibrahim Wad Mahmud's base at Gwarayo near Jerok (probably by British-led troops in 1904),[31] and we may well imagine how he would value stories of the former glories of the black Sudanese people, perhaps especially the Funj Kingdom of Sennar.[32] Mythical elements combine in Dawud's story, but the provision of riverboats by white people to leave Omdurman might well have happened in late 1898. His stories of his grandfather also seem well based. In 1906, Nickerson Bey was on a trek through the Burun country and reported, 'There is a Burun Sheikh called Faragalla living...on the Khor Tombakh. He is a powerful man physically, and claims authority over a big district. Is very loyal on account of his release....Most of the Burun Sheikhs have very little authority. There are a good number of repatriated Burun slaves along the Khor Yabus; they act as "missionaries of government".'[33] He mentioned various small villages dotted about five miles apart, including Jalei (still the local pronunciation of Chali), Faragalla, and Abu Cora; and that the northerly villages call themselves 'Uddug, a branch of the Burun'.[34] Nickerson heard of Burun villages two days' march south of the Yabus, 'but I had no camels and did not go there'.[35]

If Dawud's own forebears formed a link to the state system of the old Turkish government and had reason to be grateful for the arrival of the British, there were also others who took positive steps to welcome the Anglo-Egyptian government presence in the southern Funj. Among

[30] 'List showing number of Regulars, Bashibazuks, Civilian Employés, and Families of deceased government prisoners, found after re-conquest of the Sudan' (at Omdurman, 2 Sept. 1898), *SIR* 60 (May–Dec. 1898), appendix 41: 69.

[31] El Kaimakam G. S. Nickerson Bey, 'Dar Fung and Burun country' (20 pp.), National Records Office (NRO), Khartoum, Dakhlia I, 112/17/102: 19. An abbreviated and slightly different version was published as 'Report on Dar Fung', *SIR* 145 (Aug. 1906), appendix B. Subsequent page references are to the latter.

[32] Wendy James, 'The Funj mystique: approaches to a problem of Sudan history', in R. K. Jain (ed.), *Text and Context: The Social Anthropology of Tradition*, ASA Essays 2 (Philadelphia: ISHI, 1977), 95–133.

[33] Nickerson, 'Report on Dar Fung', 7.

[34] Ibid. 9.

[35] Ibid. 8.

these were Abu Magud, known to the Uduk as Bamagud, who went to Jebel Gule and Roseires in about 1902 to ask for government help in resettling those who had been displaced to Jebel Ulu.[36] He was thought to have spent many years previously in Roseires, Kosti, and Sennar, and he famously persuaded 'MisMis' (Kaimakam Smyth Bey[37]) to pacify the southern Funj area. In fact, Dawud emphasized a connection—that Faragallah's father had been a member of Bamagud's (matrilineal) kin-group. As a result of the repatriation facilitated by the new government, both from Gule and from the 'protection' of the Ethiopian border sheikhs, the valleys of the Ahmar and Tombakh were populated again by grateful people and thus firmly knitted into the fabric of the modernizing colonial state. The map is scattered with names of government chiefs old and new, reflecting this. In the Tombakh valley we find 'Dar Abu Magud' for the whole area now known as Chali, as well as a specific site 'Abu Magud'.[38] Villagers in the 1960s remembered other local chiefs of the early twentieth century, including one Idris, after whom two villages are named on the old map. Like Faragallah he had returned from captivity in Gwarayo in the Ethiopian foothills (and could equally have served the government in pre-Mahdist days). His brass crest, said to have been presented by the British, though in appearance almost certainly of the Turco-Egyptian period, still happened to be treasured in my old hamlet of Wakacesh (Figure 2a). A 'Dereig Effendi' appears in my notebooks but I now believe this must have been an elided pronunciation of ''Abdel Farag Effendi'. 'Farag' and ''Abd el Farrag' appear as villages on the map, and a photograph taken around 1930 by A. W. M. Disney, the Assistant District Commissioner (ADC) in Kurmuk, shows Farag Effendi at Chali (Figure 2b). Known by various other names, including Gandal, he was *wakil* or deputy to Bamagud, taking over from him when he died. Tocke, an elderly lady in Bonga, now blind, spoke to me in 1994 about the old chief 'Gandal' as a wise man who along with Bamagud had foretold many worrying things to come (see Chapter 10). Chali 'el Fil' on the old Condominium map records the residence of El Fil, successor to Idris after a spell in prison in Wad Medani where he learned good Arabic. El Fil had married a Koma

Figure 2a. Old brass crest, once kept in Wakacesh (photo, 1966)

Figure 2b. Farag Effendi at Chali (A. W. M. Disney, 1929–30; Sudan Archive, Durham 717/1/178)

woman in exile (or rather, in captivity) at Gwarayo in the Ethiopian foothills, from where the British enabled him to return. His son Talib, whose story runs through several chapters of this book, succeeded him as Omda of the district. Chali 'el Arab' on the map almost certainly indicates a seasonal camp and watering place for the nomad Arabs.

The northern settlements of Uduk speakers came to be known as Currara or Kurara in the early twentieth-century literature. I can only make an outside guess that this might be linked with the 'Abu Kura' which was apparently the name of Faragallah's father. Pirie was of the opinion that they had a totally different dialect and were not a 'Burun' group; and were rather 'the people of Kur or Kurara'.[39] Meanwhile those who had fled southwards entrenched themselves in the hills to the south of the Yabus valley, just beyond any easy reach from tax collectors or other agents of government with or without camels. This separation between the northern and southern groups of Uduk speakers, which we can date at least back to the early nineteenth century, could in part account for the differences in accent and vocabulary between them, along with various differences in customary practice I have discussed in earlier books.[40] The people of the various hills in the southern Funj were certainly regarded as good subjects for anthropological study, and as evidence I have selected another of Disney's photographs of *c*.1930 to illustrate the lively 'Hill Burun' musical scene (Figure 3). This is a flute ensemble characteristic of the Blue Nile Borderlands as a whole, known to Arabic speakers as *zumbara* and having several Uduk variants which can now be seen being reinvented in the refugee camps, as discussed in Chapter 9 below.

Dawud's story was diametrically opposite to the stories of a basically southern 'origin' I had heard in my original fieldwork, from somewhere south of Jebel Bisho. His story, however, was not one of 'tribal' origins but rather the specific story of a family, or cluster of families, who had been co-opted into government, and perhaps also military service, in one or more previous historical eras. The connection with the Turco-Egyptian period was clear, and could arguably have been built on even

[39] A. M. Pirrie, 'Report on the Burun Country', *SIR* 155 (June 1907), appendix A: 4. See also E. E. Evans-Pritchard, 'Ethnological observations in Dar Fung', *Sudan Notes and Records (SNR)*, 15/1 (1932), 31–4.

[40] James, *'Kwanim Pa*, 236–41; *The Listening Ebony* (Oxford: Clarendon Press, 1988), 356–62.

Figure 3. Hill Burun band (A. W. M. Disney, 1929–30; Sudan Archive, Durham 717/1/165)

earlier times.[41] Dawud's picture of the nineteenth century falls into place in some very interesting ways. It certainly provides some evidence for the long-term history of a divide among the Uduk people, between those who were drawn north as the tentacles of government moved south, and those who made themselves scarce by sheltering in the hills. The reputation of MisMis as a saviour of the people was long-lasting; among my recordings from the 1960s is a song commemorating his actions. Moreover, this view of long-term processes drawing some into the orbit of the state throws light on why curious claims to kin and cultural links with the Uduk are sometimes heard among communities further north. In Khartoum in 1988 I heard a tradition that the Kadalo of the Blue Nile valley above Roseires were freed slaves with former

[41] Gule was a key southern outpost of the Kingdom of Sennar, and its people, blanketed as the marginal 'Hameg', actually ousted the Funj dynasty there in the late eighteenth century. We know from James Bruce, who travelled through Sennar in 1772, that there was a large encampment of 'Nuba' to the south of the city, people recruited from Jebel Dair and Teglai in the Nuba Mountains and Fazoghli on the Blue Nile. James Bruce, *Travels to Discover the Source of the Nile, in the Years 1768–1773* (Edinburgh, 1790), vol. iv, 419–20.

Uduk connections. One old man had claimed kinship with El Fil, father of Omda Talib of Chali;[42] and William Dhupa once told me of an old lady in a shop in Wad Medani who spoke '*twam pa.*

My discussion of Dawud's story may seem a digression, but in the way it points to the contrary pulls of seeking help and support from government, and keeping as far away as possible from its embraces, it introduces some of the main themes of this book. These contrary tendencies, I now believe, not only produced the 'difference' between the northern and southern Uduk themselves, but are still evident as alternative directions of movement, even allegiance, opening and closing during the various phases of the civil war. The people did at first assume in the 1980s that they would be safe in the hills near Jebel Bisho, though bombers and long-range artillery put paid to that illusion. There are long-distance separations on a new scale now, in that quite a large Uduk community is now based in Khartoum and Omdurman, along with a scattering in other towns of the northern Sudan, while the vast majority have become refugees, initially in the orbit of the SPLA and only now beginning to return from spending most of the last twenty years over the border in Ethiopia.

THE MAKING OF THE MODERN
FRONTIER: 1898–1956

The police post established at Jebel Kurmuk acquired a connection by motorable road and an Assistant District Commissioner in 1927, as the southernmost government presence in the Southern Fung District with its HQ at Roseires. Kurmuk *zeriba* (as explained, an enclosed traders' HQ) was described by later officials as a 'den of thieves', where Kalo, a 'notorious bandit', was hunted down in 1929 (his son Nogo 'an amusing rogue').[43] Up to 1928 all the 'Burun' peoples, to the south of the Ingessana and west of the Bertha, were under a *Muawin*, Nimr Mohammed, who was himself an ex-slave *Muggadam* of Idris Ragab of

---

[42] My informant was Pastor Paul Rasha. He also claimed the Kashankoro people were formerly Uduk, but enslaved and living among the Bertha.

[43] 'Hanbook [*sic*]: Southern Fung District, Blue Nile Province', Roseires archives, 1959, 2, 14.

Gule, 'more loyal to his old master than to the Government'. He was retired and an ex-*Ombashi* (Corporal) Hamdan Damus, 'member of the family of the Mek of Jerok' (that is, the family of the previously executed Ibrahim Wad Mahmud), was given charge of Kurmuk and all the Burun hills. However he 'went off the rails fairly swiftly' and fled across the border, leaving the various Burun hills to look after themselves.[44] Meanwhile, in the far south, Sitt Amna, wife of the notorious Khogali Hassan, had been allowed to settle in the first years of the century with relatives and dependants on the Sudan side at Mortesoro among the southernmost Bertha, and in 1923 was appointed Omda over that area and the Koma villages beyond the Yabus. From there she carried on the slave-trading business, eventually being arrested in 1928. The stories about her are legion.

The layout of Kurmuk today reflects its strategic history: built around a parade ground with flagposts in the middle, it is a self-consciously 'frontier' post. Figure 4a shows its newly constructed centre photographed by Assistant District Commissioner Disney in about 1930, sporting the British and Egyptian flags of the Condominium. By this time it was already being used by the Royal Air Force for aerial reconnaissance and border patrols, as shown in Figure 4b. In 1936 the Italian invasion of Ethiopia led to the promotion of Kurmuk as a fairly large frontier district, with a District Commissioner of its own. Changes continued, and in 1938, in the context of the developing Condominium policy with respect to the northern and southern Sudan, a meeting of governors and District Commissioners was held at which it was decided to withdraw the 'primitive pagan tribes of Mabaan, Uduk and Koma' from Kurmuk, and allocate them to Upper Nile Province.[45] Boundaries were drawn accordingly, and it was in this new context of belonging to Upper Nile Province that the Sudan Interior Mission was granted permission to start work at stations on the White Nile among the northern Dinka, at Doro among the Meban, and at Chali among the Uduk.[46] The first taste of modern war came during 1940, when the. Italian occupying forces in Ethiopia invaded and bombed Kurmuk and

---

[44] 'Hanbook [*sic*]: Southern Fung District, Blue Nile Province', Roseires archives, 1959, 14.

[45] Ibid. 3.

[46] Lilian Passmore Sanderson and Neville Sanderson, *Education, Religion and Politics in Southern Sudan 1899–1964* (London: Ithaca Press, 1981), 240–4.

Figure 4a. New Merkhaz at Kurmuk (A. W. M. Disney, 1929–30; Sudan Archive, Durham 717/1/98)

Figure 4b. RAF planes at Kurmuk (A. W. M. Disney, 1929–30; Sudan Archive, Durham 717/3/6)

nearby localities. Doro was bombed, perhaps suspected of harbouring troops, and three American missionaries were killed. British and allied troops moved in 1941 from the Sudan into Ethiopia as a part of the liberation of the country and the restoration of the Emperor. After the war the importance of Kurmuk was somewhat reduced, as the whole extent of the former northern and southern Fung was amalgamated into one Fung district. It was 1950 before a new temporary British admin-istration was posted to Kurmuk, and further administrative develop-ments were planned to meet the growing economic significance of the area. A new reorganization, in 1953, involved the reinstatement of separate northern and southern Fung districts within the Blue Nile Province (HQs at Singa and Roseires respectively), with Kurmuk a sub-district of the latter. This upgrading of Kurmuk meant a reconsid-eration of the district borders. It was decided to re-transfer the Uduk and Koma *omodiyas,* centred on Chali el Fil and Yabus Bridge respect-ively, back to Kurmuk's sphere. The change, essentially made for local reasons, had larger implications too, because the western and southern stretches of the district boundary served as the line newly defining the Blue Nile and Upper Nile provinces.

In sum: what had been a fairly open zone on the southern extremity of an old northern province was first transferred in 1938, on 'ethnic' grounds under the premises of the old Southern Policy, to Upper Nile Province: and then, in 1953, just three years before independence in 1956, two of the three *omodiyas* or chiefdoms which had by this time been fashioned out of the area were transferred back from 'the south' to 'the north', along with an established Christian mission. The Meban *omodiya*, with its main town Boing, remained in Upper Nile. The shifts in district organization of this time led directly to some of the tragic consequences for the people, evident today, on both sides of this border. Almost intractable complications will surely continue, as this is the very border, between the Uduk and Koma on one side, and the Meban on the other, which divides the north from the south under the peace agreement of 2005. Under the terms of this agreement, the southerners have been promised a referendum which could theoretically result in the secession of the south.

A little further south along the frontier with Ethiopia, developments in the Condominium period also laid the foundations for later patterns of co-operation and conflict. Trade of the modern kind was positively fostered in the early twentieth century between Ethiopia and Sudan along the Baro-Sobat valley, fostering the growth of several towns, especially Nasir in the Sudan and Gambela in Ethiopia. These were also valued as stages on an alternative route from the Sudanese plains into the hills, up to the important trading centre of Fadasi in the western part of Ethiopia's Wallega Province. Local communities, especially Nuer and Anuak (sometimes spelled Anywaa), used to move up and down the Sobat valley with relative ease, and without much regard for their specific Ethiopian or Sudanese citizenship.[47] The town of Gambela was firmly in place as a trading entrepôt by 1904, and because of the importance of this trade route, a political arrangement with the imperial Ethiopian government was made to give Gambela and the 'Baro Salient' a special status within Ethiopia. A British consulate was put in place, and access was facilitated for traders from both sides. A rusting steamer from the British days could still be seen near the town's bridge well beyond the post-Mengistu era.

POST-IMPERIAL TRANSFORMATIONS OF POLITICAL SPACE: 1956–2006

The main events of the post-imperial period on the Sudan side of our region have taken place in the setting of a weak state challenged by armed resistance originating in the south of the country. With the passing decades there have been shifts in the political character of the central regime, and also in the direction from which the southern-based movements have sought external support—Ethiopia for example has sometimes been a political ally for the southern opposition, and at other times for Khartoum. The discovery of substantial oil reserves in the south and its borderlands in the mid-1970s had the effect of drawing more and more external actors into the politics of the region, deepening conflicts and complicating international efforts to implement the peace agreement for the south and find ways to control the violence in Darfur.[48]

[47] Douglas H. Johnson, 'On the Nilotic frontier: imperial Ethiopia in the southern Sudan, 1898–1936', in D. L. Donham and W. James (eds.), *The Southern Marches of Imperial Ethiopia: Essays in Social Anthropology and History* (Cambridge: Cambridge University Press, 1986), 219–45. Reissued in paperback with new preface (Oxford: James Currey, 2002).
[48] Douglas H. Johnson, *The Root Causes of Sudan's Civil Wars*, updated edn. (Oxford: James Currey, 2006).

At the time of the Sudan's independence in 1956, the political failure of the Anglo-Egyptian Condominium to hand over a viable unitary state to their successors was already clear. The transfer of power by the British to the Sudanese was essentially a legal fudge.[49] The anxieties of the southerners had been expressed clearly for several years, and violence in the far south, which was to lead to the first civil war, had already broken out. Sudanese nationalists were already blaming the British for their artificial protection of the southerners from the spread of modern development, the Arabic language, and Islam; and blaming the various missionary bodies for encouraging opposition and resistance. The first military coup in Khartoum happened in 1958, after only two years of 'democracy', partly with the aim of putting an end to the rise of a federalist political movement in the Sudan's 'marginal' areas, but this move only stoked the fires of full-blooded separatism in the south. By 1964 a popular uprising against the heavy-handed rule of the Abboud regime brought back civilian rule, and a phase of somewhat muddled democratic politics dominated by the leading families of the old northern religious parties. Again in part because of the deepening problem of the civil war, a second military coup led by Gaafar Nimeiry took place in 1969, notoriously supported by the Communist Party of the Sudan, with a modern socialist programme and a promise to establish the equality of all citizens. Nimeiry's stance secured the confidence of many southerners and he managed, with the help of Ethiopia—itself gradually moving towards modern reforms—to secure a peace agreement with the Anyanya movement in 1972. Under the Addis Ababa Agreement, a devolved regional government for the south was set up with its capital in Juba.

The peace lasted little more than a decade. Few of the underlying causes of the civil war had really been addressed. The Southern Regional Government was far short of the resources it needed to implement its own programmes, despite the discovery of substantial oil reserves in the Upper Nile area; and the secular socialist programme of Nimeiry in the north was under increasing pressure from militant Islamic groups drawing their inspiration from the more radical religious movements of the Middle East. Nimeiry himself was drawn into the orbit of Islamic

[49] Douglas H. Johnson, 'Introduction', *Sudan, 1942–1950: British Documents on the End of Empire*, series B, vol. v, part 1 (London: Stationery Office, 1998).

politics, and also diverted from his original vision for the country by the rise of regional opposition in the south to the administration of Abel Alier. Civil war broke out with the Bor Mutiny in May 1983 and the founding of the Sudan People's Liberation Movement and Army (SPLM/A) under the leadership of John Garang.[50] In early June, Nimeiry declared the 'redivision' of the south into three parts, thus abrogating the Addis Ababa Agreement and dismantling the southern administration based in Juba. This new armed opposition secured early dramatic successes, partly with the support of the revolutionary socialist regime (introduced below) which had by now established itself in Ethiopia. Having lost the confidence of most southerners, Nimeiry was thrown out of power by another popular uprising in Khartoum in early 1985.

After a year's transitional government under Suwar el Dhahab, elections returned some of the old leaders from the traditional religious families of the north. Sadiq el Mahdi as Prime Minister introduced new ways of combating the insurgency in the south, now threatening areas of the north itself (such as the southern part of the Blue Nile Province, the site of my main case study). Straightaway in 1986 he established official pro-government militias, especially among the nomadic tribes, mainly 'Arabs' but also 'Fellata' which is the common name for Hausa- and Fulani-speaking West African long-term immigrants in the Sudan. These migratory herders could be regarded as patrolling the frontiers with the south, in Darfur, Kordofan, White Nile, and Blue Nile provinces. He also introduced the scheme for 'Popular Defence Forces', recruiting youngsters from the main towns and elsewhere for training and potential front-line assistance to the regular army in the civil war. These additional armed elements provided effective reinforcement to the government side and contributed to the very heavy programmes of counter-insurgency mounted in the front-line areas of the war (which

---

[50] John Garang de Mabior: Dinka from Jonglei Province; a refugee student in Kenya during the first civil war, he was educated first at Grinnell College, Iowa, USA, and the University of Dar es Salaam, Tanzania, before joining the Anyanya; a captain at the end of the war, he was absorbed into the Sudanese army and rose to the rank of lieutenant colonel; during this time he obtained a Ph.D. from Iowa State University in Agricultural Economics; he became one of the founders of the SPLM/SPLA and was chairman and commander-in-chief from 1983 to 2005; following the signing of the CPA he became First Vice-President of the Sudan and President of the Government of South Sudan, but died in a helicopter crash in Uganda on 30 July 2005.

the southern Blue Nile soon became) during the late 1980s. By early 1989, Sadiq's government was forced by a combination of military failure in the south and political opposition in the north to seek a peace settlement with the SPLA. This was aborted by the military coup of 30 June organized by the National Islamic Front, but fronted by the unknown figure of Omer el Beshir, an army brigadier who had served in the oil fields of Upper Nile.

The National Islamic Front, reconstituted in 1985, represented an extreme form of modernist militant Islam, the latest outcome of a tradition cultivated by the Muslim Brotherhood in the Sudan since the early 1950s. Within a few months the 'traditional' *hudud* punishments of the *shari'a* law, such as the execution of heretics, and the amputation of hands and feet for thieves, along with the establishment of places of torture ('ghost houses'), darkened the political and social life of Khartoum and other northern towns. Although the SPLA was newly threatened by the Islamist coup, and was shortly to be weakened by the fall of the Mengistu regime in Ethiopa in 1991, the Sudanese civil war continued, and before long the movement was able to build up its influence again in several parts of the north as well as most of the south. It was only after a further decade and a half that, under sustained pressures from the international community, the Khartoum government of Omer el Beshir and the SPLM/A under John Garang reached a Comprehensive Peace Agreement, signed on 9 January 2005.[51] This settlement provided for the sharing of political powers and wealth as between the central government, the north, and the south, as defined by the northern boundaries of the southern provinces of Bahr el Ghazal and Upper Nile at the moment of independence in 1956 (Map 1). A key provision of the agreement was that the people of the south should have a referendum after six years, to decide whether they should remain part of a united Sudan or become independent. Thus, the 1956 line could shortly become a new international frontier. The consequences for those living along it are only gradually emerging now as a set of very difficult issues. For example, in the southern extremities of the old Fung Province, peoples like the Uduk and the Meban who have long regarded each

---

[51] 'The Comprehensive Peace Agreement between the Government of the Republic of the Sudan and the Sudan People's Liberation Movement/Sudan People's Liberation Army' (CPA), Nairobi, 9 Jan. 2005.

other—and still do—as 'kith and kin' could find themselves living in different countries.

In the course of the peace negotiations, the Sudan government attempted to ignore even larger and more blatantly pressing issues concerning the definition of 'north' and 'south'. They eventually had to recognize the fact that three areas lying north of the old provincial boundary lines were either partly occupied by the SPLA itself, and had been for many years; or that parts of their population wished the SPLA to speak for them; or both. These areas were given special provisions in the peace agreement. Abyei in particular was allowed its own eventual referendum once an international commission had determined its northern boundaries. The SPLA-occupied parts of the Nuba Hills and the southern Blue Nile were incorporated as part of newly designated federal states within the north, to be known as 'Southern Kordofan' and 'Blue Nile' respectively. The boundaries of each of these new states included considerably more territory and population than the zones actually occupied by the SPLA, and particular provision was provided in each case for balanced local representation and human rights. Implementation of the provisions of the agreement has been making very slow progress. This is partly because of the unexpected death of John Garang at the end of July 2005, but especially as a result of the escalation of armed resistance in Darfur in early 2003 which led to full-scale civil war in the far west. This struggle can be best understood as a younger cousin to the long years of the southern-based war, structurally similar and historically linked, though the pace has been faster and international attention much greater.

Events have been no less dramatic on the Ethiopian side of our Blue Nile Borderlands region, but I can deal with the story only very briefly here. With the rise of political criticism among the professional elite and students of imperial Ethiopia, leading to the reforms of the early 1970s fully supported and even introduced by the Emperor Haile Selassie, a gradual transformation of the old order was anticipated. No one expected how sudden, drastic, and bloody the transformation would be; Don Donham has provided a powerful analysis of this revolution, comparable in its effects upon relations between government and people to the French Revolution of 1789.[52] Subsequent years bore out the

---

[52] Don Donham, *Marxist Modern: An Ethnographic History of the Ethiopian Revolution* (Berkeley and Los Angeles: University of California Press, 1999).

comparison too. The man who eventually emerged in 1978 from violent struggle among the revolutionary leaders themselves was Mengistu Haile Mariam. He was able to establish, with the support of the Soviet Union and various eastern European countries, a system of centralized state socialism some have compared to that of Stalin. As mentioned above, Mengistu lent support to the young SPLA from its formation in 1983, providing among other things supply routes, training facilities, a radio station, and—particularly important for our story in this book—sites which could be made available to the UNHCR for the establishment of camps for refugees from the Sudan. Some of these camps were extremely large; in particular, that at Itang, on the Baro river downstream from Gambela, officially had around 400,000 people registered by 1988. Though this figure would have been too high, allowing for the fact that registrations are rarely removed, even for reasons of death, the number of people present by 1991 or so was almost certainly a quarter of a million. To anticipate a little, this included (unexpectedly to almost everyone who knew anything about them) some 20,000 or so of the Uduk-speaking group, the *'kwanim pa*—the very 'we ourselves' or 'us lot' (now separated very far from their relatives in the major cities of the northern Sudan) whose fortunes and misfortunes I trace in the chapters that follow.

Armed opposition to the Mengistu regime in Ethiopia mounted in the late 1980s, culminating in the success of the Tigre-led and western-supported coalition which took power as the Ethiopian People's Revolutionary Democratic Front (EPRDF) in 1991. The SPLA was no longer welcome in Ethiopia; Mengistu had left, the radio station had to close, along with the bases, and the SPLA itself recognized that it had to organize the evacuation of the refugee camps. Hundreds of thousands of people had to walk back, partly through flooded rivers, to the eastern Upper Nile in the middle of the rainy season—including the Blue Nile refugees, each year further and further from home.

The new Ethiopian regime pursued a new policy of regional devolution, in theory allowing each of its constituent peoples a high degree of local autonomy.[53] The problematic aspects of this policy became particularly clear in some of the western regions, such as Gambela where Nuer–Anuak rivalry was inevitably built into the demographic structure;

---

[53] Turton (ed.), *Ethnic Federalism*.

or Beni Shangul-Gumuz, a region of many minorities, stretched out
along the border, and difficult to administer because half is north of the
Blue Nile river and half south of it, with no bridge between them. One
has to travel far from Assosa, its capital, into the central highlands to
cross the Blue Nile Gorge before taking a route leading out again to the
northern part of its territory within the regional state. Although also
socialist in orientation, the new Ethiopian government, under Meles
Zenawi, was keen to break ties with the Mengistu regime and its former
patrons. Western support was welcomed, and a relatively warm relationship developed with Khartoum.

One of the key problems on the Sudan side was that the SPLA itself
had split, partly because of the 1991 collapse of support from the
Ethiopian side. The leadership in the town of Nasir on the Baro-
Sobat river, downstream from Gambela, was perhaps the most immediate victim of this collapse, having been so dependent upon Ethiopia,
and now facing a massive influx of returnee-refugees. Under Riak
Machar[54] they made a bid for a takeover of the SPLA as a whole, and
for the deposition of Garang. This bid led to internecine warfare
between the Nasir faction and mainstream SPLA forces based further
south, from late 1991. It weakened the ability of the Nasir leadership to
run its own affairs and look after the destitute under its own protection,
and eventually Khartoum was able to seduce Machar over to its side.
This was the situation in which a return wave of desperate people,
spearheaded by a new faction among the Uduk themselves who were
totally dillusioned with the SPLA, sought safety in Ethiopia again in 1992.

Into this mix of competing national and world interests over the last
half-century, which saw the rise of a Cold War 'global' frontier between
two former imperial territories, other players have made themselves felt.
The old Sudan Interior Mission stations had to be handed over to locals as
all foreign missionaries were deported first from the southern Sudan, and
then in 1964 from the Nuba Hills and southern Blue Nile, because of

---

[54] Riak Machar: Nuer from Unity State; after obtaining a doctorate in civil engin-
eering from the University of Bradford, UK, he joined the SPLA in 1984 and rose to the
rank of alternate commander; leader of the Nasir faction that tried to oust Garang in
1991, he subsequently joined the government side and signed a formal peace agreement
with Khartoum in 1997; claiming that the government had violated that agreement he
reconciled with Garang and rejoined the SPLA in 2002; at time of writing he is the Vice-
President of the Government of South Sudan in Juba.

supposed sympathies with the Anyanya rebel movement. But in the later course of the second civil war, a new generation of evangelical missionaries mounted high-profile campaigns in the Sudan, flying medical help in to remote areas (including the southern Blue Nile), dashing in with briefcases stuffed with dollars to organize the buying-back of slaves, and broadcasting accounts of atrocities.[55] The older mission organizations took a much more moderate line in supporting educational projects, even the SIM 'changing its spots' by accepting contracts with the new Ethiopian government to work on education in the refugee camps for Sudanese, while avoiding evangelism as such.

The Sudan and Ethiopia have been the scene of a vast increase in international aid and humanitarian activity, along with varying media interest, since around 1972, which saw both the response to the famine in northern Ethiopia and the opportunities for development in the southern Sudan opened up by the Addis Ababa peace agreement. The UN and most of its branches have worked almost non-stop in both countries ever since; along with a growing variety of non-governmental organizations (NGOs), both large and small. The NGO movement has also caught on in these countries themselves, and indeed today we see an increasingly strong stance by the governments, and even regional local governments, of these countries against the creeping influence of outsiders on local affairs, through their access to funding, their ability to prioritize projects, and to offer better wages to educated youngsters than local employers could. The influence of academics, whether international or local, has been extremely marginal, except in so far as they have been ready to take short consultancies themselves and write reports.

Looking back, it is difficult even now to be sure that peace, return, and rehabilitation are just around the corner. Looking back, as so many of the displaced from the Sudan–Ethiopian border do now, to the convulsions which began in 1985 and literally exploded over the whole region from 1987 for at least six years, we can say that *here* at the turn of the 1990s was the defining set of events; *here* were the times, and *here* were the places of action, scattered up and down the Sudan–Ethiopian border, where decisions were made—about crossing borders, joining armies, declaring

---

[55] Website postings are often ephemeral. Those of the following organizations indicate the tone: Christian Solidarity International (**www.csi-int.org**); Samaritan's Purse (**www.samaritanspurse.org**); World Magazine (**www.worldmag.org**).

religious faith or national identity. Actions were taken during those years which, unknowable at the time, on reflection affected subsequent prospects of life or death. Everything that has happened to the people since then, how they have fared in one political grouping or another, whether they have ended up still in Ethiopia, or back in the Sudan, or Uganda or Kenya, or in one case even Yemen, not to mention the USA, Canada, and Australia, was set in train during this crucial six-year period of turbulence and disaster between 1987 and 1993.

It was of course, the period marking the end of the Cold War. The fall of the Berlin Wall led directly to the end of the socialist regime of Mengistu in Ethiopia in 1991, and hence ended that source of support for the SPLA. More or less at the same time as the Ethiopian government was being weakened by armed resistance, approaches to peace talks with the SPLA by the Sudanese regime of Sadiq el Mahdi were pre-empted in 1989, by the Islamist-backed coup of Omer el Beshir. Through signing the peace agreement with the SPLA in early 2005 he and his cabal retained their grip on power. Despite the inauguration of a complex Government of National Unity, representing the whole country, the next period saw a severe escalation of the war in Darfur, specifically of counter-insurgency, and accusations of genocide against the regime and its allied militias, recruited mainly from the nomad groups. Following a partial and fragile peace agreement over Darfur in 2006, those who dictated policy in Khartoum continued to defy all levels of international opinion, including the authority of the UN, over the recommended deployment of peacekeepers beyond the inadequate African Union forces they had originally allowed. There are deeply uncomfortable implications for a lasting peace in the south of the country, let alone the three transitional areas, including the new Blue Nile State, for which extremely delicate constitutional safeguards have been agreed on paper.

CONVERSATIONS BETWEEN THE GENERATIONS

Memory is not only the capacity of individuals; it is partly the product of exchange and sharing, and the patterns which such interaction takes in the living society. Conversations between people of different ages, especially generations or cohorts who were brought up at specific eventful periods, can be a vital process in shaping the patterns of memory and expectation.[56] In the case of those people whose memories form the core of this book, the generation born from 1980 onwards has grown up in conditions similar to those of people born from 1890 onwards. Story-themes about the past tell of rushing about in the bush; looking for protection and even justice from some manifestion of 'government' or another, or alternatively looking to escape to some ideal freedom from governmental interference. In the 1960s, I met members of the generation born from 1890, already elderly. They remembered the disruptions and displacement of the late nineteenth century, and their adventures of that time. One could guess these experiences might have resonated with their own grandparents' stories of the disruptions of the 1820s–1830s, whose results were recorded by Schuver among others. By contrast, those born from around 1920 experienced relative calm up to the 1980s, when again major calamity overwhelmed the southern Blue Nile. Intergenerational conversations over nearly two centuries now have been shaped by a pragmatic, political, and moral contrast between images of peace and prosperity on the one hand, and of destruction and suffering on the other. The motif of a continuing swing between these opposed states of being no doubt gives the current under-thirties, born since around 1980, a very strong indication of how they should place themselves in relation to the past. Looking back 'from here', the older generations can at the same time speculate on the way that patterns recur. Some of the memories I have recorded from older people recall the past making of statements which now, in the light of events, appear prophetic; for example, hints that it was known even in the 1930s or so that the people would one day have to flee home again, or even that motor vehicles and aeroplanes, initially an amazing wonder, would one day return to attack the people (for examples, see Chapter 10).

WHERE ARE THE PEOPLE NOW?

As I complete this book, in the first weeks of 2007, it is uncomfortable to have to accept that most of those who were finally settled in the

---

[56] This theme is developed by contributors to Wendy James and David Mills (eds.), *The Qualities of Time: Anthropological Approaches* (Oxford: Berg, 2005).

refugee scheme at Bonga near Gambela in 1993 are still there, fourteen years later. It is true that the UNHCR, in early 2006, embarked on a repatriation programme for Sudanese refugees in Ethiopia, starting with a convoy of 500 from Bonga who were returned to the Kurmuk district in April. There was reported to be a joyful homecoming to Chali, and further repatriations resumed in early 2007 (see Epilogue). But the shadows of the ongoing unrest in parts of the country, north and south, and the open continuation of armed struggle and severe counter-insurgency in the giant western region of Darfur, still hang heavy over any Sudanese homecomings. Add to this the uncertainties built into the 2005 peace agreement itself, which promises a referendum to the people of the south after six years; if they vote for secession rather than to remain part of a united Sudan, regions like the current Blue Nile State, especially its southernmost parts, will find themselves up against not only one international frontier but two. The special constitutional provisions for this small piece of Sudan's jigsaw can scarcely make up for the problems that the people of the Kurmuk district, in particular, will face. The constitutional provisions, though accessible from early 2005 on the internet, are themselves not widely understood, and in fact both UNHCR reports and surveys undertaken among the Bonga refugees indicate a good deal of unclarity—official reports refer to the return of refugees in western Ethiopia to the 'south' of Sudan, as do at least some of the refugees. In Bonga the homeland of the great majority is in 'the north' as defined by the peace agreement.

The majority of those individuals whose voices, and sometimes faces, appeared in my first two books about the *'kwanim pa* have not survived the last two decades. Hada, among the most elderly, the specialist in spiritual matters of *arum*, died in the first refugee camp near Assosa, probably 1988; Tente, the expert to whom I owe my better-quality understandings of the ideas behind the healing and celebratory rituals of the cult of the *ŋari/*, the ebony diviners, fled with the others back into the Sudan when that camp was sacked and evacuated but died in the bush, when the people had retreated from bombing and artillery fire into the hills south of Yabus in early 1990. Tente's sister Saba died in the wretched swampy camp of Nor Deng near Nasir in Nuer country, where Uduk refugees had been allowed to settle in the rainy season of 1991. Another sister, Nyane, died alone on the trek back into Ethiopia in 1992, not being able to keep up with the dash to Gambela away from

armed clashes at Itang. She was left under a tree, I was told by eyewitnesses who later found her body. Another of Tente's sisters, Lungke,
whom I had known in the 1960s, made it to the 'safe haven' of Bonga
where I saw her in reasonable health in 1994; but she was on the point
of death when I returned in 2000, and I found myself attending her
funeral. In the meantime, others who played some role in my earlier
ethnographies had already been scattered far from the core of the
'*kwanim pa*. Pastor Paul Rasha Angwo, the first and for many years
the only ordained pastor in the Blue Nile Province, found himself
stranded in Khartoum at the time of the devastation of his church and
surrounding villages in 1987. Together with some church elders he had
gone north for a conference, and could not immediately return. He
remained in Khartoum, trying to gain news about the dispersed refugees
and seeking support for their cause, until 1992 when he died in hospital
there of complications connected with high blood pressure.

My main research assistant, Shadrach Peyko Dhunya, after completing some years of schooling in Khartoum and Omdurman, found
himself in political trouble after the Addis Ababa peace agreement of
1972. He approached the authorities about the possibility of a referendum being held in the southern Blue Nile, giving the people the option
of rejoining the southern region as against remaining in the northern
Sudan—a provision which had been indicated in the peace agreement.
He was reprimanded, but soon after found himself in Kurmuk prison
for over a year in connection with an unrelated offence, of which he was
later found quite innocent. On his release, he left the district altogether,
eventually finding a post as a headmaster and then as a senior education
official in Wau, Bahr el Ghazal (a town which remained throughout the
war in government hands). He never returned to the Kurmuk district,
and scarcely ever visited Khartoum again (where some of his relatives
continued to live). He remarried in Wau, and spent the rest of his life
there, dying of illness in 2004.

Other young men who helped me with my work in various ways
became involved in the civil war and have not survived. For example, in
1969 I was escorted on a trek into the hills south of Yabus by Philip Suga
and William Dhupa. We got on well, and had a lot of fun—we had to
cross back over the Yabus river on our return, which was in flood. The
two men first swam over carefully with my tape recorder and personal
luggage held high, then returned to launch our donkey and guide it

across, firmly held on both sides, and finally returned to do much the same with me. I never saw Philip again—he joined the army in the peaceful decade of the 1970s, and died of illness in the early part of the war while stationed at the garrison in Malakal. I did see William Dhupa again in Chali in 1983, but soon after this he joined the SPLA and received a bad wound in the leg somewhere in the Nuba Hills. After some time at Natinga near the Kenya border, an SPLA camp for the injured (where there was very little medical help), he was assisted to rejoin his own people who were by this time in Bonga; I learned he died there in the late 1990s.

These dismal stories could continue. But happily I can also report the survival, to the time of writing, of other good friends and co-researchers from before the war. William Danga Ledko is a senior and respected leader in the Bonga scheme; he became chairman of the Refugee Committee there in 2000 and held this post for a couple of years. Essentially an ironic observer rather than any kind of activist, his commentaries on the present, and memories of the past, and expectations for the future, run through the various chapters below. Others whom I knew in the 1960s who also appear in this 'ethnography of survival' include, for example, Martha Nasim Ahmed (whose post-mission education was cut short but whose career in the world of humanitarian and development work has blossomed); by 2005 she was firmly back in the Sudan, where she became a member of the Assembly in the new Blue Nile State. The story of what happened as a result of civil war to the one small locality of Chali el Fil and its outlying villages of the Kurmuk district is many-stranded; no one picture can be given. In this book I trace some of the different, and sometimes directly conflicting, pathways that individuals have taken. Over time it is impossible to miss the fact, nevertheless, that pathways do not simply diverge for ever; they cross and recross each other.

If the modern technologies of war and the easy spread of armaments have helped divide an infinite number of small rural populations who once survived through self-sufficiency but now depend on patronage, the modern technologies of easy travel and electronic communication have at least favoured the extension of personal links over wider and wider distances. The internet may have fuelled many of the major global language networks and the social activities they support, but the telephone, the mobile phone in particular, has given a new lease of life to many of the world's smaller vernacular language networks, linking diasporas and even protagonists on opposite sides of civil wars. The richness of a mother tongue can still be compelling in the life of those who may have lost touch with it on a daily basis. A language like *'twam pa* (speech of the homeland) may no longer relate to the local fields and forests but it serves well to tap into historical and personal memory, even drawing from such knowledge some true insights into the great events that are shaping the world. It is to such 'home-language' networks that we could say people still 'belong'; *that* is where they may be found, even in the great cities of North America. In this respect, the 'vernacular communities' of the world today have more ways of surviving dispersal than in previous historical times.

To help the reader follow the connections over time between local, regional, and global events as they have shaped the story of the Uduk people told here, a chronology is included in the Appendix. This also indicates when and where I was able to make a series of visits to the people in exile, and to hold the conversations upon which the book is based.

PART I

THE STRUGGLES FOR
KURMUK AND FOR CHALI

1

Projects, Targets, and the Recruitment of the People

The recruitment of individuals from the periphery into the central institutions and deployments of the state has a very long history in both the countries we are considering. One of the most ancient kinds of such recruitment has been as armed supporters of the powers that be, whether through feudal obligations or physical capture through war or raiding.[1] Military slavery has played a part in the very formation of the historic kingdoms of the region; one of the most interesting cases being that of the mainly Arabic-speaking 'Funj' and later 'Hamaj' elite of the old Kingdom of Sennar on the Blue Nile in the Sudan. Arguably the earlier Funj, and certainly the later Hamaj, rose to power through processes of recruitment from the peripheries, through trading connection, strategic marriages, and also forcible conscription into the armed forces of the kingdom. The explorer James Bruce commented, in the late eighteenth century, that 'slavery in Sennaar is the only true nobility'.[2]

During the early Condominium period in the Sudan, local traditional leaders were sought who could be relied upon to assist in the administration of districts. Where these were not obviously available, it was a not uncommon pattern for individuals to be given the responsibility for local administration simply because they had acquired some Arabic and knew the ways of government, perhaps for example having had a spell in prison. This is how the first civilian Uduk chief (following Idris,

---

[1] Douglas H. Johnson, 'Sudanese military slavery from the eighteenth to the twentieth century', in L. Archer (ed.), *Slavery and Other Forms of Unfree Labour* (London: Routledge, 1988), 142–56; 'The structure of a legacy: military slavery in northeast Africa', in 'Ethnohistory and Africa', ed. E. Steinhart, *Ethnohistory*, special number, 36/1 (1989), 72–88.

[2] Bruce's *Travels*, iv. 459.

mentioned in the Introduction) was instated—El Fil, nicknamed thus 'The Elephant' because of his size, was appointed Omda after his release from jail in Wad Medani. It is ironic that so many others recruited into the ranks of authority have had similarly little choice ever since.

Recruitment of another kind, into the economy of the country as a whole, initially affected only a few individuals who found temporary jobs while in town, or seasonal agricultural work near to home. Some of the first cohorts of youngsters who had a few years at the mission school, but then dropped out of their own accord to seek adventure in the wider Sudan, gained diverse experience of its towns—for example William Danga, who appears in my earlier books and whose story and verbatim commentaries run through this account too. Others completed the SIM programme in Chali and by the early 1960s were beginning to go on to secondary school elsewhere—Martha Nasim Ahmed, for example, was sent off to mission boarding school at Doleib Hill near Malakal, and Shadrach Peyko Dhunya, my original key assistant, went on to Juba Technical College.

AGRICULTURAL LABOUR DEMANDS

The opportunities to leave the Chali area, and indeed economic pressures to do so, increased enormously from the early 1970s. From the perspective of Khartoum and the dry Sahelian belt, lands to the south and towards the Ethiopian mountains, with their greater rainfall, were always beckoning. During the years of Nimeiry's government, the Sudan's aim was to become a breadbasket for the Middle East, and there was a vast expansion of large-scale mechanized agricultural schemes spreading southwards in the whole grassy savannah belt. Much of this expansion was financed by the Islamic banking system towards the end of the 1980s. This meant that in the Blue Nile Province, as elsewhere in southern Darfur and Kordofan and northern Upper Nile, opportunities for seasonal labour expanded greatly. By the mid-1980s there were extensive schemes in the plains to the west of Damazin, and lorries would traverse the villages of the region recruiting labour especially for the harvest.

Men recruited as seasonal labour into these big mechanized farms were among the first to experience the shock of reprisals following the

1985 arrival of the SPLA guerrillas in the Blue Nile—and the counter-insurgency, spearheaded by the newly created militias of 1986 among the nomad Arabs, which followed soon after. There is abundant evidence of the massacre of labourers on mechanized farms across the savannah belt bordering the south in the late 1980s. What we can now see as a series of incidents seems to have started in the Blue Nile, with reprisals in 1987 against labourers on schemes in the area of Jebel But, south of the Ingessana Hills. Some of those described to me as 'our lads' were there. I have been told of the way they were picked out as 'Udukawi', partly through recognition of the typical facial mark of a circle with a cross. I was given a first-hand account by one young man, Gusa Hodiya, who narrowly survived summary execution by the local Arab militia (see Chapter 2), and have heard of many such atrocities. The best-known incident of this phase of the war was in 1988 at El Diein in southern Darfur, which has since been well documented.[3] A parallel episode of violence against unarmed 'southerners' occurred at the end of December 1989–January 1990 at Jebelein on the White Nile, near to the borders with the Blue Nile Province. After a row about working on Sundays, labourers on the large mechanized farms there had been shot at and done their best to retaliate with the 'white weapons' which were all they had—that is, swords, throwing sticks, knives, and so on, no firearms. The officials witnessed the aftermath of this, and related incidents at the island of Musran where Arabs had rushed in from Jebelein and massacred a number of Shilluk Muslims who were gathered at the mosque there. These incidents, together with others being reported from Kordofan, especially the Nuba Hills, and southern Darfur, seemed to mark a real rise in racial feelings across the country, a new drawing up of the lines between 'Arab' and 'black'. These incidents, in retrospect, were clear signals of the slide towards war on a larger scale.

As part of the wave of new entrepreneurial activity in the large-scale agricultural sector then being encouraged by the new government, the NIF party, and the Islamic financial institutions, Osama bin Laden established a base at Jebel Kadum in the southern Blue Nile, an isolated hill in the wide plains to the east of the Ingessana Hills, during the period of his residency in the Sudan (1992–5). Here he ran mechanized

---

[3] Ushari Mahmud and Suleiman Ali Baldo, *Al Diein Massacre: Slavery in the Sudan* (Khartoum: n.p., 1987).

schemes and also other projects, such as constructing a new road towards Kurmuk (which played a significant role in the later military struggles of the area, even though it still ends short of its target). In fact, he was right there in the southern Blue Nile at the time of the post-Mengistu honeymoon between Sudan and Ethiopia, when the SPLA was severely weakened, while the Beshir army was getting into its stride and advancing southwards. Osama was in the southern Blue Nile Province at precisely the time that the Sudan government was agitating for the refugees to return home, through its consulates in Assosa and Gambela, 1992–5.

THE NATIONAL ARMY AND PEOPLE'S MILITIAS

Extremely significant too were the patterns of recruitment into the national army and auxiliary armed elements, which started during the 1970s decade of peace and continued after the resurgence of war in 1983. There is a long history in the Sudan of recruitment from the peripheral regions of the country, and a career in the military has always been an attractive opportunity to move out of the rural subsistence economy. Very few, of course, ever return to it. I should make it clear that from the point of view of the peoples of the southern Blue Nile, in the past there has been no problem for individuals about being absorbed into the orbit of the Sudanese state, from the time of Sennar up to the present. Successive governments in Sennar, Khartoum, and even perhaps Omdurman during the Mahdiyya, have been seen as protectors and patrons, to whom appeal can be made. The Uduk like their neighbours on the whole have not, until very recently, had any major occasion to rise up against 'the government', and many of the older (and mostly non-literate) in exile now speak of waiting for 'our own real government' to 'call us back home'. From the start, even the Sudan Interior Mission established its key links with the north rather than the south, and unlike some other Christian bodies, the SIM has been able to maintain a working relationship with successive governments in Khartoum up to the present. Freehold property was acquired in the 1940s in Omdurman, and even after the 1964 deportation of missionaries working in the rural areas they continued supportive work with the cluster of evangelical churches based in northern Upper Nile and southern Blue

Nile which came together in Khartoum as the Sudan Interior Church. Sila Musa, of staunch Christian parents, nephew of William Danga, had charge of the bookshop there from the mid-1960s for many years, and following work with humanitarian agencies in the Blue Nile during the war became an Assemblyman in the new Blue Nile State in 2005. Most Uduk in fact, especially the older generation, see no contradiction between their church affiliation and their basically feeling part of national civil society, and comfortable in the north. Of course a rift was opening up between the new Christian elite in Chali and the community of traders and the government-appointed Omda, especially after independence. But young men saw no problem about joining the police or the army as a career move, especially during the 1970s when Nimeiry was encouraging this, appealing to patriotism and the need to help defend the unity of the country, both just before and especially after the Addis Ababa Agreement.

At the age of around 24 Stephen Missa Dhunya, full brother to my original research assistant, Shadrach Peyko Dhunya, joined the military academy in 1971. He graduated two years later as a first lieutenant. I remember hearing this news myself with great surprise at the time. They posted him to Damazin, and he worked between Damazin, Singa, Kurmuk, Geissan, and Kosti for seven years. Stephen explained many, many years later, when he had already retired, that those were good times. There was peace, because of the Addis Ababa Agreement, and no active situations. 'There was nothing. Every Christmas we would go home and celebrate, I would take the army to go from Kurmuk to spend Christmas at Chali. I was also posted in Yabus, I opened the Yabus post.' I recalled the small police post on the far side when I had been there in the 1960s. 'That's right—but I brought everything to this side of the river, we opened the garrison on this side, leaving the police further away from us near the bridge. Really it was very nice, we used to go from Yabus to Chali to celebrate Christmas there. Sometimes we would go on a picnic to Boing.'[4] In 1980, he was transferred for two years to Shendi, north of Khartoum, and then to Malakal, well to the south. By this time the first stirrings of renewed insurgency were beginning to be felt, with the appearance of 'Anyanya Two' rebels crossing back into the Sudan from Ethiopia (these had refused all along to accept the Addis Ababa

---

[4] Stephen Missa, UK, 14 Sept. 1996.

Agreement). Stephen led 126 men to tackle them at Akobo. Shortly after this he was sent for further training to the United States. He departed in July 1983 (that is, only two months after the mutiny of troops at Bor which relaunched the civil war). He was successful academically, and this led to his later career in the English department of the Army College in Khartoum, rather than on the front lines of the war.

Another early recruit to service of the state, though into the police rather than the army, was David Musa, brother to Sila Musa in Khartoum and also nephew of William Danga. David joined the police and before the war broke out was stationed for seven years in Nasir, Malakal, and Daga, in Upper Nile Province, where he married a Nuer wife, and learned something not only of the ways of the government but also of the Nuer language. David became an extremely helpful guide to me at various points in the saga of the long road, the multiple displacements of the 'kwanim pa after 1987, and it was particularly sad to hear of his death, from illness and complications of an old gunshot wound, in Sherkole refugee camp.

While it was necessary to have some educational qualifications to join the police, young men could join the army as ordinary soldiers without any schooling. This became a significant opportunity especially during the drought years of the early and mid-1980s, coinciding with resurgence of civil war and calls from the government to youngsters all over the country. From interviews in Khartoum in 1988, I can estimate that while five years previously there were only about ten of 'our lads' of the 'kwanim pa who had joined up, by this time there were about two hundred, stationed all over the Sudan. As part of the 'regionalization' of the north, Nimeiry had created Damazin as a new HQ for the southern Funj, and called on all to serve their country by joining government service such as the police and army through their regions. Some of those who joined up, and not only from the Blue Nile, had in mind that one day they would be able to protect their own people. Even after the burning of the Uduk villages by government forces and allied militias in 1987, young men continued to join the national army. By mid-1988, four were in training at Shendi, and other Uduk youths were serving in the army not only at several key places in the south (including Nasir), but also more surprisingly at Gineina in Darfur and Port Sudan on the Red Sea coast. Several had already been killed in battle against the SPLA, for example near Soda in the Ingessana Hills in 1985, and in

1987 there were deaths in action at battles for Jokau, Kurmuk, Geissan, as well as one killed in an ambush between Aweil and Wau and another on Malakal airstrip. Nevertheless the tide of recruits continued, right up through the 1990s at least, both into the regular army and the PDF.

A conversation with Stephen Missa in the mid-1990s offers some light on this. I was asking about work opportunities for rural men who had found exile in the capital city, many in semi-legal squatter zones on the outskirts. They have to pay taxes and buy food somehow. They might join the army as a form of employment, but also, he explained, because it gave them training. 'Training' in the use of arms, and the discipline required to use them effectively, was valued for its own sake, even if it was only the fixed-term training provided for the PDF recruits (who had to hand in their weapons at the end of their course). There was no problem for Christians about joining up, it was 'just a job'. 'If there is any call for the PDF to go to the war zone, then they will call you, announce on the radio or in the newspapers...that we want registration number so and so to go to the war zone....This is for ordinary people. For young men who are students, they have to do what they call national service, and if you don't have this certificate you will not enter any university or will not get any job.'[5] Military service in the 1990s was a requirement if you were to seek promotion in any branch of government employment. Occasional bad news seemed no deterrent: for example the news I heard in Karmi, about two Uduk lads serving in the army who were on their way to defend Juba in mid-1992 when their plane crashed and all on board were killed.

A younger brother of David and Sila Musa's had joined the military in the early 1990s in Khartoum. He took a period of leave and was back home in government-controlled Chali in March 1995, when the SPLA attacked the Yabus garrison at the southernmost tip of the Kurmuk district.

As a soldier he went to the garrison there and said, 'I'm a soldier on leave and because of this I have come to help.' So they gave him a uniform, and a gun. He worked for the army.... So he went to help, in some of the tanks that were in Yabus. Then someone shot him! They shot him here, with a gun. Yes, the guerrillas! ['*kwanim bwasho*, lit. people of the bush].... —*I see, he went to join with the army people in Yabus, and the SPLA fellows shot him, in the knee?*—Yes, he

5 Stephen Missa, UK, 13 Sept. 1996.

was just shot, at random, he doesn't know if it was a *wathim pa* [Uduk person] or not—he was just on the side of the army. He's now hospitalized.—*Why had he joined up in the first place?*—I don't know. I didn't want them to join the army. He just ran off from Mayo [a squatter settlement south of Khartoum], we didn't know about it. So many of them, not only this lad. They thought, let's go and join the work over there. . . . He wanted to take the training.—*But why do these youngsters join the army, when they know the army is killing their people? . . . I mean do they feel that it is a good government and they want to fight for this government?*— No. They don't think that way. I believe it is just for the job.[6]

A rather older man I call 'Sitale' had joined up in Khartoum and found himself posted to Chali itself, his home area, in the early 1990s. He became a sergeant-major and was given the particular responsibility of recruiting a local PDF militia, from the smallish population who had re-gathered there from 1992 onwards following the re-establishment of the government garrison. The group included both returnees from SPLA country further south, and some home-comers from the towns of the north. Stephen explained that it did not matter whether you were old or young, Christian or Muslim, everyone was pressed into the PDF. The PDF force he trained in Chali in the mid-1990s would later come to change sides, as just one of the swings of fortune on the front line of this civil war; and 'Sitale' himself was arrested but later released, in circumstances to be sketched in the next chapter.

THE SUDAN PEOPLE'S LIBERATION ARMY (SPLA)

Far away, many years after the event, in a civilian occupation and setting to which he had gratefully returned, Peter Kuma Luyin told me how he had finally been driven into joining the SPLA and leading others with him. He offered his story quite spontaneously: 'I haven't really told you why it is that we all left Sudan.' We went down to the riverside for privacy. I have here selected only a few details from his very long account, which bear on the general situation that affected not only himself but many others. Even before the missionaries left, there were problems with the Muslims living in Chali—for example, there had been an attempt to build a mosque on mission-allocated land in 1962—

---

[6] Stephen Missa, UK, 13 Sept. 1996.

but after the deportation things got worse. Peter had already been working at the mission clinic, and when an incident took place in 1965, and Pastor Paul was ready even then to flee to Ethiopia, he was himself briefly arrested and imprisoned. By 1966 he was in school in Roseires, and that year the church in Chali was burned down for a second time. 'And there was a man in the army, he was a friend of mine—he had come to Roseires with the army—he said "We've come from a little place with a church there, it's called Chali." And he didn't know this was my home. "We were supposed to attack the church," he said. "But we looked at the people there and saw they were very poor and we left them alone." I kept quiet and thought over what they had said. . . . Later they began to insult the Uduk people. "Very bad, all Christians, *kaffirs*." I heard what they said and I saw there was going to be a problem there.'

By 1970, Peter had moved back to Chali to work in the clinic. He remained at this work for many years until the SPLA attacked Boing in 1984 in the nearby Meban country of Upper Nile and then began to infiltrate the Blue Nile. Then one day he took a sick woman to the hospital in Kurmuk. He sought out the house of a certain Catholic priest, not knowing this man had already left for the bush—that is, by implication, gone over to the guerrillas.

If we'd known he had run off we wouldn't have gone there. We'd have stayed somewhere else. Anyway we slept there, and a group of police came along, with guns. They arrested us in that house, seized us, took us to the prison. Then I took out my papers, papers from the clinic, and said, 'Hey! don't you know me? I'm a medical worker, I'm not a political person, I'm a medical worker.' He said, 'Huh! You people are followers of the rebels.' They took me and put me in the prison. Then after 24 hours, they freed me. I said, 'Why do you accuse me, when you don't know me, you are a black person yourself, you yourself could be with the SPLA.' 'Where did you know [this priest] from?' I said I knew him because of the church. 'The Christians know each other. Christians often go to stay with him, we know him. It is not because we know the SPLA, the SPLA is not present here, it is very far away. We are living in the north, why should we go to the south there?' Anyway he kept us in the prison longer. Then the doctor came and was angry. He said, 'This man used to be at the school here, when would he have known the SPLA? He has just brought in a sick person.' That day I became very unhappy. . .

I was working with the government, but this was the result. I was not with John [Garang]. 'I am with the government, along with you, so why do you arrest me and put me in prison?'... [After they] attacked Boing over there, the talk grew, and suspicion focused on the Uduk. People were stopped for no reason, there was no peace in the church, people were complaining. Then they arrested me again. Took me to prison. I asked them, 'Why do you put me in prison?... I don't know the SPLA, I don't know anything about it. I live in Chali, I haven't been anywhere else.'...

Then later, in 1986, in November, no December, [the government soldiers] killed some Meban, four of them. They brought them and killed them at Jebel Chali. They tied them with rope, brought them and killed them. Then they sought out others and put others in prison. They blamed the people of Beni Mayu, cursing them, saying, 'Ay! the black people, they are the ones spoiling this place.' The local Bunyans were saying this. They were making this political talk about people. Then, they started to say things about me. 'That Kuma, he may be a person of the government, but he's going to go off into the bush, like that man John, John Garang, that chief leader of theirs'...

They were about to put me in prison. I thought, right. I was in pain because people did not believe me, so I thought I would leave the country, go away from Sudan.... I looked for people who knew the way to Ethiopia.... I hadn't done anything wrong, but I was always being arrested, imprisoned, imprisoned, imprisoned, I was fed up. And since there was so much trouble in Chali, I decided to go.... I took the track to Dul.—*Were you alone?*—I took my lads with me, maybe ten of them, or maybe up to thirty of them. 'Where's Assosa, where's the path to Assosa?' 'The path's over there, carry on, there are lots of your people over there, they will lead you to Assosa.' Then we were found by some soldiers of the SPLA, they stopped us, saying, 'Where are you going?' 'We are fleeing from the Arabs, they are creating trouble for us, so we are running away. We're going up there.' 'OK,' they said. 'You go and stay up there.' And others, who had fled before, I found them there, people who had fled from Beni Mayu.... They were about to be killed there....

Then everyone began to flee, to flee from home, because things became worse. Some people were tied up, some were killed at Belatoma [in the Yabus valley]. It was awful, and people said, 'What are we going to do? Everyone will be killed.' I went back to have a look, to see, and I found about 120, or 130 of our lads... and after about a month, they took us to Assosa.

From Assosa they took us to Itang.... They asked us—they asked me: 'Now, some of your people are going to be killed over there, and what are you going to do about it? Do you want us to give you guns to help your people, or what else are you going to do?' We said, yes, we wanted guns. We wanted guns to help our people.... 'All right', they said, 'you can have guns, and... you can go and lead your people.' ... Then we were taken to Bilpam, and we learned to use the guns. ... We trained for four months.'[7]

Bilpam was an SPLA headquarters and training camp set up with Ethiopian support in the Gambela region, a couple of hours' walk downstream from Itang and across on the south bank of the Baro river, with access by ferry. The first cohort of Uduk who trained there formed the core of the *katiba al nishab*, the Arrow Battalion.

The stage was thus set. By 1986 there were considerable numbers of Uduk men in the government army, stationed in various parts of the northern Sudan. There was also a small but growing contingent who had joined up with the SPLA and were prepared to support the insurgency. It was not to be long before some of these young men found themselves facing each other in battle, as happened both in Chali and Kurmuk as I describe in the next chapter; and there were soon to be officers of significant rank on both sides. With few exceptions, the fighting men joined up without a strong ideological commitment to the national or rebel cause. When blame was attached to people's behaviour it was only rarely a matter of the behaviour of the leadership on either side, but of local actors who had done the right thing or otherwise. The violence of 'Arab' soldiers or militia in the long course of the civil war was almost taken for granted; but accusations and blame were typically piled upon local Bertha traders, or known groups of the Rufa'a nomads, who told tales, passing information to the garrisons. On a frontier like this, as in every civil war, there has surely been a deepening not so much of animosity between all northerners and all southerners as such, but certainly a deepening spiral of local fears and suspicions about treachery between neighbours. The Arabic-speaking local traders, typically from Muslim Bertha families, the ones dubbed 'local Bunyan' by the Uduk, the ones who often used to be blamed for the troubles of the past, these are the people who receive probably more than their fair share of blame today for bad things that have happened to the Uduk. But we should also note that a son of the main shopkeeper in 1960s Chali was among those who joined the SPLA: and all in all, the decades of civil war divided the Bertha, as all other groups in Sudan's frontierlands, against themselves just as happened with the Uduk.

---

[7] Peter Kuma, Bonga, 24 Nov. 1994.

KURMUK: TWIN TOWNS AND THE STRUGGLES
OF 1987–1997

On my first visit to Kurmuk in late 1965, a couple of friendly policemen invited me for an informal afternoon's visit to the shops and bars on the other side of the little ravine constituting the international frontier, to the Ethiopian Kurmuk. A certain amount of normal trade was passing through these twin towns to Assosa in Ethiopia. At that time the 'old' Sudanese civil war was felt to be very far away in the remote south, and no one seriously envisaged the possibility of it ever reaching so far north. Kurmuk at this time did not have vital strategic significance. But conditions on the Ethiopian side of the frontier were soon to change that, as John Young has shown.[8]

Who were the people of Kurmuk then? There were northern Sudanese merchants belonging to families, some long settled, from Khartoum and the central Blue Nile, and some visiting merchants from across the international frontier, many of whom had intermarried with those on the Sudanese side. There were locals from the various indigenous tribal communities in the border region, such as Bertha, 'Burun', or Uduk, working as servants or labourers, and speaking Arabic comfortably as a second language to their own. The long-time residents also included a couple of Greek merchant families, who still acted as a channel of communication to the nearby Christian church at Chali (following the missionaries' deportation in 1964). There was a considerable transient population of the national Sudanese elite—civil servants, police, teachers, health workers, and so on, nearly all of whom were on temporary assignment. Most of these professionals saw posting to Kurmuk as a kind of exile. There was no army presence there as far as I am aware. There was a feeling that the town was everybody's town. The sensitivity of Kurmuk, and Chali, as strategic outposts of the Blue Nile Province, and in a way the northern Sudan as a whole, sharpened up greatly over the next decades. This was especially so with the resurgence of civil war following the Bor Mutiny in May 1983, and the founding of the SPLA with support from the Ethiopian government.

---

[8] John Young, 'Along Ethiopia's western frontier: Gambella and Benishangul in transition', *Journal of Modern African Studies*, 37/2 (1999), 321–46.

This is not the place for a detailed political or military history of the succession of battles for Kurmuk which took place over the subsequent decade and a half, as the front line of the civil war moved north and south several times over the southern part of the Blue Nile Province. But a concise outline is needed, as the background to understanding the fate of the small village of Chali to its south, and the people who once lived in or near it.

The first assault on Sudanese Kurmuk by the SPLA resulted in its capture on 16 November 1987. This was launched from the Ethiopian side of the border, from bases at the nearby hill of Jebel Dul, and another at Khattawarak. The SPLA had already infiltrated the southern parts of the Blue Nile Province which had provoked severe counter-insurgency measures by the forces of Sadiq el Mahdi's government across the region. These had caused many young men to join the movement, and informed the claim of SPLA radio, broadcasting from Ethiopia, that the population of the town welcomed the SPLA soldiers.[9] Salva Kiir Mayar Dit,[10] in overall command of the forces in Blue Nile, reported the killing of 300 soldiers and capture of the garrison with a large quantity of armaments. The spokesman said the whole battle was recorded on video by the SPLA, and denied any foreign participation, though the government Sudan News Agency claimed there was Ethiopian and Cuban support. The SPLA shortly after reported that southerners, Ingessana, and other black men had been rounded up in Damazin and many of them cold bloodedly killed in revenge,[11] something for which I have also heard eyewitness reports. The government mounted a high-profile campaign across the Middle East to raise support for the recovery of Kurmuk, and the neighbouring border town of Geissan which it had also lost to the SPLA. These were represented as cities of the Arab homeland (*watan*). Assistance was

---

[9] See Radio SPLA transcript, 1 May 1987, quoted in detail in James, 'The multiple voices of Sudanese airspace', in Richard Fardon and Graham Furniss (eds.), *African Broadcast Cultures* (Oxford: James Currey, 2000), 207.

[10] Salva Kiir Mayardit: Dinka from Bahr el-Ghazal; a veteran Anyanya guerrilla from the first civil war, he was absorbed into the Sudanese army in 1972 and was deputy chief of military intelligence in Malakal at the time of the Bor Mutiny in 1983; a founding commander of the SPLA, he served in various senior capacities, becoming John Garang's deputy before the signing of the CPA; he became First Vice-President of the Sudan and President of the Government of South Sudan on Garang's death in 2005.

[11] Radio SPLA transcript, 28 Nov. 1987, quoted James, 'Multiple voices', 207–8.

forthcoming from Iran and Iraq and the tanks rolled south, with air cover. The recapture took place about a month later, by which time (according to the SPLA) the rebels had decided to leave with their captured equipment and loot. The regime's presence was reinstated, but the town population had mostly left—the merchants to the north, and the ordinary people of the area across the frontier to neighbouring kith and kin or to the refugee camp of Tsore, near Assosa.

In the course of 1988 and early 1989, Sadiq's government moved cautiously towards a peace agreement with the SPLA, which was making significant advances. However, any conclusion was pre-empted by the National Islamic Front-supported coup of Omer el Beshir mounted on 30 June 1989. In the Blue Nile, while Kurmuk and the main garrisons were again with the government, the SPLA had a presence in the more outlying rural areas. The new regime made some unconvincing offers of talks, but as early as October 1989 decided on a dry-season offensive, starting with a campaign to clear the country between Damazin and Kurmuk of SPLA elements. Forces based in Damazin attacked the SPLA positions at Surkum, Denderu, and Maiak, to the west and north-west of Kurmuk, on 16 October. After seven days' fighting the SPLA claimed to have repelled the attack and inflicted severe losses. Reinforcements sent during this week allegedly refused to advance beyond Denderu. This situation led directly to the second assault by the SPLA upon Kurmuk.[12] This attack, led by Commander William Nyuon Bany,[13] came from the Ethiopian side, the bases in the Assosa district. Kurmuk was captured on 28 October, and this was quickly followed by the fall of four small garrisons to its south, including Chali el Fil on the evening of Wednesday, 9 November. Appeals were made to 'patriotic and nationalist elements' in other regional garrisons to change allegiance, and the government started demanding the disarmament,

---

[12] Recordings of Radio SPLA made personally by W. J.

[13] William Nyuon Bany: Nuer from Jonglei Province; an Anyanya veteran of the first civil war, he was absorbed into the Sudanese army as a sergeant but rose to the rank of major; he was a founding commander of the SPLA in 1983, eventually serving as Garang's chief of staff; initially loyal to the mainstream SPLA following the Nasir split in 1991, he subsequently joined the Nasir faction in September 1992, shortly after the failed SPLA assault on Juba; based mainly in eastern Equatoria, and liaising closely with the Sudanese army in Juba, he succeeded in harassing the SPLA throughout the early 1990s, until he reconciled with Garang and rejoined in April 1995; he was killed in an ambush by Nuer forces of the Nasir faction in January 1996.

arrest, and even court martial of those who had fled the Damazin Military Area. Amid great furore the government again moved south to retake Kurmuk.

The southern Blue Nile, its strategic importance underlined by the presence of the nationally crucial hydroelectric scheme at Damazin, had by 1989–90 become a cockpit for the wider conflicts of north-eastern Africa. Mengistu had threatened Beshir that unless he cut off all support to the growing Eritrean and Tigrean movements he would make sure that the SPLA took Damazin after Kurmuk—in which event the Sudanese government would surely have fallen. A very high-level meeting then took place between Sudanese and Eritrean political leaders in Damazin to make a joint assessment of the situation. The Oromo Liberation Front (OLF) had not been proving very effective in support of the Sudanese, so in response to Mengistu's threat the Eritrean People's Liberation Front (EPLF) agreed to send a brigade of crack troops. They came down by road, and joined the Sudanese forces in retaking Kurmuk. The Eritreans then moved in to capture Assosa, scattering SPLA and refugees alike, and went on right up to Begi where they left a company of OLF troops (pretending it was an Oromo operation). These in turn were soon to harass the retreating Sudanese, regarded by this time as all 'southerners'.

This all happened at a time of rising political, and racial, feeling in the Sudan, marked, for example, in late December by the massacre of southern labourers on a large cultivation scheme at Jebelein (more detail is given above). It was only a few days after this event that the Sudanese and Eritrean forces converged southwards on Kurmuk. The former population of the town had largely disappeared, but with the re-establishment of government control, many farming and merchant families of West African origin, mainly Muslim Hausa speakers from the middle part of the Blue Nile, were encouraged to settle in and take over homes there.[14]

There were men from all the surrounding communities who took part on one or another, or both sides, of all the military struggles for Kurmuk and other places in the Blue Nile. An early case I heard of in 1988 of people who recognized each other across the lines was at Hilla Sherif, near Geissan, where William Dhupa (with the SPLA) and Idris

---

[14] Group interviews with displaced Hausa women, Nasir, 28 July 1991.

Ruthko (with the Sudanese army)—who were 'brothers' in a broad sense at home—faced each other in combat. The same fateful choreography drew friends and relatives to the key contested spots in struggles for Kurmuk itself. While the government campaign to retake Kurmuk at the end of 1989 was officially named *jundi Allah* or 'Soldiers of God', young men found themselves 'defending Kurmuk' not always for ideological or clear political reasons, but often just because of the situation in which they happened to find themselves. The Nationalities Service of Radio SPLA rather naughtily translated the Arabic call into Dinka as 'soldiers of *nhialic*', and into Shilluk as 'soldiers of *jwok*'—vernacular terms for the Divinity on high. On the occasion of the second capture of Kurmuk in late 1989, there were some dramatic encounters between kith and kin. By this time there were quite a few Uduk men who had either joined the regular army in Damazin, or even in Khartoum, and found themselves defending the town as it was attacked from the Ethiopian side by others whose language and voices they recognized. I have been given a graphic account of how those on the guerrilla side shouted a warning to their fellows on the government side before they fired, and proceeded with their superior knowledge of the geography to take the town. It was Stephen Missa who first described the scene for me (partly in English), though he had not been present:

Did I tell you that they were fighting among Uduk, in Kurmuk there?—*When was that, before, you mean?*—Yes, there were Uduk on this side, and the Uduk on that side.—*This was 1989?*—Yes.—*Tell me about that, why not. We have nearly finished this side of the tape. You carry on.*

These lads, our own youngsters, some of them were on the side of the government [i.e. stationed at Kurmuk]. And others came with the SPLA. You remember Kurmuk? There's the little Kurmuk hill here, and that's where the *'kwanim pa* fought. Here and there, here and there. Gradually the lads began to hear, there were some people over there speaking *'twam pa*. Across there. They were talking. 'Is that you fellows over there?' 'Yes, we're here.' 'Move over a bit, move over, get away from here! We're going to fire one of these really big guns!' He ran away and hid, and shouted, 'Fire it, you can fire it now!' while he was hiding. Then another said, 'I'm going to fire another big one, this is a really dangerous one! You take care of yourselves!'

That's how it was. Then, the Uduk lads here, the ones with the SPLA, they knew Kurmuk very well. There was this little path to Kurmuk, not the one by Kurmuk *zeriba* [round the south of the hill to the west], but through Kurmuk Shimi [a village to the north]. A very narrow path, up and over the hill. . . . The

Uduk lads ran this way…leaving [the other SPLA troops] behind them, ran, ran, and climbed up Jebel Kurmuk. The garrison was just between the smaller hill, and the *hafir* [cattle reservoir] on the side of Kurmuk *zeriba.—Yes, OK: the garrison is between the big mountain and the hafir.*—Those fellows were running, running—*Round the back of the mountain like this?*—They climbed the top of the mountain.…They attacked those people from behind. The people put their hands up.—*Put their hands up, those of the government?*—Yes. They took the whole of Kurmuk, that group.[15]

There were 'very many' Uduk men on the government side, perhaps fifteen or twenty scattered between different units. On the SPLA side there were also 'very many', though a good number died.

I can counterpoint Stephen's account with an eyewitness description by a young fighter who took part on the SPLA side, whom I shall call 'Jasper'. He had been led off from his village, Pam Be, in early 1987 at about the age of 12, and recruited from the first refugee camp near Assosa a couple of years later into the New Funj Forces of the SPLA. He gave me this frank account some twenty years later, in the USA where he was by now resettled. After completing their training, his cohort were given guns in mid-1989, shortly after the coup of Omer el Beshir. They were sent 'to fight the Oromo' close to Yabus Bridge, that is, elements of the OLF fighting Mengistu, who were allied with the Sudanese army there, partly to protect an unofficial refugee settlement of Oromo nearby. 'Jasper' was shot in the collarbone and side, taken for just over a month's treatment in Assosa, then sent back to join the fighting for Kurmuk, by now aged 14 or 16, he was not sure. I shall follow through some of his later adventures in subsequent chapters.

Reinforcements were soon being sent down from Damazin by the Sudan army, but the SPLA had ambushed them on the road where it crossed Khor Ahmar north-west of Kurmuk. No reinforcements could arrive, so the SPLA troops approached the town directly from the north-east side, through the village Shimi on the old road. The government soldiers in town were now rather cut off, along with those on the south side of the mountain near the hospital and *hafir*. We were speaking in a mixture of English and Uduk.

Kurmuk was a very complicated fight. At Shimi, there were Oromo, standing there with Arabs. The Arabs made them fight us there, because we had some

[15] Stephen Missa, UK, 13 Sept. 1996.

Ethiopian troops helping us. And in Kurmuk Shimi, there was a trench like this, you could stand up like this inside and see the people right up there and shoot them. A very big hole.—*You mean, with guns?*—No, with grenades. You throw the grenade, and they run out and you shoot them. There were no Uduk on that side, most Uduk were on the *hafir* side, and inside, close to the hospital. And some close by the Ethiopian Kurmuk. That's where they were communicating, because they were throwing a lot of bombs, from the Ethiopian Kurmuk...just by shouting. The Uduk were hiding and shouting from their trench close by here, and the Sudanese army were over there in their trench, just shouting back....

There were Ethiopian troops behind us; and most of the Sudanese army south of Kurmuk mountain.... That's where they had their big weapons, like howitzer, and machine guns. And yes, some of the *'kwanim pa* were in the army, coming round the mountain, they saw us there. The SPLA climbed up to the top and put their radio there, and the radio-telephone made a connection with the others. The army threw a big bomb from the *hafir*, and destroyed it, and killed maybe six people up there....

The ones in the garrison near the hospital were cut off, had no food, no ammunition, they just stayed in their trenches. I was there on the side of Kurmuk Shimi but I did not climb the mountains, I came round the side.

We took many places at that time. We took Kurmuk, Ora, attacked Chali and took it, and Yabus Bridge. The Arabs were afraid and ran away.[16]

The pendulum was, however, beginning to swing the other way. The end of the power of Soviet-backed states was by now in sight, and the Ethiopian government fell in 1991. The change of government there severely weakened the SPLA, and it lost many of the places it had controlled in the southern Sudan (and a few in the north). However, relations between Ethiopia and the Sudan had cooled again by 1995 and it was not long before the SPLA regained strength, regaining military support from Addis Ababa and finding a new generation of recruits from the refugee camps in Ethiopia.

A training centre was set up at Dimma in 1995, under 'Tigrean' officers who gained the reputation of being good professionals. On graduation, the old pattern was re-enacted: these new soldiers were sent, with some Ethiopian help, to attack the Sudan garrison at Yabus Bridge in March 1996. From there, they took their time but moved north during 1996 to take Kurmuk again at the beginning of 1997. Like

---

[16] 'Jasper', USA, Nov. 2006.

the first and second occasions a decade before, the assault was mounted from the eastern (Ethiopian) side. Once again the southern Blue Nile was pivotal to the regional struggles of the Horn of Africa: Ethiopian tanks went right up to the outskirts of Damazin, and the town was briefly evacuated by government forces. But this time, they were bolstered by stronger talk from Khartoum in explicit support of holy war, *jihad*, against the infidels and enemies of the state. Radio Omdurman, the national station, broadcast a report of an address given in Damazin by Hassan el Turabi, Speaker of the National Assembly, in early February. He was particularly critical of the Ethiopian support which had been lent to the SPLA.

Dr Turabi . . . stressed that the aggression was instigated by arrogant powers who did not care what happens between neighbours. He called all the people of Sudan to *jihad* and (?to support) [*sic*] the *mujahedin*, saying that the National Salvation [Revolution] brought religion into public life, and revived the tradition of *jihad*. He said past regimes had lost the Islamic sharia, prostrated themselves before foreign powers and humiliated the homeland.[17]

Despite the ratcheting up of rhetoric from Khartoum, and the increasingly sophisticated nature of the war weapons involved, this time the SPLA hung on to the town of Kurmuk and its satellite garrisons. The veteran journalist and politician Bona Malwal visited Kurmuk in August 1997, travelling from the Ethiopian side, courtesy of the Ethiopian government and as a guest specifically of SPLA Commander Malik Agar, originally from the Ingessana Hills area between Kurmuk and Damazin.[18] Malwal reported that people were 'already speaking of the difference between being yourself, administering yourself, and being in control of your own future rather than being ruled by "foreign" officials from Khartoum with their superiority complexes'. He continued:

I was pleasantly surprised to discover the determination of the people in and around Kurmuk to remain free of Khartoum's administrative stranglehold. . . . Kurmuk has been captured and overrun by the SPLA in the past. . . . Back in

---

[17] Translation from the Arabic, in BBC Summary of World Broadcasts, Middle East Series. ME/2840 MED/10, 11 Feb. 1997. A fuller quotation may be found in James, 'Multiple voices', 214.

[18] Malik Agar: Ingessana from Blue Nile State; former SPLM secretary in southern Blue Nile and a popular SPLA commander; at time of writing he is Minister for Investment in the post-CPA Government of National Unity in Khartoum.

1987...the government in Khartoum whipped up a racial hysteria claiming that black African hordes from the South had overrun a Northern Arab town. Observers could have been forgiven for accepting such hysteria until they found out the truth about the people of Kurmuk. The people of Southern Blue Nile are very much a black African people and are definitely non-Arab.[19]

He explained that while many were Muslims, they did not accept the policies of the NIF. The authorities had constructed a new and elegant regional headquarters at Kurmuk, where everything had been inscribed with Koranic verses. The SPLA decided to secularize everything in the building, which now flew the SPLA/M flag.

Though the SPLA never did succeed in its oft-threatened move to take Damazin, its control over the rural areas of the region waxed and waned several times over the next few years. For example it managed to take the far western outpost of Jebel Ulu in 1999, even withstanding aerial bombardment there, though it lost Geissan. However, it held on to Kurmuk firmly right up to the signing of the peace agreement in 2005. For all intents and purposes the writ of the SPLA still began at the 'truck-stop' village of Denderu halfway to the Ingessana Hills, and extended westwards to Jebel Ulu. A report by Abdel Ghaffar Mohammed Ahmed of May 2006 gives a picture of roads littered with broken military hardware and infrastructure in poor condition, very little commercial activity or public services, and no proper water supply. The plains from Denderu northwards were visibly under large, former mechanized cultivation schemes during the period of government control in the mid-1990s, but south of there the landscape was better wooded and much as it used to be before the war. Kurmuk was a dilapidated and sorry sight, physically; but at the same time full of young people with hopes and aspirations. Former fighters were yet to be re-employed usefully, but an interesting sight was of uniformed SPLA soldiers flocking off to pray at the mosque on Fridays. Two primary schools were operating, one run by SPLM staff and one by staff appointed by the Comboni Mission, all trying their best to juggle the sensitivities of Muslims and Christians and to adapt a curriculum designed by the SPLM for the southern Sudan. All teachers were from the southern Sudan or East Africa and English was the medium of

---

[19] Bona Malwal, 'In Kurmuk the thoughts are all about defeating the NIF regime', *Sudan Democratic Gazette*, 8/88 (1997), 8.

instruction. Kurmuk is certainly remote from other parts even of the new Blue Nile State, including the capital Damazin, and in practice, at the time of writing, is yet to be satisfactorily integrated into the administration and development of the region as a whole. In effect, it is still run in practice by the SPLM.[20] A couple of NGOs, including Samaritan's Purse and the Irish GOAL, have been operating there with a number of local projects, and in 2006 were joined by new young recruits to the SIM (the initials now standing for 'Serving in Mission'), intent on helping plan a new secondary school at Yabus Bridge (formal permission was still being awaited as this book went to press).

Although, since 1953, the Uduk have tended to be regarded as 'southerners' within the north, 'southerners' have always played a variety of roles integral to the history of 'northern' regions. The definition of all 'marginal' places has shifted, and the history of individual lives and allegiances has been extraordinarily complex. As the quotations from recent reports show, these complexities do not make much sense if reduced to 'African' versus 'Arab', categories which in any case are newcomers to the discourse of this 'transitional' region. In microcosm, we could perhaps regard aspects of the Blue Nile State as reflecting within itself the complexities of 'identity' and social relations over the country as a whole.

---

[20] Abd al-Ghaffar M. Ahmed, 'Visiting Kurmuk: crossing to the SPLA/M controlled area, March 15–16, 2006', May 2006.

2

Chali: Rooting up a Sleepy Village

> We '*kwanim pa* don't have guns, we don't know how to
> fight, we ask for security from the government, and the
> government attacks us. So we just run into the bush
> like wild animals.[1]

The violent events again and again shaking Kurmuk had their consequences for every village in the district, whether on the Sudanese or the
Ethiopian side of the frontier. And just as a focus on a small but strategic
place like Kurmuk can throw up the nature of the key moves in the
choreography of the international and national struggles taking place on
a broad scale, so the internal history of a tiny place in a sensitive locality
like Chali el Fil can illuminate the replicating patterns characteristic of
the front lines of civil war itself. This is especially clear in its initial
phases, when accidental or personal circumstances can throw people
onto one 'side' or another of a split whose significance inevitably
deepens over time.

The family of Luyin Thilo is a poignant example. He and his wife
Tukka were baptized in 1956. They chose the baptismal names Obadiah
and Milcah, though neither really stuck. At that time of the newly
independent government, it was apparently official policy to give
every child a Muslim name if they did not have a Christian one. The
SIM itself did not require any change of existing name at baptism, but
the view of local Christians was that all baptized people should take a
biblical name. Luyin and Tukka had a flourishing family, who came to
provide leadership in several of the new modernizing sectors over the
next decades. Among the eldest of their children, originally educated in
the mission school, Martin Luther Lipa became a pillar of the Chali

---

[1] Moses Chidko, senior educated man displaced to Khartoum, August 1988.

church, as Pastor Paul's right-hand man, returning from exile to Chali whenever war conditions permitted, playing an important role in the Christian community. The next younger son was Peter Kuma, trained in medical work at the Chali mission after primary school. Peter, who was introduced in the previous chapter, joined the cause of the SPLA, and became its first Uduk officer. Their sisters Phoebe and Estor became key women's leaders in the context of the refugee camps to which most of the people fled from 1987. A younger brother Luke, however, joined the national army and died in its service. Luyin himself had retired to the northern town of Singa where he died before the outbreak of the war; but his widow, after initially attempting to flee with others to Ethiopia in 1987, gave it up from exhaustion, returned to Chali, and eventually managed to join the growing Uduk community in Khartoum. Representing the vanguard of the rising educated generation just established at Chali before independence, the ironies of this family's fortunes mirror the divisive effects of rising national conflict at the level of local communities, especially upon any emerging educated elite among them.[2]

By May 1983, just before the resurgence of war, which is when I last visited the Chali area, with my husband and children in tow, the village had acquired a mosque and *mahad* (Islamic Institute), along with a garrison in addition to the old police post. The church was running its own affairs under Pastor Paul Rasha Angwo, as part of the autonomous protestant Sudan Interior Church whose network reached westwards through Boing in Meban country to Melut on the White Nile among the northern Dinka. The local 'chief' or Omda, Talib el Fil, lived between the Christian village, near the old mission station, and the market centre dominated by the Muslim trading families (termed 'Bunyan' by the Uduk). The Omda along with some of his immediate family and few others was a Muslim, and maintained his own network with government and trading circles in Kurmuk town and northwards. There was still something of a church school, along with a government

---

[2] The baptismal list at Chali began in 1946, and by 1951 twenty-nine names were recorded. By 1953–6 there were fifty-seven, including many people who appear in this book: Paul Rasha, Martin Luther Lipa, Ruth Panjeka, William Danga, Peter Kuma, Solomon Shiwa, Gideon Shokup, Shadrach Peyko, and Suske Wupko. The next 'peak' in the list was of 167 for 1960–1, when we find among the names Martha Ahmed, Rebecca Puba, William Dhupa, Stephen Missa, and Hergke Kinna.

primary school. Chali itself served as administrative and market centre to a large rural hinterland of scattered hamlets where the pulse of local life still ran on a different, arguably 'vernacular rural' rhythm. Economic activities were largely subsistence in character, a few animals adding to the resources of the small but determinedly self-reliant communities of cultivators. There had been a spread of Christian practices and the building of small churches in the outlying hamlets, especially following the rising profile of Islam in Chali itself, as I have described in my earlier book *The Listening Ebony*. Chali lay on the south side of the seasonal stream, the Khor Tombakh, and a key part of its own 'periphery' consisted of a string of hamlets on the far (northern) side.[3] It included some of the villages which had acquired small churches during the mission period, such as Gindi and Beni Mayu, and also others which had not been part of the Christian network until very recently—and in this category were the hamlets of Pam Be, including 'my old hamlet' of Wakacesh (Figure 5).

INITIAL ASSAULTS AND REPRISALS, 1984–1987

Events moved rapidly in Chali from the initial resurgence of the Sudanese war. In brief outline, the general story (based on a variety of sometimes very personal testimonies I have heard) is as follows. The SPLA moved close to the Blue Nile Province in its first year, attacking the garrison at Boing in Meban country, Upper Nile Province, in April 1984 (as well as sites in the Ingessana Hills). From their bases in Ethiopia they then began using forest pathways through the hamlets in the southernmost extension of the Blue Nile Province about November 1985, as they moved through to the northern Upper Nile. They avoided the main truck road through Chali itself, but passed close by, along the northern bank of the Khor Tombakh. The guerrillas were described by local villagers as mainly 'Dhamkin', primarily Dinka and Nuer (though Shilluk can be included in this term), normally regarded as dangerous strangers from the south. They would make demands on the villagers, but also sit and explain their cause.

As the government realized what was happening, harassment of the civilians around Chali increased through 1985 and 1986. People were

---

[3] See James, *'Kwanim Pa*, maps 4 and 5, pp. 26, 29.

Figure 5. New church at Wakacesh, May 1983

arrested, interrogated, and some tortured, prompting young men to join the rebels and go for training at Bilpam Base, near Itang in Ethiopia. At the same time there was a heavy demand for labour on the mechanized agricultural schemes to the north, and men who declined to join the rebels could opt to go for this work. After a year of drought when there had been strife over the distribution of food aid, the harvest of 1986 was a good one, which ironically contributed to problems around Chali as the people were suspected of passing food to the rebels. This was the year when the local nomad Arabs, the Rufa'a, along with many other groups across the middle belt of northern Sudan, were armed as a government militia, and they began to play a significant role reporting movements of the people to the garrison.

One Sunday morning in the rainy season of 1986 a group of about fifteen guerrillas arrived at Beni Mayu church, and settled down for the night. They were quickly reported to the authorities by a village elder.

About forty soldiers set off, overheard on the way asking how many rebels there were, and thanking God there were only fifteen. They attacked in the middle of the night, killing two in the church and wounding three. There was blood all over the church. Quite a number of soldiers were also killed. From that time the government would not let anyone from Beni Mayu come into Chali to buy anything or to get medicine. Their chiefs were ordered to report there, but refused to go. The pastor and church elders in Chali were repeatedly called in for questioning by the military; the Omda threw blame upon them for encouraging youngsters to join the rebels; a list was demanded, which the Omda provided and the church forwarded to the military in Kurmuk, of those who had indeed joined up.

On 25 November 1986 an assault force of guerrillas crossed over from the Ethiopian side, through Babarras, a Bertha village in the border hills, with the aim of attacking the garrison at Deim Mansour. Captain Tayeb Musbah of the Chali garrison immediately sent for the pastor's Land-Rover and took it towards the Ethiopian border to help fight the SPLA; then they took it in the other direction to get more guns and ammunition from Boing in Meban country.

Not long after this a warning message arrived from the SPLA announcing they were going to attack Chali and that all the Christians should retreat to the bush. After Christmas word came from Yabus saying that a guerrilla force had arrived from Bilpam, and there had been a heavy engagement. When the Chali garrison heard that 'the Uduk were coming home' they called for reinforcements from all over the region. The guerrillas set out from Yabus for Chali, but they were tired and had run short of ammunition. So they turned eastwards— planning to stock up on the Ethiopian border. They encounted a party of nomad Arabs, who are normally on their way south at this time of year. These ran to Chali to report. The government reinforcements blocked the road ahead of the guerrilla party, while the Chali troops came up from behind them. They were trapped; there was 'very hot fighting' for some hours, and deaths on both sides. A good number of guerrillas then quietly came back to visit their families by night, some staying on a while, but warning people that they would return one day and take over Chali.

There were several further minor skirmishes in the district in early 1987 while the harassment of civilians intensified. The small church at

Gindi was burned by the army in January. The pastor and some church elders finally got their Land-Rover back in working condition, and in mid-February left for a much-delayed meeting in Khartoum (by a bush road as the main roads were now mined by the SPLA). At the end of March, the soldiers went through the rural villages of Chali's hinterland, torching all the huts and churches. Local youngsters now part of the SPLA then returned by night to collect up the scattered civilians, and take them to Ethiopia. The Rufa'a Arabs, now gathered at Chali, were supplied with arms, and sent off to clear the Uduk villages in Bellila. The Omda remained behind at least for some time, together with some displaced people from the outlying hamlets, and from Meban villages further west. The cluster of Christian families around the church itself was left for a month or so longer, and then it too was attacked and burned and the people either had to leave for Ethiopia, try to make it north (a few from Khartoum came down to rescue relatives), or take shelter with the garrison.

The first fall of the Chali garrison to the SPLA took place immediately after the first capture of Kurmuk in October 1987 (see Chapter 1). The remaining locals then had no choice, and were escorted off to the refugee camp near Assosa. After the return of government soldiers to Chali a couple of months later, a few returnees began to show up from the north—including the Omda, and a little later his wife. Within less than two years, when the SPLA returned in a fully professional manner after the second capture of Kurmuk, they too had no choice but to accept an escort to Ethiopia. They might not have survived at all had there not been local men among the rebels who knew them personally.

The tenor of accounts relating to this early period when 'the war arrived' in the southern Blue Nile is often highly specific with respect to places, persons, and even the details of narratives which might or might not be of historical significance but strike individuals vividly at the time. The character and behaviour of individual traders, soldiers, or rebels are key points of every story-line, rather than political or ideological generalities. Local people, perhaps especially those in positions of power, are held reponsible for what they do; blame is rarely displaced to remote political leaders or movements. There are good Muslims, soldiers who try to maintain some kind of fairness to individuals, people like the local *halab* or 'gypsy' meat-trader who unties suffering prisoners, at least one army captain who apparently comes to regret what he has done; the rebel fighters are regarded as a great nuisance at first, and not really seen as heroes until much later; and there are (known but unnamed) traitors among the people themselves who give information to the security. Above all, there is little talk of 'southerners' and 'northerners' at the start. As the civil war deepens, however, the testimonies below show how categories and causes and public figures, as distinct from local individuals, become the representatives of good and evil.

ESCAPE TO THE NORTH: DISPLACED
TO KHARTOUM

The above summary is based on written notes I was shown by people displaced to Khartoum in 1988, along with interviews I held there at that time. I will now quote from some representative eyewitnesses I met there, who were either recent escapees from the southern Blue Nile, or persons normally resident in the capital city who had been down there to visit and perhaps rescue relatives.

Stephen Ruthko had been working for some time in Damazin and in Khartoum, and on a visit to Chali in April 1984 saw some of the immediate consequences there of the SPLA attack on Boing nearby in Upper Nile. The soldiers had been seizing people, tying them up, and beating them, and some people had died. A soldier asked, 'Where has this fellow come from? From the north, really?' The local officer said, 'You should not wander about. If you wander about you will be arrested.' So he went straight back to Kurmuk, where he and three others were indeed arrested. In Damazin they saw others from the agricultural schemes who had been arrested, and some from Yabus. These had been 'seized and tied, not tied in an ordinary way, tied very horribly'. They were asked if they had guns, and some guns were found. But some other soldiers said, 'These are not the guns of the rebels, these are their own guns.' There was argument about whether they should be killed, but they survived.[4]

Gideon Shokup was an elder of the Chali church, but had left with Pastor Paul's party and was now resident in Khartoum. He told me of his personal arrest, shortly after the initial advance of the local SPLA

---

[4] Stephen Ruthko, Khartoum, 2 Aug. 1988.

recruits in late December 1986—and their discreet return to visit their families by night afterwards.

Some had wives, some had children, some stayed with their father's people, they all came to see their own people, some stayed, even a fortnight, among the people...And after this, after three days, the army sought me out, and arrested me...at six in the evening. They put me in the prison, and asked me lots of questions. I told them that I didn't know anything. I told that I didn't know these people. And they kept me in prison for one day, from Tuesday to Wednesday. And the people of the church gathered to pray to God for me. They prayed to God, and God heard their prayers, and those people freed me in the afternoon, at four o'clock...[5]

A month or so later, in mid-February, there was a further skirmish with the SPLA at Khor Bodi not far from Chali. It was on the day that the church party was to leave for the meeting in Khartoum. It was a genuinely historic day, a major turning point for Chali—but what still rankled with Gideon was the slighting manner of the army officer towards them.

And on that day...the army came again and surrounded us in the settlement. Surrounded the church village, with the Chali Uduk all inside...because they thought that we were hiding guerrillas among us....

We woke in the morning to find all these soldiers...they said that if they found just one guerrilla there, they would kill all the Chali people, all the Chali Uduk people, they said. But they didn't find anyone. They found no one. Not one. Later in the morning when we were to go, we reported to the chief army officer that we were going to Khartoum.... And that chief officer, he got up with a gun, and we didn't know if he was going to kill one of us or what. Then he drove a car backwards, and hurt two of our party...And he didn't say sorry.[6]

The pastor and his companions did reach Khartoum, have their meeting, and again had to wait for the car to be properly fixed. They were still there when they heard the dreadful news from Chali: the army had first gone southwards to the Daga valley in the Upper Nile Province to do a *natafa* [Arabic; 'search and destroy'], and then carried out the threats they had made to burn the villages. Co-ordinated with this campaign at the end of March 1987 was an excursion of armed nomad Arabs from Chali to Bellila, where they killed many civilians.

---

[5] Gideon Shokup, Khartoum, 5 Aug. 1988.   [6] Ibid.

Gideon had heard that the remote outlying Uduk village area of Pan Gayo had been completely eliminated. This news, however, like some other second-hand reports of deaths and people being burned in their houses, turned out to be exaggerated. There were indeed some cases of death under tying and torture, for example a boy called Teso died this way in Chali. But in another case, I heard in Khartoum that Koya Beshir had been tied, that battery acid had been poured on his hands and they had rotted away as a result, and he had probably died. In fact he had just survived after treatment in Ethiopia, and I was to meet him three years later (see below).

Meanwhile, the Rufa'a Arab militia was pursuing its own agenda, capturing children, both boys and girls, and raping women in Bellila. Men were killed as they were coming from the agricultural schemes at Jebel But (I quote below the testimony of one who only just escaped this fate). Stories were legion of maltreatment and killings there, which I am not in a position to confirm; for example, one was being led, weak from a beating, and they asked him if he was Uduk? He said no, he was Meban, and some of the Wadega soldiers said they should leave him, but others killed him anyway. Nomad Arabs killed the Uduk man Hajko Gongosh, who worked in the dispensary at Wadega, allegedly in front of the police. At the same time I heard evidence of individuals struggling to stem the tide of opportunistic violence. My informants in Khartoum had heard that the capture of some Uduk and Meban children in Bellila was reported to the army in Chali, and when this was reported they actually went to retrieve them. Only two children were thought to remain with Sheikh Nayar el Kineita of the Rufa'a, working unpaid, as slaves, herding goats. But the nomad Arabs were becoming very aggressive. They 'had been given guns by the government', and would kill a defenceless person and take their foodstuffs. 'But a guerrilla has a gun, and the Arabs don't kill him. The Arabs will flee.' And the reported rapes of women by Arabs in Bellila were later matched by the behaviour of the soldiers in Chali: they seized women, threatened them with guns, 'and did wrong'. I heard statistics, though in the hearsay circumstances of Khartoum these could scarcely be reliable, and there was a sort of poetic moral logic to the numbers—I was told one day that 308 of their people had been killed, that is 'three hundred Uduk and eight Meban'. The sense of a common grief and shared appalling dilemma as between the Uduk and Meban was deepening, a point to which I return below. The emotional empathy was right, but the statistics were probably the other way round: in terms of deaths from violence, the Meban almost certainly lost more people in the war, even at this early date, than the Uduk.

Tabke, wife of the veteran church loyalist Moses Chidko, sister of William Danga, and mother of both David and Sila Musa, was in Chali when the outlying villages were burned. Now rescued and living in Khartoum, she did see the reasons why the army had become so angry, when 'our boys' had returned to revisit their families after the initial attack. 'So they said all of us were SPLA guerrillas ['*kwanim bwasho*, lit. people of the bush]. They said all of the people were rebels [Arabic: *maratin*].... That's why they burned the houses.' She herself had been roughly treated. 'You know [so-and-so]? They seized him. And the day they arrested him, we were going along, and the soldiers attacked us—I was slapped on the face here, '*duw! wep!* Because we were going to see him. The soldier hit me on the face here, and I fell down. I was carrying the children. We were just following that fellow to find out what they wanted to do to him.... My head ached badly after that.'

When the SPLA boys came to the church village to escort people away, Tabke was nevertheless surprised—the church group had never really seen the guerrillas or as yet had their houses torched. However, she made a start on the trek to Ethiopia with her children, under gunfire from the garrison. Their party was soon exhausted and came back. They were ordered to stay near the market area.

We were living at the church village.... About 7 o'clock in the evening they came: 'We have come to take you away.' We said we didn't know anything about this. I got ready; there were a few cattle, and I said 'Hassan',—that little boy Hassan who's here now—there were no grown men—'Hassan, up you get and untie the cattle.' Hassan untied them, and I put him on the donkey. We went on a little like that, and the guns fired right over our heads.... We went on, and God prevented the guns from stopping us....

We went on until the moon was high, right into the bush, in the night, led by the boys, on until the dawn found us still going.... The children were very tired, and one of our girls couldn't go on. She collapsed and said, 'I won't be able to make it there.' So I said we should go back home. 'If the army are going to kill us let them kill us.' I led them, we came back, we got home when the sun was here in the evening, the day after we had left.... There was some water left in the houses of the people who had gone, and ... we ate....

We slept two days. There were others who were going to return, but the army came along the road from Deim Mansour, from Kurmuk . . . and fired on them with guns, and they fled away for good. . . . The soldiers chased them and shot at them, shot at them. People fled and threw everything down.[7]

Among the government soldiers, Timothy Mona (son of the first Christian convert at Chali, and close friend of the group who had decided to return) suggested to his colleagues that they speak to the party quietly. But 'a certain captain' ordered shots to be fired both in front of and behind the group to halt them, which naturally sent them back towards Ethiopia. The army then came over to the church village, demanding to know where Tabke and the children with her had come from. They required everyone to move to the central market area, where some other women welcomed in Tabke. She could visit her own house in the day but had to sleep in Chali centre. It was about a month later that her son Sila arrived to rescue her and anyone else who was willing to go north.

On his journey, leaving Khartoum on 5 May 1987, Sila found village after village in his homeland 'didn't exist', was 'completely burned down', 'there weren't any people', there was nowhere to stay and no animals around at all. He found his uncle William Danga, who had been on foot to inspect the damage to all the surrounding villages, and who told him of the army's rampage through them. It began to rain, and for a couple of days there were no trucks going north. Sila witnessed the looting of the church property, particularly noticing how the captain took for himself the old plastic Christmas tree which had served Chali for decades:

At the time we were there, the soldiers went up the road to the church. They took beds, anything in good condition, they took it. What I know precisely is that they took the Pastor's trunks, his bed, and the fridge. The fridge is in the barracks, it was taken by the army. And the beds were taken for them to sleep on, with the bedclothes. Beds to sleep on. I found the fridge in the army barracks.

When we left, we travelled with some of the army. The captain was called Tayeb Musbah. He took the Christmas tree, the one in the church there, he took it too. He took it to Kurmuk. And also the Pastor's chair cushions, and some boxes.—*What did he do with the Christmas tree?*—He took it to his house.—*To decorate his house?*—Yes.[8]

[7] Tabke, wife of Moses Chidko, Khartoum, 10 Aug. 1988.
[8] Sila Musa, Khartoum, 10 Aug. 1988.

Tabke herself told me something of the difficulties of their journey north. They kept being questioned by men looking for a way to arrest her son. 'Those people of Garang! Where are they going? . . . You attack people, and now where are you going?'

I conclude this section with an account by Gusa Hodiya of his arrest and torture in 1987. Gusa had been looking for seasonal work on the agricultural schemes, but without success, and was on his way home, resting near Jebel But.

Then our brother, Sora, Sora Mushwad, was asked by a Bunyan [a local Bertha man], 'How are you.' Then another man came and called him, and they went over there and stopped, and talked and talked and talked. Then he asked us to call the others. . . . We went there and those people said, 'Their people have killed a neighbour of ours at Dawalla. We should take these people to the government.' They took us away.

They took us away, and we went on and on, and then they took our things away—our throwing sticks and spears, the things we were carrying, we gave them up. We rested for a while, and they said they were taking us to the government. The police. We waited on the ground. We waited, and they went to see the government. The government said, 'Ay. We don't want these people. If you want to deal with them, you may do what you wish with them.'

They kept us, until some Arabs [Rufa'a] came. They asked us questions. 'How did you come from your home?' We said that a man called Somolia brought us from our home area, to work on cutting sorghum at his place. I told the Arab all about it. The Arab said, 'Really? We know that Somolia brings many Uduk to work at Jebel But there. Leave these people, they haven't done anything.' Others saw this. They asked us questions, 'Really, really? Did Somolia bring you?' 'Yes.' And we went to work at the flour mill at Somolia's place, but the money was very little, so we went to another man, called Osman, to cut sorghum at his place and go home. They went and talked, this and that, this and that. 'A man was killed in Wadega.' We decided we should go. But then they seized us. We were not fleeing, we were still there, and they seized us. Some of the fellows saw they were carrying rope and tying our hands behind our backs—and they ran off. Four of them fled, and left four of us. We sat there, and they brought rope and tied us. They took our things, leaving just a few clothes on. We stayed there. About seven, they took us away, pushing us along into the bush there, and said, 'You can go to Damazin on foot.' 'You have been making politics [Arabic: *siyassa*] and you want to kill us.' We went on, obeying their words, we went on into the bush there. Some Arabs were there at a little hill. We went on.

Then we stopped. I said to Sora, 'To tell you the truth, you know I am a Christian and I don't want to die for no reason, without seeing the government face to face. If I see the government face to face, and they kill me, as others killed Jesus for the truth, I will die in front of the police.' And then the Arabs came rushing forward along the road. And he said, 'You do what you can; I shall stay as if I'm dead.' . . . Then they beat us.

They struck us, and I fell down on the ground. But I got up, I don't know how. . . I ran a little, I don't know how I got away from there, I thought I was dying, what shall I do, I ran on there, and I saw that I had got away some distance. I stopped. I untied myself and I went on, it was a bright moon. I went on, and I stopped. Then they killed the boys with guns, *'do, 'do*. Two boys. And the other one, they beat him until it was finished with a stick.—*Who was shot?*—Sora, and Limam. And Nyaha, he was killed with a wooden stick.[9]

Gusa ran on looking for help and rest, a moving story of terrible courage and persistence. After several days with occasional rest in outlying places he arrived at Gule.

I asked some Meban boys there, 'Brothers, are there any Uduk here? [he uses the Meban term, Ocon]. 'No, there aren't any Uduk, no Uduk,' they said. So I went on to Gireiwa, to see if there was any Uduk person at Gireiwa. I went on, reached there, and I found a *wathim pa* there, a chap we had left behind . . . from Pan Gayo.[10]

Gusa's story continues. Among other things he was questioned by the police at Roro, near Gule. He was asked whether he knew Pastor Paul; and where he was now, answering that he was in Khartoum. But they just said, 'Huh! All of you are rebels. You have all become rebels.' Fortunately they let him go, and eventually some Meban friends collected money to help him get to the relative safety of the Uduk community in Khartoum. It was in one of their houses that I heard his story. Gusa concluded by saying that he wanted to return to the work of God, since it was the God of the Bible which had kept him alive. He was due to be baptized shortly.

---

[9] Sora Mushwad, Limam Pisko, Nyaha Karabu.
[10] Gusa Hodiya, Khartoum, 15 Aug. 1988. A fuller version of Gusa's story is published in James, 'Civil war and ethnic visibility: the Uduk on the Sudan–Ethiopia border', in K. Fukui and J. Markakis (eds.), *Ethnicity and Conflict in the Horn of Africa* (London: James Currey, 1994), 155–8.

ESCAPE TO THE SOUTH: DISPLACED TO NASIR

The testimonies I heard in Khartoum were confirmed, in equally and more graphic detail, by accounts from many individuals I talked to later in various places of exile. It is striking that the attribution of blame and responsibility to individuals for what happened is even clearer among these sections of the Uduk people who later found themselves in really appalling circumstances. I will quote first from three first-hand accounts I heard in the swampy camp of Nor Deng near Nasir, by 'observers' who were never physically attacked themselves but witnessed violent events at close hand.

William Danga described first how the SPLA, members as I heard later of the Mosquito Battalion (*katiba namus*), began to appear in their hamlets, and how this provoked the government garrison.

Before, when we lived around Chali, everything was fine. Everyone was content cultivating their fields.... Then, SPLA people began to pass through the villages on the other side. From Borfa, to Gindi, to Iyanwosh, and Penawayu, and to Pam Be. Then they went on to Meban country.... But they didn't cross the valley to Chali itself. They used to come to us all the time, bother people, cut goats, and eat goats, and take beads from the women, and their clothes. And all this was a great nuisance to people. They behaved very badly. Sometimes they would do bad things to the women.

And then the government post, the one in Chali, took a very stern view of us. They thought... all the '*kwanim pa* as far as the Meban border, were helping the SPLA with food.... They said, 'Up to Bigin, we ought to kill all the '*kwanim pa.*' People had to live with this fear, just live with the fear, live with the fear, the fear....

Then one day in the rainy season the SPLA men came and slept in Margo's church [at Beni Mayu]. And Margo's people gave them fresh corn to eat, and gave them a goat to cut. Then the government came at night, and fired on the church from up on the hill there... they killed three of the SPLA people dead that day. And the rest split up and ran away....

William was of the view that the local army captain was doing these things on his own responsibility, not just following orders from outside. He directed the blame rather towards the local Bunyan merchants who had put him up to it, planting evil things in his heart (or, in the strict Uduk idiom, 'Liver', the physical and psychic seat of emotions[11]).

---

[11] A full account is given in James, *The Listening Ebony*, 70–3.

The man, the government man in charge of Chali at that time, was called Tayeb. Tayeb Musbah. He's the one who did this. The people in Damazin didn't hear that he was doing these things against the *'kwanim pa*. He did it on his own, together with the merchants living in Chali, and the Bunyan Bertha there in Chali. They told him lies to trap him with wicked words, they planted wicked ideas in his Liver. Saying the *'kwanim pa* were very bad, they really admired the SPLA and were giving them food. . . . People were afraid of Chali.

If a man wanted to buy clothes, he would have to give the money to his wife to go. And there was a lot of cursing in the market place. 'You're all women of the SPLA! John Garang's women! Garang's women over there!'

It happened like this because the SPLA would take that route [through our hamlets]. They'd eat goats. If they found beer, beer made for work parties, they'd help themselves. They'd take it and finish it up, while people were still in the fields. If they found women cooking food, they'd take it. No one *gave* them anything. They seized the goats by themselves, and cut them, right there. They harassed people, forcing them to carry boxes of ammunition and equipment in relays from one village to the next, right on to Meban country over there. And the government accused the *'kwanim pa* for no good reason. . . . That's why they decided to burn all these villages.[12]

William explained how a skirmish in March prompted them to put their plan into action, with the help of reinforcements called up from Yabus Bridge who arrived with enormous guns. By this time he had himself moved from Wakacesh to the vicinity of Chali. One morning he saw the army moving down the main road in silence towards Pam Be.

People were just sitting drinking beer, they didn't know what was going on. People just saw the huts they set on fire. And people fled off and scattered in the bush. They left the villages empty. They burned all the houses, all over the place, completely. People's huts were burned, the grain stores outside were set alight with long stalks. They kindled the stalks and used them to set the food stores alight.

Then they crossed the valley and took the path to Wakacesh . . . they burned the church and when they'd finished in Wakacesh they went to Kalagorko, they went to *pam* Bwawash, and they went to burn the houses in Kuseje, finishing all the houses, and then fired the big guns. They fired them a lot in the bush for no good reason.

From that day, people took off, and fled. They slept in the bush. . . . But the SPLA then said, 'OK, the Arabs have burned your food stores, so what are you going to do about it? Wouldn't it be good for us to help you? We'll help you. We're going to lead you to the SPLA place in Ethiopia there.'

[12] William Danga Ledko, Nor Deng, 22 July 1991.

William saw the attack on the church settlement which followed about a month later (see Figures 6a, 6b). He himself seems to have been recognized as harmless by the officer Salih, who was described to me later by others as the intelligence chief in Chali.

At night, there was a terrible thing from the government.... They fired the great guns in the centre of the village, from the garrison there. While we were there, myself and Yuha. When I heard what had happened, I called Nyorke over [his then wife], and said, 'Nyorke, there's nothing good for us here. Our little children, you must take them to Bumma's place [a mile or so from Chali centre]. And if anything bad happens I will run and find you there. I will stay here and look after the goats, and keep them tied up here.'...

The Chali people were afraid, afraid, fear was with the people, and they thought, 'We can't live like this, we should follow the Pam Be people. That way we may live. If we stay here, we will be tied up and killed.'...

First thing in the morning, I showed up in the market place. Salih saw that I was there, and saw that Balasit was there, and a few others were there, and they went off looking for people in the bush, shooting their guns, shooting, shooting, saying they would shoot everyone and kill them. The '*kwanim pa* had gone to the bush... And from that time, no one could sleep in their own houses.

They gathered everyone together, to sleep in their place, *pam* Bunyan [the market/garrison area], every day. You would eat in your own house, and then in the late afternoon, you would bring your things and sleep in *pam* Bunyan. At that time, Tabke was still over there at the church village, and I would go to eat there. But while the sauce tasted good, the food itself was not good; because the Liver was upset. You would taste it once or twice and then not want any more. For your stomach didn't want to eat. Things in the village were not good. We waited there a bit, and went back to *pam* Bunyan, and brought everything with us.

Then in May, they started again. They set the houses on fire, in *paŋ* Gwami, *pam* Bumma there, they burned the houses, burned the whole of Chali, all over. They burned it down. And there was corn stored in one of the huts, I had tried to help one of the women who was a sister of the Omda, called Thadke. I was already going up to get the corn, when they started burning the house. I managed to get some of the corn down.... They burned all the houses in Chali. It was a terrible thing they did.[13]

One of the soldiers pursued William, wanting to know if guerrillas had been coming out of the bush and hiding guns. William said, 'Fine, carry on, carry on. You can search my house for guns... If you find any,

---

[13] Ibid.

Figure 6a. Destruction of Chali church area, May 1987 (anon.)

Figure 6b. Destruction of Chali church area, May 1987 (anon.)

you can kill us all. You can kill us all.' He searched, and then escorted William and his companions off to the garrison. 'There we met Salih. He was the one who had ordered this, and we met him.... [Our escort] said, "These people have come from outside—they were living with the John Garang lot." Salih said, "What!—these people weren't living outside; these are my people of Chali here, I know them." He said, "Ay! You go home." So we went home again.' They had to move in to live close by the garrison itself, and were allocated tasks.

Martha Ahmed was a key person among the Chali church community. Like William Danga, she is also someone I have known for decades. She was a teenager when we first met in late 1965, having recently returned to Chali from her secondary school in Malakal, because the rising tensions of Sudan's 'first' civil war meant it had closed down. She told me later, in a temporary transit camp in Ethiopia, how the end came about for them. It was also a very circumstantial, highly detailed account, almost as if things might have been otherwise, if the soldiers had not come in the way they did, and not been answered in the way they had that Saturday afternoon. The soldiers had explained themselves and given a preliminary warning. Martin Luther was there in the church, with Mona and the other elders, when they arrived and announced they were intending to burn the church. 'Martin said, "All right. You can burn it but I shall stay inside."' That afternoon they just had a good look around the place and left, but were soon to return.

It was April. We were the last to go.... We Chali people had no choice, because the government were near us, we were living near the office, the police station. They said, 'Your people have all gone off into the hills, so are you going to run away too?' We said we were going nowhere. 'We shall go on keeping you here, but if you run off anywhere, we shall burn your houses.' And indeed they really did burn our houses, in the night, early on the Sunday.[14]

My third witness to the cruel destruction of Chali comes from Marzouk Taj el Din, originally from the locality of Gerebin further north in the Blue Nile Province. He had become a teacher at the Islamic Institute in Chali, and had fled with the main body of the people over to Ethiopia and thence zigzagging down to Itang and subsequently Nor Deng near Nasir in Upper Nile, where he spoke to me. As not only a Muslim, but a

---

[14] Martha Nasim Ahmed, Karmi, 26 Sept. 1992.

teacher at the Chali Islamic Institute devoted to his pupils there, including many Uduk children, his important testimony, in Arabic, is particularly poignant. It takes a very general form, but then he and I had not met before. However, he clearly trusted the Uduk refugees and they him.

I first met these Uduk when I came to Chali in 1972. After two years, the Islamic religious teachers came and established the Institute. They wanted to teach the Koran. I found a position with these teachers [*fugara*], and I helped to teach the Uduk students. There were 120 of them. The problem that developed was this. The Uduk were extremely hard-working cultivators, and the conflict began because the animals of the nomad Arabs were eating their crops. There used to be no problem, but the Arabs started coming to the farms, and would throw down the sheaves of grain stored in the granaries and in the trees, and give them to their animals. A farmer would come, and complain, and the Arab would beat him. If he was able, the man would go and report this to the police, but nothing was done about it.

So this was the main reason why some of the Uduk youngsters decide to leave, and join up with the SPLA. Armed groups then came back and before they got to the villages there were conflicts with the nomad Arabs. The Arabs then realized they were fighting with the Uduk, and they regarded them as all on that side together. The order came that if you see any Uduk, at home or not, you should kill them. That is why all the Uduk left for the bush. The soldiers were going round the villages and burning them. But since they went to Ethiopia, and up to now, there is no real problem with these people.[15]

Encounters in Nor Deng provided an opportunity for people to impress on me, who had last seen them in 1983, why they had originally left home. I heard many more graphic accounts of specific ill treatment and horror around Chali than I had previously done in Khartoum. People I knew had wandered around in the bush so long, looking for others, that they died of thirst and their desiccated bodies were only found later. This happened to the respected village elder Mathir, who had been kind to me. Gamu, another senior man of great goodwill, became weak from lone wanderings and then died by the side of the road on the way to Langkwai, and was left unburied. The torture carried out by security people in several places, including Chali, was uppermost in the minds of many.

I heard a remarkable survivor's story, from Koya Beshir. As mentioned, I had been told in Khartoum that he was probably dead. Koya's

---

[15] Marzouk Taj el Din, Nor Deng, 28 July 1991.

hands and lower arms were indeed paralysed. After being tied for a good part of a day, and then no doubt infection having set in, the flesh had sloughed off over a couple of weeks and the bones were showing through. His sisters had to feed him by hand. By extraordinary good fortune, with help he managed a donkey journey to the Assosa camp and was then transported to hospital in Nekemte, where he remembers the skin transplant and the kind help he received over some seven months from the doctors there. He got back to Assosa in November 1987, where people were glad to see him—'they thought I had died in the hospital there'. In this conversation, William Danga was asking the questions.

We were at home, and they started insulting us, saying I was a rebel, while I'd been at home all the time. I hadn't been to the bush at all. This happened in April, when people were tied up. They tied me up ... tied up at the wrists ... I was going to the market.

—*And they just saw you?*—No, they came in a truck, the soldiers, and were taking people who had been shot at Beni Mayu there, to hospital in Kurmuk. ... They saw us, and ... they arrested us straight away.—*How many were you?*—We were two. Myself and my brother Tadko. They took us off and tied us up straight away.—*The two of you?*—Yes. And in his case, they didn't do much, perhaps they knew he was a big man. But I was younger, and they tied me up terribly.—*And then what, did they free you?*—No, we were just tied with the rope, and then that *halab* [Arabic; 'gypsy'] called Mayiser, he's the one who freed us.—*Mayiser was the man who did the work of cutting meat, he was a butcher?*—Yes, he was a merchant, a meat merchant. ... He was not a soldier. He's the one who freed us from the rope.[16]

At the Ora garrison not far away, some young men from Gindi were badly treated, and I heard several times of one called Epa who died there. William explained: 'Things were done which are not normally seen. Some people were tied up with rope, and howled like dogs, *uweer, uweeer, uweer,* the people tied up cried at night. They howled at night, and in the day, yes. Because they were treated with chilli ... poured over the fire, and they would have to breathe the smoke.' When William was taken along with a party of workers to cut bamboo south of the Yabus, in April 1987, he saw some prisoners at the bridge there. These young men had come home from work in Damazin, were told they were 'banned people', and after questioning were tied up. William saw

---

[16] Koya Beshir, Nor Deng, 7 Oct. 1991.

them having to go outside to defecate, while tied up. Six of them were later taken to the river-edge and shot. Five died, but one survived to tell the tale and was now with the refugees. Waca Basal had fallen down into the hole in the river-bed with the others, but he had not been hit by the bullets. He lay still like a dead person until the soldiers had gone away. Being thirsty he drank the water even though there was blood in it, and managed to creep away. He found a Gwami village where the people untied him, and then an Uduk village near Jebel Bisho, where the women washed him and looked after him. I did not hear the story from himself, but from one of the chiefs of the Yabus area I had known for a long time,[17] a man who had gone to ask after these prisoners and was told they had been taken to Damazin. A local hill used for executions (I heard much later) became known as 'Damazin'. Knowledge of such humiliating experiences and cruel actions, and these kinds of stories, told so coolly and plainly, lay always beneath the irritations and deprivations and further sufferings of the day as the years of exile went by, whether in the cities or urban barracks of the northern Sudan, or in the refugee camps and the bush stations of the SPLA.

GUERRILLAS' REASONS, HEARD LATER

Counterpointed with the civilian accounts above, I insert here an account of these events from the guerrillas' perspective that comes from an interview many years later in quite a different place, and under different circumstances. I have already quoted from Peter Kuma's explanation of why he decided to join the SPLA, and led others with him, and here he continues his story with a description of the initial attempt at liberating Chali, and the way it was foiled. The guerrillas set out in November 1986 from their training at Bilpam Base near Itang, accompanied by a certain Dhamkin who knew the road, and some Meban. Peter described how they were attacked by the soldiers posted at Yabus Bridge (the very post we know had been set up initially in peacetime by Stephen Missa—see Chapter 1), and their advance reported to the garrison at Chali by nomad Arabs.

---

[17] Joshua Leko, Nor Deng, 6 Oct. 1991.

When we got to the Yabus, we had to scatter; there was the army. Ay! *eh, ehye, eee,* was there any peace?—there were many soldiers. And we were only about 150. The army came with vehicles, maybe four of them, looking to attack. And we felt we were willing to die like our own people had, we were not afraid. I told our boys, 'OK, this is it, let's go, down to the road.' Then while we were on the road, they fired the big guns, *bum, bum, bum, bum,* and we attacked them, attacked them and chased them, they ran and left us the road, when the sun was about here [indicating: about midday], in January.

Then we went on, towards Jebel Chali, from there to Puduom, then we crossed the road and drank a little water, and *Hay!* Guns sounded again. We were found by the nomad Arabs, they had been told to attack us by the soldiers. Then we went off towards Dul. The army closed the road ahead of us. There were many, many soldiers. About sixteen vehicles. Sixteen.—*The nomad Arabs sent word to call the others maybe?*—Mm. Yes. At the time we were fighting in Yabus, the news went along the main road. They heard and came in large numbers, stopped the road ahead of us, . . . ay ay. We were just there, and they fired the very big guns, the big ones, shooting at us there. It was impossible for us to fight back, it was getting very dark and we were very hungry, we didn't find anything, we were thirsty. We drank some water in a hole, the vehicles were so many, a whole lot of tanks were firing over there, they killed some of our boys dead, four of them. They died, and others were wounded.

Then we divided up, and some of us made our way to Dul. . . . And I thought, what are we going to do. Our people are all going to be killed. I thought it over, and I sent word to a senior man. At that time, Kerubino[18] was there. The message did not arrive quickly, and we waited.

Later I thought I would go home and see how the people were. Because people were leaving. . . . People were being tied up all the time, put in prison, so I thought I would go and lead people out. Could I manage this? I would go and see, and bring them. So then we went. There weren't any Dhamkin. It was just our own boys. We went off, about 130 of us. We arrived among the Uduk villages the next day, after dark. At dawn we looked around the place, looked for a way to lead people out. Then the nomad Arabs ran and told the army about it, and the soldiers came and found us, and attacked us, *kar kar* with guns, and

---

[18] Kerubino Kuanyin Bol: Dinka from Bahr el Ghazal; a veteran Anyanya fighter, he was absorbed into the Sudanese army and rose to the rank of major; one of the leaders of the Bor Mutiny, he was a founding commander of the SPLA in 1983; renowned for his guerrilla exploits on both sides of the Sudan–Ethiopian border, he was imprisoned for plotting to overthrow Garang in 1987; freed by William Nyuon Bany in 1993, he joined the Nasir faction and subsequently raised an anti-SPLA militia for the government in Bahr el Ghazal; he rejoined the SPLA briefly in 1998 but broke with Garang again and returned to Sudan; he was killed in September 1999.

killed one man, one chap. We were not all killed, though they were many, and they shot at us with big guns, but didn't get us.[19]

As indicated from the accounts above of visitors to and escapees from Chali, the real problems for the civilians there did not come from the initial SPLA advance as such. This was a foiled attack. The problems came from the greatly intensified reprisals and counter-insurgency drive of the armed forces against the civilians, especially the burning of churches, houses, and food stocks. Peter's story continues, and indicates how the feelings of the new guerrillas hardened and their political anger widened in the course of 1987 as a result of these reprisals. Reference to the local traders not just as 'Bunyan' but as *jellaba*, a Sudan-wide Arabic term for petty traders which was acquiring heavy racial overtones in the south as the war progressed, is just one indication of this.

And by this time they had closed the tracks, putting guns in various places, cutting off the roads, and they were afraid. They were afraid, and so they set the church on fire, at Hashu's place [Joshua Hashu, pastor of Gindi church]. They burned the church, and then they set fire to people's huts. Some old people were burned in their houses, and they died, maybe four... in Beni Mayu, and in Pam Be. Some elderly grandmothers died in their houses, they were burned. And they set fire to the stores in the roofs, the grain was burned.

So then I said, we should lead everyone from here, because the Arabs are going to kill everyone, we should take them to Ethiopia. There's no way people can live here, because of these evil *jellaba* [Arabic; 'petty traders']. . . . The *jellaba* sided with the army because they are Muslims. That is the reason why we had to flee into the bush, and why I led people into the bush at that time. The nomad Arabs burned people's grain; so how are people to live? There was no food; everything had been burned; better for us to change things.

That's the original problem we had, and why we fled. We did not flee just to join the fighting, no. This was not the story. We went in great sorrow and suffering, because of the disturbances. This business made me very unhappy, which is why I led people away openly.[20]

FIRST BRIEF CAPTURE, 1987

Not everyone left in March–May 1987, however. The very small miscellaneous community left in Chali had to live right at the garrison and

[19] Peter Kuma Luyin, Bonga, 24 Nov. 1994.   [20] Ibid.

became totally dependent on them through the rainy season that year. This included Omda Talib (see Figure 7), and also William Danga. His story of that rainy season continued with a strikingly intimate portrait of what things were like after most people had left. Individual idiosyncrasies loom large among the dramatis personae on this small stage. One of these was the captain of the garrison at that time, Tayeb Musbah, whom I have already introduced and who was later demonized by many. William saw more than one side to his character during the tense period after May 1987 when almost all the civilians had deserted Chali.

They gave us a lot of work to do. Building houses, building, building, building, every day. There was no peace. No peace at all. They harassed people all the time. Until I spoke to one of the senior men. I said, 'The month is almost over. It's nearly June. And what are we people going to eat? You keep us building, building, building, but what are we going to eat? Would it not be good for us to go and sow some grain? We need to sow sorghum, and maize.' Last year's harvest had all been burned. Our harvest which we would have eaten. They said, 'All right, you can build one more house, and then tomorrow you can

Figure 7. Omda Talib el Fil, Chali market area, May 1987 (anon.)

go.'... We went off and planted maize, did a little cultivation, and in the rainy season we found we could finally settle down and live with them. They didn't do anything bad after that.[21]

Most of the trading families in Chali, who had previously been on social terms with the soldiers (and blamed by many for informing on the people), had by now been frightened away. Personal conversations then began to take place between the soldiers and the remnant locals. William told me of conversations he had with Tayeb Musbah, who reportedly felt himself let down by the traders. They had first encouraged him to scare away the *'kwanim pa,* and had then deserted the place themselves. These conversations were in Arabic, but relayed to me in Uduk.

One day, Tayeb Musbah looked around the place and saw that the Bunyan, the Chali merchants, had all gone, completely, they had all fled to Damazin. All the Bunyan had gone. So Tayeb then said, 'Ah, so that's it, the Bunyans have deceived me.... Aha. The merchants have tricked me! I have chased all the Uduk people into the bush, and now they have gone too and left me here. I can't believe the merchants have done this to me.' And he started to cry.—*What?*— Yes, he was crying. He said, 'I've made a big mistake, chasing out the *'kwanim pa* to the bush.'—*Huh, this was really Tayeb Musbah?*—Yes, he was thinking back over things, thinking what terrible things he had done. Everybody had disappeared.

So they started searching along the road, saying OK, let's see if we can find any old people on the road to Ethiopia, comfort them, and bring them back. They searched the road. Old people would not have been able to make it. They found some and brought them back.[22]

There is further testimony to the complex position of the Chali garrison captain from a note written by Pastor Paul soon after the events in which he mentions that this officer had apologized to his daughter for what had happened, saying that he was deceived by some traders and four Uduk men.[23]

William's then wife, Nyorke, had meanwhile moved off to Ethiopia with the other escapees, and he set up house with another girl whose family had all left. When his nephew Sila Musa had arrived from

---

[21] William Danga Ledko, Nor Deng, 22 July 1991.

[22] Ibid.

[23] 'Third Report from Chali el Fil', typed document signed by Pastor Paul Rasha Angwo, 4 June 1987 (copy supplied by him to me).

Khartoum wanting to escort various of his relatives back there, William refused, saying that he wanted to stay and see what would happen next. He did not have long to wait, as in November that year Kurmuk was taken by the SPLA from the Ethiopian side. He was with others in the sorghum fields when they heard about it. All the government soldiers in the small garrisons south of Kurmuk, such as Deim Mansour and Ora, ran to Chali for shelter. Then the SPLA started to improve the road southwards from Kurmuk, bringing the big road grader. They fired 'the big gun' from Ora in the early afternoon. People were sitting quietly drinking beer at home after their work in the fields, and a shell flew overhead and landed in the thornbushes, towards Pam Be. Another one came and landed in Bumma's village, part of the Chali complex, and another. William explained: 'People didn't run. People didn't run, they were afraid because the soldiers in Chali would have killed them if they'd run outside.'

However, as things got worse they felt they had no choice, and so came out carefully to have a look at the road, and managed to slip away down the river-bed past the old mission garden.

Ayee! They were shooting at people, firing the guns directly. And people ran, throwing themselves down into the river-bed and then dashing into the bush. Because the government was shooting at everyone.... — *Were some killed?*— No, no one was hit that day. The tall grass was very close, and people all rushed together into the grass. And there was the river course, people hid themselves in the river course.... We slept in the bush, while the SPLA soldiers came and finished them off.

In the morning, when we had slept we went back to Chali. We found the SPLA soldiers there. They said, 'Where are you going? This place is very dangerous. The fighting's still going on, plenty of it, you must go. Your people have all gathered together at Assosa. What are you going to do here? In the middle of all these vehicles? You must go.'

And yes, indeed, they escorted us, escorted that time.— *Were these SPLA Dhamkin, or the Uduk men?*—Dhamkin.... And they escorted us away, as far as Ora.... Then, the government soldiers appeared, and they fought again. They fought and fought, and then they said, 'You can't stay here in Ora, you must go on all the way.' One Dhamkin, he was a soldier [SPLA], he said, 'OK, I will escort them.' He led us off. He found some others, and they were five altogether, and they took us to Langkwai.... — *And how many were you?*—Hey! We were very many. We were a hundred or more. Little children, and women, we came along and slept on the road, slept on the road, slept on the road. One afternoon, when the sun was about here, we arrived at last. . . . The *'kwanim pa* recognized us, and told the UN people, who were Ethiopians, they hurried to find us. . . . They wrote people's names down. . . . And it was a very senior man of the SPLA, Kerubino, he was the person who got foodstuffs from the UN to give the *'kwanim pa*, at that time.[24]

Although the SPLA had temporarily taken Chali after their capture of Kurmuk in November 1987, they did not hang on to either place. There was a hue and cry raised over the rebel capture of the 'northern Sudanese' town of Kurmuk, even a 'town of the Arab homeland [*watan*]' (see above), and after a month or so, the government retook it. This sharpened up racial animosities in the Blue Nile Province generally, and 'southern'-looking men in Damazin (such as Ingessana, Uduk, Meban, and Dinka) were rounded up and imprisoned, some beaten and thrown into the river. One man I had known was killed in this way, Moses Cenka.[25] I heard later from some foreign aid personnel that many bodies were seen floating down the river at this time. The government reclaiming of Chali soon followed that of Kurmuk. By this time virtually no one was left, though Omda Talib seems to have managed to move in and out with the help of the traders and the garrison. He soon sent for his wife who had gone to Damazin, as she explained to me later on, and as I report in the next chapter.

A song dating from 1986, but in circulation for years afterwards, captures the sense of shock and indignation felt by the ordinary villagers when the violence of the state was unleashed upon them, experienced not so much in the abstract as through the malicious acts of traders and soldiers against individual local residents. It refers to events in the village of Borfa, near Gindi, the closest Uduk settlement to Kurmuk and the main truck road. Men, including a younger brother of Borfa's main sheikh, Awad Chingwo Chito, were arrested, tied up, and interrogated. Among them was another chief, Shabe Yulud. As with many songs, there is more than one voice here. The last line is in the voice of Chief Shabe himself. In addition to these local, personal references, however, 'northerners' *as a category* has clearly acquired a new prominence. Here right in the middle of this Uduk song 'northerners' appear not as local

---

[24] William Danga Ledko, Nor Deng, 22 July 1991.
[25] Interviews, Khartoum, Aug. 1988.

'Bunyan' or even 'Arab' in the usual local sense of 'nomad Arabs', but are
distanced through the standard Sudanese Arabic literal term, *shemaliya*.

> Ask Yakoba, where is the home we knew,
> How is the homeland?
> The women are living on their own,
> Where are the men, where?
>
> *How did that come to be,*
> *Oh Northerners!*
>
> Our men were tied by the Sudanese
> He's tired of crying:
> The chief is exhausted with crying,
> He was tied with his hands behind,
> How do you like that?
>
> Yakoba, go and see what's happening,
> Ask Yakoba, where's the home we knew?
> The chief was tired with crying,
> Chingwo wailed as though he would die;
> Wailed like a little child.
>
> Chief Shabe is exhausted,
> Tied with his hands behind.
> Can this be the Northerners, indeed?
> Mother, cry for the children!
> The women are alone,
> Where are the men?
> 'I'm here, I'm tied, tied up.'[26]

[26] Wel Ragab of Borfa; recorded by Granada, Karmi, Jan. 1993.

3

Chali: Front-Line Garrison

How can I carry the children,
And make it to Chali?
The men were chased away.
Doctor, come and set me free!
My foodstores were set on fire.
Children, let's take the left-hand path
Let's flee to the SPLA
The way the people fled,
Along a tangled path

John, come and give me freedom!
The baboons are calling in the hills
As I run away to Chali.
But now our Chali's smashed to pieces!
The people have fled and left it cold.
The lions are grunting in the deserted village, *awu-wuh!*
Wild things are calling in the old village, *awu-wuh!*

I cry for my home
I am exhausted from crying
The infants are dying from crying.
The great grain sheaves were burning.
Please show me the way
Tell me the way the people went,
The narrow way

Look, everyone's gone from Chali!
Please release me from this yoke,
Come and redeem me,
Great leader of the SPLA!
The chickens are dying in the bush.[1]

[1] The words of this song were composed about 1988 by Denge, a Bellila woman, recalling how she had fled from her home towards Chali and found it already destroyed.

LIVING WITH THE SOLDIERS, 1988–1989

Omda Talib el Fil seems to have avoided getting too closely involved in the events surrounding the initial destruction of his district. He was certainly present in Chali, however, after it was reclaimed by the army in early 1988, and then he sent for his wife Hergke. She had spent a year away, partly because she needed treatment for a bad leg. She had relatives in Damazin, including a sister's son with the government. I quote some passages from a very long conversation with her in Bonga, five to six years later, about this precarious period. They were among the very few who stayed with the Sudanese garrison right up to the end of 1989 when the place was decisively captured again by the SPLA and they had to leave under SPLA escort. At the time we spoke, her husband was not present because after some years of displacement he had managed to return 'home'. Hergke really did seem not to understand at this point what the war was about, and why none of us, including myself, could go back to Chali (or Khartoum, where she erroneously assumed I was based). Her mention of 'three years' in the Chali garrison seems to refer to the whole period—three rainy seasons—from the original flight of the people in early 1987. She had evidently missed the brief SPLA takeover in November that year, when even William Danga's group had been obliged to leave. My quotations from her account pick up the story from early 1988. She first describes the generally calm situation in Chali under the government garrison.

The army soldiers said, 'Come and stay over here. We will look after you here.' ... Yes, we found a little food; the army brought us grain, and gave us grain, and opened a shop for us, we bought things from the shop, bought clothes, and wore them. That's how we lived. They said they had no problem with us any more, we lived there all right, they looked after us, we were OK. We were there for about three years, in the homeland there. In Chali there. I lived together with the Omda, the two of us, but the youngsters had all gone, they had been taken to Langkwai.[2]

She appeals to 'the Doctor', that is John Garang, then leader of the SPLA. This version was sung by Dangaye Chalma in Bonga, 18 August 2000. I had heard him sing it six years earlier, and noticed that his animal calls, *awu-wuh!* which had originally sounded like baboons, now included an unmistakable hyena.

  2 Hergke Kinna, Bonga, 3 Nov. 1994.

She had been staying with relatives further north when her husband insisted on her return, eventually escorting her himself with army protection. She told me how her marriage had then become very difficult because her husband had taken another wife—a Meban girl from among the refugees in Chali—while she had been away.

I went from Damazin as far as Singa, and I lived in Singa. Then I came back from Singa and I heard about it. His young son came and told me: 'Father has married again!' I said, 'What? your father has married, and I told him not to marry after I left, because I was going ill like that to Damazin, how can he marry like that?' I was upset. He sent me a letter, for me to go home. . . . Then he came and collected me. . . . We were taken by the merchants. We came together with the army. We reached home and got out of the lorry by the shops. I opened my compound, and I found the woman there in my house! I found her there, and she was heating water in my saucepan outside! . . . I told him, 'You have made her a co-wife when all my people have gone, and there's nowhere I can go in protest!' Because everyone had gone, gone to the bush . . .

I brought the big holdall, and put my clothes in it, and I went to look for a truck to take me back to Damazin. He said, 'You can't go there, you will be beaten by them, I promise you!' . . . And he kept on arguing.[3]

SECOND BRIEF CAPTURE, 1989

This tense situation continued at Chali up to mid-1989, when in fact it deepened as a result of the Islamist-backed coup of Omer el Beshir on 30 June that year. Strengthened in its resolve, the SPLA returned in force to the Blue Nile Province, taking Kurmuk on 28 October (see Chapter 1). Their quick and professional capture of the small government garrisons to the south followed soon after, Chali falling on 8 November. I return to Hergke's account of it below. This is how it was announced on Radio SPLA news, 11 November 1989:

SPLA units of the New Funj, under the command of the Chief of Staff Commander William Nyuon Bany, have captured three [inaud.] army garrisons of Blue Nile Province over the last seven days of heavy fighting. The army garrisons are: Deim Mansour, Ora, and Chali el Fil. The strategic garrison [inaud.] of Chali el Fil fell to the gallant forces of New Funj last Wednesday

---

[3] Hergke Kinna, Bonga, 3 Nov. 1994.

night, at 7.30 pm Sudan local time. Chali el Fil is the administrative centre of the Uduk people of southern Blue Nile. A great amount of military hardware, including [inaud.] heavy artillery has been captured in Chali el Fil. In a later development, the offical spokesman of the SPLA has disclosed to Radio SPLA that the command of the New Funj forces has already entered into negotiations with the patriotic elements in the nearby garrisons of Khor Yabus, Meban, and Geissan for the Sudan army soldiers in these garrisons so to effect a peaceful withdrawal within the next 48 hours, starting at 15.00 hours Sudan local time Thursday, 9 November 1989.

Meanwhile, the details of the military equipment captured in Chali el Fil are as follows: Two 120 mm mortars, two jeeps mounted with 160 mm mortars, 1 Bedford lorry, 1 lorry, five 12.7 mm anti-aircraft guns, six Gronov machine guns, two Fikris machine guns, two 82 mm mortars, 100 GM3 rifles, 1 [?foster?], 1 missile anti-aircraft Chinese made, 1 Russell long-range radio, and lots of ammunition of different types. The correspondent says that further stock-taking is still going on, and if completed, the results will be read to you as soon as they arrive Radio SPLA.[4]

On 20 November, a special broadcast was made to celebrate the liberation of Chali. This included a recording of the address given in late 1986 by the SPLA leader, John Garang de Mabior, to the newly graduated recruits of the Arrow Battalion at their training base at Bilpam near Itang in Ethiopia. The announcer referred in Arabic to the recent fighting in southern Blue Nile, how Garang had started the struggle in 1983, and how the Arrow Battalion graduating in 1986 were the first people from Blue Nile to join the SPLA. Garang spoke in colloquial Arabic, congratulating the new fighting force, explaining the cause, and inspiring them to carry the struggle to the Blue Nile. His address was translated piece by piece into Uduk by Peter Kuma, now appointed their commanding officer. This was the one and only time I have ever heard the Uduk language on the radio. My recording was not very clear, but the key points of the address went as follows:

Good morning, Arrows!
  Roar of welcome
There are many different groups among you people in Blue Nile, and speaking many different languages. But we are united.
  Cheering crowds. Joyful cries, and singing of the special call-and-response song for the new Battalion, in Arabic:

---

[4] Radio SPLA, English news, 11 Nov. 1989. Recorded by W. J.

Aiwa! I've got my Kalashnikov, firing *rege rege rege!*
The Arrows are full of anger,
We're chasing off to ambush the enemy!

We are very happy in welcoming you to join the struggle.

The fighting is under way across the Sudan. Some say it is just a problem in the land of the black people here. But this is not the reason. The war was created by Suwar el Dhahab, and Sadiq, and Nimeiry, and the problem comes from the leadership in Khartoum there, not from the ordinary Sudanese civilians. They said the problem is just one of the south, and they blame the southerners. But we have a right to fight because they don't treat us as equals. This is your problem in the Blue Nile too, and I want you to take the struggle to the Blue Nile.

Continued singing and cheering:

Let us take our guns to the sons of the bourgeoisie[5]

The power of the battalions rests on the support of the people. And where are the people? Some here are from your own home of Chali, and there are Bertha, and Ingessana too, mixed with some from the Nuba Hills.

There are so many groups of people in the Sudan, and I don't mind where everybody comes from. The people from Khartoum address us, as the people of Sudan, through a microphone, but do they know the people of the Sudan? And Sadiq el Mahdi, Nimeiry, did these people ever come to visit you? They just stay in Khartoum.

The first rebels were called Anyanya. They left the government of Khartoum and went to the bush to fight. They fought hard, and then they said, 'Come back, we will give you a government in Juba.' But then some said, 'We don't accept that you just give us a government in Juba; we black people want to separate and rule ourselves.' But we don't want to divide the country. Our struggle now is for the whole Sudan. There are people suffering in all sorts of places, like you in southern Blue Nile: in Darfur, and far away in northern Sudan, and even in Khartoum itself.

Song (an old one sung by many battalions), cheering[6]

Thanks to Radio SPLA's correspondent with his tape recorder, the message could later reach far and wide, to friends and enemies alike and the uncommitted displaced across the Sudan and Ethiopia. Even in my hotel room in Nairobi, where I was spending part of a sabbatical, doing peripheral research because I could not 'get to the field', I felt a

---

[5] An Anglicized French term adopted via Marxist discourse into Sudanese Arabic and used in SPLA parlance for northern Sudanese soldiers.
[6] Radio SPLA, 20 Nov. 1989. Recorded by W. J.

kind of nostalgia for a lost home now liberated as I heard this programme about a place in another country I had personally known. The
1989 'liberation' was achieved by the New Funj Forces, led by William
Nyuon approaching from Kurmuk, having just captured that town for
the second time. The takeover was almost uncomplicated by the presence of civilians. However, as explained, the Omda was there with his
wife Hergke and a few others at the garrison. And there were Uduk men
among the government soldiers, some of them no doubt recruited
locally over the previous couple of years as 'Popular Defence Force'
militia. While the SPLA fighters were mainly 'Dhamkin', they also
included a substantial Uduk contingent, at least some of whom had
been part of the original failed assault of 1987.

The tiny group around Omda Talib living at the garrison were put in
a very precarious position by the arrival of the rebels. Their lives were
immediately in danger. However, a couple of interesting things happened, which are no doubt characteristic of the way things go on the
front lines of civil war anywhere. The Uduk men on the rebel side had
gone to spy out the situation in Chali; the Uduk men among the
government soldiers had heard their own language, and insults were
exchanged. And after the attack, when the SPLA fighters found the
Omda's group who had fled to the bush, some hotheads indeed wanted
to kill him, but the Uduk officers argued he should be spared. The Uduk
soldiers who had been defending Chali and its civilians then decided to
change sides, and later helped escort the Omda's group off to the refugee
camp at Assosa. My summary here is based on four quite different
accounts from people who spoke to me in later years: first, my old friend
Peter Kuma who was by then operating in an administrative capacity
with the SPLA, having looked into disputes between refugees themselves and with the military since the time of the move to Assosa.
Second, I have an inside view from 'Jasper', the former SPLA fighter
quoted earlier, who took part in the attack on Kurmuk in 1989 and then
was party to the follow-up assault on Chali. Third, the Omda's wife
Hergke told me of these events and her experiences. My final source is
Omda Talib himself, who told me in Nor Deng in 1991 how he hung
on as long as he could but eventually agreed to leave for Ethiopia, under
protest. He was finally willing to accept the SPLA officers' promise that
he would shortly be able to lead his people back home.

Here is Peter Kuma's sensitive, even gently regretful, description of the 1989 takeover.

We were there!—and if we hadn't been, well, our people who were living there—you see the Dhamkin are not very wise, they would have killed them. At that time, I cried a lot, because I am not a man who likes fighting for its own sake. I know how to maintain proper discipline. I was with Paul at that time, Paul was killed dead, Paul Yolgo. . . .

The Chali fellows themselves went first, to spy things out, and I gave them instructions. . . . They would go at night into the village there, to see the soldiers' place . . . We attacked Chali and the army fled. They didn't fire on us. We fired *bum bum bum*. . . .

William [Nyuon] said, 'You ought to go and see those boys of yours.' Because there were Uduk lads in the Sudan army. They had heard '*twam pa;* they insulted us, and we insulted them in exchange. I said, 'Yes, I will go, but we want you to come too.' And they heard us, and thought we would kill them in the bush.

When we had taken Chali, and the traders had gone, gone towards Bellila, we looked for the Omda. The Omda had run off, and some of the youngsters were angry and wanted to kill him. I told them, 'No, no, you must not kill him, he is one of us, but he has been afraid to get politically involved, because the government would kill him.' We took him away, brought him over, there was no problem about it, we took him to Assosa.[7]

The account of the attack on Chali I heard twenty years later from 'Jasper', who had taken part, was much more graphic, and impersonal—where personal factors of sympathy for the civilians might have been thought to come in, they are absent. Speaking partly in English, his tone was fairly harsh and the category terms of 'Sudanese Arab' and plain 'Arab' are the language of the rebel fighters.

Yes, I fought in Kurmuk, and we went along to Deim Mansour, we chased the Sudanese Arabs from there (they didn't fight—very soft), and went on to Ora, where we had a little fight, may be two or three killed and eight injured from us, and we killed almost twelve of them, most of them ran away, and we went on to Chali. We fought from 10 at night until 1 at night, and they ran. We captured Chali!—*They went away without firing?*—They ran, but they fired a little bit. We had a very big machine gun that time in Chali . . . with forty-one barrels [it was in fact a rocket-launcher]. People fired it and it burned all the houses and

---

[7] Peter Kuma, Bonga, 24 Nov. 1994.

the Arabs were scared and they ran.—*And you were part of this group that took Chali?*—Yes, I am.—*Tell me, what did you find there?*

Well, a lot of surprises! We found clothes, and shoes, we had a very good day, and found a lot of food. The SPLA, they can go for a month and not find food like that. We found plenty of food, and besides we ate a lot of meat, goats, and pigs, and chickens, everything.—*Were there civilians in Chali at that time?*—Yes, there were civilians in Chali at that time, but in the night when we fought, they fled away behind the church, towards Jebel Chali, hiding behind a little hill called Kwoj.—*This included the Omda?*—Yes, it did include the Omda, and his wife Hergke. They were in there.—*I know, they have both told me about it!*—Even I went and ate food with them, at that time.—*In the*—No, inside there in Chali. They ran away, but our troops, we captured some people and some soldiers, some people didn't run away from inside, they give us the information and we just went after the civilians and brought them back. *And then you ate in their house?* Yes.

And how was the Omda then? Was he calm, was he angry?—The Omda was very nervous. He was beaten by one of the Meban with a bamboo stick, whacking him as you would a rat. He was being beaten, but one of the senior officers, Abu Zeid, a nephew of the Omda, came up and stopped it. That was inside in Chali, after they brought them back. He had a star, and said, 'Oh no, this is a senior man, he must not be beaten.' *He was on the SPLA side?* Yes. He tried to kill the Meban fellow, but they separated them, they caught him and they didn't let him near the Meban. And the Omda at that time was very nervous.—*And Hergke too, was she nervous?*—Yes, she was kind of nervous too, but she was OK. We ate meat there, we caught pigs, and they boiled goat meat for us at Hergke's there.[8]

Hergke's own account of the upheavals in Chali, caused by the sudden arrival of SPLA fighters and (to her) the quite unexpected need to flee her home country, scarcely touches on the politics of the situation, but is highly personal in its reminiscences. She recognized that some of their own youngsters, indeed some quite close relatives, were among the guerrillas. This was just as well, as there seem to have been two separate occasions, in the bush and back in Chali, when the Omda was in danger. Hergke was distraught as she recalled the people they had been forced to abandon.

Yes, the SPLA came . . . and took Chali, while we were there. . . . Our boys said they were afraid because we '*kwanim pa* were living among the government soldiers there, and they took charge of us and led us away. We had to leave some old people there on the ground, even my own mother, I left her on the

8 'Jasper', USA, Nov. 2006.

ground.—*What was she called?*—Wakke. I left her on the ground. . . . What was I going to do, it was beyond me. The Omda said, 'No, Hergke, we have to go, let's go. It is not good for you to refuse.' I said, 'But my mother is lying down there, and what shall I do for her?' I said, 'I'm going back!' He said, 'You are not going back. You will be killed by these youngsters if you go back.' I said, 'All right. Let us go on.' But I kept on thinking the same thing, we went on and I kept thinking; we had left them behind. These are the ones we had left: my mother as I said, and Dhulke, and Kana . . . and a Bunyan woman called Shinkir . . . helpless people, these helpless people we left so many of them behind. People from various other villages, I don't know their names. There they were on the ground, sick on the ground. I looked at them from my own front door and left them behind me. And there was nothing I could do for them, nothing.

I asked Hergke what had happened on the day when the SPLA came, was there fighting?

There was indeed fighting at Chali . . . We ran. I got the key and shut up the house. I left all my clothes in the hut, all of them, my things I had brought from Damazin, I left them all, I didn't bring anything. I came with one dress and one *tob* [a full Sudanese robe]. . . . —*And the Sudan soldiers, did they run too, or what?*—The Sudan fellows? They stayed there, stayed there up to about six o'clock here [evening], but then they escaped and they were gone. They disappeared, they were gone. But they didn't fire any guns. They came out of their trench quietly, and moved off. . . .

We ran to the bush, and slept there. About six o'clock in the morning, we packed the basket and put it on my head . . . we were setting off, and then the youngsters turned up. The SPLA had come for us . . . Some of our lads, and some Meban. These boys beat the Omda, while I was standing there. Beat him.—*Beat him?*—Yes! Beat him, beat him, and there was nothing I could do. He said, he said, 'Why are you beating me for no reason like this, you shouldn't beat me. I should not be beaten.' One man then said, 'Don't beat him. Bring him along.' They took us home!—*Back to Chali?*—Yes, they led us back to Chali, and we had to stay with them.

. . . And they took us to a senior man. . . . He greeted us, and he—*Who was this senior man, what was he called?*—He was called William Nyuon. He sat us down, and arranged for us to get some food . . . He was a big chief of SPLA, they said. He, he, the Sudan men had already left, and they were the ones living in the village now. . . . People brought us things, and we ate. . . . And I thought, and said, 'Omda, I'm going over to our house there, and see how things are.' He said, 'No! [Arabic: *La!*] Nobody is allowed to wander around.'

Hergke told me how they slept at the garrison for two days, and then were allowed to visit their own house. Everything had been looted or broken or burnt, including her mattress, which her son in Khartoum had given them. She appealed to the fighters:

I said, 'Really, if you have any feelings at all, youngsters, just give me a sheet, and I can sleep.' Because we had taken our two blankets off to the bush. I said, 'You, you are our own boys, you have all those sheets there, just give me one sheet and I can wrap myself in it.' Because they had taken all the dresses, they'd taken them, and the shoes, everything, not one thing was left, they left nothing for me. . . . The food cooking, and a pan of stew, they took it too.

. . . Then they told us, 'We are going to take you to Langkwai.' I said, 'Will I be able to make it there?' 'We will lead you slowly', they said. . . . And they didn't argue with us, or explain why people were fleeing from Sudan. 'You see us, we are SPLA', and we didn't ask questions.[9]

It was when the decision was made to abandon Kurmuk (for the second time) that Chali had to be evacuated too. The SPLA could no longer take care of the Omda's group there. As yet there was no sign of the Sudan government soldiers returning to the district, and so they had to accept the SPLA offer of an escort across the border to the refugee camp near Assosa.

For Hergke, the abrupt arrival of the SPLA in 1989, their takeover of Chali, and their rude and rough behaviour had been the beginning, and indeed the cause, of their suffering. She never made any criticism of the Sudan army soldiers, who had provided protection for them when nearly everyone had left Chali. She spoke nostalgically of returning to 'the Sudan', that is, the Sudan of their homeland as it used to be, and of the old government authorities that her husband had served all his life. Both she, and William Danga, focused particularly on the personally aggressive behaviour of the guerrillas, rather than on any big cause; they pointed to the kind actions of a few of the government soldiers, or even the SPLA fighters, sometimes by name. As in the other civilian testimonies I have heard, they do not praise or blame distant leaders; they observe the massive power of the *hakuma*, the government's breaking of a mission vehicle, the burning of houses (and later aerial bombing)—as well as the terrific sounding guns of the SPLA—as something over which they have no more control than over the powers of nature.

[9] Hergke Kinna, Bonga, 3 Nov. 1994.

You have to be pragmatic, to go with the demands of the situation inflicted on you at the time. Both Hergke and William had plenty of previous experience of surviving 'authority'—they were both mission drop-outs, and in fact as childhood sweethearts had been married in church under the benevolent eye of the missionaries. Hergke maintained something of a Christian allegiance while agreeing much later to marry Talib el Fil, who as a Muslim had several successive wives more or less in tow. These sort of things were not held against them, by and large. A similar kind of tolerance towards persons seems to be extended to the political or military arena. I have rarely heard, at the local level, of individuals in the front-line zones being blamed for supporting one side or another. Certainly in this relatively early stage of the war in the Blue Nile, individuals on whatever side were praised for personal decency or blamed for personal cruelty, but not for being caught up in one or another armed organization.

Omda Talib himself, as 'loyal to the government' as any chief could possibly have been in the circumstances, given the geographical location of his territory could not completely avoid the the embrace of the SPLA. After finally being obliged to cross to Ethiopia in late 1989, he then had to flee south with everyone else when fighting came to the Assosa district. I talked to him in the rainy season of 1991 in the displaced camp at Nor Deng near Nasir. He saw the predicament into which he had been thrown very clearly, and spoke to me then of the way the 'Arab government' had made it impossible for his people to remain in the first place, emphasizing in particular the way they had armed the nomads.

Did they carry guns?—They carried lots of guns! Yes, from the government! And then the soldiers of the Arab government, they would dress up like nomad Arabs, and take their guns with them. They would herd the goats.—*Regular soldiers?*—Yes, regular soldiers.—*Wow!*—This is what their soldiers were doing. They would herd the animals, disguised like that. The soldiers would come along with the animals, the cattle, and sheep. You would think they were nomad Arabs, Rufa'a, but no, they were soldiers. They would carry guns, riding on camels. They would come with long sticks like this, and if they were looking for someone they wanted, they would appear at the first sign of dawn, and kill them. Before dawn.—*Terrible.*—It was terrible.

Davis Sukut, who was helping me with the final polishing of these translations in 2006, asked if I had not seen on the TV what was happening in Darfur, and pointed out the similarity of these camel-riding soldiers in nomads' clothing to the notorious Janjawid of our present times. Omda Talib then explained how the 'Arab soldiers' had burned all the villages and then ordered them to live near the garrison, and how the SPLA attack came. They were fired on with heavy artillery, and when the Arabs (*sic*) saw how many SPLA there were, they came out quietly and ran off, to Ulu, and But, and Damazin.

Reinforcements were being sent south from Damazin by the government, but these were ordered to retreat, because there were so many SPLA forces in the region. Many small garrisons were also abandoned by the government soldiers, at Ora, Deim Mansour, Yabus Bridge, and Doro. The only one left in government hands was Boing. Omda Talib told me how the soldiers scattered in the bush, as his own group had to from Chali. His account went on as follows:

The thing which made me leave Chali, was when they [SPLA] fired the great gun on Chali. They fired and killed people all over the place. So we fled to the hill there, to Jebel Chali. The SPLA attacked the Arabs and came out tracking us all, because we ran from that place where everything was on fire. Then the Dhamkin came and seized me there in the bush, and led me away and kept me for seven days. I remained with them for seven days. Then they said, 'Right. You can't stay here. We are now taking you off to your people there in Langkwai.' They led me off. The senior person in charge of our people there had given instructions, 'If you find Omda Talib, don't kill him. Because he is like a bull who is among them. If he is killed, then the Uduk people will disappear, all of them. Don't kill the Omda. Just bring him along.'

He claimed that the SPLA promised he could bring his people home soon.

They took us off, saying, 'We are going to bring you to the SPLA people over there, you can greet your people, and then you can lead your people home.' That's what the SPLA told me. I could bring the people home. And I was very happy, thinking this was what they really meant. So I agreed to go.—*How many were you and your group?*—We weren't many, yes, we were only about thirty. Mostly women, there were just six men. . . . They said, 'You can stay here and rest, and go back to Chali in April, and start cultivating in your places there.' That's what the SPLA told me.

Later, everything changed, it didn't happen. The SPLA themselves suddenly escaped back to where they came from, all of them. None were left in Langkwai. They fled, every one, every single one. The people in charge just went off and left us Uduk among ourselves. We had to leave on our own: God [*Arum*] led us like that, led us on and on . . . to Itang.[10]

The victory over Chali was brief, and by January 1990 those SPLA present there would have had to flee south, along with their comrades making a hasty exit from Kurmuk. Those on the Ethiopian side had to leave their bases in the Assosa district and they converged back in the SPLA-held territory of Meban in the Upper Nile Province. Of course the refugees in the camp near Assosa also had to leave, including the recent influx fleeing the SPLA rather than the Sudan government. The story of their subsequent continuing flight onwards and southwards is told in Part II. The Sudan government forces were soon back in Chali, probably quite early in 1990. There would have been no need to maintain a large defensive station, particularly after mid-1991 when the Ethiopian government fell and the SPLA was severely weakened, while the Sudan government mounted strong campaigns to regain large areas of territory in the far south. From 1992 it consolidatd its position once more in the southern Blue Nile, and did its best to encourage returnees from the war zone to the south. Former residents who had moved north to Khartoum and other towns were hopeful that they might now return home in safety, and so Chali and other places in the Kurmuk district received an influx of returnees from both directions over the next few years. A minority of the displaced Uduk, including Omda Talib (but not his wife Hergke, who went with the majority back to Ethiopia), did manage to return from the Nasir area in 1992–3. I pick up the story of this partial 'return to Chali' under the extending influence of the Beshir government in Chapter 6. Those who did return, from both north and south, were to be unceremoniously frightened out of the place and into a new refugee camp in 1996–7, with the third advance of the SPLA into the Blue Nile. But first I have to describe the extraordinary multiple treks which took the people from Assosa, to Itang, and as far away as Nasir in the first place.

Before leaving the topic of how the war first came to Chali, it is important to review some of the ironies and reversals that emerge after hearing so many different memories and explanations. I hope it is plain that I do not see the unfoldings of the Sudanese civil war in this region as a simple conflict between two clear parties, or two well-defined

---

[10] Omda Talib el Fil, Nor Deng, 22 July 1991.

projects. War projects can perhaps be seen in clear outline only from the remote and protected centres where they are planned and funded. They need not even be seen as rational projects by those who fund the proliferation of arms, especially the traders in small arms.[11] On the ground are ordinary people, almost without previous experience of political intrigue and co-ordinated violence outside their own village networks, let alone the workings of modern war, caught up in a situation not of their own making. There is a background historical canvas, of course, of which some, like Dawud Lothdha quoted earlier, are well aware—a history of alternate entanglement with, and escape from, predatory states. Individuals have long moved in and out of service to the state, or even to local powerful overlords or even slave traders, while retaining some flexibility in their relations with the 'home' community. A good deal that went on in Chali during the uncertain interlude of mid-1987 up to late 1989 illustrates this in the modern situation, adding an element of irony, and even a note of tragedy, to the events of this pivotal time, at this pivotal place.

I have introduced the figure of the garrison chief at Chali, Captain Tayeb Musbah. He was represented to me, at the time of my original 'fact-finding' in Khartoum in 1988, as a vicious man who personally carried out various acts of war and atrocities. He has also been more recently demonized as a fierce Arab by Christian campaigners on the internet, commentators who seem to have listened to exaggerated stories about his evil deeds via the evangelical networks and then exaggerated them further.[12] However, it became clear to me in interviews at several of the displaced camps I visited in later years that this man was not a northern Sudanese or Arab in any straightforward sense. As perhaps exemplifies the origins of many who have been caught up in the military institutions of the Sudan over past centuries, he was the son of a local woman, one of the '*kwanim pa*, and a man of one of the nomad Arab groups, the Rufa'a. His mother was a sister of Solomon Shiwa, one of the key church elders in Chali, a man who had been resident in Khartoum for some years before the war. It is not entirely clear how

[11] Kennedy Mkutu, 'Pastoralist conflict, governance and small arms in North Rift, north east Africa', doctoral thesis, Department of Peace Studies, University of Bradford, 2004.

[12] See, for example, the propaganda put out in 2002 by Dennis Bennett, then director of the Seattle-based 'Servant's Heart'. He accused 'Taib Musba', among other things, of killing 15,000 Christian Uduk (**www.worldnetdaily.com/news/article.asp? ARTICLE_ID=26672**).

this unusual marriage was formalized. One version suggested that bride-wealth was paid, but former missionaries testify that the woman had been taken to hospital in Malakal, and when they returned to collect her she had simply disappeared.[13] As I have explained elsewhere, the Uduk do regard children as essentially belonging to their mother's continuing line, even if married off elsewhere, though they recognize that claims are much weakened when bridewealth is paid.[14] The churchman did at one point visit his sister when her husband's group were encamped near Chali and suggest she come 'home', but she had no real links with her people any more, and I suspect she may not have remembered much of the language. Her son Tayeb was brought up as an Arab. I had heard William Danga speaking with others about her husband once bringing her to see her people in Beni Mayu, pointing out how the children were very dark and looked like some of their own relatives. I asked about the story.

We were talking about his mother, she once brought along her children, and her Arab husband too. Her husband was from the nomad Arabs, and they came from over there, herding sheep. They built a house near the truck road, but when people began to recognize the mother, her husband took her away. They went away, but they came again and lived near Chali there, and her brother, Solomon, Solomon Shiwa, came looking for her, wanting to take her from her husband. And she had said, 'I've had enough of going around with the Arabs, it's not good for me to go away far from here again. But I've become like something sold, in marrying here. I'm now married to him.' So she told her brother Solomon 'No', as she had learned the ways of the nomad Arabs, and would not know her home properly again.

And then she called her little son Tayeb, after the name of her mother's brother, who was a chief in the Yabus valley... and she told her child, 'Our own hill at home is called Pena Wayu (Beni Mayu).' And Tayeb used to go from Chali to grow sesame there with his people at Beni Mayu, paying them on a daily basis. But he didn't explain himself, that he was a person of Beni Mayu. And gradually, people began to hear about this, but didn't ask him. They didn't ask, and he stayed quiet and acted as though he was from somewhere else....

And so he went to seek work with the army?—Yes, he was a captain in Chali there... Yes, he's the one who burned the houses. He's the one who burned people's houses.[15]

---

[13] Barbara Harper remembers hearing this story when she moved from Doro to Chali in 1954.

[14] James, *'Kwanim Pa*, ch. 4.

[15] William Danga Ledko, Bonga, 29 Aug. 2000.

Another man commented that this story shows how good the Arabs are at getting the slaves to fight among themselves. He used the word *ciŋkinal* in this sense, though in other contexts it could mean foundlings or orphans. This case illustrates particularly clearly the appalling internal dilemmas for a community on the frontier between northern and southern Sudan, however that is defined. A 'slave' boy brought up in the far north could of course find himself in the government army, or in the old days the Sultan's army, and pursue a brilliant career. In fact in the old days of the Funj Kingdom the polity was partly in the hands of millitary slaves. But if that 'slave'-type child is brought up on the frontiers of the state, whether then or now he is in a tragic situation, having to attack his own mother's people. As the years since 1987 have passed, I have heard more and more details about the particular ironies and involvements of the key actors in the original drama of Chali's destruction. There was even a softer side to Tayeb's personal character, which William Danga mentioned in a conversation they had after almost everyone had left Chali in mid-1987, quoted in the previous chapter. According to this testimony, the garrison captain apparently came to regret what he had done. However, Tayeb Musbah was in command again in 1999, defending Jebel Ulu from the SPLA, and was later promoted to the rank of brigadier. He was then posted as military attaché to one of the Sudan's Middle Eastern embassies.

LULL: AND THIRD CAPTURE, 1997

The precarious group of those 'resettled' at Chali from 1992–3 on were able to live in reasonable safety for a few years. Then, following the souring of relations between Khartoum and Addis Ababa in 1995 and the revival in the fortunes of the SPLA, they were startled by the assault on Yabus in March 1996. As was their custom, the SPLA sent letters ahead to the Chali garrison, warning of their planned attack and ordering the civilians present to leave. 'Yes, they wanted the civilians to get out. And if the garrison was ready to fight, they should stay there in their trenches, and if they were not ready to fight, they should leave with the people.'[16] The guerrillas had remained in Yabus a couple of

---

[16] Stephen Missa, UK, 13 Sept. 1996.

months after taking it, and were now threatening to move north. When the letters arrived and the news of the threat spread, Sila Musa (from Khartoum) was already in Chali, and had to run with the others to the bush. He had found his wife, but not his parents, who had already gone to Renk in Upper Nile. Returning to Chali from the bush where he had first run to hide, he found it empty and searched for the people. As he had once done in 1987, he gathered up those who agreed to come with him back to Khartoum. Many agreed. Some travelled 'the way the people once came in the past [that is, the late nineteenth century], in the direction of Ulu, first to Bellila on foot and then Ulu'[17] and some came through Kurmuk. Others, including the Omda's group, had evacuated Chali to camp under the trees at Yilejada, and here the SPLA boys found them, a re-enactment of the situation of seven years previously. By the time Sila came in search, the party had already been escorted further south towards Jebel Chali, and on to Yabus.

When the advance warning came from the SPLA, in another 'replay' of 1989, the militiamen of the 'Popular Defence Forces' trained by the sergeant-major 'Sitale'—perhaps a hundred men—'just dispersed, and disappeared. They took the guns they had been using and went, took the path to the SPLA, and helped escort the Omda's group.' Their instructor was arrested and interrogated in Damazin, but later saved by the lucky chance of some good interpersonal relations. When the deserting soldiers from Chali got down to the Yabus, they recognized some prisoners of war there taken by the SPLA. One was a particular intelligence man they respected, because he had always been fair and friendly to them when stationed in Chali, and had reported abuses in the prison. So they spoke to the senior SPLA man in Yabus about this, asking that he should not be harmed. He was released, and went up to Damazin. There he found the former sergeant-major 'Sitale' in prison and requested his release, explaining that it was this man's trainees who had saved his own life. In this case as in so many others we can just glimpse through these stories how elusive are the front lines of civil war, especially when even the official lines move back and forth over a period of years, and personal ties, obligations, and debts, even debts of life, override the formal choreography of the oppositions of conflict.

---

[17] The reference is to flight in the 1890s; see James, *'Kwanim Pa*, ch. 2.

After the flight of civilians in February–March 1996, one party north to Khartoum and the other to Yabus, and the desertion of the militia, there was yet again not much left in Chali besides the garrison. Government garrisons were also present in Boing, and in Kurmuk, where reinforcements were expected. By late 1996, the SPLA was still firmly hanging on in Yabus, in Daga to the south, and also in the Ingessana Hills, to the north of Kurmuk. In Kurmuk town itself most of the merchants had left, but the local government was still in place. The SPLA had regained its strength, partly from the new recruiting programmes on the Ethiopian side, and was even threatening Damazin. In January 1997, Kurmuk was captured—for the third time—and as described in Chapter 1, this time the SPLA hung on to it. Chali also fell, as before, with a large number of other small government garrisons in the region. So many civilians of all remaining categories were leaving the Blue Nile Province, and neighbouring parts of Upper Nile, that the UNHCR and Ethiopian government set up a new camp for refugees at Sherkole, near Assosa, not more than a few miles from the former site of Tsore (Langkwai), where the Uduk had originally found refuge in April 1987. As the SPLA managed to secure a lasting hold over parts of the southern Blue Nile, it seemed, by the year 2000, to many people inside and outside the country that there would surely be a peace settlement before too long, and that the various communities in exile would be able to return home.

PART II

THE LONG ROAD, 1987–1993

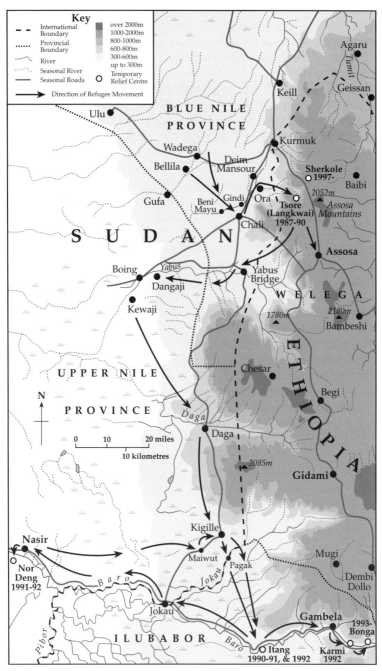

Map 3. The Long Road

4

Initial Refuge at Assosa and Why it Failed

I need a warmer place like Dul!
Sadiq made me flee from death to Ethiopia.
'Stop buying these goats,' we said,
The poor things were left behind.
They call us 'Uduk', we're wretched too;
Tayeb sent me towards death.

Jebel Kurmuk was taken by Salva:
'You people, look they've taken it!
There's only Damazin and Singa to go!'

But you can go there in civilian clothes,
Go carefully, creeping low.

Death is now released in Langkwai!
Is that the death we have to live with now?
We 'Uduk' are wretched in our death.
The poor goats were taken by the Arabs,
And some were eaten by the forest fighters,
Our wealth is finished.

I'm not sheltering here for fun,
The heavy guns made me escape,
Their sound puts the fear of death in my Liver![1]

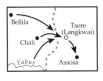

The initial 'flight' to Ethiopia included a rushed march over parched red-soil lowland and then a scramble up several thousand feet of steep ravines and scree slopes of the escarpment to a cool, even chilly, site where the SPLA had agreed with

---

[1] Composed by Kwata Kwayke, of Pam Be, who died in Langkwai, in middle years. The 'heavy gun' was explained to me as an 82 mm mortar, requiring about four men to handle it. Sung here by Dangaye Chalma, Bonga, 19 Aug. 2000.

UNCHR and the Ethiopian government that the Blue Nile people could stay for a while. Known to the Ethiopians as Tsore, this site already had a familiar name among the 'kwanim pa, Langkwai, where their grandfathers had once hunted in the forests behind Jebel Dul. There are graphic memories of this first trek. Yapmaka, a son of my former staunch friend and informant Tente, told me about it.

We all had to run. A women would carry two children in the headbasket, and one on her neck. We were very thirsty, until we arrived at Biding, near the mountain of Jerok... those who arrived first were taking water from Biding back to others behind. We could rest here because there were no Arabs. They were following us on the Sudan side, but did not come as far as Biding. They stayed in Ora. From Biding we went to Dul after three days. People dug for *shwa'b* [a wild root]. People were collecting baobab fruits and I don't know what. Then the message came for all the people to leave Dul and go up to Langkwai, right up into the mountains.[2]

On listening to this tape, many years later, Davis Sukut added his own commentary as a person lame from childhood. They got a lift for the steep part of the trek:

We people who were lame or old or blind or whatever, were told to walk to Khattawarak [an SPLA base], where we would get a lift. We walked, with one soldier as escort, from morning and got there at three o'clock. It was high up, we were zigzagging... there was a lorry waiting for us to go to Langkwai. [One soldier from his own village] went with me to the lorry, put me in the lorry, and we went to Langkwai—then we waited for those who were walking all the way up.[3]

Some of the sheer geographical difficulties of this trek to Langkwai (and the subsequent problems of leaving it in a southerly direction) can be imagined from the aerial view of the region in Figure 8. Yapmaka's story continued:

It was really steep! When you looked back, all the people looked like little kids, they were so small, and far away, right over there in the distance. You were so tired, but you just had to hold on to a tree to rest. There was a path made through the bamboo clumps, and as you went you held on to them because it was so steep. Then gradually we came out and found the better ground. The Bertha village looked close, but in fact it was quite off. Yes, we all came

---

[2] Yapmaka Tente, Bonga, 10 Nov. 1994 (video).
[3] Davis Sukut Burapa, USA, Nov. 2006.

together, the track was *wanya-wanya-wanya,* winding, it bends around so you
are close back to where you were before.—*Who was leading you?*—'*Kwanim pa*
led us [meaning their own youngsters, now of the Arrow Battalion]. We
followed the others…when we got there, it was not really a village, just an
overgrown place and there was a brick building made with cement and zinc on
top. It was really just bush, and we were surprised because we had heard so
much about the name. When we got there we had to rest our legs under the
trees. Then they cut us some corn, and we built a few huts, and after ten days we
had a village.
   —*And your father was with you?*—Yes, he was fine at that time, very strong,
and lived for two years in Langkwai. The third year he got ill.[4]

It is in the nature of things that the researcher is not normally 'there'
when the worst sufferings are being endured in a war zone, or when
military action or forced flight is actually taking place. But like journalists, academics can sometimes pick up a story later on, and even
make contact intermittently over a period of time and find the same
people as the situation changes. In the course of the successive displacements, the core of the Uduk people travelled some 650 miles on foot
between 1987 and 1993, leaving the 'northern' for the 'southern' Sudan
and meandering to and fro across the international frontier. Some
stretches were in rough mountain country, some in flat, arid bushland,
and some literally wading for miles through the floodplains of the Baro-
Sobat valley in the rainy season, as Map 3 shows. They would pull up
swamp grass and pile it up to make a bed above the water level. On key
occasions for the main parties, there were SPLA escorts, but for many
sections of the sometimes haphazard trekking, and for many laggard or
splinter groups, there were none. It is this long journey, especially the
empty stretches where many small parties suffered accident, illness,
hurried childbirth, hunger, thirst, and death along the way—not to
mention banditry by armed ambush, and hostile fire—that the people
refer to as *bway tur,* 'the long road'.
   It so happens that I was able to make contact with core groups of the
displaced at two quite significant turning points in this saga, at Nor
Deng near Nasir in eastern Nuer country, southern Sudan, in 1991, and
a year later at a transit camp called Karmi near Gambela in Ethiopia.
I then had two opportunities to visit the UNHCR scheme at Bonga

---

[4] Yapmaka Tente, Bonga, 10 Nov. 1994 (video).

Figure 8. The Ethiopian escarpment from the air, looking west

further inside Ethiopia where most of the survivors were settled from 1993 onwards, a few beginning official repatriation to their home area in 2006. This part of the book traces the epic story of the long road, its geographical twists and turns, and its physical and political hazards shared by the surprisingly closely knit core of the people who stuck together over this time. A new leadership did emerge just before the final dash back to Ethiopia, leaving a significant minority, including many of the 'old guard', behind in the Sudan; and inevitably there were large numbers of individual scatterings and small group departures of all kinds over the years. The main thread of the story in the rest of this book follows the fortunes and setbacks of the core group who eventually came to regard Bonga as 'home', while the concluding Chapter 11 traces some of the far-flung scatterings and often unexpected reunions which created a very lively outer network of connections. However far and wide the network extended for vernacular speakers over the last decade and a half, Bonga has provided, in the absence of 'Chali as we knew it', a moral centre of sorts, a tangible reference point on the map for people spread across several countries, including today not only those of the immediate region but also the USA, Canada, and Australia.

The initial place of refuge for the Uduk was Tsore in the Assosa district. I could not get there but secured accounts from a distance. I knew something about the place from my Khartoum visit in 1988, and took some comfort from the knowledge that it was a 'known' place, a one-time hunting ground. I learned much later that Tsore was known to the military as 'Kilo 27', its distance from Assosa, and that it included a site known as 'Green Book' where Sudanese dissidents had gathered in the 1970s. Under the patronage of Colonel Gaddafi of Libya, they had spent time there studying his 'Green Book'. Even Sadiq el Mahdi was remembered as having sheltered there. The site was mooted in the mid-1980s as a camp for Oromo who had already been displaced by disturbances in western Ethiopia and the border region, but the priority was changed following events around Kurmuk and the large new influx of Sudanese. The UNHCR established the Tsore camp in 1987 in conjunction with the Ethiopian Refugee and Rehabilitation Commission (RRC), and the Ethiopian Red Cross. The functions of the former were amalgamated in January 1989 under the new Administration for Refugee (and later Returnee) Affairs (ARRA). It was made clear to me in Addis Ababa in 1989 that no foreigners were allowed to remain overnight in any of the refugee camps, though brief visits to Tsore had been made by representatives of the SIM. However, there were some very capable and friendly Ethiopian staff who knew the place well. There were said at the time of my enquiries to be some 26,000 Uduk there, though this might well have included a good number of people from even less well-known minorities (and by late December there would be some 40,000 people of many backgrounds registered in the camp).

Ato Matewos Beraki was particularly helpful in outlining life in the camp. Tsore was regarded as a model refugee camp by the authorities, and the Uduk as model refugees. Indeed they have a tradition that in the old days when they had to move, they would always carry a few seeds in a large snail shell, to plant some other place, some other time. The agencies noted that in 1987 this set of refugees had arrived in reasonable condition, in 'family and clan groups', with 'chiefs and priests' in place, bringing their own seeds and tools. Ato Matewos had first lived there in a leaky tent but had overseen the growth of a well-organized settlement. On registration, the new arrivals had to declare name, tribe, religion. In many cases, even personal names were being recorded in writing for the first time ever; the form of names was expected to be in the standard Arabic or Ethiopian pattern of self, father's name, and father's father's name—something quite strange for the matrilineal bias in the way that Uduk think about the continuity of the family. Making lists of course became a very familiar chore over the following years in a string of other camps, but even a decade later I saw some lists where people were using their mother's brother, not their father, as the named relative in the next generation. Nevertheless the recording of identities at borders continued to be something of a personal, as well as a collective, rite of passage.

Tsore camp, or 'Langkwai', was about a mile on the south side of the main road between Kurmuk and Assosa. It was laid out in four quarters of a circle. One quarter had the offices and buildings such as the clinic, with a child patient room, the examination room, and so on; a concrete school block was under construction for the local teachers to use. The people's plots were grouped according to the chiefs of their former village clusters, and arranged in straight lines. One could sit in the middle and survey the whole camp. Each plot had a little room for cultivation, though people would 'pick their maize too early' and roast it for eating, before the proper harvest time. The government was considering bringing in tractors and clearing a large area between the settlement and the road, so the farming could be 'done properly'. Ato Matewos had noticed that they liked hunting, and boys would practise throwing sticks through loops thrown in the air. There were various co-operatives set up and 'participation' was a strong theme in the life of the camp. I also heard impressions from one of the Sudan Interior Mission people in Addis Ababa who had visited the previous year. The people were wearing very few real clothes, just wraps of sacking in some cases, but although they looked so impoverished a couple of thousand had come out in force to greet their visitors *singing*, that is, singing hymns. The SIM was able to send down a container of clothes, and more recently had sent blackboards, chalk, exercise books, and wind-up cassette recorders with Bible texts in Uduk and Meban. For the seventeen wood- and grass-built churches, they sent one church bell each.

Some years and many hardships later, William Danga reminisced on their time in Langkwai, where 'the *'kwanim pa* ate their fill. They ate wheat a lot that year, ate their fill and became very fat.' He had arrived by Christmas 1987, and remembers how they were all given blankets, and sorghum, and cooking oil, and clothes. William regularly helped chief Soya Bam with the distribution of supplies for the Pam Be group.

Other things, sugar, I would prepare it carefully and give it out.—*Sugar too?*—Yes, sugar too, but there wasn't any tea! The UN didn't bring us tea leaves, only just the sugar by itself. But people could buy tea from the shops. The Gomasha shops. People could buy it for themselves. . . . It worked like this, the UN would give you oil, you could put a little aside and sell it, and the rest you would use it yourself. Clothes, what had you got? And how many blankets? . . . eventually people could save up and buy a goat, or a sheep, there were plenty of sheep! . . . That place wasn't at all bad.[5]

The mention of such a luxury as sugar once having been given out by the UN (almost unbelievable generosity in retrospect) always tended to reduce listeners in later years to helpless giggles. But to me the really astonishing thing was William's casual reference to going shopping in Gomasha. He mentioned the mango trees there, and market days on Saturday and Tuesday, with Bertha (Watawit) and Wollo merchants. This 'Gomasha' (accent on the first syllable), about an hour's walk on the other side of the main Kurmuk–Assosa truck road, was the very same name, and almost certainly the very same place, where just over a hundred years before, Schuver had visited the notorious chief Mahmud Himmeidi. Here he had been offered one of the 'Gomasha beauties' with 'clear ringing voices' (see the Historical Introduction). These girls had almost certainly been abducted from the nearby valleys opening down to the Sudanese plains, and very probably included some of the *'kwanim pa* displaced by Turkish raiding. The great-granddaughters, as it were, of those beauties were now there again, having also been forced to leave their homes and seek protection of a kind in the Ethiopian hills.

In fact, modern Gomasha and its immediate region, now up against a precisely defined and active international line of conflict, indeed the

5 William Danga Ledko, Nor Deng, 22 July 1991.

front line of the Cold War, was a more complex and dangerous zone than it could ever have been a hundred years earlier. Although a civilian refugee camp, Langkwai was dominated by officers and men of the SPLA. They were of rather diverse background, including Latuka, and Murle, and Nuba, but were perceived as mainly Nuer and Dinka, and in the eyes of at least some of their protégés no doubt had a glamorous appeal. They are remembered as tempting Uduk girls away with gifts of dresses and perfume, though sometimes treating them roughly. The girls with a little education—usually from Chali itself—with perhaps rather more 'modern' ways than those from the outlying hamlets, were especially popular. A couple of dozen girls at least were remembered as having gone off with soldiers and never having been seen again, though occasional news about them arrives. The scattering of women through marriage ties or informal liaisons with SPLA soldiers was a continuing source of unhappiness among their Uduk relatives throughout the years of exile (a theme I return to in Chapter 11).

While it is true that the initial relationship with the SPLA in Assosa district was a positive one, it gradually became more complicated. Uduk lads who had joined the Arrow Battalion and taken part in the first assault on Kurmuk in 1987 were now occasionally dropping out of the military and being absorbed into the refugee community. William Dhupa, who as I have mentioned in the introduction had travelled with me south of the Yabus in 1969, was one of this first cohort. He continued to work with the SPLA during the refugee period in Assosa, but found himself with few resources and became a civilian again, marrying a Meban woman. When he and his wife had to leave with everyone else they settled down to cultivate fields in Meban country along the Yabus, rather than go on down to Itang (though he rejoined the struggle in 1992, serving in the far south and the Nuba Hills, where he was seriously wounded). However, the late 1980s were a period of growing strength for the SPLA generally. Certainly from early 1988 and possibly before, recruiting did begin among the refugees and civilians in Assosa district. Here Salva Kiir Mayar Dit, the victor of Kurmuk, raised and trained the 'New Funj Forces' at the site called Green Book near Langkwai. As mentioned, the site has its own history as a place of refuge in the Blue Nile Borderlands, particularly remembered as a place where Sadiq el Mahdi had found temporary shelter in the early 1970s.

William Nyuon later took over leadership in the area. He received large numbers of newly trained fighters from what was then the Ethiopian army and SPLA base at Bonga in the Gambela region, and he moved the Assosa training site to Sherkole. Ironically, both Bonga and Sherkole sites later became refugee camps (1993 and 1997 respectively), though this could not have been anticipated in the heady days of the late 1980s. As explained in Chapter 1, William Nyuon led the big assault on Kurmuk in October 1989, followed by the capture of small garrisons such as Chali to its south. These disturbances caused new waves of refugees, fleeing both SPLA and Sudan government advances, to seek shelter in Langkwai. In Geissan a similar situation obtained as the result of a similar history, and people fleeing from that border town were also received in Langkwai around New Year 1990.

News about the refugees leaked out from the Assosa district very slowly, the first letter to Khartoum being from Hannah Weyak to her husband, Pastor Paul, about a year after the move, but no direct contact or reunions were ever made. My own plan for a possible visit was completely written off when the place had to be evacuated just a month after the Addis conversations above. Although it had been impressed on me by the Ethiopian authorities that Tsore was a civilian camp, no one was under any illusions about the close proximity of SPLA posts in the area. Nor was it a secret that the new Sudanese government of Omer el Beshir was intent on pushing back the SPLA, especially from the recently acquired territories in the 'northern' Sudan like Kurmuk and Geissan. Armed opposition to the Mengistu regime, in Eritrea and in northern and western Ethiopia, was also known to be spreading, with an element of Sudanese support. It was in fact a combination of these developments which led to the sudden news of the sacking of the camp at Tsore. In the last week of December, the SPLA decided to evacuate Kurmuk and leave it for the Sudanese government forces and their allies to retake. This happened quickly, with the assistance of Eritrean troops who had been strategically placed at Khor Ahmar on the new main road to the north-west of the town.

A large force composed of both Eritrean and Sudanese soldiers then came across the border in the first few days of January 1990. Targeting the SPLA base at Khattawarak near Dul on the way, they moved by night up the road from Kurmuk towards the Ethiopian government garrison at Assosa. The refugees at Tsore were told they were not a target and should get out of the way, which was not easy, for by early morning on 4 January the Assosa garrison was responding, and shells were flying up and down the road in both directions. The refugees escaped as best they could towards Assosa, a few going all the way to the town but most taking a right-hand turn and following the slopes and valleys south-westwards down to the border. Together with some of the fleeing SPLA soldiers, most of the refugees made their way through very rough mountain country down towards the Sudan and Yabus Bridge. Others did not survive this journey, and I shall return to their stories.

In the next three chapters, I describe what happened to the Uduk refugees from the time that the relatively safe and familiar 'haven' in the Assosa district was sacked in early January 1990. They found themselves locked into an unpredictable zigzag of journeys which for the core of the population seemed interminable. From a safer place in the United States, twenty years later, Davis Sukut expressed the way they had felt completely baffled, uncomprehending, as they rested occasionally on the long road, as to why, *why*, these things should be happening to themselves, again and again, apparently alone among the peoples of the world. Wiser perhaps as anyone would be from a distance—as Davis himself is now—this was a powerful feeling of the time that we need to try and understand. There is now quite a large body of UN and NGO reports from this period, but inevitably they deal mainly with material conditions at those points where the displaced have come to rest for a time. They do not often throw light on the atmosphere, the long treks, the wilderness between such places, or the basic reasons why people have had to keep on moving. At three such places, and basically four points in time, I was able to undertake short consultancies for these bodies myself: Nor Deng near Nasir in mid-1991; the transit camp of Karmi near Gambela in mid-1992 (and early 1993 when I was consultant to a TV documentary[6]); and the Bonga refugee scheme, 1994 and 2000. On each occasion I have tried to fill in the blanks, the wilderness experiences, as best I could through tapping into memories and reflections. Each of the next three chapters opens with a short summary describing the place as it was at the time of my visit; and continues with an explanation of the key reasons on each occasion for

---

[6] *Orphans of Passage*: Disappearing World, War: Granada TV, directed by Bruce MacDonald, 1993.

renewed flight, followed by a collage of discussions, reflections, and hopes drawn from taped conversations.

It gradually became clear to me that the character and content of memories, and even the kind of issues that people are willing to discuss, keeps changing. For example, during the time that the Sherkole site was a sizeable military training camp, not far from the refugee camp at Langkwai, there were some problems of discipline, the kind of thing that does not often get reported in the UN or the aid agency literature. Academic fieldworkers of whatever kind tend not to hear about the military side of 'refugee stories' either, and in my own case, it was nearly twenty years before I heard that SPLA men had been looting the local Bertha villages in the late 1980s, that the Uduk as such were blamed, and that seven of them had been executed by firing squad. Other unsavoury details of goings on came to my notice only when they had, as it were, become history. For example from the time that an SPLA presence was first suspected by the security in Chali, I have now heard more than once that some men were engaged as paid informants. Of course I was not present in Chali or Assosa at these times, and indeed almost everything I have reported here I learned after the event. The following chapters are written on the basis of a series of fairly short field trips over the following two decades, and all include some first-hand observation along with conversations close to actual events. But in these next chapters I have tried to distinguish between things learned close at hand, and retrospective conversations held years later and in distant places. Civilian suffering from hunger, illness, and death, along with immediate needs, especially those that feed into the categories of the UN and agencies, tend to dominate most conversations with the anthropologist on the spot. It is through later reflections that the picture becomes more complicated, and, especially once the fighting is over, the military aspect comes to the fore.

One of the underlying aspects of the sojourn in Assosa, and indeed of the trek as a whole, not always visible to me at the time has turned out to be the key importance of the real-life role of armaments, especially small arms, to displaced communities. Although the problem of the spread of small arms has only recently been recognized in academic and other reporting on the world's local wars, the presence or absence of arms is quite central to many of the events that take place. We need to understand what gives the people themselves a sense of power, some 'anger in their bodies', some strength. The theme does return to guns. We might recall that the Uduk were first disarmed in 1956, at the time of Sudanese independence. This was not a major upheaval, as there were only a few guns hidden around the villages. However, they were all confiscated. The theme of having guns, of getting the training to use them in self-defence, or the humiliation of having them confiscated, or looted, becomes quite compelling in the stories of the long road.

Some years after the initial period of guerrilla activity (1986–9), Peter Kuma (who had now given up military activities and was doing sterling work for the humanitarian agencies) explained their feeling about this to me. In the later refugee scheme at Bonga he was reflecting on the fact that the people no longer had guns, or power, and were entirely in the hands of the UN—that is, dependent on their protection—protection which by this time had proved ambiguous and fragile from the time of Assosa onwards.

There are no guns here. Nothing. We have no power here. And we *'kwanim pa* here, we are just followers. The UN is in charge here, and the government. If the UN had not given money for this land, we would not find any peace. And they give us food, so there will be peace. And because of this, I give instructions all the time, that people should live quietly. Leave the problems alone, we don't have any power. We have no power here, the UN is in charge of us. If anything happened here, the *'kwanim pa* I think would not survive, because we have no guns.

A gun helps a person to lead the children along and look after them, as happened before. Look at myself, I have no power. Nothing. This is very hard for me at the moment. Because guns helped the men before, helped the Uduk, that's why we survived up to now. Because we could deal with the problems we found. We were very strong. And where can we find the strength now? We can't. If we had guns we could look after the village properly. If a man has a gun he is able to live. Because he can look after his people properly. But the Uduk now have no power.[7]

In the event, as the political pendulum swung to and fro, there were new opportunities among the refugees for recruitment into the SPLA, especially from 1995. Some young men at various points, boys and men so young they scarcely remembered their homeland, did join up, and I shall tell their stories. But despite the commentary above, armed activity has not been the main key to survival of the displaced over the last two

---

[7] Peter Kuma, Bonga, 24 Nov. 1994.

decades. It has been rather the exercise of will and foresight through more basic means—survival skills in the bush, decisions to move, to plan for the self-cultivation of crops where possible, and to seek the security of patronage where it might be available, even under contradictory circumstances. The story when summed up sounds as though all 'the Uduk' moved together, and indeed it is truly remarkable that so many did act in concert at crucial points, but rival factions did emerge and splinter groups did strike out on their own. Not all the latter survived, and the rhetoric about survival through sticking together has understandably become a key theme in the people's discussions with each other and with the agencies.

In the circumstances, the refugees had been well cared for in the Tsore refugee camp, under the *de jure* authority of the Ethiopian government of Mengistu Haile Mariam, the auspices of the UNHCR, and the local *de facto* overlordship of the SPLA. But in the context of the ongoing sea-change in international and global politics, this relatively 'safe' situation could not last. The Berlin Wall fell in November 1989, as Kurmuk was being struggled over for the second time, and inside western Ethiopia armed resistance was building up decisively against Mengistu's rule.

5

Blue Nile South: Ethiopian Turmoil, SPLA Protection, 1990–1992

> Our dreaded in-law! It's droning on, *diling diling*
> Anto-no-ov! It's droning closer, *diling diling*
> Mancole, the 'Small Arms' Battalion!
> Anto-no-ov! It's droning closer.
>
> The coffee's all spilled over in the grass
> It made us tip the coffee on the ground
> *'The guards will surely seek me out, but it's three days now!'*
> How are you in Kewaji? *We're fine.*
> *How are you in Dangaji?* We're fine.
>
> Civilians of Kewaji, are you all right?
> *Civilians of Dangaji, how is it?*
>
> O Battalion 'Mancole'!
> Our dreaded in-law, here it comes again[1]

When I heard the news that the Assosa camp had been evacuated under fire, in early 1990, and some months later that the people had shown up in the notorious Itang refugee camp much further south, I was astonished, and began to think about visiting there. But by early 1991 it was clear that the Mengistu regime was in a fragile condition, and in April that year during a conference visit to Addis Ababa I met Russians who told me that they and the Cuban advisers in Itang were already leaving.

---

[1] Uduk children's song, Nor Deng, 1991. The song's main theme is the fearful sound of the Sudanese Antonov, which first circled over the people and released bombs as they returned from Assosa to the Yabus valley. It was dreaded 'as one might one's parents-in-law'. As with many other songs, there are different voices in the 'conversation'. 'Mancole' is in the Jum Jum or Wadke language, meaning literally 'small arms', which is what these recruits had apparently been given in Assosa. A deserter's voice is heard, hoping he won't be rounded up. When the refugees are divided between the SPLA posts at Dangaji and Kewaji further south, they call out to each other.

The road to Nekemte itself was closed. The following month, the government fell. And one month after that, I heard from my husband who was on a consultancy with the UN Operation Lifeline Sudan that the Uduk and other Blue Nile displaced were coming down the Baro-Sobat valley and arriving in the Upper Nile town of Nasir, held by the SPLA. I was glad to accept a consultancy to visit there in late July–early August and provide background on these unexpected 'returnees'.[2] The Nasir faction of the SPLA then, at the end of August, made a bid for leadership of the movement, provoking internecine conflict which made the situation of the stranded 'returnees' even more precarious. I returned in late September–early October and did a follow-up report.[3]

The conversations I had in Nor Deng, the site across the wide river Sobat from Nasir to which the Blue Nile displaced had been directed, were mainly about the terrible treks since Assosa, and what was to happen next. At the same time people were very glad of an opportunity to tell me (as someone who knew their original home area) precisely why they had been obliged to leave. Some accounts of this kind have been quoted in Chapters 2 and 3. Here I draw on more circumstantial stories of what happened in and around Chali in the late 1980s. I met people who had suffered torture at that time, and heard of many others who had died of ill treatment, or thirst, or illness, including people I had once known well. I also heard of some I knew who had become fighters with the SPLA and had taken part in the original battle for Kurmuk. However, Nor Deng was not the kind of place where I could actually speak to fighters. It was later on, and in other places, even other countries, that I heard testimonies from fighters themselves and began to understand the military side of the story of the flight from Assosa, back into the Sudan, again into Ethiopia at Itang, and back once more to the Sudan, to our current setting close to Nasir in eastern Upper Nile. Similarly, it was only on subsequent visits to the Uduk refugees, when they were, unbelievably, back in Ethiopia for the third time, that I began to hear about the underlying military tensions of Nasir itself in 1991–2.

[2] Wendy James, 'Background report and guidelines for future planning: Nor Deng centre for Sudanese returnees, Nasir' (Nairobi, UN, WFP/Operation Lifeline Sudan, Southern Sector, Aug. 1991). Cf. also James, 'Managing food aid: returnees' strategies for allocating relief', *Refugee Participation Network*, 13 (1992), 3–6.

[3] Wendy James, 'Vulnerable groups in the Nasir region: update on Nor Deng (Blue Nile returnees) and resettlement proposal' (Nairobi, WFP/OLS Southern Sector, 15 Oct. 1991).

For this reason, in each of the sections that follow, I first illustrate the sort of conversations I had in Nor Deng itself about current problems and a particular portion of the journey, and then draw on later conversations to indicate some aspects of the military side of events.

Nor Deng was an old Nuer encampment on very, very slightly raised ground near the Sobat river bank, still with a few local Nuer homesteads nearby. It was adjacent to the historic site of 'Old Nasser', the original Turco-Egyptian *zeriba* founded by (and named after) a slave trader turned government official in 1875, though this poignant echo of the past was not known to the new arrivals. Nor Deng had been designated one of seven sites for the large numbers of displaced people returning from Ethiopia as the rainy season was already under way in June 1992. It was identified specifically as a site for those displaced from the Blue Nile, who included not only Uduk but some Bertha-speaking 'Funj' from Geissan, a small number of Burun from the various Kurmuk hills, and Koma from the Yabus. There were considerable numbers of Meban from the adjacent parts of the Upper Nile, 'traditionally' closely associated with the Kurmuk district people, and also substantial numbers from remoter parts of the southern Sudan. All these people were transported over the river in small rubber dinghies or local boats. Building materials were minimal, mainly consisting of a few sticks and some green plastic sheeting unofficially dropped by UN planes along with the first sorghum (Operation Lifeline had to operate within very harsh limitations from Khartoum, permitting aid only in the form of grain). It was a ghastly site for the displaced. 'Overcrowded' would be a mild term, and literally no means of escape should there have been any attack upon them from air, land, or river (Figure 9).

Even more basic, for the very first time, it was not possible physically to retrace your footsteps back to any part of the Blue Nile homeland—you were stuck firmly on the far side of the great river Baro-Sobat in flood, with no bridges and no locally friendly contacts, sometimes literally stuck in the mud of that swampy place. You could only cross back if given a place in a small boat of the UN or the SPLA. No wonder a significant minority of the Itang returnees offered a place in Nor Deng, including many southern Uduk, and Meban, had refused to cross to the south bank of the river, preferring to hang around on the north bank and risk a trek back 'home' at the first opportunity. The population who agreed to be transported over in a series of small boats

Figure 9. Nor Deng and the Sobat from the air, July 1991

were in a way 'captured' by the SPLA, and henceforth firmly under their control. The commanders even expected them to cultivate on land which they could see was too heavy, liable to flood, and infested with a grass called *saga'b* which stifles the roots of crops. One of the Nuer commanders had already got people working in his 'private garden' and people feared, with reason, that if they did plant they would not be able to keep their own crops. It turned out to be a very heavy rainy season, and by the time of my second visit in September, much of Nor Deng was truly flooded, some of the shelters that people had by now built almost afloat. Adults were afraid of their children falling in the river. Women collected concrete fragments from bombed buildings in Nasir, and hammered them into grinding stones (Frontispiece and Figure 10). They also learned from the Nuer, specifically from a Nuer woman long married into their community, how to improvise 'hearthstones' from dried mud (Figure 11).

Figure 10. Pake and Tumke (wife and niece of William Danga), preparing a grindstone from the remains of a bombed building

There were no supplies in place to greet the returnees. There was no land transport, and the ground was too wet for cargo planes to land. As part of Operation Lifeline, the World Food Programme arranged some emergency air drops of grain from Kenya in early July, and UNICEF sent small planes with modest supplies for medical help and children's feeding. These efforts were far from adequate for the many thousands of people in the seven centres for returnees around Nasir.[4] For a period of about two whole weeks, for one reason or another absolutely no food supplies reached Nor Deng. I witnessed part of this hard time. People were using what wild resources they could, including various types of

---

[4] Douglas Johnson, 'Increasing the trauma of return: an assessment of the UN's emergency response to the evacuation of the Sudanese refugee camps in Ethiopia, 1991', in T. Allen (ed.), *In Search of Cool Ground: Displacement and Homecoming in Northeast Africa* (London: James Currey, 1996).

Figure 11. 'Hearthstones' made from mud: learned from the Nuer

leaves (*jipi, ba'th, kath, saa*), wild okra (*karis*) and mushrooms (the tiny *cinjolo*, and larger *dish*), a tiny plant with pea-like seeds in pods (*malampo*), small snails (*homo'd*), large water snails (*kwali*), fish, and python. Men explored the surrounding thin bush for honey, and children caught locusts. The people were frustrated because there were none of the wild roots they were used to eating in hard times, because the ground was regularly flooded. A little food could be had from local Nuer, but rarely for money, and where Ethiopian dollars were acceptable, the price was twice that in Itang. The only goods in demand were things supplied by the UN. Exchange rates were punitive, including the following: 1 blanket for 1 large fish; 1 large plastic jerry can for 1½ panfuls of grain; 1 empty UN sack (very valuable item here) for half a panful of meat. Arrangements of a politically very complicated kind were under way for some weeks before a barge arrived from Kosti via Malakal with the UN flag, carrying UN grain courtesy of the Khartoum government (Figure 12). The *El Mugren* arrived on 27 July, and further

Figure 12. Arrival of the UN barge, 27 July 1991

deliveries followed. These supplies certainly averted a major loss of life through starvation and hunger-related illness in and around Nasir.[5] Many individuals I had known well in the past did not survive their stay in Nor Deng, and others would succumb in early 1992 after they were re-transported across the river to the north side. I noticed that William Danga had a brand-new UN-supplied *moloda*, or hoe, under his green plastic shelter. Would he be using it to plant some crops? No, he said. He would be using it for digging graves.

CONVERSATIONS IN NOR DENG

Omda Talib denounced Nor Deng; he declaimed to me emphatically that the place was like a prison. There was no way they could leave, there was nowhere to grow crops, people were selling their UN blankets and sheets to the Nuer for the sake of a little food for their kids. He explained carefully however that they were grateful to be able to stay with the help of the UN, and as yet they had no clear indication of an alternative either from the Arabs or from the SPLA. He was enthusiastic about a move to the drier areas upstream, such as Kigille: he painted a somewhat rosy picture of how two crops a year would grow there, how there were wild animals for meat, etc. He announced that he knew how to speak the truth, having worked once for the English, as well as the Arabs, and having had dealings with the missionaries. He might not have much English, but he did, he claimed, speak straight to the point, and tell the case as it was.[6]

The plight of women and children on the long treks and in places like Nor Deng was particularly severe. There was a strong commitment, for example, to the idea that people should continue bearing children, as many as they could manage, in order to compensate for the deaths of so many people, young and old. But childbearing in current circumstances was desperately difficult, as Rebecca Puba, a trained midwife, knew only too well. I had known her in the old days, when she was married to my main research assistant, Shadrach Peyko Dhunya.

---

[5] 'The return to southern Sudan of the Sudanese refugees from the Itang camp, Gambela, Ethiopia', UNICEF/Operation Lifeline Sudan, Nairobi, 31 Aug. 1991.

[6] Omda Talib el Fil, Nor Deng, 22 July 1991.

Figure 13. Sunday worship, Nor Deng, October 1991

I've had a lot of work from early this morning, because of our women giving birth. There is no rest. They keep calling me. The births are hurting women a lot. We midwives have no rest.—*Now Rebecca, what was the situation over childbirth like in Itang?*—It was all right there; there were a lot of births, a large total. But on the long road, there was a lot of miscarriage, from blood loss, because of the weakness from the long road . . . and now, the children are getting ill, from the long road. . . . And now, in July, a lot of women are giving birth . . . some twins too . . . only Arum is there. . . . There are women who help me, yes, but we don't have any cloths to wrap the little babies. And some women who give birth, don't have a blanket to warm themselves.

—*Have they sold their blankets?*—Yes, they've sold them because of hunger. . . . I do have some help, there are eight midwives altogether now. If a case is difficult, they call me. And I can sometimes call Peter Kuma, who is an experienced doctor. Sometimes there are conditions that I can't deal with.[7]

I found myself pressed into service as a messenger from the displaced people in Nor Deng to their relatives, at least the accessible ones, the

---

[7] Rebecca Puba, Nor Deng, 22 July 1991.

Christians in Khartoum, with whom there had been little communication for at least four years (Figure 13). At the people's request, I took many photos for relatives and made several tape-recorded messages which were later sent on. Some were simply personal family messages, such as Suske, Pastor Paul's first wife, addressed to her children: 'Bulus, Nathan, and Banuni, Cliff, I am anxious to know how you are. I am worried about you all, what work are you doing, if you hear these words from me...Rachel, Mary. Lidia, and Diye is with me here. I send greetings to you all...I am very thin, my Liver is crying for my children all the time.'[8] Hannah Paul, Pastor Paul's then wife, who was very ill and weak, also sent a moving message, speaking slowly with greetings to the people in Khartoum and requests for their prayers. She spoke about the hunger and the illness in Nor Deng, but also mentioned they had heard that Paul himself was ill and they were praying for him. She sent greetings to the new small Uduk churches in Khartoum and Omdurman, as well as to the established one in Mayo on the outskirts of the capital. 'I am ill from the time in May when we left [Itang] but am getting a bit better. We may not see you again.'[9] Hannah died shortly after this.

THE TREK: ASSOSA TO ITANG

(i) Civilian accounts

Other messages I taped in Nor Deng for relatives in Khartoum were factual reports, sometimes based on notes which people had kept along the way. William Danga sent one such message to his sister's son Sila Musa in Khartoum, mainly listing the key events of the fighting after Sila escorted his mother Tabke away from Chali in 1987, and then places where family members had died (Hada in Langkwai; Tente, Sija, Kanyke on the long trek south—all of whom I had known well from our village in the old days). Titus Solomon Gathe, of the core Chali church community, delivered a detailed and unemotional

---

[8] Suske Wupko, first wife of Paul Rasha, Nor Deng, 22 July 1991.
[9] Hannah Paul, Nor Deng, 7 Oct. 1991.

itinerary from memory, on the basis of written notes which he had kept during the trek. I quote from his testimony in sections in order to provide a framework for some of the more fragmentary recollections which others were keen to give me. It is a remarkable account from one who had long been lame. The first section gives details up to the first return to the Sudan from Assosa. I have a closely corresponding account based on a written diary from Idris Mochko, which generally matches the accuracy of Titus' chronology of the movements of his own group.[10] He had already been playing a key role in helping register the lists of household heads and dependants at various places for a succession of 'authorities'.

We left Sudan on Saturday, 11 April 1987. We left at 8 o'clock from Chali, through the night, cutting the border between Sudan and Ethiopia at a place called Abu Nazir. We slept at a place called Yin Kutha-E, for two days. Then we went to Biding, and on to Dul, on the 14th. Then we slept one day at Dul, and then went on for two days on the road to Langkwai. And we were hungry on the road, and there was nothing to eat. In various Bunyan villages in Ethiopia a lot of people sold a few things, dogs, and things we were carrying, and clothes, to buy maize and beans and sorghum, to boil and toast them so we had something to eat. We got to Langkwai on 17 April. It was a place for 'refugees' [English], and the Uduk were living there near Assosa. We stayed there about three years.

Until 4 January 1990, when the Ethiopian fighting started there, and we fled to Assosa. We stayed one day near there, sleeping just beyond Assosa, at a place between Assosa and Mekelle. At Mekelle there we rested a while, and we then set off from Mekelle to Yabus. And at Yabus, we stayed there until an aeroplane

---

[10] Idris Mochko Waku gave the following dates for the movements of his particular group: they left Bellila on 4 April 1987, when nomad Arabs took off their goats and cattle and killed the pigs. On 6 April the local traders (Bertha/Arabic speaking) burned the church, and the nomad Arabs attacked at midday, killing many elderly who could not run away. They arrived at Langkwai on 18 May. They left Langkwai early on 3 January 1990, as the *hakuma* (government, army) of Eritrea was fighting the *hakuma* of Ethiopia; then another *hakuma*, of the Oromo, appeared in the mountains and attacked them on 6 and 7 January; they were in the Meban area up to 28 April when there were attacks from the government troops at Boing, and they left for Itang. They fled from there on 26 May 1991. After two days they returned to obtain foodstuffs from the warehouses but after fourteen went on to Pagak, from where they had to depart for Nasir. It was not possible to sleep during this trek, because of walking through water so much of the way. They arrived at Nasir on 27 June 1991 (handwritten memo later provided to W. J.). Nor Deng, 7 Oct. 1991.

came and attacked us at Yabus there, and so we fled to Wora Dis. We stayed there five days, and again, there was an Arab attack and we went to Bwawosh. Again we stayed five days, and the Arabs attacked us again, and we fled to Bugaya, and a place called Cez. We stayed there another few days, and people said, 'Let's go to Meban country'. We set out from Cez towards Dangaji. We stayed there in the thornbrush until some Meban found us, who had come from Khartoum, and they gave us news about you who are living there in Khartoum. Then, we went from Dangaji, towards Liang, and from Liang, to Kewaji, and in Kewaji they divided us up, some went to Dongoje, and some to Kantusha, others to Dar Saliya, others to a place called Pumke. Then again, word came that people should go to Itang.[11]

I heard many stories of different sections of the trek from Assosa onwards. Here are the events of the assault on Assosa, in Willliam Danga's words:

[The rebels said:] 'We are going to fight the Ethiopians for our land. We don't want to attack the SPLA. You just go, leave here.' But they [the SPLA people] didn't pass this word on properly, they refused to tell us. And through the night, while people were sleeping, some began to hear about this, gradually, and started to pack up their things. Some didn't pack up, they didn't get ready. The the guns sounded, *beerreeer, beemmmm,* Haaa! It was bad. People fled in the night, they woke up and ran.... It was the New Year, January.... Yes, this fighting came from the direction of Kurmuk, and reached the people at the refugee place there.

Then the Ethiopians started firing big guns from up in the hills there, shooting, and the whole mountain caught fire.—*The soldiers of the Ethiopian government?*—Yes, they were shooting a lot. But the others, they waited, and waited, until the refugees had all gone.... Airplanes were going around, Ethiopian ones ... they were flying around, far away. Then in the afternoon, when the sun was about here, the Oromo started shooting from there, the direction of Assosa. While people were still coming along the road, and had not yet reached Assosa. They fired from there! The *'kwanim pa* were coming along, and they split up, some took the way to Assosa itself and some went to the right. They slept in scattered places. They continued coming, and near Assosa, they went to Makelle, from Makelle up a hill, and then on down to Kubri [Yabus Bridge]. At Kubri, they met up together, and had some rest.[12]

---

[11] Titus Solomon Gathe, Nor Deng, 6 Oct. 1991.
[12] William Danga, Nor Deng, 22 July 1991.

Among the few exhausted individuals who left the main party to seek shelter in the town was Yukke, wife of Hada, who had been my neighbour in the old hamlet of Wakacesh in the 1960s. Her relatives had not been aware of this, and most people assumed for years that she would have died. But Yukke figures in one of the surprising stories of survival that came to light later. I eventually saw her again in the year 2000, when she had just been rescued and brought to Bonga (see Chapter 11). The majority of the refugees took a right-hand track away from Assosa town, through a deep ravine in the mountains and down to the Yabus valley. As William mentioned above and many others have testified to me, they were shot at on the way, by soldiers of the Oromo Liberation Front or their supporters among the Bertha-speaking people of the hills. Traversing a particularly steep slope, some dropped their belongings under fire, and even their infants, who rolled down into the bottom of the ravine (but again see Chapter 11, for a remarkable story of one such infant's survival, and reunion with his people, though he grew up speaking another language).

As the refugees returned 'home' across the Sudan border to Yabus Bridge, the Sudanese air force arrived (at this early date in the guise of an ageing Russian cargo plane) and dropped some bombs, though no one was hit. Of course along with the fleeing civilians there were large numbers of SPLA fighters retreating from Kurmuk, Dul, and from Geissan. William Danga's account continued:

So we found them there at Kubri, many of them. And there was this vast amount of coffee! Ay! People piled it up like this, and kept on drinking. Then the Antonov appeared, and attacked people there. Some had been there five days, some only one day, as people were coming in small groups, small groups. As it attacked people they all scattered and fled, and left things on the ground.

We all fled to a place called Wora Dis. After a few days the government came, from Chali, came up thinking the *'kwanim pa* were there, living in Kubri. Then they discovered that people had gone from Kubri, into the thornbrush there, and right away.

The people went on to Bugaya that day. If someone was ill, people would leave them on the ground. Leave them, not dead, still a little alive, but there was no way to carry them. . . . A person would die on their own later later. There was no way. Plenty of people died on the way, some of them were ill and had to be left. Not buried. Not buried, just left alive like that, many of them.—*Is there anybody that I know who was left like that?*—Some you know, Bocke, whom

I once took to Medani because of her eyes. They left her alive, she had not died . . . in the place where they fled from the plane. . . .

We came on, and arrived at Bwawosh near Bisho mountain there, and stayed there, just a few days. Again, the government approached from Boing, because some Meban had told them 'the Uduk' were at Bisho. . . . They came along by Marinyje's village [on the north bank of the Yabus river]. The great things were fired from *pam* Marinyje, and found Bisho mountain there. The guns reached there. People fled again from there . . . and waited behind the hills.[13]

Tingke Tira, relative of William's wife Pake, was with some others digging for water in the dry river-bed when the firing had started from Yabus Bridge, and as they fled she got separated and continued on her own with children, all the way to Cez, south of Jebel Bisho.

I was down there getting water from the sandy river-bed, and the Arabs fired their guns from over there, from Marinyje's village. I was in a deep hole and I couldn't get out. I fell over and got all muddy and then managed to run but left all my things behind. I cried. I went past some of the women boiling meat and left them too, and ran on, and dragged off my children away from my husband who was just sitting under a tree. We ran and ran towards Cez. It was very hot and we were very thirsty. We went on up to about *this* time [early evening], just by myself with the children. My husband stayed behind, because he said the Arabs were far away, but I was frightened and shivering, and had left all my things. I went on and slept under a *bat* tree. I thought my mother would die, and I would be all alone. . . .

When I got to a Meban village, I asked where the people were, and they said, they're over there where you see the fire. You can go and rest there. Are you alone? I said yes. A brother of Soya called Pebway found me, and called me to come over. We stayed there and he said you can look for your people in the morning. I found them, my in-laws. . . . I was trembling, shivering. . . . We had spilled all the water in the grass, we had no cooking pots, nothing, I had left them behind. . . . [14]

Tingke's panic was partly because she had already been frightened by the Antonov bomber at Yabus Bridge. At that time she had been firing the grass in the hope of killing rats, and Pake had been gathering a few lime fruits. They suddenly had to pack everything up on their heads, leave the limes on the ground and run away, because of the plane which had appeared. 'We were shivering; we were all there at Kubri when the plane

---

[13] William Danga, Nor Deng, 22 July 1991.
[14] Tingke Tira, Nor Deng, 5 Oct. 1991.

came, and it seemed to stay above our heads, and then fired bombs behind us. We went very still and watched it, but we were trembling. It fired twice, but the bombs went in the bush.' When the big guns were fired later, while she was at the river, Tingke was terribly afraid because she thought the plane might come again.

The hilly region around Jebel Bisho, to which they retreated, had been a key place in their stories of the nineteenth century where people had sought safety from slave raiders, not always with success.[15] Having always thought of the hills as a place of safety, they were all shocked to find that artillery brought up to the Yabus river by the Sudanese army was able to shoot several miles southwards, and so they retreated further south and west, seeking shelter with the SPLA at their posts in Meban country (Kewaji and Dangaji).

Titus Solomon's spoken diary for 1990 continues:

So then we were told the way: myself and Zakaria Garshu, and Philip Khamis, he led me from Kewaji, to set off for Itang…we went through Rabub, and from Rabub where we stayed nine days, and then we set out for Lul. We rested and then went on to a place called Lul Two. We slept at Lul Two, and at dawn we set off for Buldit. From there, we went on to Pekesh country [Ganza], at a place called Pai Thes. Then we left and went on to Daga, and on to Dhana-maya, Dhanamayan Caga, where there were elephants. We slept there at Maya two days, and from there went on to Kigille. We arrived in Kigille on 5 March.

We went on from Kigille to Maiwut, sleeping on the way, arriving on the 6th, staying the 7th, 8th, and leaving Maiwut on the 9th on the way to Pagak. From Pagak, we stayed there from 10 March until we got instructions that people should build huts in Pagak, so we built huts. Then on 10 April, when the huts were finished, the command came that people should go to Itang. We rode in a truck and got to Itang, and from the 10th people all started coming to Itang, up to May.[16]

It was in the villages near Jebel Bisho that Tente, who had become ill in Langkwai, finally died. Here is the continuation of my conversation with his son Yapmaka, describing what must have been a harrowing three months after leaving the Assosa area:

What was his sickness?—His body was aching in the back, and he couldn't walk, and he was getting old.—*Did he go to the clinic?*—Yes, he kept on going, to the

---

[15] James '*Kwanim Pa*, 56–8.
[16] Titus Solomon Gathe, Nor Deng, 6 Oct. 1991.

clinic in Langkwai. But he didn't go to Assosa. He completed the year there, and after Christmas, we didn't even have time to celebrate the New Year. We had to flee. We finished the year by running to Yabus Bridge. He was very tired from this sickness, I led him and held his arm, and we went to Bugaya. He died in Bugaya.—*And you buried him nearby?*—In a little Meban village nearby. There were many who were ill and died there.—*I was very sad to hear this news when you first told me in Nor Deng.*—I buried him, and then followed people to Itang. I didn't want to leave him, so I stayed with him. My wife was saying, 'Let's go', but I said, 'No, I'm staying here, if something happens to us, let it be. It will be all the same for those who have gone on ahead of us.'

I arrived in Itang on 8 July. I didn't have a hut, and it was raining that day. I was taken in by the people of my father. After five days they gave me a tent, but there was water everywhere and nowhere to put it. At last I found a dry patch and I put up the tent. I was really tired.[17]

A major problem for those who left Assosa was that the open grassy plain of Meban country stretching southwards to Nuerland, between the swamps to the west and hills to the east where various Koman groups lived, was the front-line zone of the war. No national or international aid had ever reached this area. The SPLA and Meban chiefs between them could not feed the refugees (and as I explain below, I learned later of military tensions there which were a crucial factor in the subsequent forced migration south). Under SPLA order they had to depart for what to them were the unknown southern regions, Nilotic country way beyond the familiar hilly geography of their home area. Trekking from late February for several weeks, they arrived at Pagak on the frontier, where, as Titus explained above, they stayed for a month expecting that the UNHCR would establish a new reception centre. This did not materialize, and the people had to go on, right down to Itang inside Ethiopia on the Baro river where there was an immense refugee camp for southern Sudanese. Most of the surviving people from the Blue Nile arrived there by June or early July 1990, some in a pitiful state, having lost many to malnourishment and illness on the way. William described their hopes of 'being met by the UN' at Pagak.

David [Musa] knew the way, and Shingwo, they went ahead and led the people. They went on and arrived at Pagak. They started work and built some huts. The UN people came and met them there.

[17] Yapmaka Tente, Bonga, 10 Nov. 1994 (video).

And a big man in the SPLA, the UN accosted him—*Who was this?*—The senior man in the SPLA, John Garang. The UN warned him, 'If anything happens and the Uduk are lost, we shall hold you responsible.'

From then, he did not sleep; he sent his people to prepare things, along with one white UN person, who saw us and said, 'Ah, you are the *'kwanim pa,* I know about you.'... They told him that all the *'kwanim pa* were on the way.... And he went back and gave orders to send foodstuffs to Pagak so that when the people came, and were tired, they could be given something to help them go on to Itang.... They came on to Itang in small groups, small groups, right on to June, when *'kwanim pa* were still arriving. Some arrived at Itang in July.[18]

Ayoub Shingwo described some of the ways they managed to stagger on from Pagak. They often trekked during the night, as before, when it was cooler. Twice vehicles came to Pagak to transport the sick, but the rest had to leave their new huts, in the pouring rain, carrying the very small grain rations they had just been given, along with some *shwa'b,* a wild root they had collected in the Daga valley. They killed a few animals for food, including the *yes* (a large rat-like creature) and the python. On the way they sold what clothes they had left to the Pur people (a Koman people I have called Shyita, known in Ethiopia as Opuo). Taking pity, the Pur actually gave them grain for the children.[19] It is interesting that some Pur people were reported as saying, when they saw the Uduk streaming southwards at this time, 'The Ce Parka are coming home.' Our observer from the early 1880s, Schuver, reported 'Kebarga' as one of the important 'Gambiel' villages, which might just be their reference to the one-time settlements of Uduk in the hills between the Daga and the Yabus.[20] When they arrived in Itang, the Ethiopians gave them tents, and when these had run out, they started to build their own huts (at a site officially named 'Village 6', informally dubbed 'Assosa').[21] Later arrivals ('Assosa Group 2') were allocated a further place outside the main site of Itang, on the west, at 'Village 4' near the police post at Tarpam.

---

[18] William Danga Ledko, Nor Deng, 22 July 1991.
[19] Ayoub Shingwo, Nor Deng, 22 July 1991.
[20] *Schuver's Travels,* 337.
[21] Multi-Donor Technical Mission, 'Report of mission to Western Region Sudanese refugee camps', Addis Ababa, Feb. 1991, 3, 9, 13.

(ii) Military aspects

It was only a long time after these events that I came to understand something of the 'war' aspects of the long trek of the Blue Nile refugees. I would like to mention here a particularly important military factor which crucially precipitated the epic flight from the 'known' country around the Yabus valley and the Meban villages right down to Itang. I learned this from the one-time 'child soldier' whose adventures I have already introduced. 'Jasper' casually remarked that 'the worst place' on the whole trek was Dangaji. I asked why; surely Nor Deng had been the worst place? The answer (partly in English) was very clear; there were games being played between government and SPLA commanders in this front-line war zone, following the army's advances south in early 1990 and the retreat of the SPLA from Kurmuk and the nearby bases in Ethiopia. The army wished to entice back the disappearing civilians, while the SPLA commanders wished to keep control of them and prevent them going of their own accord. The Uduk men on the SPLA side were disarmed at Dangaji and Kewaji in about February 1990 and imprisoned, in case they decided to escort their own (very hungry) people back across the front line. The army based at Boing nearby nevertheless seemed to have reached some agreement with the local SPLA commander, because the nomad Rufa'a Arabs were apparently bringing in some grain supplies. This fragile situation broke when the government soldiers came out of Boing and attacked the SPLA posts at Dangaji and Kewaji, burning them to the ground. This, it is now evident, was the crucial event which forced the SPLA out, and the civilians hundreds of miles south into unknown territory.

I don't know if you have the story yet.—*I know the Meban chiefs didn't have enough food for you*—We were there and the SPLA commander, he arrested the Uduk people, and took away their weapons for no reason. All the Uduk guns, were put away. Even myself, I was catching fish in the river, and they caught me from the water there, took my gun, all my weapons, my things, and took me straight to jail, for a month, and 26 days, nearly two months. I don't know why. For nothing. They said the Uduk soldiers were trying to take the refugees back. At that time we were in Dangaji, Kewaji, Dar Sagiya. They didn't want the refugees to go back to Bwawash [near the Yabus]. I am lost to explain this, it is a very complicated story. . . .

—Did the people want to go back?—Yes, some wanted to go back, but the SPLA didn't want them to go, and they blamed the soldiers, saying they might escort the civilians back to Kubri. They put them all in prison in Kewaji, almost two months, many of us, about forty-six of us.*—Who was the commander?*—He was known as Kai Yabas, he always had a pipe, he was a Nuer.

They had distributed the Uduk in different areas, some in Kewaji, some in Dangaji, some in Kantusha, and Dar Sagiya. At that time the nomad Arabs were still coming. That commander, he had a connection with the nomad Arabs and with the government soldiers in Boing. But God was with the Uduk. There was nothing bad happening to the civilians.... Yes, they took the guns only from the Uduk. The Meban, and the Nuer, they had their guns; they took only those of the people from the Ethiopian side, the Blue Nile people....

They wanted us to live there. But there was no food. And Boing was very close. Then after about two or three months the Sudanese army came, they fired on us, and chased the SPLA from Dangaji, setting the buildings on fire. That is when the *'kwanim pa* left, all the way to Buldit and on and on, there was no proper escort....

—If the commander was talking to the government in Boing, why did they attack you all?—I think they changed their minds. When they attacked Kewaji, [the commander] ran away at the same time as us, and got to Itang, but people made a report about him ... he was put in jail there, and I think he died there in jail.[22]

THE TREK: ITANG TO NOR DENG

(i) Civilian accounts

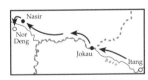

A French documentary film, *Famine Fatigue*, which I happened by chance to see on TV in mid-1990, includes footage of the Itang camp and harrowing scenes of the newly arrived Uduk from the Blue Nile.[23] Martha is seen helping to check up on the sick and the dying every day, who are carried through the mud to a 'clinic' tent. We see in this film that Martha is herself pregnant, and would know from later

---

[22] 'Jasper', USA, Nov. 2006.

[23] *Famine Fatigue: ou le pouvoir de l'image*, a co-production, La Sept/Point du Jour in association with Temps Présent (TSR), 1991. Director Patrice Barrat. The scenes of Itang may be found about thirty-six minutes into the film.

conversations that this baby died in infancy as she had no milk. The new arrivals were at the bottom of the pecking order in this enormous camp, run in practice by SPLA officials, and there is evidence that over the subsequent year they did not actually receive all the humanitarian aid to which they were entitled.[24] The death rate was high, and Itang 'the first time' (the second time had yet to happen) is remembered as a place where four or five, or even ten, were buried in one grave. Informants remember too that during that year, all the young men had to carry guns—that is, for the SPLA—and a number of boys were led off 'to school in Kenya' along with many hundreds of southern Sudanese youths, often ending up in battle situations with very little training (see some accounts below in Chapter 11). There were weird and unexpected outbreaks of what has to be called religious hysteria among the starving children, which I first heard about in Nor Deng and are described in Chapter 10. William Danga himself reported being very weak and having to attend the special feeding clinic. Ironically, after the departure of the Ethiopian officials and the SPLA leaders with the political crisis of the following year, the local Anuak people encouraged various needy groups, including our refugees from the Blue Nile, to take what they needed from the warehouses.

I was nearly about to die myself. I was extremely thin, from being ill from this and that so much, I had a terrible cold. I arrived at Itang, and went to the clinic, and they looked at me. I was extremely thin. They said, 'You should try this soft porridge at the feeding centre, and they will give you some small biscuits, your blood should improve.' I used to stay at the feeding centre there every day, from the morning. They would pour a little out and I would drink, something for people who are very ill, very thin. I began to get a little better.

We stayed there at Itang, and people improved a little, got fatter. The food supply was all right at first, but later it got very short. The Ethiopians would distribute the things, sometimes one way, sometimes another way—*Why?*—I don't know; there was plenty of grain, the lorries would bring it all the time. But they didn't distribute it well to the people, after dividing it up in the warehouse there. In fact there was a lot of sugar, and lentils, and 'juice' [English]. It was brought by the UN, for people like us. This juice was made from a type of meat, and had beans in it—*'Soup'?*—Yes, yes, 'soup'—there was plenty of it, but they hadn't given it to people.

[24] Multi-Donor Technical Mission, 1991.

Just recently, when people fled from there, we found these things in the warehouse, and helped ourselves, as we were leaving Itang. And all that sugar, it was spilled out on the ground in the warehouse, you walked into the middle of it like sand![25]

By May 1991 the turmoil in Ethiopia had reached a head, and the government fell. Most of the Uduk camped for two or three weeks just outside Itang, living on these food supplies—including things, as William tells us, they had never received before. After this, most of the Uduk were forced to join the main body of returnees moving down to Nasir.

Titus Solomon's laconic itinerary recorded for the Uduk in Khartoum continues, and concludes with an earnest appeal for prayer to God (Arumgimis):

We stayed in Itang, and then the Ethiopian fighting started again, and drove us out of Itang. We set off on 25 May from Itang, in order to return back to the Sudan. We stayed in the bush seven days, and then five days in another place, and then set off for Pagak. Then in Pagak, the word came that we should go on towards Nasir.

We came to Nasir from Pagak through Jikau, and to Malwal Goz, and then through many small villages, until we arrived in Nasir here. Right now we are in Nasir, and today we are longing to meet up with you again. Pray to God [Arumgimis] for us, and we shall also pray for you, that Arumgimis will improve things for you, and for us, let Arumgimis prepare the way, and settle things in the country, so that we can meet again properly, in the Sudan there.

As for our lives here in Nasir, some food has come from Kenya, by aeroplane, and some from the Sudan by barge, through Kosti. We are living in a little place called Nor Deng, alongside Nasir. And at the moment we don't know where we can go next. We don't know if we'll be able to go back to the Sudan [i.e. home area], or go somewhere else, we have no idea. But I want to ask you to pray to Arumgimis, that he should find a way for us, so we can all meet up again. That is my word, the word I am sending you today in Khartoum; and please greet everyone, all of you living there in Khartoum. And thank you.[26]

With the evacuation of Itang, the horrors of the trek resumed, this time including bandit attacks. The border was not really controlled by the 'authorities' from either side, but by local groups of armed Gaajak Nuer, who took the opportunity to loot travellers, for their clothes and pots

---

[25] William Danga Ledko, Nor Deng, 22 July 1991.
[26] Titus Solomon Gathe, Nor Deng, 6 Oct. 1991.

and pans, blankets and mosquito nets, and especially for their guns if they could get away with it. Firing in the air and shouting their demands in Arabic, the looters were not interested in money. If the travellers were in groups with sufficient firearms of their own, they would probably be all right. But woe betide the odd individual with such a possession. Mary Ahmed's son was killed for his gun as he went for a bathe in the river, on the way out from Itang.

My young son Ayoub Hajko had been singing in a church group, and he went down to the river. It was a Sunday. He went to the river, and he told me to boil some beans for him, 'I'll come back later and eat them,' he said. And I was glad he was coming back for something to eat. I prepared the food, and when it was ready I put it aside. I waited. A child came up; my sister Sare. She said, 'Mary, Mary! Your son Ayoub has been attacked by the Dhamkin, by the Gaajak!' I said, 'What? When he went to bathe?' 'Yes! He was attacked, I don't know if he's dead, so I came to tell you, your son is shot.' I went and called Martha, and we ran. We ran and found him dead on the ground. I took hold of him, I tied him, and people carried him. We buried him. Took him home, washed him, and buried him. He was just killed for no reason, while going to bathe. The Gaajak are not good people. Very bad. The Dhamkin have killed many, many of us.[27]

Martha added some details about this incident on a later occasion. She reminded me that the Anuak had been killing any of the 'tall Dhamkin' they found who had been trying to loot the abandoned warehouses. Her group were still halfway between Itang and the border, living off the supplies they had themselves collected. Martha heard the shot as Ayoub was attacked at the river, by two men, 'the real Dhamkin, with those long guns' (that is, not the SPLA with their Kalashnikovs).[28] David Musa, one-time policeman in Nasir and travelling together with his Nuer wife Elizabeth Chol, was ambushed by gunfire and their party was looted on the way, close to the border. In Nor Deng, David did not tell me that he had sustained a wound from one of these attacks, and the bullet had lodged in his body (I learned of this later, as a factor contributing to his early death in Sherkole in 2001). As we talked in 1991, he did tell me more about the long-term reputation of the Gaajak. 'I know from the time I was working with the police in Sudan there, they used to come from Ethiopia and attack people.

---

[27] Mary Ahmed, Karmi, 19 Sept. 1992.
[28] Martha Nasim Ahmed, Karmi, 20 Sept. 1992.

They used to cross the border and attack people and run back. They had no quarrels on the Ethiopian side, they were respectful of the Ethiopians. They had these long guns from years ago.'[29] The imperial Ethiopian government certainly used to be in the habit of arming border communities as frontier guards of a kind; I know from my own work in the mid-1970s that some of the Koma groups were thus asked to carry arms for Haile Selassie. In any civil war situation there is likely to be a strong temptation for self-help projects by groups with access to arms in unpoliced areas.

William Danga recalled hearing the sudden explosions at Itang which signalled the departure of the soldiers of the Mengistu regime. It was not a conflict as such, but the sound of these soldiers setting fire to their own buildings and ammunition stores at Tarpam, very close to one of the Uduk refugee sites.

People heard the sounds exploding, but someone told us that there wasn't any fighting.... The Ethiopians of Mengistu were at this place called Tarpam, the garrison was there. The '*kwanim pa* didn't know what was going on. But they had set fire to their own buildings. The Ethiopians set fire to their own buildings...and their ammunition [lit. 'seeds of the fire'] was inside.... The explosions sounded *Buuuw! Buuuw!* [30]

William agreed that this deliberate destruction would have been to prevent others from taking the arms supplies after their departure, though the Oromo fighters were still far away. However, this is what prompted the people to scatter into the bush once again, but as explained, with Anuak permission they hung around for two or three weeks, occasionally returning to collect food supplies. An SPLA officer then came and instructed them to go on to Nasir, because a UN plane was coming to Nasir with food; in fact, he reported, it had already come twice. But the first plane they actually saw ahead of them was the Antonov as it came to bomb the border town of Jikau. At Jikau, the SPLA gave them four cattle for meat, and apologized for not having more but so many people had already passed through. They went on, even selling off the clothes they had made for themselves from the fabric of the tents they had been given in Itang. The whole trek was very hard, having to go through the floods and the rain,

[29] David Musa, Nor Deng, 22 July 1991.
[30] William Danga Ledko, Nor Deng, 22 July 1991.

carrying so many children, but only one woman seems to have died by the wayside on this dreadful stretch of the trek.

It was a hazardous journey for everyone. Many had tried to evade the demands of the SPLA that they should go downstream across the border and all the way to Nasir, but only a few managed to sneak away. The Omda himself had been threatened with death.

Reports had reached the Operation Lifeline headquarters in Nairobi of the sudden influx of hundreds of thousands of Sudanese from Itang and other camps in south-western Ethiopia downstream to Nasir.[31] An advance party went to meet some of them at Jikau on the border, by chance also witnessing the welcoming bombing raid by the Sudanese air force.

(ii) Military aspects

The evacuation of Itang and the mass return to the Sudan may have looked spontaneous to the refugees themselves, and was certainly completely unexpected to international officials. It was even recommended by some that the people showing up in Nasir should be sent back to Ethiopia, where there were facilities and supplies for the displaced, whereas there were none in Nasir. But the move back 'home' was not unexpected for the SPLA leadership. Video footage taken by the SPLA itself shows debates under way at Itang in the dry season of 1990 about whether or not, and when, the people should return home. Then, on what must have been 25 May or a day or two later, Commander Taban Deng Gai appears on the video listening to the BBC World Service announcing that Ethiopian insurgents have entered Addis Ababa.[32] The SPLA then escorts several hundred thousand refugees back to the Sudan, that is, through flooded tracks and across rivers to the upper Nile swamps at the height of the rainy season. On the video we can hear

[31] Alastair and Patta Scott-Villiers, and Cole P. Dodge, 'Repatriation of Sudanese refugees from Ethiopia: a case study in manipulation of civilians during civil conflict', *Refuge*, 14/1 (1994), 19–25.

[32] Copies of this video footage taken by the SPLA were circulating in Nairobi in the mid-1990s.

Taban Deng Gai: Nuer from Bentiu; he was employed by the Chevron oil company in the Sudan before joining the SPLA in the 1980s; he was in charge of distributing relief supplies in both Itang and Nasir; one of the commanders leading the Nasir split, he subsequently rejoined the SPLA and is currently Governor of oil-rich Unity State.

and catch sight of a few Uduk women and children boiling and eating snails. Many had wanted to return home, northwards back across the front line of the civil war, and some did—a few of whom were shot by the SPLA. I pick up the story below of those who went north to escape the orbit of the SPLA between 1990 and 1995 in the hope of settling back home.

There was never any secret about the fact that a good proportion of the men were expected to carry arms for the SPLA in Itang, 1990–1. I had not appreciated at the time of my visit to Nor Deng how many guns had survived the journey from there, though most of the looting was in fact directed at weapons rather than saucepans. I learned much later that some guns did make it to Nor Deng (and beyond). The large headbaskets carried by women sometimes provided a hiding place for weapons on the journey.

And along with such details, I heard many years later of the way that the SPLA had transferred a good number of soldiers to the assistance of the Ethiopian forces of Mengistu in April–May 1991, just as the Gambela region and the whole of western Ethiopia was falling to the armed opposition, particularly the Oromo Liberation Front. The SPLA men now faced a very difficult time fighting inside Ethiopia, and many of them, including a number of Uduk men, did not survive, dying near Dembi Dollo and even Gimbi. 'Jasper' happened to be part of the contingent transferred to the aid of the Mengistu troops as the other SPLA came downstream to Nasir, and, remarkably, emerged again from the maelstrom in Ethiopia to rejoin his people in Nor Deng.

After everyone left Itang, some of the Uduk SPLA were sent to Pagak and on to Meban country, but some were sent inside Ethiopa to Dembi Dollo and Gimbi.

I was myself sent to Gimbi. The Oromo troops were very heavy, they chased us, and the place where they put the kids was here, and another base there for the adults [indicating]. A lot of Oromo, they chased us from here to here, and the big city was here, and a lot of troops came and encircled us. We were in the middle, no way to go, and we ran here and there, and there was a big mountain on this side. And a little path here, we ran along it, but those other people had no way, and most of them died, they had no way to go. Just a few escaped.

They were shooting very, very heavy bombs [*sic*], because the Dembi Dollo government had been taken over by the Oromo among themselves, and the Mengistu troops had already left. The SPLA was sent a warning from Dembi Dollo, that the government there did not want the SPLA to stay in this place, but to go back to the camp near the border in Itang. Because we had been sent from Itang to fight. They said, 'We think it is better for you to leave, and not continue fighting.' They gave us three days to leave. The Oromo commanders did not want to fight us. 'It's not your war.'—*Were there many southern Sudanese with you?*—Yes, they were crazy [*sic*], they said the SPLA did not want to leave that place without using bullets. Yes, there were Nuba, and Dinka, and Nuer, and Shilluk, a lot of tribes. We chased [the Oromo] for two days . . . the heavy troops of Oromo were still there . . . maybe from inside Dembi Dollo, they came and encircled us. . . .

And how did you escape?—We opened a way here, a door, not for us, for the Ethiopian troops only, the ones we were supporting. In this place we stayed six days, while the guns were sounding. They tried to capture people alive, and that's where I got shot—in my hand. A lad from Bigin was shot almost by accident, he was not killed. . . . We were about two hundred, and 34 escaped from this side. . . . On that day we fought from 4 a.m. and broke them, firing at them, made an opening and got away. We went on, leaving Dembi Dollo to our right . . . and spent many days and finally found the Mengistu troops. That's how we escaped, we went with them, there were about ten thousand of them, and we were very hungry, they gave us food.

—*And you were a small group, with some others, Uduk and Dhamkin too?*— Yes. We came down to Gambela, spent one day, they came and chased us around again, 12 o'clock midday, everywhere was fighting. Then I got down to the Anuak place, close to the riverside, and down to Itang. And people had left, they were just outside, camping, and going back to collect food.—*And you then came on with them to Nasir?*—Yes.

We are lucky to have you here [in North America]! Yes, I have been in nasty situations, I still feel confused, and I have dreams about it, all the time, those mountains we were in, that tall mountain, going up, and falling down, going up and falling down.

Yes, that's where a lot of Uduk got stuck, mixed up with Ethiopian troops of Mengistu. A lot of kids were lost and we don't know what happened to them.[33]

This young man and I might have crossed paths in Nor Deng, but this kind of testimony could not have been put to me at the time. The level of affairs at which the SPLA leadership was managing the fortunes of the displaced, not only the civilian majority but also, and particularly, the fighters among them, was largely unseen by visitors and outsiders, perhaps especially those dedicated to 'helping the innocent' and there-fore committed to turning a blind eye to politics and war. I went on

[33] 'Jasper', USA, Nov. 2006.

hearing disturbing and strange things, especially after the event, as my own series of visits to the *'kwanim pa* in exile continued. Some of these came to my knowledge not through any plain conversation or interview, but through translating and discussing songs, as happened in this case.

> The vultures are spreading their talons over the slopes of Dembi Dollo!
> They sold my brother to the war,
>
> But there's only the wind blowing in my eyes as I look back.
> The Red Cross found the boys,
> Found them on the Dembi Dollo mountain.
>
> *'Who will tell Ala where I've gone?'*
>
> John, come and tell me where to go!
> 'Look down, forget your hope of his coming'
> Which way shall I go?[34]

This song became well known in later years, when it could still bring tears to the eyes of grown men. It was sung for me in 2000 by Hosiah Dangaye Chalma, but the words were originally composed by a woman. Ala, also known by the name Twambunyan (a name I remember from my first fieldwork), is here mourning the disappearance of her brother Kama Lisan. He was one of those 'sold' by the SPLA to the Ethiopians, to help defend them against the Oromo fighters inside the western part of the country as the Mengistu government fell. Ala, with everyone else, was fleeing from Itang towards the Sudan border in 1991, and as she did so, kept looking in hope over her shoulder to the mountains of Dembi Dollo. But her eyes just felt the wind, and all she saw were vultures circling, spreading out their feet as they came down. She imagines him saying as he dies, 'Who will tell Ala?'—and her appeal to John (Garang) is fruitless. After singing this song, Dangaye commented to me, 'Yes. Death has really bought us.'

[34] Hosiah Dangaye Chalma, singing words originally composed by Ala, sister of Dangaye's own mother, from Pam Be; Bonga, 18 Aug. 2000.

6

The SPLA Split: Refugees on the Edge

'Hey, nice girl, "Malei"!'
Mal Magwar! And how are you?
I'm fine!
Oh, 'Malei, Mal Magwar'!

Oh my, the young girls' cheeky bottoms in Jikau!
And how they look in Nasir!
And how they were in Itang too!

You should have a boy-child soon
And I can call him 'Daddy'![1]

THE TREK: NASIR TO MAIWUT AND KIGILLE

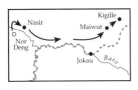

From the time of Assosa onwards, but particularly in Itang 1990–1 and from its evacuation back to the southern Sudan, the Blue Nile refugees were thrown together with the SPLA soldiers, here mainly Nuer and Dinka, and also with (mainly Nuer) civilians in the Gambela region of Ethiopia and the eastern Upper Nile of Sudan. Flirtation and brief relationships were not uncommon—mainly between the SPLA soldiers and refugee girls—and a few reports of forced sex. There were also instances of marriage, often leading to problems even when happily entered into, an issue to which I return in Chapter 11. The children's song above captures a teasing exchange between a soldier calling to a girl with the Nuer greeting 'Male!' and her replying—in an Uduk version of the friendly Nuer

---

[1] Children's song, Nor Deng, 7 Oct. 1991.

response 'Mal mi goa!' The chorus then comments archly on the girls' provocative behaviour on the long trek.

Despite tensions, the friendliness of this song matches a reasonable level of respect and mutual co-operation between the guerrillas and those refugees who found themselves obliged to share their fortunes from the sacking of Assosa up to their arrival in the Upper Nile. However, this did not last. In between my two visits to Nor Deng, the SPLA was shaken by a split when on 31 August the Nasir commanders attempted a coup against John Garang's overall leadership. This made things much worse for the returnees stranded in the Nasir area, the most vulnerable of whom (including the Blue Nile people and also the 'unaccompanied minors' from Itang) were clearly being used as pawns in the competition for humanitarian aid. Abuses began to accumulate through the later months of 1991. My own reports of August and October, which recommended that the Blue Nile people should be allowed to move back closer to the dry land and the border hills, where they had reasonable relations with local people such as the Koma, and where they could cultivate and thus contribute to their own support, had little impact. The situation worsened generally by November as internecine warfare developed between the Nasir faction and the mainstream SPLA across the Upper Nile and Jonglei provinces. The UN was then permitted by the Nasir leadership to assist the Blue Nile refugees to cross from the south to the north bank of the Sobat, and settle in a tract of barren ground beyond the airport, where they were supposed to be more content. The site was ironically dubbed by one of the key medical workers 'New Chali', along with his 'New Chali Hospital'—in line with the SPLA vision of the New Sudan.

I did not witness any of the events I describe in this or the next section, but am relying on what I heard from afar, and later when I next caught up with the core of the Uduk refugees back in Ethiopia in September 1992. The themes of hunger, and the search for food, dominate the stories I heard of their troubles on the Nasir side of the river, the move upstream which was eventually allowed, and the disastrous conditions of their lives in the hoped-for respite of Maiwut and Kigille, near Pagak. These themes also dominated the efforts of the relief agencies, and in retrospect we can see they helped shape political and military decisions, sometimes through manipulation of the agencies by governments or guerrillas. After the early food drops, OLS officials managed to work out a scheme with the Nasir SPLA commanders, and the Sudan government, whereby a barge would bring food aid upstream from Khartoum and Kosti to Malakal, and thence either by barge itself or truck to Nasir. This northern supply route had to be endorsed by the growingly ambitious regime of Omer el Beshir. Quite soon the negotiations had become an instrument in the hands of the government, backing Riak Machar and his colleagues in the gamble they had launched against Garang.

From the point at the end of 1991 when the decision was made to transfer the Blue Nile refugees back across the Sobat river, conditions for them deteriorated. Some of the refugees refused even to set up shacks there, as it was so inhospitable. Food aid was unpredictable and much destined for the Blue Nile people was appropriated by others. There were some edible roots here because the land was drier, and a little more honey could be found in the thorn trees. But bandits roamed the grassland and bush, looting and attacking both women and men seeking these wild foods. The split between the Nasir faction and the mainstream SPLA of John Garang had caused serious warfare further south, and this resulted in fear and suspicion both within and targeted at the displaced communities around Nasir. Suspicion of the Uduk in particular was almost certainly a factor in the decision to transport them from the south side of the river to a place where they could more easily be monitored, as well as being more accessible to visitors and journalists as evidence of Nasir's dire need for international aid. It was also around this time that the remaining guns they had discreetly brought with them from Itang were (largely) confiscated—the implication being that the SPLA-trained fighters among them were no longer trusted. Law and order generally were breaking down under the authority of the Nasir leadership, and their soldiers were partly out of control. The killing of one Uduk man in particular, who resisted having his fish appropriated by the soldiers, was reported to Riak Machar and yet nothing was done. There was some fighting along the Sobat itself, and by early 1992 there were killings of suspects, including Dinka professionals and aid workers and Nuba soldiers of the SPLA itself, in Nasir.

Estor Luyin put very clearly the distressing things which had been happening in the Nasir area, after I had left. Her reference to being treated as *ciŋkina/* means they felt they were scarcely regarded as human beings. She goes on to emphasize how, on the contrary, they are *'kwanim pa*, in the sense of decent people with moral standards who know how to look after wandering strangers.

After we crossed the river from Nor Deng, we sat for nine months with hunger. We lost any way of managing. We went in to dig wild potatoes [*se'd*], in the forest, but the wild potatoes were soon finished...then we found Dhamkin wandering in the middle of the forest, and they chased us.... And they began to attack women, and beat them.... And the women ran away, and cried out, and called for the men, and the men came. And the Dhamkin searched them and beat them on the head with guns, saying they would shoot them. People cried out, they wanted the wild potatoes because the children were hungry, but they were told, 'Go away...you will finish off our wild potatoes...you Uduk will finish things off.'...

—*Where was their village, was it near Nasir?*—Near to Nasir, we don't know its name. It was hidden in the bush, in the middle of the area of wild potatoes...they would come out and follow us, track us like weasels.... This was a very bad business of *ciŋkina*/...We said 'We shall report this to your chief, Riak Machar.' They said, 'Go on then. Go and tell him.'...They even did these things to our men. With their honey...they said it was their honey...And heglig, and tamarind. We would be eating fruits from a heglig, one person would be up the tree, and [a Dhamkin] would shout, 'Drop those fruits in your hand!'

'You should go to your homeland!' they said. 'Your land. This is our land, by right.' We said, yes, we knew, but the UN said we could stay here, among them. If they say we should go, we will go to our homeland. It's not that we don't want our home! We are longing for our home....

And I told them if we were sitting in our own place, Chali there in the Sudan, where you found us before, and the Dhamkin had come, the Uduk would have given them beer to drink, a place to sleep, food to eat, water to drink, and a good place in our huts to rest.... We are *'kwanim pa* [emphatic]. We are called *'kwanim pa*, because, if you see a poor person, you say 'Come!' We give them water, food, they shelter with us. But we have not found this in the land of the Dhamkin.... [2]

I heard complaints that the women overseeing the children's feeding programme were not getting their proper allowance of the special mix, that Martha for example was getting only three bags in place of the normal sixty, and being warned not to tell Dale (an American working

---

[2] Estor Luyin, Karmi, 19 Sept. 1992. Estor's final comments here recall, for example, an occasion in the early 1980s when a party of refugees fleeing Ethiopia strayed into the Uduk villages and were indeed given help and shelter.

with the World Food Programme, warmly recalled by the refugees later on). But matters were getting even worse. Armed and uniformed men would follow the Uduk to the riverbank where they were fishing, with hooks recently supplied by the UN. One man, Musa from Yabus, refused to hand over his catch, and was shot dead. Resentment at this, since 'fish are things of God [*arum*]', was compounded by the lack of action by the authorities. I asked whether they had told the SPLA; and got the reply from a man who had been strongly supportive of the movement before the split, 'Huh! Where was the SPLA there? Those people in Nasir, they call themselves SPLA, but they aren't really, what we keep hearing is that the doctor is the real SPLA, it is John Garang... we didn't know where the doctor was or what he was doing. We were just sitting pointlessly in Nasir.' I heard plenty more about this incident.

Some very bad things happened in the fishing place. We were there among all these guns, and they wanted us to give them fish. And they said openly, 'If you don't give us fish we shall kill you.' And so we always gave them fish, we did not refuse. We gave fish again and again. And then one day; this fellow did not refuse fish, but his catch was very small, and he had a wife and children at home, and the few fish he had were not enough for him to take back for them. Because of this, they killed him....

He remained there in the water, and we in the clinic there, we heard about it the next morning.... People brought him to the clinic, and we examined his body and found the bullet went in the groin here and as far as the lower buttock, there was an entry wound. We said, right, this is how he died; so you should take him to the government [*hakuma*, here the Nasir SPLA leadership] and report this to them. And we thought that something would be done. But nothing was done... he was killed and he died just like a dog....

And all those who used to come and gather in the fishing place, all wore uniform, and carried Kalashnikovs in their hands. And they brought sacks, to fill with fish. Always like that. We fished with hooks on the end of a string. The local people would sometimes chase us off—saying, 'You Uduk shouldn't fish here, go away.' Then the *hakuma* would come, guns in hand, and take fish from us.[3]

Those who were recognized by the SPLA as refugee leaders were rebuffed when they complained. At the same time they understood very well that the wider political situation, including the growing

---

[3] Dawud Hajar, Karmi, 19 Sept. 1992.

proclamations of Islamic ideology in Khartoum, ruled out the possibility of returning home in the near future.

As the dry season took hold, by March the river was too low for barges to get up as far as Nasir. It was decided to unload at Baliet, not far from Malakal. A few old lorries from Nasir, with local drivers, were sent to collect the grain, and 150 Uduk men were ordered by Riak to go and help with the unloading. But very little grain got back to Nasir. Several lorry-loads were diverted to a Dhamkin village in the bush, and stored in a series of large holes dug in the ground. 'Yes, they may have been SPLA, though we don't know really, because the word of Riak Machar is obeyed there, he is a powerful man. And some of his guards were on the barge.' 'It was that government [*hakuma*] itself doing this, while we were very hungry.' The World Food Programme monitor, Dale Skoric, realized too what was happening—according to what I was told, he would ask, 'Five lorries were coming yesterday, and where are they? Three were coming this morning, and where are they?' He arranged to have drivers flown in from Kenya, and lorries sent from Malakal to load up at Baliet. The next problem was that mainstream SPLA forces arrived from the far south to confront the Nasir faction at Baliet, and no more grain came through. The Kenyan drivers took the plane back home, and the Arab crew on the barge fled, some of them to Nasir and on by plane to Nairobi. The workers were chased and threatened as they took some small bags of grain just to eat on the way home, and to give their children.[4] Some years later, in the relatively safe haven of Bonga, I was given a very long eyewitness account of how some of the Uduk men sent as labourers found themselves under suspicion as having 'come from Torit', that is being fighters with Garang's SPLA, as they made their way back on foot to Nasir.

By April and May things had become extremely dangerous in Nasir, with 'the Dhamkin fighting among themselves', shooting being heard at night (for example when an alternate commander had been killed, 'with his children too'). Dawud Hajar, one of the key medical assistants at the Nasir clinic, heard the news in Karmi from newly arrived Dhamkin that a number of Dinka aid workers who had been colleagues of his, and of Martha's on the feeding side, had been killed. 'They were sent by the UN from Kapoeta to help with the medical work, before Riak Machar

---

[4] Dawud Hajar, Karmi, 21 Sept. 1992.

turned the SPLA upside down.' They couldn't go back because Garang had reportedly refused to allow anyone to travel from Nasir to Kapoeta.

The Operation Lifeline people had been pressing Riak Machar for some months to allow the Blue Nile refugees to move upstream to more acceptable conditions in the borderlands, and my own reports for them had urged the same. He was reluctant, but eventually agreed. Their leaders argued that they would be able to grow crops to help sustain themselves, and on 10 May they set off with eight days' rations and some seeds. I had a phone conversation with Emma Riak, the British aid worker newly married to Riak Machar, during a visit she made to London in September 1992. She seemed unaware about the relief situation generally around Nasir, but regretted the Uduk had left Nasir, because as she explained they had started bringing fish to the market, which had been very useful; 'We miss them.' A compelling account of this period and its dilemmas can be found in *Emma's War*, Deborah Scroggins's brilliant portrayal of human lives as they weave in and out of Sudan's conflict and intrigue.[5] An escort of precisely two soldiers was provided for the trek upstream via Jikau to Maiwut and Kigille, for some 15,000 or 20,000 people. One of the guards was killed by bandits on the way, while the other managed to shoot his attacker.

The people were divided up between Maiwut and Kigille. The OLS aid workers did their best to provide ongoing support, at first hoping to supply by air, and the people cleared an airstrip in anticipation. However, the Khartoum government refused to give the UN permission to add this place to their approved landing sites. A few vehicles made it through before the rains really set in, but there were struggles over those few grain supplies that did arrive. People ate their rations and began to plant their seeds and build huts. They would have fared better if the early rains had been adequate. But May and June that year were very dry. A lot of seedlings died, and replacements mainly found their way into the cooking pot. Sharon Hutchinson, my anthropologist colleague, reported from this place in June, indicating a terrible level of hunger and death.[6] The local soldiers of the SPLA, perhaps augmented by straight

---

[5] Deborah Scroggins, *Emma's War: Love, Betrayal and Death in the Sudan* (London: Harper Collins, 2003), 286–92.
[6] Sharon Hutchinson, 'Potential development projects for the Sobat valley region: a set of proposals prepared for Save the Children Fund (UK)', SCF/UK (London, 1992).

bandits, treated the people roughly and were said to have killed at least a few for interfering with crops and other reasons. The SPLA loyalist leaders among the Uduk did their best to appeal for further help from the UN but had little success. By mid-June, unrest was spreading by word of mouth among the refugees, and secret meetings were being held among a number who felt that going 'home' across the front lines was too dangerous, while the option of staying on in Maiwut and Kigille in the hands of the Nasir SPLA and local bandits, without a proper level of UN support, was almost as ominous. There was fear among the discontents that if it leaked out that they had been seriously thinking of returning to Ethiopia, they might be killed. The idea had first emerged, quietly, back in Nasir, and then suddenly, one early morning, without the knowledge of the main leaders, a mass of people made a dash across the border and down to Itang. The SPLA sent soldiers to bring them back, but this did not work.

HARD CHOICE AT KIGILLE

The plan to leave the orbit of the SPLA and the Sudan altogether, by making a bid for survival and perhaps humanitarian assistance on the Ethiopian side of the border, had been spearheaded by sheikhs and younger leaders (including some themselves with an SPLA background) from the Gindi group. They were supported by some from Chali. However, none of the key official figures in the church, the Omda's group, or the original SPLA loyalists even knew that the decision had been made, and were taken by surprise to find that so many had disappeared. Over the next few days, nevertheless, many others decided to follow.

At a 'safe distance' from the Sudan, and the 'Dhamkin' who were by now being blamed for much of its troubles, I began to hear more political detail about the split in the SPLA and how it had affected the people stranded in the Nasir area. There were explanations from both those who had represented 'the authorities' on the Nasir side of the border, and those who had decided to leave, without their permission or even knowledge. I will just quote one of each viewpoint.

Peter Kuma, who had been put in overall charge of the Blue Nile refugees in Nasir by Riak Machar, tried to reason with him over the various troubles that arose, representing the interests of the refugees as best he could:

And when we got to Nasir, Riak Machar created a split between him and Garang. They split up the *hakuma* [here, 'power'], Garang was on his own, and Riak Machar on his own. And then, Riak Machar said, 'Oh, those Uduk, they just want Garang.' They said this . . . and then they took away our guns.—*Some guns were still with you?*—Before? Yes, before, there were plenty of guns. Plenty of guns, we brought them from Itang. If we hadn't had them, would we have survived? We would all have died. Up to Nasir, we had guns among us. They were afraid, because of the quarrels among themselves, and we were one extra problem for them.

The thing which drove us out was the trouble at home, the way we were disturbed and attacked at home, otherwise we would not have gone to join the SPLA. There was no great idea of fleeing. Only the attacks we suffered, the pain of this drove us out. These things I used to think about a lot.[7]

Sheikh Musa Nayim of Gindi, who had succeeded Sheikh Mabrouk, explained to me why his group had come to the decision that they should leave the Kigille area secretly, without even informing the recognized leaders of church or 'government', old or new.

It was living in Maiwut, and Kigille, that is what made us change our minds. Saying, we are struck by hunger. . . . People got together, the day before, a few people came to ask me, Musa, shall we not go to Ethiopia? . . . I said Good. I got people together, the active youngsters. Then they formed this plan; and they concealed it. . . . because there were government people there [i.e. the Nasir SPLA], if you are to help people you have to go secretly and go, *te'b!*—*At night?*—In the morning, at about four o'clock, as dawn was opening. People went then. It was cool.—*And were the government people still sleeping?*—The government were still sleeping, because we hadn't told them. . . . But they caught us up . . . and this man . . . became angry. . . . We said, 'We ourselves are not going back from here, we are not going back there, we are going to Ethiopia.' So the government people left us, saying, 'Go on then!'

And the Chali people stayed a little longer, and then secretly followed you?—Yes! The Chali people came later . . . And others, remained behind.[8]

In the next chapter, and indeed the rest of this book, I concentrate on following the fortunes of the majority group who did make the major, and very bold—if not foolhardy—decision to return to the new Ethiopia. But to conclude the present chapter, I will sketch what happened to the minority who stayed on in Maiwut and Kigille—in fact I believe

7 Peter Kuma, Bonga, 24 Nov. 1994.
8 Musa Nayim, Bonga, 5 Nov. 1994.

they all moved to Kigille—with the short-term plan of benefiting from whatever crops they had planted that survived the season, and the longer-term intention of returning northwards 'home' to Yabus and Chali, where the regime of Omer el Beshir was consolidating its hold.

HANGING ON IN THE SUDAN

A good number of the Uduk refugees remained for a year and more in Kigille. It soon became known that one party who struck out for Chali prematurely, a group led by the senior church people Jeremiah Jeenu and his wife Kwadangwa, were ambushed by 'Dhamkin'—it is not entirely clear whether these were SPLA or just bandits—before they got to Yabus Bridge and the relative safety (then) of government protection. Two girls were captured and their father was killed trying to save them, but a substantial party reached home. This news made for caution among other would-be returnees. But even in Kigille, there continued to be harassment from soldiers, not excluding occasional trouble from the Blue Nile men themselves. Riak Machar sent messages over the border and tried to persuade various men still loyal to him to bring the people back. The old guard of church and state, mainly from Chali itself, who were left behind in Maiwut and Kigille faced a real dilemma. None had been particularly committed to the SPLA, and yet even though the Nasir faction seemed to be succumbing to the overtures of Khartoum, would it be safe to go back home, or wiser to follow their kith and kin over the border? Peter Kuma was concerned as to who would look after the interests of those who had disappeared over to Ethiopia. In August he was permitted by Riak to go and see their situation, with the hope of perhaps arranging their return or at least some kind of cross-border scheme for humanitarian aid that would benefit both sides. Peter did not have an easy time, he and some colleagues he travelled with being detained on the way and looted by bandits, and then arrested by the new Ethiopian authorities more than once on the basis of information supplied to them that they were SPLA men. Some pragmatists who had remained behind benefited from the crops that did come up, but otherwise risked problems—William Danga who had been working with the food distribution, for example, was beaten by troops out of control. Even those leaders in whom the

Nasir SPLA had placed their trust in at least one case treated civilians badly, inflicting the kind of punishments that had unfortunately become common practice among Sudanese soldiery of whatever ilk. When this man did eventually join the others back in Ethiopia, he was feared and shunned.

The core of those who stayed in Kigille, including Omda Talib el Fil, and Pastor Martin Luther of the Chali church, managed to keep a low profile for a year or so. But news about their location and willingness to return did get around, and one day a party of 'Popular Defence Forces' showed up to escort them north. Returnees from the war zone were generally being welcomed, especially from 1993, though as we shall see anyone who might have been a rebel fighter was still the object of suspicion. The southern Blue Nile community based in Khartoum, including several hundred of the *'kwanim pa* by this time, made a point of keeping track of their own returnees and helping them move on further north if necessary.

Omda Talib had made very clear to me his plan to go home when we spoke in Nor Deng. After what he called 'forty days on the road' eating wild leaves like goats, he had wanted to go straight back north from Itang, but was persuaded by news of UN help and a death threat from the 'Dhamkin' to come down to Nasir with the others.

I agreed to what they were saying, because I heard that your people, the people of the aeroplanes, the white people had shown up, bringing grain to a place called Nasir. But I said no, I preferred to go to Daga. I tried to refuse. But because of the Dhamkin order I had to agree, as maybe they would kill me if I refused. I was afraid, very afraid. Because they might kill me.

They said I might run off to Chali. And I said, 'Yes! I want to die in my Chali. I don't want to stay in the lands of other people.' If God [Arum] helps me I will go back home. Living like this in the bush like antelopes, I don't want it at all. People have become like the hyena—it is his thing, to run around in the rain like this. But how can human beings [*'kwanim pa*] live in the middle of the water? But as for the government; I don't know who is the person who can protect me and my people. But God [Arumgimis] has been looking after us, and people have been praying and doing everything they could.

Although a lifelong Muslim, and knowing I was not a practising Christian, Omda Talib had found it possible, in speaking to me in *'twam pa*, to speak about God. The first reference was the somewhat uncommitted 'Arum' (which I spell thus to distinguish it as a 'modern' short word for God, a usage much more common today than a generation ago, different in sense from the older *arum* which permeates the world of living things) and the second was explicitly the Christian God of the Bible, 'Arumgimis'. Though introduced by missionaries, the latter was the most effective for him to use between us at a time when everyone fervently hoped there might be some hope of human salvation. He had certainly never used this term to me before. He then addressed me as a representative of the international aid community:

But we thank you very much [Arabic] for what you are doing, bringing us a few things and letting us rest a little in the shade. But we are living, up to now, like the antelopes. This is awful for us.—*Really indeed like antelopes!*—We are just antelopes! Don't say we are living in the homeland of the Dhamkin, we're living as antelopes in the bush! Just wild animals, *hayawanat* as the Arabs say. We're in the land of strangers for so long.

Do we have a government [i.e. here in Nasir]? A government ought to say, 'Yes, settle down here a while, we are the government. These are very poor people, they've been fleeing, living in the bush.' Do we have guns? Are there any guns? We are people with absolutely nothing. And they chase us out. We are completely wretched. Is there anyone among the Uduk with education to represent us? No one. Uduk just look for food, and take off their hoes to cultivate. That's all. We cannot fight the government. For government, what do you need? Do you have vehicles, or guns, or planes, or factories to make things? The Uduk don't know these things. . . .

Metal things, we don't have them. We just live with God [Arum], God just gives us a place to grow our food. We don't have people complaining, 'Let's fight the Dhamkin, let's fight the Meban!' No. It's not like that.[9]

Omda Talib also impressed on me how well they had got on with the Bertha when he and a few others had stayed on in Chali in 1988–9 (see Chapter 2). He mentioned that Bertha were hungry at that time, and had come over from Ethiopia with cattle, goats, and chickens, which the Uduk had acquired through the fruits of their own labour—sorghum, sesame, and tobacco. This was fairly unusual, but might reflect the ongoing disturbances in Ethiopia itself, and the warm links between the Sudan government and the armed opposition in western Ethiopia, as did the camp for displaced Oromo on the Yabus (up to its sacking in

[9] Omda Talib el Fil, Nor Deng, 22 July 1991. On the imagery of the antelope, see James, 'Antelope as self-image among the Uduk', in Roy Willis (ed.), *Signifying Animals: Human Meaning in the Natural World* (London: Allen & Unwin, 1990).

mid-1989). Omda Talib then explained how having acquired all these animals from the Bertha, they suddenly had to leave. We know from 'Jasper' that at least some of them were soon eaten by the SPLA, and we have the Omda's assurance that the nomad Arabs herded off the rest.

RETURNS TO CHALI AND RENEWED FLIGHT

The Sudan government forces in 1992 had been able to make major advances southwards, retaking important places and territory in the southern Sudan. A small civilian community gradually developed in Chali again under government protection, consisting of returnees from both north and south. There was also a growing number of Meban, especially women, displaced to Chali from their homes in the Upper Nile Province to the east. All were gathered into one settlement near the market place and garrison, or on the main road to Kurmuk, while the outlying countryside and former village areas fell into neglect. Among those who returned from Khartoum were William Danga's sister Tabke and his brother Yuha, who had been rescued in May 1987 by Tabke's son Sila Musa; Sila himself joined the Sudan Interior Church humanitarian relief effort to support returnees in the district. The Islamic relief agencies were also very active in the southern Blue Nile: Dawa al Shamla, under a very active commissioner; and Muwafak al Khairiya, 'The Blessed Agreement', whose associations with the National Islamic Front became the object of much public discussion.[10]

My first descriptions of conditions in Chali come from Khartoum-based people I met in Nairobi who had visited Chali in 1994–5, and my second are from interviews by Alex de Waal in the Ethiopian town of Begi, south of Assosa, in mid-1996. By this time the Blue Nile had been disturbed for the third time by advances of the SPLA and government responses to these. Omda Talib and others who had reached Begi after being displaced (in some cases for the second or third time) gave accounts of the situation in the hope of securing external aid.

---

[10] 'SIC resettlement programme 1993', Derek Spriggs (SIM Project Coordinator) and John Awet (SIC Project Coordinator), 23–30. For the controversy over Islamic agencies, see African Rights, *Food and Power in the Sudan* (London, 1997) and *Africa Confidential*, against which Muwafak al Khairiya sustained a libel suit over many years (eventually settled out of court); but after the attacks of 9/11 the organization found itself accused of pro-al Qaida activities.

Phanuel Dhunya, younger brother of my former main assistant Shadrach Peyko, had been down to Chali in March 1995. We were speaking in English, in November that year. He mentions the ill treatment of Sabanaya Moses, son of Moses Chidko, who turned out to be among the interviewees in Begi a few months later.

What was it like?—Yeh . . . I was able to stay with them for three weeks, and I was enjoying life with them there. But still, there is that mistreatment from the government side. They are still calling the resettlement people rebels. . . . They don't trust them that they come back fully, but there is that tendency of accusing them, they are still SPLA, they are not citizens. . . . Life is still full of confusions, in Chali. Even if you want to go to Wadega, you have to go to them and they give you the letter, it is not just like that you can just decide to go. No. Even if they happen to see one of us, a stranger for them from Khartoum, they have to call you.

When I was there in Chali, there was a conflict between Sabanaya and one of the army. They try to tie him and beat him up, and most of the people they had to run and take their sticks, ready to fight with them. . . . And then we talked with the second captain, the one who was in charge, and he said that, er, he will not be very pleased if the citizens mistreated or insulted his army, and he is giving that privilege for the soldiers to do what they want, for the citizens.—*Is that what he said?*—Ya. Especially on the side of girls [i.e. with respect to the issue of girls]. That is what now they are trying to do, rape the girls.—*Has it happened?*—It happened, it happened, you know we had some Mebans there, and they were the ones causing this problem. Because they came and they tried to make a friendship, and they were brewing this African beer, where the off-duty soldiers would go and drink.—*This is in Chali?*—In Chali, ya, because now, half of the population there are Mebans.[11]

Because there were signs already that the civil war was coming north again, Phanuel explained how he thought they would tighten their grip further on the civilians, collecting them and putting them in camps for their own safety should the SPLA attack.

I heard accounts of the difficulties facing the few young men who had 'returned home' from Bonga, and whose loyalty was therefore particularly suspect. Another young man I met in Nairobi told me (again in English):

I remember, Miss Wendy, there was a boy who came alone from Bonga. Because back in Bellila his father got a lot of mango trees, so he felt that he should go

[11] Phanuel Dhunya, Nairobi, 19 Nov. 1995.

back and be in charge of them, his father's mangoes.... He reported to the soldiers in Yabus. It is close, and he said I am from Uduk and I am going back for my resettlement. So they accepted him and they wrote him a letter... And [in Chali] they said that, OK, no problem, let him go, for settlement....

But the thing which is very discouraging: when he left Chali and went back to Wadega, there he met those army soldiers, whom they were fighting when he was in the SPLA. [Another voice] *So, there are some people who still recognized him, in the garrison?*—Ya, in the garrison of Wadega.... And then, those Berthas in Wadega, living around the army, they tried to plot to kill him.... Until we [in Khartoum] sent the word that 'Let this boy come up from the area.... And he has come back up to Singa now.... —*So it is not easy if you come back home.*—Not easy.[12]

Two young men who came back to Chali were said to have been imprisoned and tortured until they died. Returning from the refugee camps in Ethiopia was also hazardous, though some made it, and were able to get their letters of permission to resettle from the Omda (himself sometimes in Kurmuk).

Within a fairly short time the SPLA did indeed advance quite rapidly into the Blue Nile again, attacking and capturing the Yabus post in March 1996. This and subsequent attacks and their consequences were recognizably patterned in the same ways as before, but the scale and intensity of polit-ical/religious ideology and military activity were heightened on all sides. In early 1996 Chali was again alarmed by the news of the SPLA takeover of Yabus, and the threat sent by letter from there to the Chali garrison itself. The Omda's group were once more frightened out of the village, and escorted down to the Yabus, under SPLA guard. Omda Talib and a few supporters, however, including Moses Chidko and his son Sabanaya, were among those who had an opportunity in August to talk to a group of aid workers visiting the nearby Ethiopian town of Begi (in fact their cross-border plans did not materialize). What follows is based on the interviews held at that time. Some of the representatives at the meetings had been displaced by the SPLA advance itself, but most by the government soldiers coming in response from Renk, through Boing. In early April villages in the Khor Tombakh had been attacked by helicopter gunships, and then the ground assault came along the same route, burning villages all the way

---

[12] Group discussion, Nairobi, 19 Nov. 1995.

to Chali. In May two other villages were burned by a force moving out of Chali.

Moses (or often, in an Arabic-language context, Musa) Chidko and his wife Tabke had spent many years in Renk and also several in Doro, where he was doing medical work. When they heard that Omda Talib had returned to Chali, Tabke returned there for a year. At this time the National Islamic Front (NIF) was much in evidence in the region, along with the security and associated organizations, and inevitably the Christians were somewhat conspicuous. Moses remained in Doro, site of an old SIM mission in Meban country near Boing, which the army had turned into a training place. The Islamic agencies were there, and would collect up children in the evenings, to be taught about the Koran around a fire. They asked Moses to become a Muslim but he refused. In July 1996, as soon as he heard the news that Chali had been threatened, he came straight there, and with help located the Uduk in the bush. At first, people were taking food from their houses to cook in the bush, but 'this was before the aeroplanes'. In his interview, Moses took the opportunity of sending greetings to his family; three sons were in Khartoum, one a driver, one a pastor, and Sila, an administrator; Tabke at this time was in Yabus with four girls. Even Douglas and I were mentioned (we had once stayed with Moses and Tabke in Doro).[13]

Sabanaya talked of his year as a primary teacher in Chali. He was one of three Christian teachers out of the total of five. The Muslims taught religion but there was no time for Christian teaching. He and the other teachers were expected to clean buildings and even dig and clean trenches. The organization Muwafaq al Khairiya ('The Blessed Agreement') had opened a big *khalwa* (Islamic religious school) in Chali, called 'Hamesh Koreb'. They failed to get the 1,000 children they expected, and so took off some of the regular primary school children for 'language courses'. When Yabus was attacked, Sabanaya was elsewhere but responded to the government appeal for all those with training to come back to Chali and take up arms with the militia. All the Uduk, Meban, and Bertha were getting this training. Because he refused to carry his gun while going to collect his salary from Ora, the soldiers confiscated it. Ora was then attacked by the SPLA, and with

---

[13] Moses Chidko Kengi, interview with Alex de Waal, Begi, 18 Aug. 1996.

others Sabanaya spent several days running around, ending up in Yabus.[14]

It is no accident that the *khalwa* at Chali mentioned in Sabanaya's testimony had been given the name 'Hamesh Koreb', or that the head of the *khalwa* was a man called Ishaq, who came from Hamesh Koreb. He 'did not greet women', according to Sabanaya. Located in the eastern Sudan close to the Eritrean border, Hamesh Koreb had become a byword for the new Islamic movement. A *khalwa* was first built there in 1951 by the religious leader Ali Betai, and by 1972 it had one health centre. By 1995, still under the leadership of Ali Betai and his family, the centre at Hamesh Koreb had extensive land, a hospital with the status of a university teaching hospital, three schools, and a religious institute with boarding facilities. Visitors included President Omer el Beshir, who engaged a personal religious teacher there and returned with him to Khartoum.[15] Hamesh Koreb had attracted the attention of Osama bin Laden during his years in the Sudan (1992–5) and soon gained fame (or notoriety) as one of his training camps.[16] However, it was captured by the National Democratic Alliance (an opposition alliance including the SPLA) in March 2000. Bona Malwal reported that they found it then an Islamic education centre catering for 40,000 children, mostly southern Sudanese.[17] These represented a new generation of teachers to be sent out all over the country.

Omda Talib el Fil explained to the interviewers at Begi how oppression had increased in Chali by 1996, though he appeared—understandably—to be conflating events at different dates. He complained about the way that people were forced to be circumcised, which related to the recent period, but also goes back to Tayeb Musbah, the officer who gained notoriety in 1986–7. He described how Omer el Beshir had sent the 'Popular Defence Forces' to collect him from Kigille (some of these were Uduk men). 'They came at night. I was caught. They told me to go and bring my people back to Sudan. I had received a letter before from

---

[14] Sabanaya Moses Kengi, interview with Alex de Waal, Begi, 19 Aug. 1996.

[15] Birthe L. Nautrup, 'Sudan in the context of civil war: marginalisation and Islamisation among the Hadendowa', in M.-B. Johannsen and N. Kastfelt (eds.), *Sudanese Society in the Context of Civil War* (Copenhagen: University of Copenhagen, North/ South Priority Research Area, 2001), 101–3.

[16] *Africa Confidential*, 39/17 (28 Aug. 1998), 2.

[17] *Sudan Democratic Gazette*, 11/121 (July 2000), 7.

the youth in Bonga, which said: "We will not come back to Sudan except by arms."' He claimed that there had been 500 Uduk with him in Kigille, but while they let him go, some of them refused to leave under the militia escort. It was agreed in group discussion that this happened in June 1993. On arriving back home in Chali, he was shocked by the way 'the Arabs'—that is, anyone coming from the north—had spoiled it.

The Arabs had their agencies working there but we were not helped by them. They were just teaching people the Koran, to say all the time, '*Allah hu akbar*'. By force. . . . Even the Christians who were taken into the [government militia] were made to shout these things. The military intelligence people were there. Most of them were working in these Islamic aid agencies.

For me, I was put in prison for one month and three days. I was just praying to get out of Chali. I was accused all the time of sending youth to the SPLA. . . . The military intelligence asked me to write a letter to all the Uduk in the SPLA areas to come back. I refused. They said, 'The SPLA have no weapons and no food, they are just eating wild fruits.' I said, 'This is our life. I came here with my people, you did not assist me. My civilians do not want to return to Sudan, they would rather stay in the land of the Ethiopians, and become part of Ethiopia.'[18]

Omda Talib had, however, been warmly welcomed after the SPLA advance by Commander Malik Agar, now in charge of their forces in the Blue Nile. He stated his wish that relief organizations would bring food and medicine to Yabus, and that they had already prepared two airstrips. Their hopes were in God.

As a direct result of the continuing advance of the SPLA, which took Kurmuk again in January 1997 (see Chapter 1), the UNHCR and new Ethiopian government set up a fresh centre for refugees at Sherkole (the one-time SPLA training camp near Assosa). Many of those who had to flee for the second or third time from Chali, including those still most loyal and deferential to the authority of a somewhat imagined 'Sudan government' of the old school like Talib el Fil, the indomitable Omda, were among those given shelter in Sherkole. He took the opportunity of visiting Bonga over the Christmas holidays of 1997, where I understand he exhorted the people to stay on in Ethiopia until there was peace in the Sudan. Unfortunately he did not live to see the agreement of 2005.

[18] Omda Talib el Fil, interview with Alex de Waal, Begi, 18 Aug. 1996.

He retreated quietly over the border to his own district around the year 2000. I had news of him as late as 2003 but he was not to live much longer. Omda Talib had never wanted to spend long in Ethiopia. His homeland was by this time firmly under the SPLA, but as his testimony above indicates, by this time he had no problem about this.

Sherkole continued to receive a variety of refugees and other categories of Sudanese living in Ethiopia, including many rounded up from the towns. The Uduk who found themselves sheltering at Sherkole in 1997 were to spend many years there, which were to include Moses Chidko's last, though I heard that Tabke made it back to Chali as part of the initial repatriation of 2006. In the following chapters, I shall be tracing the story of those who did not take the option of returning north in 1992–3 from Kigille, but made the alternative decision to cross back over the international border, initially in secret, and put their fate in the hands of the new Ethiopian government. The children, and grandchildren, of those who made this decision were to grow up well beyond the frontiers of the Sudanese state and with little inclination, until the peace agreement of 2005, to return. However, their move to escape the Sudan of the Nasir faction and of Omer el Beshir in this way was a truly desperate decision, and brought its own hazards.

7

Escape back to the New Ethiopia

THE TREK: KIGILLE TO ITANG, GAMBELA, AND KARMI

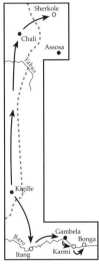

I have never had an opportunity to catch up with those refugees who decided in 1992 to remain on the Sudan side of the border, even though they had to decamp again in 1997 to Sherkole. But I was able to meet up with the majority faction in July 1992, after their desperate dash back to Ethiopia, in the transit camp arranged for them at Karmi, just upstream of Gambela. I was phoned that August by Lucy Hannan of the BBC World Service, then based in Addis Ababa, who said she had heard that I knew something about the Uduk tribe, and was it true they were 'dying out'? I learned from her that they were showing up in Ethiopia again, in small groups, and a story soon appeared in *The Guardian* describing them as 'a small ethnic minority from Sudan' having 'suffered all the disasters that plague the Horn of Africa', trapped between Sudan's political and religious north–south divide. They had arrived in Ethiopia 'carrying little more than their Bibles and starving children, and followed by a pack of emaciated hunting dogs'. Emmanuel Jajal is quoted as giving various declining figures for the population, estimated in Gambela at this time as 10,000.[1] I had already been invited to a refugee

---

[1] 'Sudanese tribe hounded out', Lucy Hannan in Gambela, western Ethiopia, *The Guardian* (3 Aug. 1992), 7.

studies conference in Addis Ababa in September that year, and was able to arrange a local consultancy with the UNHCR to go down afterwards to Gambela and Karmi, to provide some background on this unexpected reappearance of former Blue Nile refugees.

When the vanguard of the Gindi group had arrived in Itang, they knew they would need a spokesman to explain things to the Ethiopian authorities and whatever relief agencies they could contact. Dawud Hajar, who had substantial clinical experience, was an obvious candidate, but it had become his role to stay behind on these moves with the sick people, and try to bring up the rearguard. So they had arranged for Emmanuel Jajal to take on the position of key spokesman for their initial arrival back in Ethiopia, because he was another of the very few who could speak English (following initial education at the government school in Chali, in the years following the expulsion of the missionaries, he moved to Khartoum and took English classes there).

I was met in Gambela by Emmanuel, also known by his personal name Mola. He soon gave me the official story. The 'ethnic' factor was becoming very prominent.

We left the Sudan because of hunger, and we Uduk have come to Ethiopia to find some peace. We are still in difficulty, who is going to help us find a place? We were 26,000, and not many are left. Many have been lost. There is nobody to ask for us. Now you have come. It would be good for you to help us, find a place separate from the Nuer people. We don't want to fight. We want to rest and live here until things have been put right in the Sudan. We want to plant things; and first of all, we want to have schools. We have been in the bush for too long; my heart [Liver] says, this is not good for children. I am telling you so you can tell the senior people in the UN. We want peace and a place to cultivate, and schools. I want the eyes of the Uduk to be opened. That is my word, and thank you.[2]

Before describing Karmi, I shall sketch how lucky the majority of this group were who made the unexpected return trek to Ethiopia. There were not only the usual hazards of finding food and being looted, but after they made it to Itang, they ran into large-scale violence which was not of their making, and they had to flee further upstream to Gambela. In addition, UN and governmental bodies on either side of the border at first could

---

[2] Emmanuel Mola Jajal, Karmi, 21 Sept. 1992. The figure of 26,000 refers to the maximum registered under the name 'Uduk' in Tsore camp, 1989.

scarcely believe this return evacuation had happened, and were at a loss to explain it. It took a long time for the agencies on the Ethiopian side to react, as they were engaged in finally closing down the major relief programmes in the south-west. Having allowed a temporary move to a nearby transit site at Karmi, they finally gave permission for the 'new' arrivals to stay in Ethiopia for ninety days while longer-term plans were discussed.

> So what can we eat?
> With all the children too?
> I dig wild roots
> The Dhamkin ask, 'What's this, what's that?'
> Why's the UN denying us our grain?
> My feet are blistered
> We're from the long, bitter road
> With the hungry children too
>
> Oh, UN, oh!
> I've been strung along by the white people
> Riak Machar's behind it somewhere
> He thinks himself the Captain of the UN
> Oh, UN!
> Why don't you take us to Nairobi![3]

CONVERSATIONS IN KARMI

On the way back to Itang the people suffered the expected problems of food, and had to leave various sick and exhausted people again by the wayside. They bought some colobus monkey meat from locals, and dug up *kagash* roots, but many had dysentery and were not strong enough to go on. Martha said: 'We had left people from Toj up to Pekesh, some others who came later found them dead.... When we got to Tarpam first, we bought some grain, made a little porridge, and took it back to them but found them dead.... Girls, just teenagers, we found them dead. Five of them. Others were about to die ... their knees were finished. We just put some water in a jerry-can, and left them a plastic sheet.... All on the long road.'[4] They were also severely looted by

---

[3] Wel Ragab, recorded by Granada, Karmi, Jan. 1993.
[4] Martha Nasim Ahmed, Karmi, 21 Sept. 1992.

Gaajak Nuer on the border, speaking Arabic, carrying the long guns. They took clothes and medicines in particular. Martha described how eventually they made contact on the other side, and reached the houses they used to occupy at Tarpam, near Itang.

Some Ethiopians found us and said, 'Where are you going? Are you Uduk?' We said yes, and they said, 'On you go.' We went on to our own houses there. Then they looked at the children who were hungry. They sent a message to the big people.

   Then Tsehai and Negussie, we knew them, they came. They questioned us. 'Where is Martha?' I had little John, and no milk [the baby did not live long after this]. And we told them about the journey—all our clothes had been taken. They wanted to know what we wanted to do: 'Do you want to stay in Itang, or go back to Sudan?' We told them about it, why we came. 'Will you go back to see your crops later?' they asked. But we were afraid of the looting. They brought some medicine, and beans, and some meaty thing. They said they would send some food.[5]

This must have seemed an unbelievable break. But things turned out less rosy than they might at first have seemed. On getting news in early July about the re-arrival at Itang of former refugees from the southern Sudan, the UNHCR and the new Ethiopian government were extremely surprised and unprepared. As one official in the UNHCR offices in Addis Ababa exclaimed to me even in September, 'But *don't they know the refugee camp is closed?*' It had been decided that never again should there be such large camps, like the old Itang, of hundreds of thousands of people dependent on external aid. But the pressures to reopen the channels of assistance to the needy suddenly escalated.

DRAMA AT ITANG

A bare two weeks after the first Uduk had arrived 'back' at Itang and reclaimed their houses, violence broke out which had little to do with them, on the surface, though it certainly was provoked at a fundamental level by the way that relief assistance to Sudanese in the Gambela region had come to an end the previous year, and many among the massive number of those who crossed back to the Sudan then were still in great

---

[5] Martha Nasim Ahmed, Karmi, 19 Sept. 1992.

need. About ten days into July, the Nuer prophet 'Wurnyang' (Uduk pronounciation of Wut Nyang) appeared near Itang. His inspirational background and sometimes warlike activities have been described by Sharon Hutchinson, mainly for the central and western Upper Nile area.[6] He conducted a sacrificial ceremony to make peace between Nuer and Anuak, primarily for those based inside Ethiopia, while demands were being presented to the authorities both in Gambela and in Itang for the re-establishment of food assistance. These demands were not accepted, and there shortly followed an attack by his armed followers on traders and Ethiopian police in Itang. My friend David Musa was there.

He is from Wundeng, from Fangak. They are just people of *arum*, and Wurnyang is one of those people. Speaks powerfully in the Dhamkin language. I saw him myself there. A very, very tall man. Yes, he is called Wurnyang. He is like a *ŋari/* [Uduk 'diviner']. He collected a lot of people together in Nasir, and said he would take them to Itang to find food. There were large numbers of people, including women, men, children, youths, all of them. . . . He led people, held an *arum* rite, and killed an ox for the people. . . .

They stayed at the place where the Uduk tents used to be. They had mosquito nets ['and we had nothing'—interrupter] and they used the huts [originally built by Uduk] and the school.

He went and gathered the Dhamkin together, and the Anuak; and he held an *arum* rite to reconcile them so that they would cease fighting each other. They would stop fighting. . . . I went and stood there among them, to see what would happen. . . . He was there in between the Anuak and Nuer, to speak to them; the Anuak got up and made their speech, why they had been angry, why they had fought; and the Nuer got up and explained what had made them angry and made them fight. When this was finished, he said, 'All right, from today the fighting should stop.' He held his spear high, and then speared the ox. Yes, one beast. The ox fell down on the ground, and then people were content and dispersed . . . I wanted to see this for myself. I watched it.[7]

David elaborated his impressions later. He was the only Uduk present at this peacemaking ceremony, and one of the very few who understood something of the Nuer language (having been a policeman in Nasir in 'the old days' of the 1970s, and married a Nuer wife). Because of this, they chased him away. He believed that Wurnyang had hoped to be able

---

    [6] Sharon Hutchinson, *Nuer Dilemmas: Coping with Money, War and the State* (Berkeley and Los Angeles: University of California Press, 1996), 338–45.
    [7] David Musa, Karmi, 26 Sept. 1992.

to secure food aid once again for his people from the UN at Itang, and his reputation would have soared if he had been able to manage this. He was a striking figure, not only tall but wore pure white clothes, and was shaded by an umbrella.[8]

Dawud Hajar described how the Nuer arrivals had ejected him from his own house. ' "Get out!" [Arabic]. I found my children chased out, and my hut full of guns—Kalashnikov, and great big guns, "Jiim" [GM]. What should we do if it rained? They said, "We are the government [*hakuma*], and we need to put these things inside. We are the government." . . . They said, "We have not come to do anything; we are just hungry." They denied it. But I felt in my Liver ['heart'], "Ay! If a person is just hungry, does he come with guns like that? This is something else." And they talked in their language a lot.'[9] This happened around 12 July.

After about three days, and after the peacemaking ceremony which David Musa had witnessed, Dawud Hajar then saw a large number of Nuer with long hair come singing, and dancing into the market place, with spears, even women were there. A lorry was driving in with grain for sale. The order of events is not clear, but mayhem broke out. It started with the Nuer crowd throwing out the lorry driver and shooting him dead, and the Anuak police (or soldiers) firing over their heads. Nearly all adults from the Uduk refugee group were out in the bush, the women looking for wild roots or the men for honey. A number of Uduk children were scratching around for individual grains or beans on the ground in the market area. Emmanuel Mola Jajal had emerged as the key spokesman for the Uduk, and had gone with a vehicle to arrange some food relief. Another man helping in this effort was very impressed on being given a tent of the type the Tigre soldiers use themselves.

The lorry which arrived was, I believe, a regular merchant. Dawud went on:

Then the Dhamkin did this thing, they took the lorry, took the driver and pulled him out and threw him down on the ground. Other Dhamkin took the flour off the lorry. And then, they started shouting, and singing loudly! They were singing in Nuer, and they were going around the back of the village to the market. I was coming from the market. They came flocking along, and there

---

[8] David Musa, Karmi, 7 Jan. 1993.
[9] Dawud Hajar, Karmi, 26 Sept. 1992.

were Ethiopian soldiers in the market there. They watched them as they came, and then these Ethiopian soldiers shot at them. They shot them. I ran away as they were coming this way, I was going that way, and when I heard the guns sound '*daw* like that, I ran away.

And in that place there were lots and lots of children, lots and lots; and some were brought down by the guns. And later when the fighting was over, some Ethiopians came and told me, yes, there were many Ethiopians and Uduk who died; and people fled. Some women fled and left their children; some couldn't run and remained there. Others were very hungry and couldn't run; they remained there and are still there now.[10]

The raiders were said by my informants to have included some SPLA, but also many people from the villages, and they were herding cattle too and spearing them to eat. When they first arrived, 'The people of RRC had treated them very well. They opened the stores and gave them some of those white beans.' But after the violence started, they 'broke open all the Ethiopian shops, killed a lot of the Ethiopians, seized some alive and took them away, and as for us, I think they may have taken some Uduk alive as well, this is their habit, to carry things for them, they took everything, clothes, shoes, coffee, those white beans, they took the lot.'

When the adults out in the bush heard the noise, they returned, found chaos, collected what children they could, and made a fresh effort to escape in the direction of Gambela town. They fled together with many Ethiopians, including women who could not swim.

They told us to get out of the way or we would be killed with the Ethiopians. The guns began to sound, and they killed lots, lots of Ethiopians, they killed a lot of women, Ethiopian women, some Uduk too, in the middle of the market,—*Who?*—You can get their names from the chiefs now. And they took some women, some women were lost at that time. And the Ethiopian soldiers said some Uduk girls had been seized, to carry firewood on their heads. . . . Then we fled, the guns sounded, '*dow,* '*dow-*'*dow,* '*dow,* over our heads like that, and we ran through the night. And the Ethiopians ran too, their clothes were taken, they were naked. Up to Gambela. Some were wounded, here, big wounds with blood. We went on, found Anuak on road, they said, 'Go on to Gambela.' We were about to die. We were about to die. They were very fat, and couldn't run, and we helped pull them along, and they didn't know how to swim—people helped them across. . . . And in Gambela, everyone was amazed.

[10] Dawud Hajar, Karmi, 26 Sept. 1992.

And the Ethiopians said how we had all been attacked by the Nuer, and how the Uduk were in the same position, we had all been treated like dogs. 'The Uduk helped us on the road, and helped us across the water, we don't know how to swim.' In Gambela they asked if all our people were coming, and we said some were left behind. Taken by Anuak, while some of us crossed the river. The Anuak have some of our children now, are helping them. . . . The Anuak helped us—gave us maize, when they saw the children crying.[11]

Some people again died on this trek and had to be left, including Nyane, one of the daughters of the matriarch Umpa I had known well in the old days.

The testimony of children caught up in the violent incident at Itang is painful to listen to, but I will quote from Sila Nyitha, perhaps 12 or 14 at the time. His mother and other women had been killed, but he had made it onward some months after the violence in Itang to his people in Karmi.

At the time of fighting . . . when people began to run, I ran over there, and found her [his mother], her leg was swollen up, and I said we had to leave Itang. But she said her knees were swollen, she needed to rest a little. . . . I wasn't sure where we were going, and some Anuak took charge of us. People fired guns at night. People kept us in a hut and we slept there overnight . . . some Anuaks said we could take some dregs of food and eat it. We stayed there quite a bit, and her foot swelled up quite a lot. One child was very, very ill, there were four altogether . . . and they put us on the other bank of the river. We thought that our mothers were going to be brought there, and we waited five days.

And two other little sisters [not necessarily full sisters] of mine came, and I asked them, where was my mother? They were killed, they said, killed at night. I asked if they were killed with guns, or what. They were killed with guns inside a house. And another little child was killed with a gun too. And there were three other women, they were pregnant. At night people came and led them away, while everyone was sleeping.

Next day in the morning people said . . . they would take us to Gambela.— *Who were the people who wanted to lead you to Gambela?*—The people who did the killing. The one who killed our mothers, he was carrying a gun on his back. . . . I argued a bit with the man but decided to move away from there. And I thought the others would have been brought here, but they have not shown up . . . maybe the Anuak took them off for good. . . .

I was very afraid, this was something very big that I had asked these other children, and I was very afraid, and now I am here and I am happy but this idea is bothering me, for five days now . . . that very bad man is still living among the

---

[11] Martha Nasim Ahmed, 19 Sept. 1992.

Anuak, he said he would kill me and throw me in the river, so I was careful to avoid going to the river, I stayed in the village. A man wanted me to go and live in his village very far away but I refused. I thought, if people are going to come and search, let them find me here. And another little child, a very young one like this, was taken off to a very far place . . . I'm worried that the Anuak may be taking the children further away, saying to themselves that these children are for sale, perhaps.[12]

DRAMA AT KARMI

Visually and geographically, Karmi transit camp was a great improvement on the Upper Nile swamps. The land was dry, there were plenty of trees, and nearby hills. But the Ethiopian government had not yet agreed that the returnee-refugees could stay, and in any case the site was not suitable, being too close to Gambela town, and having only recently seen severe disturbances of a resettled community from the highlands who were attacked by locals. Temporary assistance was set up quite quickly, however, and very soon Karmi was sporting new blue UN plastic sheeting and spruce little wood and grass huts and church meeting places. The immediate problem was for all parties to sort out what should happen next for this community. It was here that through a kind of benevolent collusion between the people themselves, especially the new leadership, the thinking of the new Ethiopian government, and the aid agencies, an explicit narrative emerged of the plight of the Uduk group as such. In Assosa, and in Itang the first time, and in Nasir, it was understood that many of the rural communities of the Sudan–Ethiopian border had got caught up in the war one way or another, and expected that an assorted range of individuals and families of various backgrounds would be catered for in each project. It was in Addis Ababa in September 1992 that I heard officials, both international and Ethiopian, talking of the need to 'save the Uduk tribe'. And it was sitting in Karmi a little later that I heard how the SPLA split had affected the Nasir area, and how this had helped provoke a new faction among the Uduk to leave altogether and risk a return to Itang, with a new justifica-

---

[12] Sila Nyitha, Karmi, 7 Jan. 1993. In this conversation Martha helped me talk things over with Sila, following the filmed interview he had given for the Granada documentary a little earlier (*Orphans of Passage*, dir. Bruce MacDonald).

tion of fleeing the oppression of the SPLA. There was clearly a growing 'ethnic' consciousness which became a key element in the exchanges between the refugee spokespeople and the humanitarian agencies. This sat well with the approach of the new Ethiopian government, dedicated to respecting cultural diversity and the rights of all 'ethnic groups'. The new spokespeople emphasized their fear of unfair treatment by the 'Dhamkin', the Nuer and Dinka with whom the SPLA was of course primarily identified, not only by the Uduk but also by the Anuak of Ethiopia.

By mid-1992 the Sudan government had taken full advantage of the weakened state of the SPLA and the relative friendliness of the new Ethiopian government. They had advanced far to the south-east, along the Ethiopian border, and retaken Torit, near Kapoeta in Eastern Equatoria. They established consulates, moreover, on the Ethiopian side, in Assosa, and in Gambela, and from this last place illegally approached the refugees in Karmi in the hope of persuading them to return. However, as the year wore on, more and more Sudanese from the Nasir area (where many had been stranded, unable to reach their homes across the country) began to trickle back into Ethiopia, and to join the Uduk refugees in Karmi. Some were interrogated in prison, as former SPLA fighters; all were supposed to be completely disarmed. The influx began to cause anger among the local Anuak; and also to cause unease among the Uduk as the newcomers, mainly from Nilotic groups and blanketed as all 'Nuer', set up their huts on several sides of Karmi. This was the background against which a series of important discussions were held in Addis Ababa and Gambela over how to manage the return of a steadily increasing flow of refugees from the Nasir zone of the southern Sudan. The reopening of Itang as a refugee camp was ruled out. Various options were proposed for the reopening of other former camps, at Dimma and Fugnido, and some site visits were made to places where new schemes might be developed. One of these, which I was invited to join, was at Khor Bonga, a tributary of the Baro at the foot of the escarpment (Figure 14). Bonga had been a home area of the Koma people in earlier times, but the local population now consisted mainly of a few Anuak settlers. Bonga had been the site of an SPLA military training camp under the former Ethiopian government, but apart from the straggling remnants of a market village, it was by this time unoccupied. It was officially decided

by the Ethiopian authorities and the UNHCR in October 1992 that a
new refugee scheme would be set up specifically for the Uduk at Bonga.

Perhaps inevitably, the conversations I had on my first visit to Karmi
transit camp were of a very factual, circumstantial kind about the near-
impossibility of surviving under the crumbling SPLA discipline in
Nasir. This was the key factor which had provoked the new dash back
to Ethiopia and the uncertain situation the refugees were now in. As
explained in the previous chapter, the SPLA split was the indirect cause
of the split among the Uduk refugees themselves, and a substantial
contingent, including the Omda and the old guard among the church
leaders, had not agreed to cross the border again. These were all still on
the Sudan side, and appalling things were now happening there again, as
we have seen. The militancy of the new Islamic politics was known to
many of the refugees, not only through the radio but the 'bush network'
of interpersonal communication which worked remarkably well throughout all these upheavals. David Musa, a fluent Arabic speaker, commented,
'There is no way to go back to the Sudan. Because the way of this Islamic
shari'a: they do not want *masahin*, Christians. Aha! So where could we
go? . . . The SPLA and ordinary Dhamkin loot us; the Sudan government
doesn't want Christians; Aha! . . . We don't want to become Muslims. So
this is why we decided to come back to Ethiopia.'[13]

While the UNHCR and the Ethiopian authorities were very reluctant
to open new refugee camps on the old model, they were sympathetic to
the new arrivals whose story was one of escaping SPLA maltreatment.
And new thinking about refugee assistance was in progress on the
eastern side of Ethiopia, where officials were discussing the problems
of singling out Somali 'refugees' for special assistance, when their
survival problems were more or less the same as Ethiopian Somali
'returnees' or 'stayees'. Plans for refugee-affected areas were being formulated in which the programmes of UNHCR and other UN humanitarian agencies would be co-ordinated under a 'cross-mandate' approach.
In this policy context, discussions were held at different levels about what
should be done for the people in Karmi, and field visits were made to
possible sites for a new refugee scheme (Figure 14). The idea was that this
would be a 'semi-permanent settlement' scheme, where the people would
have the opportunity to grow crops, learn skills, and thus contribute to
their own support, in a context of general regional redevelopment. Bonga

---

[13] David Musa, Karmi, 21 Sept. 1992.

Figure 14. Emmanuel Mola Jajal and Peter Kuma, on an official visit to Bonga as a possible refugee site, September 1992

was the chosen site, with the agreement of both the regional authority in Gambela and the central government.

It was following the confirmation of this agreement to allow the people to remain in Ethiopia that I accepted an invitation from Granada TV's Disappearing World series to help make a documentary film, in the ethnographic tradition, and had the opportunity to visit Karmi again for a month from the New Year, 1993. I was greatly relieved that there was the prospect of a 'safe haven' for the immediate future, but also aware of certain tensions in the Gambela region, and indeed already in Karmi during my previous visit in September 1992. One night there had been a series of explosions, and a rush of running feet as people scattered off into the bush. It turned out to have been Anuak gunmen, angry at the re-arrival, not of the Uduk as such, but of the Nilotic refugees, regarded as solidly SPLA supporters still and not welcome. The tensions escalated up to the end of January 1993, when a minor quarrel between women and children at the river led to a dangerous outbreak of fighting across the camp, on a Saturday afternoon when no UN personnel were present, and the only vehicle the Land-Rover which Granada TV's Disappearing World programme had hired. We were therefore witnesses, and in one respect participants, in the events of that weekend. I have published a detailed account of what I called 'The Battle of Karmi',[14] and here just summarize.

Towards the end of our planned month filming in Karmi, the film crew were setting up an afternoon interview in the southern outskirts of the settlement when we became aware that something was amiss. A wave of movement had spread across the camp. We were told briefly, 'We're running from the Dhamkin'. We followed the direction of the rush, and lined up with others facing across the road. Several hundred men were holding sticks, rough spears, knives, and stones. We gathered that some Uduk had been attacked by Nuer from the direction of the river. In a body, though without obvious leadership, the men flowed over the road, holding their makeshift weapons high. They were attempting to block the Nuer in the riverside settlements from joining those to our east. We crossed over too, and met several groups of Nuer in distress, some with bleeding faces. They told us, or rather gestured, that walking in from Gambela they had been stoned by the Uduk as they reached Karmi. Demanding (in Arabic and English) of Nuer spokesmen what was going on, we were told that the Uduk had killed a Nuer woman and left her in the river. The film team wanted to cover this incident, and we insisted on being taken there. After zigzagging through the grass we were eventually shown an injured woman on the path from the river, who whimpered that the Uduk had stoned her. She was lifted up and taken to the road where several other quite badly injured Nuer were lined up. Speeches complaining about the Uduk were made for the camera.

Returning to the core Uduk area we interviewed people we knew well. They spoke of a riverbank scrap between two children, one Uduk and one Nuer. The women joined in; then an Uduk man tried to separate them. Nuer men nearby were enraged to see him handling their women; sticks and spears were thrown. The old woman was stoned

---

[14] Wendy James, 'The names of fear: history, memory and the ethnography of feeling among Uduk refugees', *Journal of the Royal Anthropological Institute* (*JRAI*), NS 3 (1997), 115–31.

by retaliating Uduk, and the rumours of her death flew. A party of Nuer men attacked the eastern end of the Uduk settlement and, in response, Uduk at the western end stoned groups of unknowing Nuer returning innocently from a day's trip to town.

Among the 18,000 asylum seekers (some 13,000 Uduk and 5,000 'Dhamkin' though actually including many besides Nuer), and a few local traders and Anuak villagers, we were conspicuous as the only outside visitors. There were no security authorities posted to the camp. We were relieved when the rumpus seemed to die down, an hour or two after it had started, and we began to arrange to take the injured into Gambela town. It was almost sunset; the next day was Sunday and no UNHCR vehicles were expected. But suddenly the fighting flared up again. What seemed like thousands more people, mostly men but also women, were flying together towards the river to attack the Nuer, shouting and hurling sticks and stones. We realized all control had gone. After a few moments of panicky cursing and swearing we decided that the driver and I should go straight into Gambela to report the situation, and the rest should hold our fort, a cluster of grass huts. I grabbed Emmanuel and another man who I knew would be respected by the authorities, made them drop their makeshift missiles, and hurried them into the Land-Rover. We raced off, Emmanuel beating the side of the car excitedly and shouting to those we passed, 'Don't be afraid! Get your weapons and *go and fight them now!*' As we reached the western end of Karmi and the tiny trading settlement, a crowd of Ethiopian merchants and their families were waving and yelling desperately to stop the car and get a lift to safety; I told the driver to ignore the crush and go straight on, which he did, with some difficulty.

We returned after a painfully long time from the town, in convoy with an army truck of equipment and soldiers, a police truck, and a UNHCR car. All was quiet. A good handful of injured Uduk had by now gathered at our place. Some had what seemed to be shrapnel wounds. Firearms were of course prohibited in this as in any refugee settlement; everyone had been screened before admission. But on film, the team had recorded Nuer huts burning against the evening sky, and two explosions as some kind of device went off. Later that night our vehicle, and the UNHCR's, ferried the wounded of both sides to the Gambela hospital; a unit of the soldiery appropriated our camp facilities as we slept, and the police started an inquiry in the morning. Reports were offered of looting, and of Nuer departing for the forest with guns. Some of the Uduk too had prudently left for the forest and no one knew if they were safe.

We left this unsatisfactory situation behind the next day, catching in Gambela town what might only have been rumours that some had died in the incident. Two years later, on a subsequent visit to the new settlement at Bonga, I first learned that at least three Nuer men had indeed been killed at Karmi, by stoning. I have not seen any official report or figure, but have since heard of higher numbers, possibly rumour.

ONWARD TO BONGA

It was this whole incident which accelerated the plans of the UNHCR and Ethiopian officials to settle the Uduk in the newly planned scheme further east at Bonga. On subsequent visits to them there I have frequently been treated to exciting and dramatic stories of the events at Karmi, which certainly marked a new turn in the saga of the epic journey. I have indicated how there was a gradual build-up of tensions about the behaviour of the Dhamkin over the previous years and how the original plea of the people on re-entering Ethiopia was to be allowed a place to settle away from them. This had not been an issue before. The key turning point was the split in the SPLA, and a shift in leadership among the refugees themselves; discreet loyalty to the mainstream SPLA was there but not often apparent.

Stragglers from Kigille, with no particular hankering after life with the Sudan government of the day, and no particular SPLA associations, came on in small groups across the border. William Danga led one such small party in early 1993, including his wife Pake, and her son from a previous marriage. They were relieved of possessions on the way by bandits, though there was no shooting. It was still a strange kind of 'rite of passage', from the insecurity of one political space to the uncertainty of another. They were among the last to leave the radar screen of the UN Operation Lifeline projects based in Nairobi, who had always been obliged to work through the political constraints of Khartoum, and now in addition the local constraints of the Nasir commanders. They were to enter what was by this time the quite disturbed political arena of Gambela Regional State, but be given more or less safe passage past Itang and Gambela town straight on to the newly established Bonga refugee scheme, well away from the recent clashes and the border zone. There was hope. And there was a moving story of new life from the wilderness, the no-man's land of that border.

William told me in 1994 how Pake gave birth after they had crossed the border, but before they had arrived at the first Ethiopian police post/garrison at Tarpam, just outside Itang. The path was very wild, and they saw elephants along the way. Pake's elder son Thany remembered the problems of cooking and eating the wild fruits and roots they had to live on.

People boiled figs and made a 'porridge', and people made *tulpe*, it was very bitter, you have to keep changing the water, and people boiled *shwa'b*, and it doesn't cook quickly, people made *mat*, by straining ashes for a salty liquid. And we ate beans.

People bought a lot of things from the Dhamkin, we bought corn, but when we ate figs our faces swelled up, and we cooked *shwa'b* and ate *se'd*. It irritates the throat a lot. People were warming up water to ease their throats by drinking. It makes a lot of saliva, people were dribbling. It was very bitter. People ate the leaves along with the new tubers.

Is there a river at Kigille?—Yes, very narrow, like the little one in Bonga. People caught fish there.—*Were there plenty, big ones or little?*—There were some big ones. And we caught *nyer* (a little one), we fished with baskets.—*And what were they like?*—Very good, they have a lot of oil, you fry it in its own oil. And you mix in some flour [to make it crisp]. And Ate [short name for his mother] would mix sesame.

What was the long road like? . . .—We were very hungry, when Ate went to dig for *se'd*, I was hungry and I cried. And part of the *cu*, you usually put it back to grow again, but this time we took it all. . . .

When we left Kigille, people began to take our things on the way, they took our cooking pans, everything. Danga tried to hang on to the cooking pans, but the Dhamkin said they would shoot him, pointing their guns.

Did you see any animals on the way?—We found elephants. They were crossing the road in front of us; we had gone ahead of our mothers, and when we saw them we ran back. The elephants then started following us!—along the tracks we were making in the long grass![15]

---

[15] Thany, stepson of William Danga, Bonga, 10 Nov. 1994 (video).

They rested for the night, on a little coloured sheet they still had, and Pake had her baby. A truck found them in the morning. William said, 'They asked us who we were, and wrote our names down, and gave us a card, and said we should ride in the truck. Pake was there with the baby in her arms. They said, "Oh, was that baby born yesterday? What is his name?" I said, "He doesn't have a name yet!" . . . They said, "No, that won't do, you should give him a name now. Give him a name and I can write it on the card." I said all right. I said, "Good. I will call him Dale." So he wrote down his name as Dale.'[16] William spontaneously gave the name of the American worker with the World Food Programme, Dale Skoric, who had been so helpful to them over the previous year in Nasir. Dale meanwhile, of course, had moved on—like the medical worker 'John' after whom Martha's baby (who was not to survive) had been named. I never met either of these aid workers; but I heard a good deal about the efforts they and their colleagues made to help the people at one of the most difficult periods of their zigzag and desperate displacement, now left behind in the flat swamps of Nuer country.

[16] William Danga Ledko, Bonga, 4 Nov. 1994.

PART III

BEYOND WORDS

8

Safe Haven? The Bonga Refugee Scheme

> The harvest birds are flocking to the red-barked
>   trees which fruit in Bonga
> They're looking for the red-barked trees
> You birds are flocking!
> Aren't you like the 'Uduk'? Oh!
>
> Yes, they say the birds are searching out the trees in Bonga
> So why should I trek back to Itang for my food?
> Should I go and peck around for beans in Itang?
> Are you going back to look for food in Itang?
>
> The children too are coming, to find the red-barked
>   trees which fruit in Bonga
> Oh yes, I had to take the Itang road,
> To find some food! For I come from far away.
> The birds are twittering *jege jege,*
> Looking for food.
> You're just like the 'Uduk', flying to the trees
> Flocking all the way from Nasir
> Chattering in a hungry chorus *jege jege!* [1]

After a series of partially chaotic scenarios extending over the best part of the previous six or seven years, Bonga was an ordered and organized place. The decision to establish this new refugee scheme upstream from Gambela and Karmi, primarily and in the first instance for the Uduk, was made in an agreement between the UNHCR and the Ethiopian government in October 1992. It was planned more or less on the pattern of other refugee settlements, unfortunately without implementing the original idea of including access to surrounding land in the plans that were posted. Rather, sixteen residential blocks were drawn to fit in

[1] Composed by David Musa, sung by Hosiah Dangaye Chalma, Bonga, 20 Nov. 1994.

the open delta area where the Khor Bonga met the Baro, giving a fairly heavy population density within a bounded area. The plans were drawn up in three days by an expert from another part of Africa, but no space was allowed in the plans for football fields or churches (though these were already much in evidence in Karmi). It was officially reported at the start that the land provided was not enough for a significant contribution to self-sufficiency. By the year 2000 two more blocks were added for 'Burun' groups (actually speaking languages of the Koman family), and more additions were made in the following years as refugees were redistributed within the Gambela area.

Various arrangements, including a list of the order in which existing groups were to move, were being drawn up at the time of my second visit to Karmi in January 1993, but the actual move was brought forward as a direct result of the violence in Karmi at the end of that month. The elderly and sick were transported by truck but most people walked, and the move was completed by mid-February. Karmi itself remained a point of first reception for the continuing stream of new arrivals from the Sudan side, mostly Nilotic speakers from distant parts of the south who could not return home because of the new waves of internecine fighting between factions of the SPLA, some being co-opted in effect by Khartoum as pro-government militias. The details or causes of the ongoing unrest in the Sudan were not often understood by UN or NGO personnel on the Ethiopian side, but they did see a point in separating 'ethnic groups' as far as possible in the refugee settlements. Once the Uduk had been moved on to Bonga, the other refugees left in Karmi were encouraged to transfer to Dimma or to Fugnido camps further south.

For the Uduk themselves the supervised move to Bonga was a tremendous relief. After six turbulent years, the middle of 1993 seemed to promise respite, a good time for reflection, for modest celebration, and even for hope. By this time most of those 'left behind' on the Sudan side of the border had either set out for the government-controlled areas of Yabus and Chali, as explained in the last chapter, or been able to trickle across the border to rejoin their kith and kin either at Karmi or in Bonga. It was a conscious choice between returning to the rather generalized conception of the *hakuma* of the Sudan, in the sense, I think, of a historic 'nation-state' rather than the current regime in power, or staying outside its orbit in a sort of suspended association with

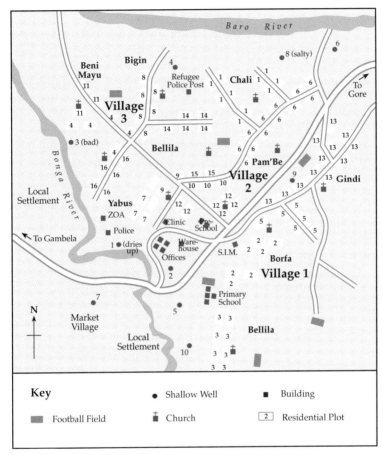

Map 4. Bonga refugee scheme

the continuing core of the armed movement still struggling against that regime. Those who had returned 'home', and those resettled in Bonga, were now thus clearly divided by the front line of the war. At this time the new Ethiopian government's relations with the Sudanese Islamist regime in Khartoum were warm and co-operative, and the newly opened Sudanese consulates in Assosa and Gambela even made contact with the refugee camps, for example visiting Bonga in person to pressurize the refugees to return home. The local authorities made it clear that such visits were illegal within international law, after which the Sudanese officials would regularly hang around the market village just outside the refugee settlement, hoping to entice them home through friendly conversation. However, by 1995 relations between Khartoum and Addis Ababa turned sour again, the consulates were closed, and there was sympathy and support once again for the SPLA from the Ethiopian side (and a new phase of recruitment into the SPLA). In 1996–7 the SPLA again secured territory in the Blue Nile, attacking and finally hanging on to the small garrisons of Yabus and Chali, and then the now well-defended town of Kurmuk (see Chapters 1 and 3). Knowing of these developments, the refugees in Bonga grew optimistic, during the late 1990s, about the possibilities of peace and of returning home soon to a newly democratic Sudan. Some older men did trek back to start up cultivation, and not a few young men who had been recruited and trained within Ethiopia slipped over the border to support campaigns of the SPLA, sometimes moving discreetly back and forth.

The Bonga scheme was initially planned as a village-style settlement for the third-time-round refugees, where they would be expected to make a significant contribution to their own support from the start and move towards self-sufficiency. The new Ethiopian authorities were strongly against the reappearance of the old-style camps where very large numbers of people were catered for on a 'care and maintenance' basis, kept quite apart from the local population, and not allowed to put down any roots locally. They preferred a more development-oriented strategy, and in many ways this was very successful over the following years which saw educational, environmental, health-care, income-generation, and skills training projects on a scale the people had never before experienced. Morale was incomparably better in Bonga than it had been for years (Figures 15–20).

In particular, there was a very optimistic start to the Bonga scheme. In the early 1990s the UNHCR and its partners were discussing a new approach which recognized that many of the problems of refugee groups were found also among locals, and that in places such as the Ethiopian–Somali border people had moved so much it was almost impossible to distinguish between refugees, returnees, and 'stayees'. The new 'cross-mandate' approach would seek to link the programmes of the various UN branches and agencies assisting Ethiopian communities in needy areas with those under the umbrella of the UNHCR, themselves aimed at protecting and helping the foreign refugee groups among them. The

Figure 15. William Danga with the new harvest, Bonga, 1994

Bonga scheme was originally set up as a pilot project under the new approach, labelled by the UNHCR a 'semi-permanent settlement' scheme. The regional government in Gambela was initially keen to support the granting of cultivation rights to the refugees over quite large areas of land downstream from the Bonga site itself, though the central government had reservations; these views shifted a few years later, with the central authorities willing to argue for a little more space for the refugees but the regional government beginning to resist this. The net result was that the original vision was never fulfilled.[2] Each house plot was supposed to be 25 metres (27 yards) square, where a little kitchen gardening could be done, but no cultivation was supposed to be allowed outside the site. I have measured a number of these plots and they were all precisely 20 metres (22 yards) square, having been measured by the same piece of rope which was that length. This meant that bureaucracies from Gambela up to Geneva were provided with a larger figure for the cultivable land available to the refugees than was the fact on the ground, and I spent a good deal of energy pointing this out but to no effect. This was only one aspect of the immense gulf that I began to realize separated the language, concerns, and indeed 'discourse' of the development and humanitarian agencies, on the one hand, from those of the refugees—something I discuss further below.

Meanwhile, the refugees began from the start to plant along the fertile river bank, but just before harvest time officials pointed out that this zone had been declared as a forest reserve and local Anuak were hired to assist in tearing up the crops. The refugees then began to clear their own little plots behind the hills and across the river, illegally, facing periodic reprimands from the officials and challenges from the locals. The number of officials proliferated over the years, and they spent a good deal of time attempting to stop the refugees hunting animals for food, or cutting down trees, or even collecting fallen wood for fuel or building. By the late 1990s there was talk of fencing in the whole of the Bonga

---

[2] Wendy James, 'Uduk asylum seekers in Gambela, 1992: community report and options for resettlement' (Addis Ababa, UNHCR, 31 Oct. 1992), 41 pp.; 'The Bonga scheme: progress to 1994 and outlook for 1995. A report for UNHCR on assistance to Sudanese (Uduk) refugees in western Ethiopia' (Addis Ababa, UNHCR, 25 Jan. 1995), xii + 79 pp.; 'Community services for Sudanese refugees in Western Ethiopia: working proposals for Bonga and Sherkole' (Addis Ababa, ZOA Refugee Care, the Netherlands, 2000), 59 pp.

settlement so that refugees could not use the surrounding forest at all, while their movements out to the growing local market village, and Gambela town, could be monitored. There were other threats too, such as to burn the little canoes they were building to cross the Baro to their cultivations on the other side. This kind of talk rarely led to action, but it certainly helped to foment resentment. The Ethiopian authorities called Bonga a 'camp' from the start, while UNHCR initially called it a 'semi-permanent settlement'. Everyone seemed after a few years to have forgotten the 'cross-mandate' approach, and certainly various partner NGOs fell into the habit of calling it a 'camp'. My own choice has been to refer to the project as the 'Bonga refugee scheme'. By 2000 its population was just over 14,000. Before returning to a fuller picture of life there, and then a survey of relations between the displaced Uduk and the international humanitarian agencies in general, I would like to illustrate how Bonga began to offer space for more reflective conversations, both among the people themselves and with outsiders, than had been possible in Nor Deng or Karmi.

CONVERSATIONS IN BONGA

It was only in Bonga that I came to realize the basic strength of sympathy among the Uduk refugees for the cause of the SPLA, by no means for the Nasir leadership they had just left but for the underlying cause, and with the reviving strength of the mainstream movement and its renewed advances into the Blue Nile Province. They certainly were never 'separatists' who wished to see an independent south, but were still in line with the stated main aims of the movement to reform the Sudanese political and social system as a whole. They were on the whole very satisfied to hear the news of the revival of the movement after 1995, and pleased at news of its renewed successes in their own homeland—such as the taking of Jebel Ulu to the west of Kurmuk in 1999. Again there was the hope that an overall peace settlement was a possibility, one in which they could return to a Sudan in which there would be, among other things, individual security, educational and economic opportunity, and freedom of religious expression.

Having outlined the circumstances in which I was present in Bonga first in 1994, and then in 2000, I now go on to discuss the more general conversations I was able to pursue there, in line with the underlying anxieties and hopes of the people themselves. These fell into four categories: ongoing concerns over what they were in fact able to do to 'help themselves' in Bonga; sharp and bitter reflections on the politics of the war in Sudan and the SPLA split, and the way these had affected them in Nasir; the violent events they experienced at Itang and at Karmi; and a newly emotional take on the original displacement from Chali and their place in the scheme of Sudanese things as a whole. Before my eyes also were a range of newly creative activities: dramatic and often hilarious storytelling about events on the journey; encounters with the Dhamkin and the 'Battle of Karmi'; newly philosophical reflections, admittedly in somewhat soft focus, even making something of a 'destiny' out of present displacement by linking it with myth and older prophecies, newly come to mind; reassessments of the meaning of received religious teaching; and music, song, fun with language, games, and sports. In this chapter, I concentrate on the first kind of straight-forward conversation, interview style, though the longer-term reflec-tions begin to make themselves heard. The following chapters will turn the focus fully onto the realm of the imagination and way that raw experience, of suffering and death as well as of physical survival, was being turned into modest but unmistakable forms of creative art in the relatively peaceful, but crowded, circumstances of Bonga, and thus the ethos of a consciously transformed, if recognizable, social world.

Looking back to the earlier phases of the whole journey, even the frightening and hazardous times, conversations easily turned to fun and laughter. In Nor Deng, for example, women did not elaborate on their raw experiences, a place and time where there were still so many fears, but below is part of a spontaneous group discussion I happened to witness in the safer circumstances of Bonga in 1994. Half a dozen women were sharing their memories of the way they were ambushed as they came away from Assosa, through the rough Ethiopian ravines and ridges of the escarpment (see Figure 8 on p.114). Their manner was sometimes suddenly hesitant, shocked silent by vivid recollection, but most of the afternoon was punctuated by crowing laughter and hilarity to the point of tears. It was after all five years after the event, the relief of getting to Bonga was still tangible, and laughter can be stran-gely cathartic. Several voices are entwined in the following summary paraphrase.

We were two days in the bamboo forest, and then over another slope beyond it, we were all together when we stumbled into this 'ambush' [English].

[Another voice] Well, we went the other way, and there was no ambush!

[Various voices, overlapping and interrupting] As we went up, they fired two 'RPGs' [*sic*: rocket propelled grenades] and Kalashnikovs at us. There was water, falling down like smoke, a waterfall yes, some of us saw the Oromo people there, behind the waterfall. Before that we were crawling over the rocks, and our hands were blistered. We saw that the people shooting had white clothes on. They were far away and looked very small. Some of us got down to the valley where we could see up, but the rest behind were those who got shot. The team of Peter Kuma were already down there. My friend, we were the ones who got down to Peter there. Some of them came back up to help. And then we went all together to Kubri [Yabus Bridge]. We got some water and took it back to give to those behind us, who had lost things, like their headbaskets.

The guns sounded, *'da-'daw, 'da-'daw!* [shrieks of laughter] But on that day some were wounded, some fell down, some died, you had to be very strong. One soldier died, he was carrying his child on his neck, he ran and fell down. He was from Bellila. Jangka from Beni Mayu, the blind singer, he died in that ambush. He was stopped by the guns and fell down and was left there. . . .

[Another voice] When we heard the sound of the guns, I threw the child on my back and tried to run. Someone said, she was wondering whether to throw away the sack she was carrying or not, to run faster? She was asking, 'Help, is my child shot on my back there?' She had no time even to wipe her nose as she ran; 'Is my child shot behind there?'

[Several voices at once] . . . When they threw the 'RPGs' the grass burst into flames on the mountain side! They came over our heads, and hit the ground in front of us, burning the grass. Bwaybonya—her headbasket got shot and the bullet went through it and it fell on the ground. One woman cried out, 'Bwaybonya's dead! Oh, oh!' [Hilarious laughter] Some trucks were coming out from Assosa, to join in the fighting, and they saw some of us people wounded and collected them up and took them back to Assosa. I collected up the kids in my arms and said, 'Let's just go on and die over there if we have to.'

[Another voice] *Did you leave a child there?*—Yes, she was a girl, she had lost her senses, in Green Book, the recruitment place for our boys at Langkwai there, she was screaming and shouting out, people were afraid of her. . . This is where we all ran to first, with the SPLA, until the first bombs hit the centre of the village and we all left towards Assosa.

[Another voice] On that steep path, the men were pushing us, pushing us out of the way and trying to get past, but one of them shouted, 'No, don't push her!' [Loud laughter] He was like a lion. Someone said she was exhausted, 'Let's go to the cave and hide', when they heard the guns, but her child said, 'No, let's keep going.' So she agreed, and they went on, and said, 'If something happens we will all die together.'

So she agreed with her kids, she walked and walked and saw the young babies left by their mothers, but they kept on walking. [All go quiet]—Yes, babies that had fallen down the steep mountainside. Nobody picked them up. They were just left there on the ground. They were thrown down as the baskets fell. This was a terrible thing. One little girl baby was very nice and plump, the baby was crying and crying, and I thought should I pick up the baby, or not, and I had to leave the baby. Those little kids, oh dear. And all the cooking pots, everything was left.[3]

I was also present at several ad hoc hilarious performances of women's struggles with the 'long shanks', that is the Nuer and Dinka. The blind lady Tocke was a particularly entertaining storyteller, especially on her own tussles with them. In this scene, she is re-enacting an incident on the way back to Itang when Nuer looters approached her group, including two of her sons, Ria and Cesh. The latter was an SPLA soldier but did not say so when asked. An officer saved the day.

Ria was sitting here, and his wife Cila, and the wife of Cesh. The Dhamkin came and asked Ria, 'Are you fellows soldiers?' The Dhamkin started beating them, and Cesh beat them back. My son didn't give them what they wanted. But we were surrounded by men with guns. I said to Ria, 'My sons, we should stay here and die!' They grabbed Ria and Cila. The Dhamkin tried to kick Cila but she dodged, and I cried a war cry [*kayi*], *yeeow yeeow yeeow!* [Uproarious laughter] When the Dhamkin spoke, I went towards them to attack them with my digging stick (metal tipped), 'If you are going to kill the only son I have, who led me from Sudan, who will lead me back? Kill me right now, use your gun and kill me now! I want to die right now, if you are going to kill my son!'

Then some of our soldiers came along, and a senior Dhamkin man took the guns away from these Dhamkin. He said to me, 'Mama, what's going on?' I said 'These Dhamkin are trying to kill us all! They will kill us with guns! They wanted to shoot us with guns!' The big man said, 'Mama, *agod!* [Arabic]—sit down!' I said, 'Mama is *not* going to listen, *not at all*! I do *not want* to sit down!' [Appreciative guffaws] The officer began to ask the looters, 'Why are you doing this to the civilians?' ... Ria was telling me to keep on shrilling the war cry; I ... started to dance a war dance [*waŋga/*], pounding my digging stick and crying the *kayi* too! My son's wife didn't join in, she left it to me!

Here in Bonga we have found a little peace, but there is no peace when we are with the Dhamkin. We would be killed by them dead, *na'd, na'd.*[4]

---

[3] Women's stories, Bonga, 18 Oct. 1994 (video).
[4] Tocke, daughter of Baske, Bonga, 20 Nov. 1994 (video).

A group of Chali churchwomen were talking very seriously about deaths on the long road one afternoon, and as so often was happening in Bonga, the conversation gradually fell into the hilarious anecdote mode. People seemed almost to want this to happen when they got together and stories of the long trek surfaced.

Coming from Nasir, we were resting, and we had to go and collect the body of the young Nuba escort who was shot by the Gaajak on the way, and bury him. . . . He got shot [by a bandit], and the other was shot back. Both died. When we spent the night, some men stayed up and walked around with their spears, guarding us. . . . A Kolnugara man was also shot; he was a trader, with a lot of money, and was carrying a large trunk with blankets; when they killed him, they took everything. He had refused to share all this luggage with his wife, and he was walking behind the others when they shot him. . . . He forgot his axe, and went back for it, and this is why he was behind the others. . . .

[Another voice, an old lady, joining in this rather serious reflection but in a different tone] We had a saucepan when we left Kigille, and I was very tired. I told the kids to go on, and I would rest and come on slowly. When we came, we found the place where this looting had happened to the people in front. They said hey, hey, put your things down. When we put them down, they asked my two boys to give them the bags they had. They asked them to open them up, and took their trousers, their fishing hooks and lines, given us by Dale. Then they came to us, myself and Matta. The Dhamkin took chickens from some of us, and saucepans, and blankets.

A senior man came and said, 'Check *what this grandmother* has!' [squalls of laughter as she enacts the scene] I struggled, 'I've only got *one saucepan*! Just *this one*, oh please!' He took his leather belt, and beat me with it on the back of the neck, *tup!* I was shrieking, 'My *one and only* saucepan!' He was a senior person, he had a star on his jacket here. They took the saucepan off me. Then they took a small plastic water can from us and used the water to wash the chicken, and used my pan to cook it. . . . That person almost wrestled me onto the ground in that place where we struggled! . . . The Dhamkin were laughing, and we were insulting them [in Uduk], 'Great disgusting backsides! Why don't you die?'[5]

When they got to Itang, her group had no saucepan to use. 'We were truly *ciŋkina/* [foundlings, slaves, kinless people; here in the sense of 'helpless'].'

Omda Talib's wife Hergke agreed with me one day that it was a great relief not to have any kind of soldiers around harassing them, or fighting each other, but she still hankered after the idea of going home, where they would be 'free' to hunt and cut down trees. She had perhaps

---

[5] A group of Chali churchwomen, Bonga, 20 Nov. 1994 (video).

forgotten how treeless and barren, and shorn of wild animals, her own homeland had become.

Yes, some people think they might pack up and go home quietly. They want to go home and hunt some meat, because the Ethiopian government says, 'Don't kill the animals, don't hunt animals here.' But this is not good, stopping people from hunting. And we sit here thinking we might just go home, always worrying about it, thinking, 'I might just leave!' because we want to do things in our way, as we please, to cut down trees and hunt animals, to eat.—*But the Ethiopian government is concerned, because you know the wild animals, they are very few, there are not many, and they think the Uduk might kill all their wild animals!* [laughter]—Yes, they think we will finish them all off... Yes, we are people who cut trees, and they are afraid of this. And people think about it, and complain, because they want a little freedom [Arabic: *hurriya*]. They don't have any freedom.—*But where is this freedom? If a person packs up and goes home, where is this freedom? Gaajak will take their things, SPLA will attack them, and I don't know what! And in Chali, there is still no peace.*—There is no peace yet.—*And there is not much help for people there. But here, there is a lot of help. You have a little clinic, you have some children in school.*—Yes, what you say is true... but nevertheless...

—*This talk of freedom, everyone in the world wants their freedom, even I want my freedom too, but where is it, where?* [laughter] *People follow this idea, they want it, but where is it?*—Well, Wendy, the thing is, they keep following us, telling us, 'This is our land, our freedom', and we say, 'Yes, we know this is your land, your freedom, we are not going to do anything. If all this talk comes to an end, if the government can finally arrange a peace, we will quietly leave you to your freedom!' Isn't that right? We have patience....

We were cursed by the Dhamkin, in Itang, and in Nasir, over the land, and now we have more of the same here.... People order us about, 'Bring "the Uduk" here, send "the Uduk" there.' They used to attack people, and take the cooking pans. You wear nice clothes and people would take them from you. They would take the wild potatoes from you, and say, 'What d'you call these things of yours?'[6]

SPACE, LAYOUT, AUTHORITY, AND SOCIAL LIFE IN BONGA

Bonga was the first 'camp' the exiles had been in where no military authorities were in charge and where there was scarcely a visible military presence. Moreover, unlike the old Assosa and Itang camps in Ethiopia,

[6] Hergke Kinna, Bonga, 3 Nov. 1994.

international aid workers were more in evidence and permitted to reside there. The 'blocks' retained something of the character of former 'traditional' named village clusters, though reassorted in their spatial relationships, and within a couple of years football fields, performance spaces, and church sites sprouted up all over the site along with various offices and NGO compounds (Map 4). Committees and projects of various kinds proliferated, through the system of chiefs (block leaders), each with their own small committee connected with the food distribution system, dispute management, women's affairs, informal support for education, and so on. Several parts of Bonga developed informal classes for primary education, organized by volunteer teachers, and held under the trees—known as 'Undershade Schools' (Figure 16). Over the whole presided a new Bonga Refugee Committee with an elected chairman and larger powers than any previous such body. In the first few years, the Committee attempted to consolidate its position and control affairs, including the setting up of a refugee police post and

Figure 16. Classes under the trees, Bonga, 1994

prison, to the point where a certain amount of internal criticism developed. Bonga became a well-known place in the Gambela region, with a flourishing traders' market just outside its limits, a lot of official and other visitors, and a rather successful football team.

I was invited by the UNHCR to carry out a 'progress report' on the Bonga scheme in late 1994, and spent about two months there, able to settle in relatively easily with the groups of people from Pam Be I knew best.[7] My second visit was in 2000, when I accepted a short consultancy with the Dutch relief organization known as ZOA Refugee Care (ZOA is a Dutch acronym for 'South-East Asia' where its work originally started). This organization had already specialized in intermediate skills training, such as ironworking, beekeeping, basketry, and weaving, and at that time was expecting to implement an extended programme of community services.[8] Conditions both in Ethiopia, and in the Gambela region, were more tense than before, and no doubt the newly active presence of the SPLA on the other side of the border made for a greater wariness on the part of officials. The UNHCR had made a policy decision in 1998 to reduce the food rations for Bonga, in what we can only assume was a justifiable hope that people would decide to return home. In practice, it was still extremely dangerous for them to do so, and I have heard of the suffering which this decision directly caused.[9] People were straying off for miles and miles into the bush and forest—almost as far as Gambela's airport—looking for wild foods, and the mortality and morbidity rates were going up. There was much greater surveillance in 2000 than on my earlier visit. I was only given permission to visit at all after a series of difficult meetings between ZOA Refugee Care, myself, and the Ethiopian government refugee agency in the capital. Part of the problem was that the government agency had its own eyes on the new UN budget for community services; but part of the problem must surely also have been government knowledge of recent SPLA successes on the Sudan side of the border and sensitivity towards foreign observers in the area. I was eventually allowed to leave for Gambela, but only with a government minder. I behaved politely in

---

[7] James, 'The Bonga scheme: progress to 1994 and outlook for 1995'.

[8] James, 'Community services for Sudanese refugees'. ZOA report, 'Beekeeping', 1999.

[9] Jody De Blois, 'The promised land: refugee experiences of the Uduk in Ethiopia', Thesis Report for Cultural Anthropology, University of Utrecht, Eijsenga, Apr. 2001, 82–5.

the hope that he would get bored after a while, and indeed he excused himself after five days on the grounds of work awaiting him in Addis. It was quite clear that I had been expected to live within the ZOA compound, and I did so for the initial period. However, I was able to get informal permission to move out and settle with my old friends for a week and a half or so, before being actually called back to the compound because a senior official was visiting from Gambela. It was a distinctly more tense experience than my first stay. But it gave me insights into the increasing 'reality gap' between officials and refugees.

This gap had struck me on my earlier visit in 1994. One day there was a sudden explosion and a girl was injured, though not severely. The UNHCR and other aid personnel were alerted, and immediately thought of mines. They ran around organizing a mine-awareness campaign, informing refugee leaders about the dangers. I had myself earlier offered to show the Granada documentary *Orphans of Passage* which we had made in Karmi, if equipment could be found and powered somehow, and it was worry about mine-awareness that finally led to some officials carting in a video player (for the first time in Bonga) with an educational programme on mines which we watched before the film (Figure 17). Most of the refugees, however, already knew more about mines than the well-meaning aid workers did, and in any case they knew that Bonga was not heavily mined—it had never been a target inside the war zone, but a protected training camp during the Mengistu period. Although some mines had been laid when the SPLA left, mainly near their HQ on high ground, the refugees considered the explosion was probably a stray cartridge mislaid at that time.

This incident, which I witnessed, illustrated for me the gulf that can exist between one kind of knowledge and another in a place where the intensively administered processes and assumptions of international aid—the discourse of humanitarian assistance—come up against the relatively powerless populations they are, for the moment, assisting. The beneficiaries may be powerless, but their knowledge of their own predicament should not be underestimated.

In writing about the expansion of 'community services' in Bonga I was very conscious of crossed wires and non-communication between the patrons and the protected. In his foreword to the 1996 version of the manual *Community Services in UNHCR: An Introduction*, the Director of the Division of Programmes and Operational Support notes that it

Figure 17. Barbara Harper in the audience watching *Orphans of Passage*, Bonga, 1994

has become recognized that emergency response in refugee situations must go beyond material relief. Whether for large groups or for individual victims of persecution, the response 'must also address their social, human and emotional needs, and help to heal psychological wounds'. The manual advocates an approach which helps people to help themselves and to help others in need, reaching and giving priority to those who need it most. Community services activities are said to rest on certain fundamental principles about human beings, which include the 'dignity and worth of individual human beings', and the ultimate goal of aiding self-help. In July 2000 a mission from the UNHCR Regional Office in Nairobi, led by the senior community services officer, visited the four refugee schemes in western Ethiopia which had been established afresh since 1993, including Bonga.[10] Their report emphasized the need to promote further participation by the community, and particularly women, in the various efforts and projects of the agencies designed to improve their lives and their long-term welfare. Families broken up by displacement were to be monitored; the institution of marriage supported; unaccompanied minors to be given support; links with other camps and across borders traced. Sports, recreation, and cultural activities were to be extended as far as possible to girls' and women's participation; group projects for income generation favoured over individual ones; environmental education given; and inter-agency collaboration and reporting mechanisms were to be improved. ZOA Refugee Care formulated a project proposal in early 2000 for an initial six-month pilot project. UNHCR was keen to have a relevant and usable data base relating to questions of assistance to the vulnerable, and ZOA emphasized the need for understanding the communities' own concepts of vulnerability and ways of supporting those in particular need. ZOA was also keen to consider how the community could be assisted now to develop support structures which would be relevant to the future repatriation phase. The working proposals offered in my report were intended to address these main questions, specifically for Bonga where I spent some weeks, and Sherkole for which I had only second-hand information (there were transport problems as it was the

---

[10] Marie Lobo, 'Community Services mission to the camps in western Ethiopia', 16–30 July 2000, Draft Executive Summary. UNHCR Regional Services Centre, Nairobi o/m in Ethiopia.

rainy season). Many of the problems perceived by the agencies in Bonga, it seemed to me, derived directly from the contradictions of working with a long-established refugee community, which is nevertheless not allowed to 'settle' but is still having to live basically off a 'care and maintenance' regime of assistance. The people are understandably trying to put down roots in their own way, but this clashes with official restrictions on the use of space and local land and forest.

On the basis of this general approach, I was able to formulate some specific working proposals for ZOA Refugee Care in the expectation that the Ethiopian government would eventually agree to the provision of funds to them by the UNHCR for the implementation of community services activities. I described the problems perceived by the agencies working in the scheme: dependency (as usual) by the refugees upon the indefinite provision of aid; over-use of the surrounding lands and forests, leading to erosion; lack of 'participation' in agency projects, especially by women; the high birth rate (I did even hear the reported comment 'they breed like rabbits'); and rising insecurity. I also described problems of the scheme as perceived by the community. They could not understand why they should be criticized for 'dependency'. They were refugees in the first place through no fault of their own, as they saw it, and they were still grateful to the UN and to the Ethiopian government for the basic security they had been given. They did not see themselves as sitting around waiting for hand-outs, but they did remember the initial expectations of 1992–3 that they would be given access to significant land around Bonga. The refugee community, like the agency community, was full of projects of many kinds. Some of these were admired by the agencies (such as the full use they had made of the domestic plots formally allocated). It is quite true that some of the refugee projects were strongly discouraged by the authorities as 'illegal', especially those affecting the immediate environment: the projects of seeking wood and other resources from the forest, of clearing fields and planting crops, and a modest amount of hunting and fishing. But they were seen as essential by the people, signalling their effort to be independent from, rather than dependent on, the agencies. Other refugee projects included the investment of time and emotional energy in church activities and to a lesser extent in 'traditional' crafts and arts such as music and song.

The basic problem from the refugees' point of view was that the agencies did not seem to recognize the realities of their situation on the ground. For example, there was a lack of attention by the authorities to the fact that their allocated plots were very small, that some households were never allocated plots at all from the beginning, and others had them confiscated, or diverted to other uses (including the setting up of agency compounds). While they understood the concern expressed by authorities over use of the forest and clearing of trees for outside cultivations, they did not feel they had been offered realistic alternatives. While officials especially in the Ethiopian government agency stressed dangers of deforestation, erosion, and a level of wildlife destruction which threatened the tourist potential of the Baro valley, the refugees found it difficult to understand why there should be constraints on raising a few crops, since the eastern side of Bonga had no existing local population. Nor was there much other productive work for men. The role of a man, in their view, was to stride out and work hard in the fields and the forest, to help support his wife and children, and his sister's children when necessary. Men sometimes said that if they were to sit around all day, just waiting for the next month's food distribution, doing nothing, they would get depressed and even 'die from all the worry' or lose their reason. The skills training offered by ZOA, and the educational programmes provided by Radda Barnen, SIM, and ARRA, were much appreciated. Income generating projects were a little hit and miss; it was not understood for example how fearful people were of falling into debt, especially debt to the various official bodies in Bonga. In my first book I explained just what a serious matter this was, and how at that time one should be strictly dependent only on matrilineal kin for help with all investment and debt. To be indebted to anyone else was almost like being part-owned by them, at its most extreme like being enslaved.[11] This point seemed still very pertinent; in Bonga, while people were willing to establish credit with shopkeepers, they were not very keen to borrow money from ARRA for growing and selling vegetables—something which ARRA tended to see as a lack of interest in 'participation'. Moreover, the refugees could not understand why local Anuak hired to work on various projects were paid, while the refugees were not—their labour was sometimes demanded on the basis

[11] James, *'Kwanim Pa*, 102–11.

of plain 'participation'. A good deal of argument circled around the right of refugees to 'incentives' rather than working for nothing on what they saw as projects of officialdom. Loans for small business activities were sometimes made to male household heads, who were expected to rope in their sons as assistants, but more often than not men would rope in their sisters' sons from the other side of Bonga—something squarely in line with the old ideas of a natural common interest and shared investment/debt with one's matrilineal kin. A man who shared profits from selling tomatoes with his own son would face criticism from his wife's people. There were several other particular problems I highlighted in my report, but the question of access to cultivable land and usable forest was by far the most fundamental.

The UNHCR and agencies were nevertheless concerned with 'vulnerable categories' and some wanted to get all the data on a computer, so that aid could be 'streamlined' and 'targeted' more effectively. In my report I tried to discuss *patterns* rather than *categories* of vulnerability, showing how these patterns were related to strengths of the community, such as the maternal family groupings (or matrilineal clans) which were the traditional unit for social reproduction, productivity, and a safety net for the weakest. However, I have tried before to explain matriliny to aid agencies without much success, and I am not at all sure how my contribution helped those officials anxious to bring in the computers. I did recommend that some efforts might be made to strengthen the marriage tie, by recognizing and registering new married households, for example, so that they could receive aid in their own right rather than borrowing all the time from the bride's and the groom's relatives. The most substantial recommendation I made concerned the setting up of a network of local Community Development Centres, below the level of the blocks. This network would work in close collaboration with the existing church groups and leaders of the new Women's Centre, to support the existing pattern of services provided by the various agencies and also to support the community's own strengths and initiatives in community life. At this local level there could be more effective collection of data, practical help for vulnerables, and a fostering of social and cultural activities throughout Bonga.

The personnel of most agencies I discussed these proposals with were sympathetic, and often very supportive of them. They appreciated that I had been 'speaking to the refugees', and indeed in their own language. But they rarely recognized the state of quasi-captivity in which the refugees felt themselves to be held. The political and military background, and even the details of the successive displacements the people had been through, were not subjects for discussion in relation to the ideals of the discourse about 'community services'. I was certainly surprised in 2000 to discover that some senior people in the aid agencies were innocent of all knowledge about the political situation, and did not know that the refugees' home area had been taken by the SPLA from the Sudan government nearly four years earlier. For the anthropologist or historian, there is a 'lack of fit' between the rosy language and reporting about human welfare as proclaimed by the humanitarian assistance industry and the life of refugees on the ground as real human beings. The refugees see very plainly, for example, the contradiction between talk of funds for cultural and musical events, psychological counselling, environmental education, etc., while they are increasingly constrained from helping themselves by planting crops in the 'empty' areas outside the cramped settlement and thus assisting their own dependants.

'The Uduk' happen to have acquired a sort of profile with the UN and the agencies, as a result of the 'bureaucratization' of their group identity. People on the ground, however, in a region like this with an extremely complex cultural and social history, are very aware of all those other minorities scattered this way and that without the same kind of 'recognition' as deserving targets of aid. I should acknowledge here the way that the Ethiopian agencies, and Ethiopian personnel of UNHCR, did have a series of smaller projects for internally displaced communities, such as for example the 'Opuo' group to the west of Gambela (the people I have called Shyita, i.e. Schuver's 'Gambiel'). And I have mentioned the inclusion of two 'Burun' communities (two different Koma groups) in Bonga in the late 1990s.

Since their settling in Ethiopia in 1992 and becoming accessible as a group of deserving poor, the Uduk have appeared variously on the radar screens of governments and international organizations. A number of academic papers, reports, and theses have also appeared.[12] The gap between

---

[12] De Blois, 'The promised land'; Sarah di Pasquale, 'A study of the Uduk church in Bonga, Ethiopia', SIM Independent Study Report, 1995; Ellen Vermeulen, 'Beyond emergency aid: possibilities of partial self-sufficiency among the Sudanese refugees in western Ethiopia', MA thesis in Development Studies, Catholic University of Nijmegen, 1998. Jan Gerrit Van Uffelen, 'Return after flight: exploring the decision making process of Sudanese war-displaced people by employing an extended version of the theory of reasoned action', Ph.D. thesis, Wageningen University, 2006.

the understandings of aid workers and locals has however remained large, and academic studies have only partly made the connections. In the setting of Bonga, by the year 2000 there was a cosy sense of purpose and rational planning within each of the aid compounds, and even in the exchanges and debates between them, international as their staff are. So there was also, though on a different wavelength, among the serried rows of small huts and stands of crops beside them, a shared and in an odd way similarly cosy sense of endeavour. In the Ethiopian official compound, you could catch this if you spoke Amharic; in Radda Barnen, Swedish; in UNHCR, English, and so forth; but in the serried ranks of huts you could really only catch it in *'twam pa*. Where the worlds of the agencies, and the refugees, meet up, there can be a real weirdness in the atmosphere of Bonga. The place looks well and flourishing, especially in the late rainy season when crops are ripening and small stalls are selling tomatoes and okra. It could be 'home'. But underneath there is no substance, there are no land rights. There is the strange role of Ethiopians and foreigners from all over the world, trying to teach the people how to make pots and baskets or tidy their fields, but crucially in different ways from those they were familiar with in the old homeland. There are odd notices around Bonga with the UN logo on, some with flow charts of various committee structures so precise they are fiction rather than a guide to reality; and others appearing to be advertisements, a large poster stating for example: 'Superior protection, Superior pleasure'—was this meant to be a joke, or a serious notice about the mandate of the UN, or a propaganda message for the birth control campaign? In terms of the latter, the experts certainly up to 2000 were speaking to a deaf audience. 'Why should they stop us having babies? So many of us have died, and these are our seeds.' One young volunteer from Japan who was supposed to be helping with family planning advice was totally ostracized—none of the refugees would even speak to her.

THE HUMANITARIAN INTERNATIONAL: BRIEF ENCOUNTERS, 1987–2006

Many of my quotations in this book are from conversations with Martha Nasim Ahmed. I first met her in 1965–6 when both of us were younger—she late teens, myself mid-twenties. She had been a star pupil of the mission school at Chali and had gone on to secondary school at Doleib Hill near Malakal. Like others of her generation, it became very difficult to continue any education after the escalation of the first civil war and the final deportation of foreign missionaries in the southern regions in 1963–4. Martha was back in Chali and helped keep the Christian group there going in a modest way for the next two decades or so until the place was overwhelmed by the second war. As evident from the conversations quoted in this book, she went through all the deprivations and difficulties of the long road and the temporary stops along the way. It was an unexpected delight then, in 2000, to hear of her meeting with Kofi Annan, Secretary General of the United Nations, and other world figures, at the Hilton Hotel in Addis Ababa. She had been up to Addis from Bonga twice before, initially escorting a party of young lyre players to join in the concerts there for International Refugee Day, 1995. Two years later she went as the women's representative from Bonga to a UNHCR meeting in Addis, and it was in that role that she was invited to International Women's Day, 1998 and introduced to Kofi Annan, who was very charming to her, saying 'Good Luck, Martha!' Speaking mainly in English, she told me about it.

Then in 1998, I was taken to the Hilton Hotel, with the other women. And there were so many people there, from UNDP, from UNICEF, people of the Development, from UNHCR, from UN. And I met someone whose name was written in the programme there, the Secretary General of the UN! I saw him!— *Did you actually greet him?*—Yes! 'I can see a young lady from Africa among you there, a sister of mine, and the only one from Sudan. She looks very short among you.' There were 170 of us, women from . . . Liberia, from Ghana, from all over Africa. And the President of Egypt, Hosni Mubarak, I saw him. And the President of Liberia [Ruth Sando Perry, briefly head of state in 1996] . . . she had been a refugee from war too and fled from her home. . . .

And we met the leader of Ethiopia, Meles Zenawi. He said he was glad to hear my voice, the one woman from Africa and the country of Sudan, from the black people there. He was pleased with what I said, that I was very glad for what the government of Ethiopia had done to protect us, and find us a place to live. We had been travelling on and on through the bush, and because of this I am now alive to meet him, as the Secretary General of the UN. . . .

He said, 'Good Luck' to each of the women from Fugnido, and Dimma, and myself from Bonga. He took pictures of me, and sent them to me. And he presented us with a cloth. I had never met a leader like this! It was a wonderful opportunity. I felt so small, like a little chicken fallen in the water, and all these women were so large! But they told me, 'Don't be afraid, let us get to know each other.'[13]

A brief encounter at the very top! This experience certainly helped Martha's confidence in pursuing women's issues in Bonga, and later working in Kurmuk for the Sudan-based local group, the Relief Organization of Fazoghli. From there, her career developed even further, and following the peace agreement of 2005, she was appointed as an Assemblywoman in the new Blue Nile State, based in Damazin.

Hers is a very positive story which builds on contacts with, and experience of, the various humanitarian and development agencies that have intermittently played a role in the story of the Uduk refugees. Less visible have been the gaps in support, the failures of information, and the actual abandonment of the people by institutions supposed to be helping them. These gaps in sustained contact, and loss of information, have usually happened when the people have moved, slowly and painfully, from one side of the Sudanese civil war to the other, or across the international frontier. International agencies almost always work on one side or the other of a war situation, or within the context of one nation-state or another. When displaced people cross between the spaces of support set up by the structures of international aid itself, they are on their own. People learn this hard fact through experience; just because 'the UN' helped you one side of the border, it will not immediately show up on the other. The one organization which has really maintained supportive contact with the people over the long term is the SIM. After the deportations, they were able to keep in touch, indirectly, with the church group in Chali through their long-term base in Khartoum and support of the HQ of the indigenous Sudan Interior Church there. After the destruction of Chali, from their base in Addis Ababa they were able to dispatch a representative to make contact with the people in the first camp near Assosa, and send down a few materials. After the flight from Assosa, they lost touch, and I believe it was my own report and letters to them from Nor Deng which helped re-establish indirect contact. In due course, on the Ethiopian side they were successful in applying for a permit to conduct educational work (but not evangelism) in Bonga. And by mid-2006, young SIM members were already active

---

[13] Martha Nasim Ahmed, Bonga, 30 Aug. 2000 (video).

on the Sudan side in the Kurmuk district, welcoming home the first repatriated people to Kurmuk and Chali. But this long-term contact with a foreign organization whose personnel actually know something about the people and their past is the exception.

Many individuals, of a wide range of nationalities—from all the continents—have done devoted work with this particular set of refugees in one place or another, but have moved on as their contracts and consultancies start and stop and start again elsewhere. Some are well remembered by the refugees, and one or two crop up in the conversations quoted in this book, such as the American Dale Skoric of the World Food Programme, and Makonnen Tesfaye, an Ethiopian UNHCR official who recognized the people when they returned to Itang, and helped them settle in Karmi and recover lost children from the Anuak villages (but was then suddenly called to work in Rwanda). Others were well liked and appreciated but have slipped into anonymity, as the refugees themselves probably have in turn. Beyond the individual discontinuities, though, is the serious problem of institutional discontinuity and the loss of memory even within single organizations across borders.[14] Reports are written but overtaken by new events which require new reports, while vast sheaves of old paperwork are rarely read and sometimes left to rot or be thrown out.[15] When messages arrive of a fresh wave of 'new arrivals' in a displaced centre, new surveys and registrations and measurements have to be taken. The people themselves become anonymized, and at the worst mere numbers, because this is the only basis on which funding can be obtained. But these head-counts by aid officials are as often as not efforts to catch up with events outside their control, to respond in a formulaic way to upsets caused in some cases by the will, and the deliberate projects, of the displaced and needy themselves.

It is understandable that the Uduk refugees have developed a healthy scepticism not only about the intentions and promises of governments but also about the role of the humanitarian agencies, including the UN

[14] See for example the clear analysis provided by Aimée Comrie, 'The politics of food aid in the Sudan–Ethiopian borderlands', in Andrzej Bolesta (ed.), *International Development and Assistance: Where Politics Meets Economy* (Warsaw: Leon Koźmiński Academy of Entrepreneurship and Management, 2004).

[15] A project by the Rift Valley Institute to place back records of the agencies online is under way in respect of the Sudan, and this promises to be most useful. See 'Sudan Open Archive', **www.sudanarchive.net**.

itself, over the last couple of decades. Right up to Sudanese independence in 1956, the only international institution to establish a relationship with them was the SIM, and its reappearance in Bonga, although it had its critics, was at least the reappearance of an old friend and genuinely welcomed. By the time of widespread food shortages in the Sudan in 1985–6, other organizations had started to make contact in the southern Blue Nile, for example World Vision, but this organization was soon expelled from the Sudan. The fragile and ephemeral nature of much international assistance has since been demonstrated to the Blue Nile displaced again and again. The evacuation to Assosa in 1987 was followed by a massive increase in the range of their encounters with what Alex de Waal has somewhat bitterly dubbed the 'Humanitarian International'. Many of their intensive efforts to assist at different points on the long treks from there have been mentioned in this and earlier chapters, along with a recognition of the limits upon their activities and fulfilling of their own goals. The politicization of aid activities and their intimate connection with the course of wars in 'emerging' regions has been lucidly analysed by Mark Duffield, with particular relevance to the case of the Sudan.[16] The situation on the eastern frontiers of the country as of late 2006 is that, finally, the plans for repatriation from Bonga and Sherkole, along with the other Sudanese refugee sites in Ethiopia, are beginning to materialize. There are limits to what can be done quickly here too; and still a worrying gap between the knowledge and expectations of the refugees on the one hand and the agencies on the other. The immense achievements, nevertheless, of the Ethiopian and international aid agencies in providing not only humanitarian assistance but also development and educational aid over fifteen years in Ethiopia, especially in Bonga, have not only been crucial in helping the 'survival' of the *'kwanim pa*, but led to very high expectations of the opportunities that will await them on their return home.

[16] Mark Duffield, *Global Governance and the New Wars: The Merging of Development and Security* (London: Zed Books, 2001).

9
Dance, Music, and Poetry

The gourd of old, how was it broken?
The gourd was broken by the *wuṯule*/

'Jaws so coarse and ugly, from crunching funeral goats!'
'Macha, just leave Bonya alone—They are the fiercest fighters!'
'You're so ugly from all this funeral feasting'!

What was the gourd broken for?
The gourd of old, how was it broken?
The gourd was broken by the *wuṯule*/ [1]

THE RESURGENCE OF DANCE

I suddenly heard of the revival of what I had assumed a 'mythical' dance, the *baraŋgu*/, in Bonga in 1994. I had never seen it before, and in fact was firmly told in the 1960s it was obsolete. It was quite a surprise, thirty years after my original fieldwork, to be called out to hear the music of this 'antique' form and see the dance. A key lyric is the one quoted above. This catchy song can be 'read' on three levels. It is a lament for death in general, evoking the old myth of the Moon Oil, once used to revive people after temporary death, until the gourd was dropped by the *wuṯule*/ lizard in a silly struggle, so that death, once died, became permanent.[2] It refers indirectly to a state of hostility between the people of Bigin in the Tombakh valley and those of Bellila (or Bonya) in the northerly Ahmar valley. This seems to have been entrenched for a long time. There is an old Bellila song 'Beef left boiling on the fire' which still makes the Bigin people feel insulted—you should take care

---

[1] William Danga Ledko, Bonga, 27 Nov. 1994.
[2] James, '*Kwanim Pa*, 74–5.

not to sing it in front of them, though it dates back several generations. And finally the lyric above incorporates a conversational exchange between Macha of Bigin village, who is warned by his own people against fighting Bellila but replies by ridiculing their over-developed jaws from gorging too much funeral meat, that is to say, being afraid of losing more people in battle. I found to my initial surprise that this and other special *barangu/* songs were in circulation in Bonga, songs I had never heard, though I knew the mythical stories associated with them.

The very name of the dance was familiar too. The story of the *barangu/* evoked the beginning of time. Everybody came; the giraffe high-stepping *tuku, tuku, tuku,* the elephant calumphing, the tortoise waddling, etc.; this happened, and that happened, people took sides, fire and language appeared with the help of the Dog, human beings began to hunt the other animals, and permanent death displaced the older cycle of a return to life, made possible by the Moon Oil.[3] There had been plenty of dance forms in vogue during the 1960s, but while they told these stories people said that the *barangu/* dance itself was no longer practised, except by one very remote group, from Pan Gayo to the north-west of Bellila.

William Danga, who had been one of my staunch assistants from the original fieldwork and knew my interests, was the person who alerted me in 1994 to the revival of the *barangu/*, and roused the relevant musicians. They got out the new gourd flutes they were fashioning, shaping the mouths with sharp knives and tuning them by soaking and partially filling them with water (Figures 18a, 18b). When the band got going, a crowd spontaneously started the hopping, skipping pattern of steps, whirling around the musicians and singing snatches of song. Those who resurrected the *barangu/* did indeed come from 'faraway' Pan Gayo, but here were huddled up in the settlement with everyone else and there was general satisfaction at the chance to join in. Young and old were also reminded, through song, of the ancient stories of

---

[3] James, *The Listening Ebony,* 31–41. It is worth noting here the antiquity of the stories about the life-giving properties of the monthly cycle and the Moon Oil stories across Africa; see, for example, Robin Dunbar, Chris Knight, and Camilla Power (eds.), *The Evolution of Culture* (Edinburgh: Edinburgh University Press, 1999). The following chapters are of special relevance: Chris Knight, 'Sex and language as pretend play'; Camilla Power, '"Beauty magic": the origins of art'; and Ian Watts, 'The origin of symbolic culture'.

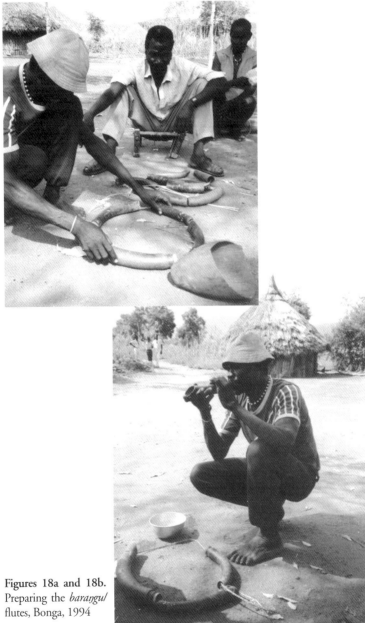

Figures 18a and 18b.
Preparing the *baraŋgul*
flutes, Bonga, 1994

fighting and death that went with the dance music. While death had become a more manageable matter since the settlement in Bonga, it had been a raw and appalling reality over the previous few years and on a scale, and in a number of manners, never before known, or even conceivable. There is a striking resonance between current experience and these old stories of the beginnings of death, and the lost hope of reappearance afterwards. But to *play such music,* and to *dance along* with others in its rhythms, is even more an evocation, a re-creation of a sensed link with a particular, and shared, past. This was scarcely appreciated by the few international personnel who noticed the amount of dancing in Bonga. One comment I heard from a UN protection officer who used to visit Bonga was 'Dancing? *Dancing?* But they are refugees; they should be working, or doing something useful for themselves.'

Besides the *baraŋgu/,* I already knew of a considerable repertoire of anticlockwise circling dances, frequently performed in the 1960s. These included the *athele/* (with beaten logs and bamboo flutes), the *bolshok* (flutes only), and the great ceremonial dance of the diviners, the *ce ŋari/,* around an ensemble of beaten antelope horns. There is some evidence that the choreography of the great moving circle was once widely established in the Blue Nile Borderlands generally (see Figure 3 on p.17, the Hill Burun band photographed in 1930). Its persistence today is, however, more than simply a leftover from the past. The circular form has a robust and lasting quality, which must be linked to the way in which it defines a special, inward space of its own, a centre to which participants orient themselves and through which they relate to each other. It is a self-referential pattern of movement, and those who take part turn their backs, literally and perhaps symbolically, on outsiders and mere spectators.

A strong characteristic of the vernacular musical style is the way that it makes use of percussive rhythms produced through ensembles of players. It is also very noticeable that the everyday working sounds of the village have a percussive quality. For example, a woman will prepare the surface of a (typically granitic) grinding stone slab by chipping at it repeatedly with a sharp stone, to produce a roughened, pocked surface, on which the grain can be effectively ground with the smooth oval hand grinder (typically basaltic). The sound carries far, a kind of resonant *tock, tock, tock* (Figure 10). Often two women will help at the task, chipping in a fast alternating rhythm on the same grinding slab, *tock-tick-tock-tick-tock-tick*. The alternative method of dealing with grain is to pound with a heavy pestle in a wooden mortar, a technique more characteristic of the neighbouring peoples who live in the clay plains but adopted easily by the Uduk in the refugee camps where there may be no stone. This too produces a resonant beat, and the muscular effort is made much easier if two women are working side by side together, either pounding in turns in the same mortar, or in separate ones, when they always tend to calibrate their movements either in unison or alternation. Threshing the grain with a wooden paddle on a smoothed hard clay surface, and winnowing it by throwing it up from a wide basket, also have their distinctive rhythms. And grinding itself produces a satisfying 'washboard' effect, especially when a couple of women are working side by side. Young children learn to join in these working rhythms early, and to help make what in effect is an ensemble of sound. Across the village, especially at harvest time, there is a rich 'soundscape' of echo and counter-echo, as women within hearing distance of each other seem to contribute consciously to the overall 'musical' effect.

Young women, and quite small girls, also play with percussion for fun. In the early rainy season, it is possible to make a set of firm holes in the newly damp ground, and tune each one up by adjusting its depth and width, and pouring in a little water if required. The Uduk style is to make six such holes in a row, though I have seen and heard the same music in a Gumuz village in Ethiopia where five holes are made, a square of four with one in the middle. Girls play this 'instrument' by slapping the holes with the palms of the hands, producing a light, bubbly music called *pumbul/*. Very often, other little girls will gather round and dance. After a few days, it rains again, the ground is turned to mud, and the instrument disappears. Another instrument played by women and girls consists of a bow, with a single string drawn across twice. It is played essentially for rhythm rather than melody, though pitch is altered by moving the thumb on the lower string and the chin on the upper. The sound of this *dumbale/* music also draws a little group of dancers, as do some of the tunes and songs of the men's lyre instrument. Especially when the latter are playing fun songs from the dance ground, the gathering crowd can sometimes add to the percussive effect by slapping their feet or sandals on the ground.

The major dance forms of the Uduk village are on a larger scale but consonant with these informal kinds of percussion music. The players themselves are adult men but all join in the whirling, encircling dance. There were several genres current in the 1960s. Most conspicuous was the *athele/*, an ensemble of eleven men, each playing a short bamboo flute in the left hand while beating a specially curved log, held between the legs, with a stick held in the right. Each flute had one note; each log had one resonant, drum-like pitch when struck, and the musical effect depended upon the collaborative rhythm of the whole. The set of flutes formed two five-note octaves, thought of as a matriline, the deepest one being the grandmother of the rest. Villages would take it in turns to hold the dance, each tending to start after the beginning of a new moon, playing one night and resting the next for several days. The sound of the evening *athele/* band would spread several miles across the moonlit, evening air, and people old and young would flock to it.

Another variant on the theme was the *bolshok,* said to have been learned from the neighbouring Bertha. The *bolshok* flutes were longer, also made of bamboo, and the accompanying percussion consisted just of short sticks beaten by a leader of the group. The music was more delicate and variable than the *athele/*, the musicians suddenly dashing around the village from place to place, seeming to escape the dancers who had to rush after them.

The dances above could be said to have been quite 'secular', though libations were usually made over the instruments before a dance series opened. However, in the past there were special ceremonial celebrations and dancing after the killing of large animals, such as the elephant or leopard (I only heard about this among the Uduk, but I have witnessed a two-week leopard celebration among the Gumuz in Ethiopia). But one of the most spectacular events I witnessed several times in the 1960s was a grand ceremonial dance that formed part of the initiation rituals of the diviners. The instruments were horns of the kudu antelope, of which any number could be brought in. They were not blown for the dance, although the diviners did blow them as signals on some occasions—they were beaten, with soft short sticks of light wood, again by an ensemble of diviner-players. There seemed to be two main 'notes'—some horns gave the lower, and others the higher, resonance. Special songs were sung, usually on the pattern of a lead singer and choral response. Some thousands might gather for the *ce ŋari/*, the horn dance of the diviners, which could last up to three days. Unlike the regular dance events, the diviners' dance went on in the daytime, in the full sun. This occasion seemed to have a well-ordered, even military air, by comparison with the regular dance. Instructions were given, special places assigned to categories of people. Groups of young men dressed in feathers and body-belts of leather would advance, feigning attack, and leap and jump together on the outskirts of the main circle, evoking parties of fighters. This whole style of ceremony and dancing was said to have been learned from the Jum Jum to the north, along with the rest of the diviners' activities.[4]

Within the range of percussion styles, there was flexibility for innovation and one instrument would sometimes 'imitate' another. I noticed a vivid example one day when girls who had tuned up a couple of sets of holes in the damp ground for the *pumbulu/* asked me if I would like to hear them play 'the horns of the diviners'. They played this time in unison, catching the effect of the massed beating of the horns in quite an eerie and evocative way. I have also heard people imitating this rather special sound with their voices.

Not only did the pervasive styles of percussion-based music play off each other, and I believe also in a distinctive way interact aesthetically with the daily soundscape and bodily working rhythms of the village, but the vocal forms of song and chanting sometimes echoed the sounds of the natural landscape too. The shrill cries and whoops of women at the dance were evocative of various birds. And very specifically, people used to say that they learned their funeral chanting, the wailing for death which was never very far from one's hearing, either close by or even far away, from the frogs. In the early rainy season, the frogs appearing from the newly flowing streams produce a striking chorus of their own, high, middling, and low croaks joining and leaving the flow of sound, combining into a sustained overall effect which could almost have been planned— to match the way that men and women, young and old, enter the funeral village with a wail and the funeral hut with a cry, starting high and falling in steps to join the collective rhythm of the chant. Movements of the animals, too, provide suggestive models for dance steps and styles. The 'frog-dance' I noticed was very popular among small boys in Bonga. Some songs are light and playful, attracting a foot-tapping audience who can add impromptu percussion by slapping their sandals on the earth. An example sung with a swinging melody and hopping rhythm 'just as it always has been' is the lyric about Tortoise being

---

[4] See illustrations in *The Listening Ebony*, frontispiece and 10 (b), after 188.

refused a drinking cup by the frogs (in this fairly free translation, English grammar obliges me to give the Tortoise a gender).

> Tortoise was lap, lap, lapping at the puddles!
> And why were the frogs croaking so?
> Off she waddled
> Denied a cup by the frogs!
> The poor thing wept as she went[5]

It goes without saying that the 'traditional' musical arts depended also on the forest and the animals to provide the raw materials for all their instruments: wood, bamboo, calabash, antelope horns, twisted grass for the strings of the *dumbale/*, animal sinews for the lyre strings, leather for the soundbox. The question arises on several levels: what has happened to their music-making as the people have endured the treks and deprivations of the long road? And closely linked with instrumental music too, the life of the dance-ground and the songs that it used to generate? Even the solo songs of the lyre-player, are they still sung, and if so, have their lyrics changed? And while church participation, or at least lip-service to Christianity, has spread to become almost general in the refugee population, is there any sign of a new aesthetic creativity livening up the old mission hymns and forms of worship?

In this chapter and the next, I take up the themes of music, dance, the arts of language, bodily discipline and expression, and religious practices, as the heart of what we could regard as shared emotional life, memory, and anticipation. Earlier chapters have drawn on a large body of recorded commentary, bringing many spoken words to the printed page. But what gives words their magic flows from the way they are combined with styles of musical or bodily performance, along with all the games and arts of ordinary life which go into the making of a shared world.

LANGUAGE GAMES

'Ancient' as *'twam pa*, the 'language of the home' might well be in one sense, up to the present it is showing resilience and capacity for creativity. A striking illustration of this is the way that old styles of storytelling about

---

[5] Sung to the lyre by Hosiah Dangaye Chalma, Bonga, 18 Aug. 2000.

hunting, and adventures in the forest, now lend themselves to descriptions of war, ambushes on the road, dodging spears, and even running from aeroplanes. Examples have been quoted in earlier chapters, but here is a brief reminder; it is Chuna, recalling in vivid and entertaining tones, and re-enacting in energetic body-gesture, some seven years after the event, scenes from the 'Battle of Karmi'.

The fight started there at the river and the village of Waskan. The stone came past us, *dayeee*! Waskan's had been attacked! 'Someone has died!' [*sic*: this was not actually the case]. The Dhamkin were on the other side in the open space near the feeding centre. I was running over to Waskan's place, *kuca kuca kuca*, and I heard them crying 'Gaajak, Gaajak!'

The Dhamkin thought the Uduk had no fight in them. They were surprised, 'Where have they got this anger from?' Uduk sent their throwing sticks, *jip, jip!* '*Eeeugh, ow-eeugh!*'—they groaned and ran away, back to hide in their huts. . . . When they saw the Uduk didn't follow, they came back, people hit them with sticks, and threw spears, and some ran off to die with spears in their body. When I was running from our place there I didn't have my throwing stick or spear, so I took a tent pole, I found some Dhamkin lying on the ground, I was about to hit them! But somebody said, 'No, no, no, don't hit them!' This was near the feeding centre, by the road, and the Dhamkin were coming back. . . . They used branches of trees as rough spears . . . but we dodged! Our throwing sticks flew back, *wip, chuu!*[6]

The vernacular tongue is relished in other ways too. One evening around William Danga's fire, I noticed that everyone was joking and teasing each other in a way which used to be reserved for specific relatives, such as cross-cousins, and termed *sor*. Here they were playing with language, and inventing insults, just for the sake of fun and wit. There is also a lot of *salkin* talk, a kind of jokey, informal banter, a wink and a nod. I heard some ragging about people with 'big ears'—why don't we collect them up and take them to the riverbank? Tana can be the chief of the big ears; another one will be his 'bodyguard'; people with small ears will be kept away and the big ears will refuse them water. They will have to go to the small river Bonga.

William explained there was something else becoming very popular, called '*twan ṯaar*, a sort of veiled joking, which can only be understood by the person you are addressing. People speak *ki ṯaar*, which I think we

---

6 Chuna Hada, Bonga, 2 Sept. 2000 (video).

could put in English as a sort of 'sideways' or 'cross-wise' language; suggesting movement in an opposite way, in a different direction. To sleep *ki ṯaar* is to lie on one's back, flat, not comfortably as usual. '*Twan ṯaar* is complicated and witty, not simply speaking fast and eliding words, which is *bor 'twa e mis*, to lift up one's speech. William explained that people were 'cutting' and changing the language, inventing all sorts of new things. Young people were doing this at the dance ground, he commented pointedly, while the church people stick to one meaning.

William, what was it you said about the youngsters changing the language?—Yes, the youngsters, the way they speak, a person will not be to able to recognize it easily or know what it means.—*Hm?*—Because what they speak, it sounds like '*twam pa*, but they keep changing it a lot. They change it, shorten a few words and speak fast, just on the surface. But if you don't listen carefully you will not catch them, they can only be heard by people who know this way of speaking very well and can say, the real meaning [lit. root] which they have changed is like this, and this. If you're part of their own actual village you'll be able to understand the meaning they've changed, but someone from outside, they won't know, thinking that's not how you should speak. It's only us who know this new language they've made up, because they are living among us.

   —*When did they start changing language like this . . .*—These days, there's plenty of this going on. Even the older people are doing it too! Right now you can hear them doing it here in Bonga. Don't you know that expression */e meren?*—Huh? '*IE meren?*' *Meaning?*—*Ata mere e?* That is to say, 'What are you so surprised at?' *Ata ti mere le ba?* There are plenty of things they have invented, it's just a kind of teasing or joking [*gwo salkin*].—*Eh?*—'*Salkin* talk.' Salkin means [he goes into part English] is what is called joking, or it's like a person making fun [English] with language—*yes, joking*—yes, joking in a different way, how to speak good fun words. . . .

   That is the kind of new talk which they have invented here in Bonga, the new way of speaking, but this is not just done by children. Grown-ups do this here. They're inventing all kinds of new ways of talking, a whole lot of them, from the dancing they do there.—*It's from the dance place?*—Mm. They're dancing in new ways, and inventing a lot of new songs, and inventing new ornaments and fashions, all from the time of Karmi, *kwany kwany kwany!* It's all just new styles, invented in this place. That's what they are doing.—*Another day I'll go and see them!*—You can go and see, see them, and the dancing. Because the dancing is now different, it is completely new.—*Really? I'd like to see it.*—It's on tomorrow!—*Which village?*—It's in Borfa today, they will dance through the night there.[7]

---

[7] William Danga, Bonga, 7 Nov. 1994.

And many new songs were emerging with the music being improvised on battered old plastic cans at the dance ground. William and I discussed how this contrasted with the local church usage, where the meanings of words, and the songs, do not change—'They follow just one meaning.' I asked whether it was not true that many Christians could be found at the dance ground these days. As his audience collapsed into giggles, he exclaimed: '*Ayee!* Many of them have got lost! They've fallen by the wayside, a lot of them, escaping excitedly like locusts! Yes, they're flocking off like locusts to the dance!'

Typical dance songs are teasing and flirtatious (though some stronger variants I heard in the later years in Bonga would be more accurately described as being about sex and drink—the Ethiopian 'honey-wine' being by this time available in the market which had grown up nearby, along with disco tapes and karate videos). A very popular one goes as follows, in which we can hear at least two voices. The suitor tried to approach a woman separated for at least a year from her husband, but was scared off by the family dog; he teases her on her preference for fashionable white socks just like the Majangir people of the nearby forests, and she counters by asking why he looks at her so; he asks what her real feelings are (in English idiom, 'heart', but in the Uduk, 'Liver'), and in an aside to others, wonders why she is still waiting for her long-gone husband. In the sixth line as quoted here (though in performance, the lines weave in and out of each other), the phrase *ata mer /e* comes in, a phrase mentioned by Danga as being part of the new 'cross-wise' talk, in 'Why d'you question me with your eyes...?'

> I was nearly bitten by the dog last night!
> She spent a whole year with her mother
> Oh me, oh my!
> The free-woman in her white socks,
> Just like an Ujang!
> *Why d'you question me with your eyes as though you know my name?*
> What are your feelings in your Liver?
> Why does that lady to go on waiting for her husband?[8]

As I have described in Part II, the lowest point for civilians on the long trek from home was at the muddy, flooded camp of Nor Deng on the south bank of the Sobat river, and the severe hunger which followed

---

[8] Recording of singing to the jerry-can dance, Bonga, 25 Nov. 1994 (video).

even when the people were permitted to cross back to the Nasir side. There was no dancing at this time, and very little music-making. Materials for the instruments were simply not available, quite apart from the fact that people were weak and many were dying. However, I heard several popular songs from a group of lads, led by Rima Puna Basha, playing their small lyres to the beat of the plastic jerry-cans. The particular style in fact was well known in the Sudan as 'Kaloshi', popularized by a number of singers from the Blue Nile. The songs are often in Arabic, but also in local languages such as Bertha, and typically include reference to places and events in the southern Blue Nile. I am indebted to Akira Okazaki for background on this style, played on the lyre, accompanied by drums (where available) and sometimes women's voices, which he has heard recently in Damazin and among the Ingessana (Gamk) people. It was circulating in early 2006 in the form of cassettes, both 'home-made' copies and more professional formats, in markets in the region. Okazaki mentioned that he was 'very impressed by Kaloshi; danceable for anyone, sounding familiar to the people of southern Blue Nile, a mixture of "Arabic" and "African" elements, and, above all, powerful rhythmic drive and something of a very local and confident way of vocalization'.[9] A typical lyric I recorded in Nor Deng, sung in Arabic (and with no particular message from exile), went as follows:

> Amuna, don't cry
> Amuna, we could be happy living on our own
> My true love
> You are the most beautiful
> Before all others
> Alone in heaven
> You are like a lovely bird
> You and I could survive in the world
> You are so hard to win[10]

Another was an Arabic-language lament for the home country (*al watan*), originally composed by a singer from Roseires:

> Here we are in Ethiopia,
> While Roseires is our homeland.

[9] Akira Okazaki, p.c.
[10] Rima Puna Basha and group, Nor Deng, 7 Oct. 1991.

We must return one day to the Sudan,
Let's return to the eastern Sudan!
Roseires is our homeland,
We must move back to the Sudan
Oh when shall we return to the homeland?
We must go back to the Sudan,
Oh let's return to the eastern villages[11]

The group in Nor Deng were switching comfortably between languages.
They even sang in Bertha, as well as Arabic and Uduk. The following
example, composed and sung by Thoha Puna Basha, is in Arabic; but in
the middle are spoken interjections in Uduk, addressed to his friends
and relatives in Khartoum, to whom I was to send a copy of the tape
(compare his lyric in Uduk, which introduces Chapter 11 below):

Wherever I go, my lyre goes too;
I stayed awhile in Ass-so-sa

[Assosa's a little town in Ethiopia,
That's where I used to live!
But we're now singing this for you in Nasir]

I lived awhile in Ass-so-sa
Do come and visit us!
Wherever I go, my lyre goes too
I stayed awhile in Ass-so-sa[12]

Inventive ways of incorporating sounds, and moving between languages, are also found in the numerous lively children's songs which can
be heard in even the most depressing of camps for the displaced. Some
of these are quoted as epigraphs to Chapters 5 and 6 above, where little
children can be heard imitating the drone of Antonov bombers (*diling
diling*), mocking military terms in Jum Jum (the 'Small Arms' Battalion)
or the flirtatious greetings of Nuer soldiers in Uduk pronunciation
(*Nyama, Malei!* And the response, *Mal Magwar!*).

I was told that *athele/* music and dancing proper had resumed soon
after the people first settled in the Assosa camp. Wood for the logs, and
bamboo for the flutes of both *athele/* and *bolshok*, were available there,
though not in Itang or Nor Deng. By the time the people reached the
transit camp of Karmi, variations of the old circular dancing reappeared.

---

[11] Ibid.   [12] Thoha Puna Basha and group, Nor Deng, 7 Oct. 1991.

The spatial and musical *form* of the *athele/* resumed, without the forest-made instruments. Old plastic jerry-cans and other debris of the international aid scene were appropriated on a large scale, and those few men who still had or had recently made lyres were roped in to help out with the songs and music. This 'baga' (jerry-can) dance continued on an enlarged and enthusiastic scale in Bonga, but the *bolshok* soon appeared there too, with the proper flutes (from nearby bamboo in the hills). Sukke Dhirmath also played her *dumbale/* instrument for me, something she took up in Bonga after many years without playing (Figure 19). It goes without saying that there were no antelope horns, as a very strict watch was kept by the authorities on hunting activities by the refugees. Nor were there visible activities by the diviners, though we set up an opportunity for them to talk and display their songs and rituals when we were making the Disappearing World documentary film at Karmi.

Later on, however, the old musical tradition was being revived in a substantial way. In Bonga itself, by the year 2000 the 'real' *athele/* logs were being prepared for use at an early date, and I was told that in the new refugee camp at Sherkole there was already real *athele/* dancing. Beyond that, and even more surprising, a recent visitor to Sherkole had seen the *ce ŋari/*, the diviners' horn dance. In reminiscing over the old days, William even came up with information about the ancient *baraŋgu/* which was new to me: that there had indeed been *baraŋgu/* musicians around in the 1960s, for example Jumo used to make the *baraŋgu/* gourd-flutes in Beni Mayu, but there was no one he could pass the 'mother-horn' on to when he died. Given all the flux and flow of 'performance' in the conditions of exile, here was a new interest in firming up the oral history of the *baraŋgu/*; so what else might be said about 'continuity'?

THE CHRISTIAN/'PAGAN' DIVIDE

In his memoir of missionary work in Africa,[13] which included several years based intermittently at Chali with his wife and family after their first arrival in 1939, Malcolm Forsberg emphasized the pull of the dance, which Christians were supposed to resist. He refers mainly to

---

[13] Malcolm Forsberg, *Land Beyond the Nile* (New York: Harper, 1958).

Figure 19. Sukke Dhirmath playing the *dumbalel*, Bonga, 2000

the *athelel*, the ensemble of flutes and beaten logs (the Uduk have never to my or their knowledge used drums, which are commonly seen in the Blue Nile Borderlands as the prerogative of chiefs and kings). 'Any Uduk could pick up a dance block, put it between his legs, pound out a few hot licks, and draw a crowd. The people were often too tired to work or talk to us, but they were seldom too tired to dance. . . . A dance which followed a beer drink lasted until dawn, or sometimes for forty-eight hours, and was lewd and sensuous . . . even women with babies saddled to their backs danced, the baby rocking to the harsh drumbeat [*sic*]. . . . The dance was especially suited to the restless impulses of the young people, who danced wildly as the drums [*sic*] waxed hotter at midnight and beyond. The older people would go home and the young ones would pair off and disappear in the bush.' Forsberg comments, 'We did not want our gospel to be negative, but we were dealing with matters beyond our control'; he told the people, 'God doesn't want us to behave like animals.' The Forsbergs were horrified to find their own infant son imitating the dance beat and the flute playing. 'We were suddenly brought face to face with the results of our living in Africa. The dance, like the snakes around us, had turned up inside our house.' The little boy would join with playmates in the village imitating the dance band, until the 'witchdoctors' called a halt to the dancing when locusts came during the rains. The Forsbergs kept closer supervision over their son, and prayed more earnestly for the 'coming into being of a strong Christian community at Chali'.[14]

Among the Uduk themselves, the dance as such came to signify the old ways; to 'return to dancing' was shorthand for having left the discipline of the church. Given the strictness of the latter, it is scarcely surprising that the dance remained as vigorous as ever, even gaining a kind of extra vitality and symbolic resonance because it was so frowned on by missionaries and the church leadership. With the departure (by government order) of the missionaries in early 1964, church discipline fell away somewhat, and the dance scene was certainly a lively one during my visits from late 1965 to mid-1969. These dance evenings of course provided opportunities for affairs and elopements and quarrels, but they were confined to networks of people who shared all kinds of other activities, including working activities based on neighbourly

---

[14] Forsberg, *Land Beyond the Nile*; all quotations from 152–3.

and kinship links, and people regarded them as basically innocent fun. There were virtually never strangers present, and I do not think that these dances of the 1960s were threatening or dangerous to girls or women (in the way that I believe began to happen in the 1990s, in the much larger dances of the refugee camps).

I was able to revisit Chali and the outlying villages briefly in 1983. The dominant change seemed to be that the younger generation had switched over to Christianity, and there were a lot of small bush churches operating. Another feature that struck me was the popularity of gymnastic exercises among the young men. There were also parades and marches and whistle-blowing. I suddenly realized the youths were imitating the training they had seen at the military garrison now in Chali. Was there dancing? If so, it was not very conspicuous; the fashion that year at any rate was for Christian activities such as football and hymn singing, as I had seen in 1967 when there was a brief season's Christian revival.[15]

Elsewhere in the Sudan, Gerd Baumann has shown how the people of Jebel Miri, in the Nuba Hills, were living in the 1970s with an even more profound pluralism, a kind of double morphology in their performance of national and local styles of dance and music.[16] A large proportion of the men were labour migrants in the towns, many were Muslims, spoke good Arabic, and were familiar with the music and dance of the northern Sudan. Even back at home in Miri, although the mother tongue of Miri was still vital, many women also knew some Arabic, and the young girls would play and sing Arabic romantic love songs (*daluka*) they had learned in some local market place or from the radio. But when the men returned home on leave, they joined in the local harvest songs and music, and when the young girls married, they had to forsake the Arabic love songs for Miri grindstone songs and other 'autochthonous' forms. Baumann argued that a balance had been reached in Miri between local and national 'identity' and that musical practices reflected this balance. While this was no doubt an apt way of seeing the plurality of Miri's social life at that time, Miri has since been destroyed by civil war, which is a reminder that any state of 'balance', even an 'internally' achieved one such as that of Miri in the mid-1970s, must be fragile.

[15] James, *The Listening Ebony*, ch. 4.
[16] Gerd Baumann, *National Integration and Local Integrity: The Miri of the Nuba Mountains in the Sudan* (Oxford: Clarendon Press, 1987).

CURRENT TENSIONS: AN INTERNAL POLARITY

Many years ago I wrote of the strange gulf that seemed deliberately maintained on both sides between the practitioners of 'village' musical styles—rhythmically complex, polyphonic, shifting, and innovative—and the strait-laced formality of the hymns taught by the missionaries at Chali.[17] Most vernacular music and song was banned by the SIM, it is true, as being part of the world of dancing and drinking, and moreover associated with the rituals of village life they dismissed as evil. In the course of the flight from home and years of exile, and their evident embrace of Christian practices, the people have stuck ever more tenaciously to the stately rhythm of the mission hymns in their various temporary camps, chanting them in strict unison under the trees. Perhaps they were afraid of straying too far from the discipline of the church, as did in fact happen at least once in Itang (as described in the next chapter).

For some of the church people I talked to about it in Bonga, however, the *baraŋgul* was no longer banished as immoral and devilish, but had now become reframed as 'Uduk custom and tradition'. The idea that such a thing as 'Uduk heritage' existed had recently been stimulated by a trip up to Addis Ababa for refugee musicians and dancers, organized by the UNHCR. The occasion was World Refugee Day, 1994, and performances (mainly by Somali, Nuer, and other well-known groups) were not only staged for a distinguished audience in the capital city but also broadcast on Ethiopian television. I know that Uduk lyre players were present, and performed. I am not sure about any flute players—I think probably not, because you need eleven men to form the ensemble, not to mention the circling dancers singing round them. On previous occasions, when Ethiopian kings and chiefs brought musicians up to their highland courts to entertain their guests, they certainly had to abandon their circle and face the audience squarely (even before the days of the television camera). When bands of antelope horn players were co-opted into the armies of the old Sudan, they had to march, in

---

[17] Wendy James, 'Uduk faith in a five-note scale: mission music and the spread of the Gospel', in W. James and D. H. Johnson (eds.), *Vernacular Christianity: Essays in the Social Anthropology of Religion Presented to Godfrey Lienhardt* (Oxford: JASO, 1988).

line, forwards. The best examples of the instruments used by all these musicians co-opted by the powers that be are no doubt safely conserved as 'material culture' in one museum or another. It is interesting that the great formative circle of players-and-dancers survives socially in rather a different way: it survives in the refugee camps, *sans* classic instruments, making do with discarded bits of modernity (shades of the Caribbean steel band?), but recognizably itself. Against this background, the circular dance, however secularized and even vulgarized, represents some kind of claim to a space for the people to be themselves, to celebrate a self-referential centre of their own, and to turn their backs on spectators.

The circular dance was thus recreated in exile, most strikingly from a cultural point of view in the reappearance from the ancient past of the *baraŋgul*, classed even by the new missionaries as 'heritage and custom'. From a sociological point of view, it was most obviously recreated in the enlarged 'jerry-can' dance, still representing—but to all and sundry, rather than just the Christians, who today tended to join in—the pole of immorality and the slippery slope to Satan. The scale of these performances had changed—Bonga was a much more crowded place than people had been used to. The formalities of style had softened up; the crowd was much bigger and louder than it had ever been in the old village days (you could scarcely hear the instruments); dancing started in the daytime and beer was often available, sometimes actually for sale, and I think it fair to say that women were more exposed and vulnerable to unwanted advances than before. The old polarity between church and dance ground was marked again, but not as a matter of total separation—it had become an internal moral polarity. The community were by now as good as 100 per cent acknowledged Christians, and yet nearly everyone seemed to cross the line without qualms. This was one theme running through the documentary film I helped to make in Karmi. The dance ground was marked by a sort of flag pole, with fragments of cloth and paper attached—rather like the old English maypole, suppressed by the Puritans. This appeared to mark, as it were, the 'place of evil', and we learned from Christians in the film how fragile relations between men and women had become, how tempers could flare, and how it had been agreed that the dance should stop at sunset. When I was in Bonga in late 1994, one or two quite serious fights blew up at the dance, and eventually the Committee

(I think in conjunction with the representatives of the Gambela police) tried to set rules and regulations.

'ENCAPSULATED' CHRISTIAN SONGS

As against the free flow of new songs and music from the dance ground, and also as I shall show below from the flourishing men's tradition of muscular topical and political songs for the lyre, Christian songs and music have been carried forward in a static, almost fossilized or encapsulated form. The first edition of the Hymn Book in Uduk, published in 1963, included ninety-two hymns, and a second edition of 1982 added a further sixteen (prepared under missionary guidance in the USA, some of these distinctly on the wordy side). This corpus has remained the almost exclusive mainstay of Christian worship ever since the heyday of the Chali mission in the 1950s. The actual tunes have been sung regularly by all the small church groups right through the succession of refugee camps that marked the history of the last generation, and indeed sung at resting points by the wayside as they trekked back and forth on the long road. My tape recordings of these hymns as sung over the decades suggest a hardening of the style, a rigid holding to the notes of the five-note scale in unison, and an almost uncomfortable uniformity of voice. I was glad to learn, in Nor Deng, of 'new' Christian songs, but these turned out to be different from the improvisations of the home or the dance ground. They were extracts from the scriptures, and from my own brief recordings they were sung to a simple tune in unison rather like the existing hymns, quite unlike the polyphonic, multivocal, and catchy lyrics of the 'traditional' genres. The main composer of these new Christian songs was a blind singer, Jangka Wormai, who sadly had been fatally shot in the ambush as the people fled down from Assosa to the Yabus valley in 1990. I explained in *The Listening Ebony* how songs were thought to come from dreams,[18] and Jangka's case was no exception. Ruth Panjeka and some friends had sung phrases from Psalms 31 and 19 for me, and explained how these words had come to Jangka as he slept in the night, and were with him when he woke in the morning. 'God [Arumgimis] told him, because he

---

[18] James, *The Listening Ebony*, 77–83.

was blind, he would have the eyes of a chief, to understand things on earth.... God gave him this perception of underlying truths [*pemen*, lit. "root"], and gave him great ability, he was better than all of us in remembering the scriptures.'[19]

In the course of my visits in 1994 and in 2000 I had the chance to talk to Barbara Harper, then working with the SIM educational programmes in Bonga after having started her missionary career at Doro, in Meban country, in 1948, transferring to Chali 1954 and remaining there up to the deportation in 1964. She had followed in the steps of the formidable pioneers 'Mary and Betty'—Miss Mary Beam and Miss Elizabeth Cridland—and had kept in touch with them over the years.[20] I asked her about the music and song scene, and why the people were so rigid over allowing new hymns to be created. I mentioned that I had noticed the hymn singing had sounded even a little harsher than before, almost too regimented and disciplined, everyone starting and ending precisely on the same note and on time. It was not at all relaxed like their own songs at home. We talked about the way the people had indeed taken pieces of scripture and put them to existing mission-style tunes during the long trek, but Barbara thought they had now forgotten them. She had a note written by John Jangka on 15 March 1998, listing some of these.[21] Perhaps this was a kind of creativity more naturally emerging in the desperate context of the long road than in the relatively comfortable and settled circumstances of Bonga. I reminded her that she herself had once suggested they compose hymns themselves. She was quite clear that it had been the church elders themselves, from the start, who had resisted the idea of mixing Christianity with the 'traditional' village styles.

Well that was way, way back. I didn't have anything to do with working with the elders at that point. This was when Mary and Betty were there, or as far back as the Forsbergs, I don't know. But it was Betty and Mary who worked with the elders developing them [the hymns], and helping them learn to take responsibility for the church. But whenever they brought out an idea about creating their own songs, the elders told them there was no way they could use the Uduk music because it's associated with the, er, traditional religion.—*Come on Barbara! You*

[19] Ruth Panjeka, Nor Deng, 22 July 1991.
[20] *The Listening Ebony*, ch. 4, includes a brief history of the mission at Chali.
[21] The list included John 14: 15–16; Matthew 5: 11, 22: 39, 28: 20; James 4: 7; 2 Corinthians 5: 17; Ephaesians 5: 3; Acts 22: 21; Mark 13: 5–6; 1 Timothy 6: 6, 21; 2 Timothy 3: 1; Romans 12: 11, 23: 23.

mean 'witchcraft'!—Yes, OK, right [laughter].—*Even the music?*—Yes, the music was associated with it, they said. And the other thing is the immorality that went along with the dance. So that kind of music. . . . I used to talk to Mary and Betty about it, but they said the elders absolutely say 'No.' Because it seems to me that what reaches your heart is your own way of doing things, you know, your own style of music.[22]

And in recent years, when she had returned to work with educational programmes for the refugees in Bonga, and was in Kenya for a visit, Barbara Harper talked with an ethnomusicologist attached to the Summer Institute of Linguistics (SIL) there, who was interested in music and songs of the region. This lady suggested that Barbara should find out about all the different kinds of music that they have, and said the first step was to get the elders to agree.

She said you'll get nowhere unless the elders agree. So I went, and talked to the elders, I talked to Michael first, and Joshua, and they saw it. I talked about, like for instance when you bring in the grain and thresh it, then don't people sing? I said, 'Is that bad, is what they sing that bad?' No, that was perfectly all right. So I mentioned about the children singing around, 'Is that bad?' No. 'Couldn't we create some music with the kind of style they use?'—*Meshing in with the Christian?*—Yes, with Christian words and ideas. So they agreed that it wouldn't be bad, now. That it would be perfectly OK. And Michael made a stab at it, at writing a song, but it was very much like an American tune, or a European tune. It had a little bit that was like Uduk, you may have heard them singing it, about 'Cayin', *Cayin and Habil*, that is Cain and Abel?—*I don't think I have, no. How does it go?*—I've forgotten the tune, but they used to sing it all the time . . .[23]

Barbara had tried several ways of encouraging the people to create new hymns, as she was aware that the Meban people were good at this. She had even taken a Meban tune herself and adapted it to a new beat, so the Uduk wouldn't recognize it. Barbara, up to the present still engaged in checking translations of scripture into Uduk (in late 2006 working her way through the Book of Exodus from her home in Florida), is keen to encourage younger colleagues to persevere with the idea of encouraging musical innovation within the Christian life of the Uduk people. But the Protestant focus on *words* has always helped define Christianity for them, while the rhythm and melody of songs still reverberates too strongly with the old non-Christian ways.

---

[22] Barbara Harper, Bonga, 1 Sept. 2000.   [23] Ibid.

LYRE SONGS: POLITICS AND MEMORY

The five-stringed lyre is played solo by a quite a number of men. There is both a well-known corpus of 'old' historical songs and a burgeoning repertoire of 'new' and topical songs growing from the older forms, even in Arabic. A song I recorded in the 1960s looked back to the late nineteenth-century raiding from the Ethiopian border hills, naming and blaming the 'Bunyans' there, and appealing to 'MisMis' (Kaimakam Smyth Bey, a British officer; see the Historical Introduction) to redeem the country. Today's equivalent songs, in the same musical style, name and blame Sudanese leaders and soldiers, appealing to John Garang to give them freedom and redeem the country.

The lyre songs often contain a sad lament, a focus for nostalgic sentiment, but can also express political criticism, directly or through satire. They can carry accusations and insinuations about individuals or groups. I have mentioned the sensitivity of the Bigin people about the very old historical song 'Beef left boiling on the fire'. I have heard at least one song which I could not possibly reproduce here because it concerns a recent (if accidental) killing, where retribution might still take place. The songs circulate essentially among Uduk speakers themselves, and make as plain as anything else could the social world they share. Song cassettes from the refugee communities in Africa now circulate in the global diaspora, their sad words but catchy tunes enlivening the routine drive to work in American cities.

The Uduk language songs are usually a little indirect in their targets. But some of the plainest and most direct cries for a lost homeland, and the need for continuing struggle, are expressed in colloquial Arabic. These 'political' songs for the lyre are sung in strong repeated pleading phrases, quite different from the subtle allusions and lilting phrases of the Arabic love song (*daluka* or *kaloshi*) style already quoted. Several by Buha Dharas, for example, were in circulation in the United States, where I heard them recently. The first presents no difficulty in translation.

> The Upper Nile is soaked in blood
> The land of Kurmuk's soaked in blood
> Kurmuk mountain's soaked in blood
> We need a new beginning

> The land of Ulu is all blood
> Where shall we go?
> Where is our land?
> The land is soaked in blood

There is anger too at the way that political leaders seem to let people down. The next example reflects badly on the way President Nimeiry, after securing the peace agreement of 1972, abandoned the cause of the southerners and precipitated the beginning of the new war in 1983.

> We men of the land are coming!
> Nimeiry deserted us, and left us to another.
> You should be ashamed.
> Fight you southerners, fight bravely!
> Oh, Nimeiry[24]

The songs in Uduk tend to be more local, more personal, referring to immediate incidents and personalities rather than national ones. Although always, to my knowledge, put to the lyre by men, the words can also originate from women. Many tell of the sufferings of the long road, and appeal for salvation, or even call for a return home, such as the following example appealing to the then chairman of the Bonga Refugee Committee (Emmanuel Mola Jajal). The alternate voice is his, suggesting people stay calm.

> Omer, why do you deny us our homeland?
> Oh my, oh me, oh my
> We are refugees in Ethiopia, but let us look back to our country
> You are the one at fault
> The world's powers should find a way for us
> Our homeland was destroyed by Omer, it's our home no longer
> The grandmothers and the children are crying to each other
> Oh, my people
>
> *Let us just eat the free food, but stay quiet, don't complain*
> *Just take your mouthfuls*
>
> Omer, why do you prevent our return?
> Ask our leader, ask him carefully
> We've had enough of travelling, as if to the end of the world
> Flocking to and fro like this, all together
> As refugees in Ethiopia

[24] Buha Dharas, both songs recorded by James Shama Pulale, Bonga, 2002.

Ask the leader, ask Mola, ask him carefully
Would he agree that we should go back home
We are weary of the long road, with the children too
Ask our leader Mola
The country is destroyed by Omer, but he says it is our home[25]

Some songs are explicitly those of the battle scene, in the voices of
men. A recent example is one which relates to the 1999 struggle for the
hill of Ulu, in the north-west of the Kurmuk district, just beyond the
Khor Sama'a. The SPLA here managed to take Ulu from the Sudanese
forces, partly through their deployment of anti-aircraft guns. According
to my information, the Sudanese commander was none other than the
notorious captain of the Chali garrison in the 1980s, Tayeb Musbah (see
Chapters 2 and 3). Note the way that the two armies speak to each other
in the song. There are many verbal as well as musical echoes with the
'classical' style of historical song, and in fact this battle took place only a
little further north than the much earlier struggles with Bellila I have
mentioned.

Where are those guns sounding?
My brothers, look, the fighting has arrived
Wayyi! Oh, my mother!
Oh 'Uduk', why are the guns sounding?
My brothers are dying in the grass like dogs
Wayyi, wayyi, wayyi

>   That name of Tayeb is heard all over
>   That name of Tayeb is now famous
>   Let him come!
>   Just come and get us 'Uduk'
>   What is it camped there in Ulu?
>   The men in Ulu have the red eyes of mad dogs!

Everything is finished in Ulu
Let's get out of Ulu Sama'a
Why are the guns sounding?

>   SPLA put up the flag!
>   *Oh Ulu, Oh! I swear by my mother!*
>   The whistle's blowing, blowing, why's the whistle blowing?
>   *Something's calling in Ulu*

[25] Composed by Timothy Kola Rehan, sung by Hosiah Dangaye Chalma, Bonga, 18
Aug. 2000.

> Why are the big birds calling like that?
> *In the name of my mother!*
> The rats are scrambling into their ground-holes[26]

A quieter style is also common, directing ironic comments or even pointed satire towards aid workers, camp leaders, and committees. The next example is composed by Wel Ragab, who advises people against giving up their old dirty saucepans when bartering for food from the Ethiopians, but only 'sell' their new ones—though people sold them all! Perhaps the people should all leave for Mettu on the Ethiopian highlands (whence come the supplies). Martha Ahmed is teased here for her pre-eminence in the relief operations of Bonga, as our 'royal lady', linking the normal Uduk word for 'woman' (*abom*) with the Arabic *malik* (King). James was a Nuer in charge of the warehouse.

> What can we use to buy supplies?
> Martha, come and buy grain for us
> The rations were to come on Friday
> But where are they?
> Oh, that tiny scoop!
>
> Starvation, move over please!
> One man got angry over the hunger
> Chingwo was angry over the hunger
> There should have been food on Friday!
> The 'Uduk' will sell off all their plates,
> Sell and sell again!
> My advice: 'Just sell the new and keep the old black ones!'
> But people sold them all.
>
> Our royal lady spoke on the radio-telephone,
> And asked for grain.
> The answer—there was no way!
> James, if you feared God you'd have opened up the stores on Friday.
> Oh royal lady, lady-queen of ours!
> James was in charge of the distribution.
> 'Uduk', let's go to Mettu!
> The 'Uduk' have no saucepans left[27]

Many of the songs have a 'conversational' structure, one person's words answered or echoed in the next line by another's. This is clear in the

---

[26] Composed and sung by Hosiah Dangaye Chalma, Bonga, 29 Aug. 2000.
[27] Composed by Wel Ragab, here sung by Dangaye Chalma, Bonga, 18 Aug. 2000.

following song where a Gindi woman, Kude Galsha, is addressing her 'brother', father of Hila, whose own name was Baga Rada. He was one of the first recruits to the SPLA but died of sickness in the training base at Bilpam. In death, he asks after her.

'Kude is cut off, she has no home'
So where shall I stay?
Oh! Where can we bury the dead?
The youngsters ['seeds'] are finished
Oh children

'Which way has my sister Kude gone?'
I could run to the north
Father of Hila, call me first to the long road
Oh my!
I have no home
Oh, oh! And the youngsters
I am crying for the children are finished
Crying, for the seeds are finished
And Hila's father has gone to the land of Garang
Oh, Hila, oh!
Oh, oh
And where has he gone?
And where can I go to hide?
We are overcome by Garang's war, and where can I go to live?
They say the boys are all taken up in Garang's war, but where shall I live?
Oh! Where shall we bury the dead?

The hyena is howling, *wu-wuh!*
The wild ones are howling in the old village
For I am without a home
As for the 'seeds'
Where shall we find them?
Father of Hila, please come home to me!
Am I to run to the north?
My brothers are all taken up in Garang's war
I want to know where to go

'Which way did my sister Kude go?
Who will look for Kude?'[28]

I asked Dangaye, widely regarded as a first-rate young singer, but who had been blind from birth, when he learned to play the lyre (Figure 20).

[28] Words composed by Kude Galsha, sung by Dangaye Chalma, Bonga, 18 Aug. 2000.

Figure 20. Hosiah Dangaye Chalma with his lyre, Bonga, 2000

He told me that as a child he used to practise on his father's lyre, but had not played in Langkwai, or Itang, or Nor Deng, or Karmi. It was only here, in Bonga in 1994, that he started to play. He did not play his father's songs, only those of Wel Ragab, and his own compositions, often putting phrases suggested by women to music. He certainly had an acute ear for goings on; here is a satirical song from 1994 which pokes fun at how the chiefs (leaders of the blocks) were too scared to stand up to the chair and members of the Bonga Refugee Committee, positioned as they were between the block chiefs and the national and international agencies. The people felt the Committee was beginning to behave too much like a mini-government, imposing fines and punishments, and exacting a share of the proceeds that could be made from the sale of empty UN sacks. The term *kayid* comes from Qa'id al-'Amm, 'Supreme Commander', here used ironically. It was the term the British used for the head of the Sudan Defence Force, replacing 'Sirdar', when this body was split off from the Egyptian army in 1925. President Nimeiry also applied it to himself, and it was used more generally for 'commander' in the SPLA. In the vernacular, songs often play cleverly upon words, something which is visible even to a non-Uduk speaker in this lyric composed by David Musa. The word *mol* means 'to be ignorant of', while the chairman's personal name is Mola, both resonating with *tul* or *tul is*, meaning 'to gather together' as for a meeting.

> *Dhan tapa hili mo kan*
> *A'Kayid thu'thku'd ee*
> *Dhan tapa dena ayidara mo ya*
> *Dhan tapa yuna shush ki yaw yaw*
> *Dhan tapa waga nyara nyana'b*
> *Dhan tapa 'ce'd 'ba kan*
> *'Kayid thu'thu'd ee*
> *Um be deni 'twal ki bir bir*
> *Dhal mol gwo o*
> *A'Kayid thu'thu'd mini mol dhan piya*
> */E tul 'kwani is dhali tor jasa gwo ma sijin 'te/ ta?*
> *Mol tul tapa is*
> *Dhan tapa dena yidara*
> *Yisa tor 'kwani jasa bway ma sijin 'te/ ta?*
> *Dhan tapa dena 'twal kan*
> *A'Kayid thu'thu'd gom ata kan?*

Dhan ta̱pa hili mo kan
Dhan ta̱pa yuna shush ki yal yal
Dhali mol gwo
/E mol t̲ula?
Dhan ta̱pa dena 'twa ki bir bir
Dhal mol gwo
Aya! Ba t̲ul uni is mo
Aya! Gana, Mola t̲ul uni is dhal mol gwo o
/E molu t̲ula!

Look out, you chiefs!
The Boss is making a mess of things
And you chiefs behave like new-wed brides!
You tremble with nerves in front of the Committee
You daren't even blow your noses
You shyly hang your heads.
But the Boss is making great mistakes!
While your mouths tremble, mutter mutter
And you don't know how to speak.
The Boss has got it wrong but he can be replaced
'You gather people up but can only speak of prison!
You don't know how to handle the chiefs!'

The chiefs are afraid of the Committee

'Why can you only threaten people with the prison?'
The chiefs are stuttering in their words
But why must the Boss make these mistakes?
Look out, you chiefs!
You daren't clear your noses
You don't know how to speak
Don't you know what a meeting is?
Ay! Have a proper meeting!
Ay! You, Mola, you have these meetings but you don't know what to say
You don't know what a meeting is![29]

In my earlier books I noted something of the extraordinary resilience of the vernacular language of the *'kwanim pa*, and how that very language defines a sense, for them, of belonging together. By this I do not mean a state of being a cosy community. It is rather a matter of belonging to a network of relations between people who reckon they are

[29] Composed by David Musa; here sung by Dangaye Chalma, Bonga, 20 Nov. 1994.

accountable to each other, of knowing who the other is within the longer history of this network. The continued survival of the vernacular, and those modes of cultural creativity which thrive within it, has something to do with this kind of belonging. In the context of an increasing use of other languages, and the spread of newly learned 'other' modes of civil behaviour—whether Sudanese national, Christian evangelical, impersonal market, or 'development bureaucracy'—the vernacular arena seems to show an increasing moral density. The use of the 'language of the home' entails a kind of commitment between those who share it, whatever their external entanglements over time, and this feeling can become a kind of 'secret' between them. But it can also be a lively space for creativity. Whether there will ever be a lively engagement between Christian and 'village' language and musical art, I do not know. The innovation and creativity so far lies largely on the 'village' side, especially the older song traditions, rather than on the 'Christian' side of hymns and prayers, which seem to have become somewhat fossilized in the form bequeathed by the original missionaries. Acceptance of the faith still has to go hand in hand with strict discipline on all levels. The next chapter shows how the brittle casing of mission Christianity, however, once did crack under stress, during the original stay in Itang, to the point where strange proclamations and behaviours (bearing a distinct connection to older cults) were too much for the church to hold back and had to be contained by 'government', such as it was.

10

Sermons, Visions, and Dreams

A woman got up in Chali church and told the people a dream she had. There was a huge hole, and her mother was in it cooking food. And the hole was hell. Her mother asked her to come down and eat some food. She said, no, no, I can't come down, I am a person of Jesus now and I can't come down where all you people are. And also, there were all these people dancing, the kind of dancing which had been going on. And the earth suddenly opened up and swallowed all these people dancing, swallowed 'em all up, and this woman apparently . . . she was now convinced not to go.[1]

This publicly shared dream, on one level, could be represented as a 'Christian' dream, but it has echoes and depths of other kinds. It clearly speaks to a sense of loss of family and kin, and to the polarized morality of social life in Bonga where the dominant understandings of Christianity are derived from the evangelical protestant tradition, and believers are supposed to see the dance ground as sinful. There have been and are still occasional contacts with other Christian traditions. There was a Roman Catholic presence in the southern Blue Nile from about the late 1970s. Father Joseph Bara had converted some of the Koma of the Yabus area, had built a church in Boing, and two in Damazin, with a house and classrooms in Kurmuk, before he was arrested in Renk in 1988.[2] I have quoted Peter Kuma's mention of his friendship with a Catholic priest he used to visit in Kurmuk, and how this was held against him politically (Chapter 1). A couple of Uduk young men had attended Catholic college in Khartoum and even started a little teaching in the Yabus valley. That region on the very edge of 'the north' had also seen Islamic teachers; the *feki* Sheikh Ahmad I mentioned in *The Listening Ebony*[3] had gained followers there, but after his move to

[1] Barbara Harper, Bonga, 1 Sept. 2000.
[2] Information noted in Khartoum, 1988.
[3] James, *The Listening Ebony*, 262–4.

Assosa, people from the southern Blue Nile no longer went to see him even after they arrived across the border in force. The years of exile inevitably led to greater contacts between the Uduk and Catholics from the southern Sudan, and it was touching to hear that Catholic Dinka women were going round the tents of the pitiful new arrivals in Itang, 1990, to sing and pray, and were even holding prayers over the bodies of those who died.[4] In Nor Deng, a number of the makeshift shelters had crosses on the top, which had not normally been Uduk practice, but here was spreading from the Dinka.

MYTHS, DREAMS, AND SERMONS IN EXILE

Despite these contacts, the physical, moral, and bodily separations which mark the protestant world-view, including those between believers and the rest, have become dominant in the discourse of the Uduk churches, partly through co-opting some of the dichotomies of the old Uduk world. There are obvious echoes in the dream reported above of motifs I have reported in *The Listening Ebony*, of the underground places of the dead one may seem to visit when very ill, and how one should avoid their invitations to share food and drink.[5] There is a very clear mapping of the realm of life and the above, with Christianity, as against the realm of the below, with death and the realm of Satan. They can never meet, as the dreamer knows who cannot join her mother, not only because she is dead but because she was not a believer. They cannot be reunited, even in the hereafter. The dream as reported also has deeper resonance, however, in the myth of the Birapinya tree, whose branches reached to the sky. People used to climb up it to the great dance. However one day an old woman burned it down, cutting off the dancers in the sky. There was no way down. Some jumped, though not all survived, while the rest were lost for ever.[6] Structurally, we could see the dream of hell as swallowing up the dancers of today and thus cutting them off from the living, Christian survivors as a surprisingly precise transformation of the old story. The three levels of sky/earth/ underground in the old myths and cosmology are maintained as a spatial framework but the moral content is polarized as heaven/earth/hell.

[4] Accounts heard from both Nuer and Uduk in Nor Deng, 1991.
[5] James, *The Listening Ebony*, 133–40.
[6] James, '*Kwanim Pa*, 68–71.

In the old stories there were two separations created among the people:
first, between those stranded by disaster in the sky, and the survivors who
made it back to earth. Second, while those on earth used to go through a
cycle of temporary 'death' and revival, when death became final, their
arum (life-spirit) would move to its underground home. There were cases
of return from death, a theme which again resonates in Christian teachings. But there was no cosmic dualism of good and evil in the original
stories, no moral colouring of above or below, there was just loss from the
living communities of people on earth through either disaster or death.
The Christian cosmic schema, however, rests on a spatial dichotomy in
the afterlife that impinges on relations among the living. Again, the
people are divided, the primary and permanent division being after
death. But this division enters into relations among the living too:
believers and non-believers can be identified here among us now. The
way the dance ground is now associated with unbelief and immorality—
by everyone, and not just by Christian spectators—makes this a tangible
marker in daily life. For Christians brought up on the myths of the
'*kwanim pa* to dream of dancers being swallowed up into an underground
hell seems very logical in its own way.

I have never heard of someone dreaming about heaven as such, or
almost reaching there, or being invited to sup with the angels. Rather to
the contrary, I heard at second hand of various dreams in circulation
which warned of the realities of the other place. For example, when
Hannah Weyak, the then wife of Pastor Paul, became very ill and died in
Nor Deng, somebody dreamt that she had not been able to find the
door to heaven. This distressed the other strongly Christian women of
the Chali group. They were saying to themselves, well, if she's gone to
hell, what hope is there for the rest of us? Barbara Harper commented to
me years later, 'And they really believed this, you know, a dream seems
to be to them something real.' I heard also of a rather different dream,
by another staunch Chali churchwoman, about Pastor Paul himself,
waking from the dead. He started calling all those with him, saying,
'Let's follow the people to Assosa.' All along the way, he was calling the
dead to get up and follow our people. So they went to Assosa, and Itang,
and Bonga, and still all along they kept calling, 'Let's go, let's go.'[7]

[7] Barbara Harper, Bonga, 30 Nov. 1994. For further comparative studies, see Charles
Jedrej and Rosalind Shaw (eds.), *Dreaming, Religion and Society in Africa* (Leiden: Brill, 1992).

By the year 2000, some indications of a new flexibility were developing within the mainstream church community. For example, the staunch churchwoman Ruth Panjeka who was now active in the (secular) women's organization pointed out that the old kinds of dancing were at least their own, as against the new disco styles being taken up by the youngsters.

We in our office are trying to help the kids, and calm them down. The way that the young people are behaving is changing. They are beginning to dance these new dances, not the Uduk dances, these are Bunyan dances and very bad.— *Now Ruth, in the old days, you church people criticized the athele/.*—Yes, but now we say the *athele/* is relatively good, because it is something of ours. It would be better for those who do not believe in God to hold on to those old ways of ours, to dance in the way our people always used to. Now as for we people of Jesus, it is true we don't want our kids to dance. But we are all mixed up together, and our kids want to go and see what the others are doing and what is going on at the dance. If we lived in our own group far away it would be easier, but it is difficult to manage as we are all living together in this foreign land.[8]

At this point, we were joined by Peter Sol, a senior elder of the Chali Christian community, who took a harder line. He wished to make his absolute disapproval of all dancing very clear.

If we live in the land of others, it is not good to disturb people with our culture [Arabic], they expect us to remain quiet here. We Christians would prefer people to stay quiet. The authorities should have a chance to get on with their work, and not be distracted by these disturbances. It is better for somebody who is protected like this, to stay quiet, and get on with cultivation rather than dancing.

It is very important in following the word of God that we should not dance, for God will not be pleased. If we follow the word of God we will be able to get back home, like the Israelites in Egypt. They were very quiet there, and prayed, and asked God to help them. We don't want to live the life we have here in Bonga for ever, if there is peace in Sudan we want to go back. If we forget about God, we will have pain, and there will be illness, and people will die. Then who can we go and cry to, to help us? There is nobody here on earth who will be able to help.

If you die in the hand of Jesus, you can be alive again when Jesus returns. The thing we want here, if we do not change to a new way of life and leave dancing, and the many sinful things that go with it, God will take his Liver [*sic*: his heart, his love] away from us, withdraw and no longer be close. He will open up a great hole in the earth, and cause the death of the people who do not listen.[9]

---

[8] Ruth Panjeka Idris, Bonga, 27 Aug. 2000 (video).
[9] Peter Sol Kul, Bonga, 27 Aug. 2000 (video).

This opinion is of course from the heart of a strongly 'fundamentalist' worldview, which excludes as totally 'other' the lives of non-believers, or of the followers of other faiths such as Islam. But the generality of the people did not have such certainty: within the complex world of competing moralities and looser combinations of certainties, their centre of gravity was rather different. The claims of Christianity and the texts of scripture were definitely a recurring point of reference, though the striking parts of the Bible were not always those of the New Testament. Suske, the first wife of Pastor Paul, was one of those who spoke very eloquently about the imagery of the Old Testament stories of the exile and how it touched their own experience. I caught her talking about this quite spontaneously in Nor Deng, and asked her to explain.

Yes, we are living like the people of old.—*What people?*—The Israelite people.[10] And I was saying that some of the women still don't know about this, but we shall wait and eventually believe, as the Israelites did. And when everyone believes, our God will lead us, to look after us in our home where we shall one day live; but at the moment, we are not going to find the homeland where we used to live. We are maybe just waiting to go one day to the land of God. We should wait, with our prayers, and keep on believing in our Livers. I am a woman who has been a person of Jesus from long ago, and I still am, with God. Arumgimis will not leave me; but I have strayed, I don't go to church, I think a lot and cry at night with tears.... Pray for me, pray for Suske a lot.

And that's why I was saying just now, we are like the Israelite people, from crying in the wilderness. They strayed, and they went into a cave in the mountains, Moses led them, he went to help them. But I have not forgotten ... I don't want to curse anyone; I was created by God, and he led the Israelite people first. And as we came from Itang, I began to really believe again, as we came through the water. And it was raining, and we were really like the Israelites of old, and I wanted to believe like them, and go on with a good will....

—*What was their life like, those people?*—The Israelite people, when they had to cross the water? I've forgotten! I don't know the story very well! But what I do remember is that they led the way, I have remembered a picture of the Israelites leading the way, and I have kept it in my Liver.[11]

The connection with former missionaries of the SIM was kept up on both sides. For example, among the taped messages I was able to convey

---

[10] The Uduk phrase is *'kwani Yahuda,* literally 'Jewish people', but since the only reference is the OT text, I translate this as Israelites.

[11] Suske, first wife of Paul Rasha, Nor Deng, 5 Oct. 1991.

from Nor Deng was a message from Martin Luther, the most senior of the few ordained pastors there, who spoke to me after a Sunday service in the open air. Addressing the Sudan Interior Church people in Khartoum, who then included Pastor Paul, he asked them to write to Miss Beam and Miss Betty, and send greetings to Mr Forsberg. He described how they would sing hymns at night as they camped by the wayside on the long road, and again in the morning. He sent greetings to his wife and family members, and the community generally in Khartoum, stating very firmly that 'We shall not leave Arumgimis. He is with us here in the bush.'[12]

I should make it very clear that I am not a complete cynic. I have the utmost respect for those of the Christian community who had rooted their own lives in its teachings, and been touched to the heart, or they would say Liver, by the love of Jesus and the power of the God of the Bible. The situations of death and suffering were such as to bring home to anyone the powerful hope that such belief could offer. I quote Ruth Panjeka again, who described in a taped conversation for her relatives in Khartoum how her dying son begged her to read the scriptures to him.

I want to tell about the youngsters who died in the hills. One was called Kadalis. I don't know all their names, but one was from *pan* Dundur. One was called Denka, and one was Sabi, and one was called Shima, a child of Muriya. And Balla, and Jedan, they were very many, I don't know all their names. I have forgotten them all. And one of Nathaniel's, and Bulus, and Thomas,—*Were these killed at Kurmuk or where?* Gambela, up the road in Ethiopia to the hills there.

And we left them behind us when we left Itang, as they went to fight people in the mountains there. And Mary Ahmed, her son Ayoub was killed for his gun, outside Itang. . . . And children of Duka, and Peter Kuma's youngest brother from Khartoum, they wrote us a letter which told us that he had died fighting with the army. And we thought we should remember him, along with those who died in the fighting here. And Kwadangwa [whose group was ambushed on the way home] and a child who died of illness in Khartoum.

And my son Thoha died in October. I didn't send you a letter. He got ill, my young son, he was about 15, he had just married, and was ill in the stomach, and he asked me to read the Bible for him, St John's Gospel, Chapter 15, and Chapter 6 of Luke. I want to remember his death; I used to get very upset in my Liver, but God calmed it down. I took strength from God, and I am now able to accept his death. He was my first-born, and I now respect him. He was a very lively child, his death was a lesson from God.[13]

[12] Martin Luther Lipa Luyin, Nor Deng, 28 July 1991.
[13] Ruth Panjeka Idris, Nor Deng, 7 Oct. 1991.

Ruth first explained this to me on the occasion of the modest memorial service (*purash*) they held in Nor Deng for all those who had died. Tiny handfuls of grain from the UN shares were gathered together, along with a few bundles of okra which people had managed to raise from the mud in the short weeks they had been there. The food was cooked, and hymns were sung around the orange plastic plates laid out for the event (Figure 21). I asked for whom this memorial was being held. It was for *everyone who had died* since they had last had an opportunity to remember them: some had died fighting as part of the Sudanese army, some had died fighting as part of the SPLA (including those who had been sent into Ethiopia to die in places like Dembi Dollo), some, like her son, had died of illness; and others had just died for no particular reason. The news of distant deaths came mainly from occasional letters received, either through the Red Cross or by the hand of outside visitors like myself. In Karmi, a year later, the Ethiopian authorities noticed how

Figure 21. The *purash*, memorial gathering and meal for all those who had died over the previous few years, Nor Deng, 1991

much attention was paid to remembrance of the dead, and I was told they would sometimes provide a little extra food for the ceremony, or at least they did once, 'so we could send his soul [*kashira/*, originally shadow or dreaming self] to Arum'.

The church groups and their activities were organized in a very open and democratic manner in Bonga as in the earlier camps. Discipline was sometimes seen to be imposed, and certainly implicit in the Rules of the Church inherited from the 1950s mission. But each church group organized its own site for a building, and meetings, even clearing a space for church crops to be grown. At the point when the 'breakaway' group left the Sudan for Ethiopia in 1992, there were no ordained pastors with them. Both Pastor Martin Luther Luyin and Pastor Jonah remained on the Sudan side. It was not long before arrangements were made by the SIC to ordain Joshua Hashu (and later, Michael Beya and others). However, the practices of each little church had continued in exile, led by a range of preachers and elders. The yearly calendar passed through its cycle in good order. I found in Bonga that the ceremonial calendar included Thanksgiving, something I had missed in the past. It was not realized there that this occasion is basically an American national festival, rather than a regular Christian event everywhere. However, Pastor Paul had seen the missionaries celebrating Thanksgiving at an early date, and decided to adopt it for everyone. The date does match quite well the season of ripening crops in this part of Africa (as in the case of the Plymouth Bay colony), so it soon acquired quite the air of a local harvest festival.

There was always something of the schoolroom in the style of Uduk sermons over the years. I heard Pastor Paul Rasha himself preaching in Chali in the 1960s, and saw him on one of his visits to the outlying villages in 1967 (Figure 22). I then had the opportunity to hear him when he was living in internal exile in Khartoum, in mid-1988. In his preaching at that time, he laid clear emphasis on the discipline of studying the Bible and working at one's faith. There is also a warning to his no doubt expectant audience of coming change, including the return of Jesus, and apocalyptic catastrophe. He used the parable of the wise and foolish virgins. Towards the end of a long sermon, Paul mentioned having witnessed Billy Graham preaching, during the time he spent working on Bible translation in the United States. The following

Figure 22. Pastor Paul Rasha Angwo visiting Wakacesh, 1967

is a paraphrase translation of part of the sermon, the original being in Uduk but with a good admixture of Arabic words.

Your faith is like a lamp, you must cherish it and work at it, and always be ready for the coming of Christ. Otherwise you will be left out. You must study the Bible in depth, and not read it casually 'like a newspaper'. It is for you to choose to listen, and to decide which way to go.... The house was prepared for the bride and groom. The five wise girls came with their lamps and enough extra oil. The foolish ones did not have any extra oil. The lamps were burning nicely, but no one knew when the groom was coming by night. The foolish girls asked for more oil, but the wise ones refused—there would not be enough for themselves.

This is a lesson, for Jesus is like the bridegroom, and he has not told us when he is coming.... Those who believe, he will lead to the land of heaven, but if you neglect your faith, you will be left behind on earth amidst your sin. It's up to you. Even your own brother cannot take you. I may be a pastor, but don't think I will go to heaven simply because of this. You have to look after your faith, like your lamp, so it shines, and this will lead you to heaven.

Before, when I was in America, translating for the American Bible Society, Dr Billy Graham and a pastor from the Baptist Church...talked about forthcoming catastrophe. No one knows when it might happen, or when they may die.... But there is protection from Jesus.... We don't know when this will happen. Now if Sadiq el Mahdi says he's going to Medani, people will know when he will arrive and will get ready. But we don't know when Jesus will come.... Do your work, and wait, do your work, and wait, for people on the earth don't know when the time will be.[14]

Both elements, of self-discipline, and of expectancy, recur in many of the later sermons I have recorded. But there seems less exhortation to intellectual study as part of keeping faith in good order, and rather more on practical advice. There is often a good deal of Old Testament storytelling, which resonates easily with everyone's daily experience. But there is a much more raw edge to the expectancy, of the imminence of God's judgement, and the resurrection of the faithful. This comes through powerfully in the memorial service for Pastor Paul, who died in Khartoum on 31 March 1992 (Figure 23). A few weeks after the refugees arrived in Karmi, shared memorial services were held across the camp over the course of a week. The first event was jointly organized by Michael Beya of Chali and elder Mathias of Gindi, who constructed his sermon around the story of Lazarus. Here is a paraphrase translation of some key sections. Michael Beya started with a set of announcements.

You children should pay attention, don't play around outside, come to the church and listen. All of us are here today because our pastor has died. And now he is in heaven. He is no longer here on the earth. His life is in the hands of God. And everyone everywhere when the world is coming to an end, God will judge, and everyone who is not following Jesus will be punished. Everyone will stand up in front of God on that day. Those of you who believe in Him will stand on His right-hand side, and those of us who are just playing about, and do

---

[14] Pastor Paul Rasha Angwo, Khartoum, 14 Aug. 1988.

Figure 23. Memorial service for Pastor Paul Rasha Angwo, Khartoum, 1992 (courtesy of Barbara Harper)

not follow Him completely, will be left behind on earth. Because on that day when He will send his Son, He is not going to explain further. Today we are honouring our first pastor, the first from us the Uduk, and will always do so.

Mathias led a prayer, and a hymn, and embarked on his sermon, using the Gospel of John, chapter 11.

We are here to remember our father, Pastor Paul. We have lost him but he is in the hand of God. He is not lost to human beings. All the churches are in his hands. They were all his. He was like a centre pole for us, the church started with him and has branches which have now spread out. We came today to honour him, and give his *kashira/* [in this Christian sense, 'soul'] to God. . . .

I am reading today from John, the story of Lazarus, who died, and Jesus came, and was given power by God. . . . Remembering Paul, if you will not be faithful to the church, who will keep the church going? We have lost the founder of the church, the centre pole, while some of you just go off and play the stones game, this is a bad thing, and you fight with people on the road. If you keep doing this, who will be the centre of the church? For those of you who are young, it is foolish to play around.

Remember the story of Lazarus, and what Jesus did. If Jesus were here now, he would do the same for Pastor Paul as he did for Lazarus. In Jesus' way, death is like a sleep only, and He could call him at any time. Paul's sisters are here in Karmi. His sister does not believe that Paul will be alive again, she does not believe. And Mary, when Lazarus died, she did not believe that he could return to life. But if Jesus called him from the grave, he could come out. Yes....

If Jesus came now, he could call Pastor Paul and we would see him, not tomorrow but today. Like Lazarus, he would come out. Everyone was afraid and moved away, because the man was *arum*. He was *arum*. Yes, and he was wrapped in the thick cloth used to bury him. And when he came out, people said, take that cloth off his body and let him go. And he walked away on his own feet. He came out of the grave and stood at the entrance, and everyone wondered and said, 'What is this?' And this is how Jesus could call Pastor Paul out of the grave.

It is a good thing that all the churches came here [to the Chali church today] to remember and share happiness with the Chali church. We are in the wilderness, but all of us are the seeds of whom? His seeds. We must continue the work of the church.[15]

There were then announcements about prayers in a rota of meetings at the smaller churches through the week.

Several great public demonstrations of Christian faith and allegiance were in evidence by the time people reached Bonga. The first was undoubtedly the highly ceremonial visit of Miss Beam and Miss Betty, the iconic early missionaries, organized by the SIM so that they could be present at the Bible Conference held there in November 1993.[16] I witnessed a mass baptism in 1994, when I would reckon at least 500 people assembled a mile upstream on the banks of the Baro river for a ceremony of baptism. I believe there had been others, but this was the largest since their arrival, and was carried out in great style by Pastor Joshua Hashu and attendants. Several dozen people, not only youngsters but adult men and women, were baptized in batches, as Joshua preached of John the Baptist in the wilderness, wearing sackcloth and living on locusts and honey before calling all the people of Israel to God.

---

[15] Chali church memorial service, in Karmi transit camp, 27 Sept. 1992.

[16] I had the opportunity to spend an afternoon with Miss Beam and Miss Cridland when they passed through London on their way to Ethiopia. They were extremely pleased at the chance of returning to the people they knew and remembered so well, and were greeted warmly when they arrived. The SIM visiting party made a video recording of the occasion which they kindly copied to me.

CHRISTMAS IN ITANG, 1990

I have emphasized the way that the churches exerted a degree of disciplinary control right through the long trek and initial years of exile. And as briefly mentioned above, this was put to a severe test at Christmas time in Itang, 1990. As described in earlier chapters, this was a very low point in the story of the refugees, following great deprivation during the first half of that year and poor-quality care even when they got to Itang camp, in the final months of Mengistu's regime in Ethiopia. The close of the year saw an outbreak of religious hysteria. Parties of young people across the camp were engaged in post-Christmas carol and hymn singing, in anticipation of the New Year, when suddenly a couple of teenagers from the formerly outlying village cluster of Pam Be had strange visions of angels and promised the people that Jesus would appear to lead them home. They rushed off to gather in the bush, and were followed by many other youngsters, including some Dinka. Eventually orthodoxy prevailed, the Chali church elders being alerted and the armed camp authorities managing to rein in the new movement.

William Danga was the first who described the events for me:

That time in Itang, . . . in the church, the Pam Be church, the youth groups invented a new kind of *arum*, a new kind of religion. They sang carols, sang carols, every single day; at night, at night, at night. After several days, they became like people who had gone crazy. They saw all sorts of things, and said, 'Those are the angels over there, they have arrived; we are going to heaven.' 'There they are flying in the sky, they they are up with the stars; look over there!'

And a great number of people rushed out of Itang, all rushing out together *kwany kwany kwany*, because of their words. They brought along a certain youngster with a whip, called a stick, who said there was a Rainbow inside it. They said, 'If you deny this, this thing will change you, this thing will strike you and you will die.' This is what they were doing at that time. Jangul, and Peter Manyjal (Yethdha), those were the two main leaders. They managed to win over many older people in the church.

And I was concerned about this. They came again, bringing some fluff from a chicken which had been cut on the ground, they brought it and said, 'This has fallen from the sky!' And again they found a bamboo stick on the ground, picked it up and said, 'This has a shining light inside it, it has *arum* in it, it has fallen from heaven and we found it on the earth.' They kept saying this and a lot of people were led astray. And clothes that were patterned: they said, 'These fancy patterned clothes are not good, they're bad; the clothes of heaven are not patterned. These are not good.' And some women took off their clothes and threw them in the bush. Beads too, they threw in the bush. And some people tore up their money and discarded it. And many cut their ration cards up, the cards they had been given to claim food. Because, they said, they were going to heaven that day. In Itang. They said the time was up. 'The angels have appeared to open the way for us, and take us up.' That's what they were doing at that time, they were inventing a new kind of *arum*.

William, not at this time a churchman, went and tried to reason with them personally before reporting this development to the Chali church elders. He asked if the Word in the Book was being changed. Was one of the churches getting lost? They had heard, and agreed it was.

I said, 'Getting lost? They're literally in the bush!' Really, they had been leading people off from the camp, emptying the place *kwany kwany kwany*, with Dhamkin too, diverting them too. Some Dhamkin believed them, and were following them, thinking they would go to heaven. They deceived people, saying, 'Look over there! There are the angels, shining white over there! Up in the mountain there. In the mountain!' Their voices had gone, they were hoarse, they didn't know how to speak properly. Some had been singing, singing through the night, singing, singing to the dawn. And then they flocked off, flocked off, they didn't seem like ordinary human beings any more. This was the new thing they did in Itang at that time. This new thing, people wondered at; when I heard this amazing story, I told them, 'You must be joking, this can't be the truth. Jesus is not going to appear in this way. This is not how the angels will appear, nothing like this has been said to happen. You are totally lost. The evil Satan must have arrived and caused this. You are starting to make up some new kind of *arum*. The '*kwanim pa* are inventing a new kind of God.'
  And everyone indeed got lost, that day. I went towards Pagak, and found them in the bush. I saw them there, they were all screaming out in their prayers. Each one was praying on his or her own; each alone, each praying alone, each alone, gathering together from morning until the sun went down. Some came from there, they were so dizzy they got lost. 'Where's my hut?'

The church elders began to mediate, explaining they were not following the true word, but were led by Satan. William recalled, 'I thought about it in the night, Ah—I must tell Wendy about this! That people invented a new God in Itang.' I asked him if this new God had a name—'Anti-Christ . . . it's there in the Bible.'

They said that if you die, you will soon be taken up. And people were very afraid. Thinking that if someone had sinned, they would be left behind. People were afraid, and then decided to follow them, *yap yap yap*. There were large numbers of them! They ignored the word of the church and left, thinking they would go to heaven.—*All the children?*—All the children, and all the grand-mothers, and the elderly people.—*Did anyone remain?*—'Right now', they said, 'The angels will lead us back to our own real home.' People carried things on their heads, thinking that they would be led back to the Sudan....

And some Dhamkin followed them?—Yes!—*and Meban?*—Yes! Everyone. I went to see the Dhamkin, they were crowding like this, into the shade of the big tree where they were gathered. They gathered together with Dhamkin, and Meban, thinking they were on the way to heaven ... they spoke in *'twam pa*, and then it was translated into Arabic, because there were Dhamkin present.... And the people were extremely thin, because they had not been eating. There wasn't any food....Ay! 'There are the angels, over there, and there, and there, flying over there, do you see?' But you didn't see them. There weren't any. 'Over there, there, in the tree there!' You'd look at the tree, and not see anything ...

Some reported visions they had seen in caves in the hills.

And a child of Badangwa, Jamia, they said she had been up the mountain and was struck by *arum* and couldn't speak. These kids were doing it, each in their own group, that *arum* business, they went up a particular hill where there was a great cave. And when they had gone right down inside the cave, they said they found a great *arum*. And this *arum* they found had grown horns on its head, and a red mouth. It was down in the darkness of the mountain. At Itang there....Jamia 'died' in there but revived again. They were all fainting. And their throats couldn't speak afterwards. They couldn't speak. For several days! Their throats were very sore. Because they were extremely thin, and had sung so much.—*And were their songs those of the church, or different?*—Songs of the church, probably....

However, the youngsters were playing games with the language of the standard hymns and prayers.

But when they were singing, the church hymn should be sung properly with 'Hallelujah', but they didn't sing a 'Hallelujah'. They made it into 'Hannaniya'. They made it 'Hannaniya.' This Hannaniya was a bad man long ago, he was a thief. As in the story of the meeting place in the Bible....

And they didn't pray to the name of Jesus. They prayed like this, to 'The God of Ibrahim, and the God of Yakub,' that was their prayer. We pray, Amen, but they left out the name of Jesus. They didn't pray in the name of Jesus. . . . They were about to invent a new kind of God. But the church was very firm, and prevented them. . . . Because they were about to start something quite new. *Very New!* [English] . . . It was something made up by those two kids. And within their own group, within the choir, they created this thing, in the little church of Pam Be. This new thing.[17]

William was quite serious that I should take note of what had happened. 'You will follow all this carefully? Follow it, and write it down, so you will understand my words carefully, and follow the story of this new *arum* which the kids, the *ucim pa*, invented. You will write it down, the young-sters did this, and this, and that, at Itang that year, just after Christmas.' He explained how people would come to the church, and be told, 'Ay! You there, you're very *dark*, you aren't going to heaven. You are very dark. You have a great *kashira/* in there. You have not purified yourself.' They also began to tackle people who had two wives, saying 'You should leave this new wife.' And 'a whole lot of people left their women! You could only keep your original first wife.' After a few days, people realized this was nonsense, and they took their wives back. 'They'd been told, "If you have two wives, you won't go to heaven. There'll be no heaven! The time is up. The angels have now arrived!"' William's account of all this, in a group in Nor Deng just over six months later, was greeted with nervous laughter, perhaps a touch of embarrassment. Although he was not a churchgoer, William had plenty of insight into the ups and downs of the Christians, having been an early mission recruit himself, and having actually led the tours of carol singing over several Christmases when young. The Itang events were apparently not entirely new; something of the kind had been started by Bellila children when they were all in Langkwai.

I heard other accounts of the strange outburst at Itang—in fact I deliberately asked about it, and other people confirmed much of what William had told me. At a gathering organized by myself and Barbara Harper in Bonga, we were discussing Christmas 'in the old days' with much nostalgia and fond memories. I brought up the subject of the strange events of 1990, and while people were uncomfortable at first, they soon warmed to the topic. Peter Kuma, then overseeing the administration of this part of Itang, was the one who had to bring the disturbance to an end, as he explained:

[17] William Danga Ledko, Nor Deng, 22 July 1991.

They were dreaming first, dreaming that people were going to go back home. And they were dreaming that *arum* told them they could go back home. They were shouting out a lot, saying, 'Let's go home, go home.' They said, 'Look at that mountain, there is an angel over there on the mountain' . . . a lot of people strayed from the word of God because they were confused. 'Is that a person over there or an angel?' . . .

Jesus is not going to show up just like that, no, you have to wait. That's what it says in the Bible. That's what I told them, it is not the Day of Judgment. . . . And I reported it to the government people, and the UN, who came and told people not to do these things. 'Don't think about going home, if you leave here you will suffer very much.' People were tearing up their clothes, and their money, saying God had appeared.

Some of the core church people, including Ruth Panjeka, explained that not everyone had gone off to the bush. Nathaniel remembered that the Chali church people themselves were accused of preventing the return home, because all should go together.

They said, 'It's only if you join us, we can go to the real Chali . . . Who is the leader of this church in Chali? Let's go.' . . . We asked, 'Why are you looking over there?' 'We are looking at the angels there, at the wing feathers they have dropped down there!' 'You should sit down and we will read the Bible for you.'

They were very, very thin, very pale, pale. A lot of kids, crying and doing a lot of silly things. It was midday, very hot, and they were very thirsty, and their eyes were all red. Peter left his work, and went to bring them back . . . in some small churches, on Sunday, you would not see anyone in the church![18]

The young SPLA fighter 'Jasper', whose adventures I have mentioned already, was serving as a military guard. He was detailed to go to the mountain and bring the people back. His account of that time, more than fifteen years later, was partly in English.

These people, their faces were changed, they were like sick people. They had a piece of glass, they would put it to their eyes like a telescope, and say, 'Your Liver is very dark'. I told them to come and read the Bible, but they didn't have time. . . . —*Were they all young men leading this?*—Young women too, they came in a group, they came to see me in my house and tried to convince me. . . .

When I went to the cave, I saw they were quite ill; Jamia, and Batha, and Dota, and Chobe. They were fainting there. They saw some evil thing that has a horn and red mouth, and they got ill and fell over on the ground. They died for

---

[18] Group discussion, Bonga, 12 Nov. 1994.

a while, and then recovered. And one died later when she came home. She was sick for two weeks and died [this was Jamia, a young married woman]. . . .

Did you go to the cave?—No, they sent me to bring them home, but I didn't go up to the cave. I heard them talking about it at home, before they went. . . . Yes, the news had spread so everyone knew the day. . . . They said God called us up into the mountains. . . .

Yes, they came to me, in my house, and said, 'You want to see Jesus?' and they showed me something on the hillside, and I looked and I couldn't see him. Then they said he was up in a tree, on a thorn of a heglig tree. I looked and there was nothing. . . . And they said they found evil things in the cave.

It was the most scary story I have ever heard, you know.

The first thing, they said God called us over there. Then after three days they changed their story, they said that God wanted us to go back to Sudan, he was calling us back to Sudan. That's when a lot of people were running across, they wanted to go home. That's when Peter Kuma got angry. It was clear this was something else, it wasn't just a religious thing, so he came to find us at the station and told us to go and bring the people back by force.[19]

He confirmed that the youngsters were demanding people's money and tearing it up, because you could not take it to heaven. He also elaborated on the way that they would 'diagnose' the condition of people's hearts (literally, Livers) by placing a glass on their body and looking through. This indeed happened to him. Davis Sukut later confirmed it had been done to him too (we were speaking in English): 'This is similar to what I told you they did to me, looking at me through a glass sort of cup, they put it right through my eyes and right through my chest, yes, against my body, and say, "You cannot go to heaven, your heart has a lot of darkness. You have to come with us and follow us, then you will be forgiven."'

It is impossible to avoid comparison here with the old methods of the diviners; they would look into a gourd of water to diagnose the state and whereabouts of a person's *kashira/* (shade, dreaming self), by holding a lighted wand of ebony wood over the surface and watching the patterns. They too would diagnose a 'dark' *kashira/*, and even prescribe plain living and diet. The old cults included apparitions in caves and figures from the world of the dead.[20] The youngsters at Itang were reinventing, to a degree, some of what the missionaries used to dismiss as 'witchcraft'

---

[19] 'Jasper', USA, Nov. 2006.
[20] James, *The Listening Ebony*, chs. 5 and 6.

and the work of Satan. They were transforming the more 'spiritual' aspects of the old methods into something more bodily—instead of diagnosing a 'shade' through manipulating elements of fire and water, they were applying a glass to a person's body, and looking through it at the physical Liver inside. The leading figures of the strange cultic movement in Itang did have family connections with specialists of the old kind; for instance I once knew Manyjal, Peter's father, as an expert diviner. One of Jangul's mother's brothers had been a leading ritual specialist, Tuda Bata, who explained to me in a quite separate context the old practices for controlling worms and flies in the fields and how the situation in Bonga was quite different (see below). It might seem that the practices introduced by youngsters at Christmas in Itang, 1990, were medicalizing the older divinatory techniques. Holding a glass against the body as a way of seeing inside it recalls the stethoscope, even more than the former common diviner's technique of applying small horns to the body to 'suck out' foreign matter. It is evident that the movement was proclaiming very explicit visions both of Jesus and of Satanic beings, as well as bodily ways of responding to the biblical expectations of return from the wilderness and judgement of all the people on Christ's return.

After giving me his own first-hand account, 'Jasper' asked me: 'Can this not happen to white people? Like seeing *arum*, and evil things in the mountain?' I replied that yes, this kind of thing is known at times to have happened all over the world, there have been comparable things in many countries, and often also in times of distress and great suffering.

LOCATING ONESELF IN A DIVIDED WORLD

I have written elsewhere about what I consider a deep ambivalence among the Uduk about the world religions, which have become best known in literal and dogmatic forms. While on the surface, especially in Bonga, the whole population was at ease with their collective Christian allegiance, there were undercurrents of doubt and even hostility. The Committee, which as I have already mentioned soon acquired its own critics, actually launched a campaign in 1994, writing letters and asking the UNHCR to expel the SIM representatives. Nothing came of this, but the Committee were reminding many people of the way that the old

Sudan government had expelled the missionaries in 1964, and were rehearsing some of the old reasons. This was mid-1994, by which time the Sudan government, now dominated by the National Islamic Front, was again in control of the southern Blue Nile, and represented in the form of a consulate in Gambela. Political talk of this kind might well have been in circulation among the various refugee communities in western Ethiopia. It also reminded people of some of the reasons why they were in Ethiopia at all. While the rise in Islamic militancy was not affecting them directly at this time, they remembered it from the 1980s back in the Sudan, and many could speak Arabic and were listening to the radio. David Musa listened whenever he could, and commented, 'And another thing people are afraid of is the Arabs [here, by the nickname "red ears"]. If you go home they say you should pray with them. People are very afraid of this. The people of Omer are now people of *shari'a* and don't want people of the Bible to live with them at all.'[21]

Being caught between varieties of religious proselytism, as so many Sudanese are, especially from the south and the transitional areas, creates special tensions of its own. There can be no easy compromise, no synthesis. For most western missionaries, the world of Islam is something 'out there', external, but for Sudanese communities like the refugees from the Blue Nile it cannot be excluded, it is simply part of the world they have to live with. They have relatives in Khartoum, even boys fighting for the national army and as 'holy warriors' for Islam in the PDF. The Omda, for whom respect certainly grew in the course of the long trek, was a Muslim. Islam has to be engaged with in one way or another, it is part of the *internal* landscape. But perhaps partly because one cannot merge together, or even reconcile, the oppositional demands of modern Christian and Islamic advocacy, there remains a space for those life-related concepts and practices stemming from what I have called the cultural 'archive'. Christian teachings, whether in the modified 'biblical' style of the scriptures in the Uduk language itself, or in English, or concepts from Arabic language discourse, have not displaced basic understandings of life and death, though they have certainly reshaped some of these, in line with the new moral dualism. We can see this, for example, in the various ways that the language has taken on terms from Arabic. A number of the apparitions reported to me in the

[21] David Musa, Karmi, 19 Sept. 1992.

context of exile have been described as *iblis*, Arabic for 'devil'. And it is common today, though I do not remember this usage from the 1960s, to speak of worrying, troubling ideas of a kind that can make you ill and even die, as *fikra*. While this is an Arabic term for 'idea' or 'thought', it does not carry the darker sense that it takes on when incorporated into Uduk.

What has happened in fact to the old practices? Some have simply been dropped altogether. For example, there used to be a ritual proced- ure called *koŋgoro/*, for protecting the ripening harvest from birds and insects, especially flies which laid eggs that turned into grubs in the budding heads of sorghum. This involved a period of quiet in the fields, restrictions on movement in the heat of the day and on sexual relations. In Bonga, a former *koŋgoro/* specialist, Tuda Bata, told me the rites were no longer done. Whereas sorghum in the old homeland used to get sick easily, 'like human beings', the UN grain was very clean and did not get these worms. He explained in fond detail all the protective and cleansing rituals he used to carry out for sorghum (maize was never sensitive in the same way). He pointed to the lax way in which youngsters now create noise and confusion, and take sweet sorghum prematurely from the fields, and he can do nothing about it.[22]

The healing practices of the ebony diviners, so visible in the 1960s, seemed also to have disappeared, along with the Gurunya rites designed to save the lives of vulnerable infants.[23] But then a number of individual former ebony diviners were still providing consultations, and beginning to appropriate modes of diagnosis and healing from the wider Sudanese context. In particular, I heard that one senior diviner from the old days, Nyethko, was beginning to take on cases of *tumbura* possession, under- stood locally as a 'Bunyan' phenomenon, but well known across the Sudan as a variety of *zar* spirit possession, typically occurring in com- munities historically linked with military slavery.[24] An Uduk man had married a brother's daughter of Sebit Robo, the Funj chief from Geissan,

[22] Tuda Bata, Bonga, 17 Aug. 2000.

[23] For the latter, see *'Kwanim Pa*, ch. 7.

[24] For comprehensive studies, see Janice Boddy, *Wombs and Alien Spirits: Women, Men and the Zar Cult in Northern Sudan* (Madison: Wisconsin University Press, 1989); and specifically for *tumbura* possession, see G. P. Makris, *Changing Masters: Spirit Possession and Identity Construction among Slave Descendants and Other Subordinates in the Sudan* (Evanston, Ill.: Northwestern University Press, 2000).

in Langkwai. She died in Nor Deng, even though she had been seen by the international medical people there. Her people themselves diagnosed her condition as possession by a *tumbura* spirit, and songs, drums, and dancing were performed for her. Nyethko learned this specialism from Elyas, whose mother was a 'Bunyan' from Jebel Jerok. Because Nyethko's group were his father's people, Elyas could hand on the ritual (known in Uduk as *arum ɲari bunyan*) without danger of contamination.

Although the full Gurunya rites were no longer carried out after Langkwai, the specialist women leaders of the cult having died on the long road, the odd *ɲari*/in Bonga knew how to tie the special cotton thread on a vulnerable baby. And of course there were new clinics and clinical methods for dealing with vulnerable children. And beyond the new facilities for healing the human body, there was an array of new rules and regulations for controlling the forest, the landscape, and the crops, as explained in Chapter 8. Sanctions and punishments were legion, but the 'regime' of punishment was administered by institutional agents such as forest guards, hygiene inspectors, agricultural instructors, and the police, rather than emanating from the intangible realm of moral and spiritual taboos connected with the responsive nature of living things in themselves.

The landscape itself used to be littered with the remains and signs of the past. Shades of the dead could manifest themselves, though rarely with evil intent, from beyond the grave. In Bonga, as in the previous administered camps, it was not permitted for burial sites to be scattered across the landscape near people's homes, but all were concentrated together in a fixed place at a suitable distance from the settlement. In a few early cases, the authorities required reburial. Strangers were buried together, and relatives far apart, which I think carried an aura of the 'unquiet dead'. Even more deeply worrying were the cases of people who had been left along the way, not yet quite dead. Each time I have talked about the trek I have heard of yet more people abandoned in this way. Women resettled in the USA were spontaneously talking to me about this many years after the event. It is partly the knowledge of so many unburied persons out there that gives the memory of 'wilderness' its power. The 'hunter's imagination' I have written about in my earlier books usually had connection with actual encounters with the dangerous animals of the wild, or with the shades of elephants, leopards, and so on once killed by one's patrilateral forebears, which could be a source of affliction for many generations following. In Bonga, hunting was strongly prohibited by the Ethiopian government, though what could you do if the odd crocodile walked right out of the river to your front door? In this as other spheres, whereas there had once been an intimate link between the bodily, the physical condition or event, and its *integral* 'spiritual' consequences, there was a new dichotomy between the material and the spiritual. Both were very 'real'. Your main worry these days over killing a crocodile might well be very pragmatic, that is being found out by the police. But at the same time there was no lack of strange visions; for example, as late as the year 2000 William Danga reported to me various apparitions that had been seen of a leopard woman, supposedly emanating from one of the new non-Uduk groups. He heard that 'she' had died, and was greatly relieved as 'she' had been bothering people.[25] Earlier, in Karmi, several people had experienced visions of something evil. Martha told me of her own strange vision:

In this place, people run away at night. They see something which they say is like a dog. It's something like a dog, but not a dog, but it flaps like this, and people run, shouting out, children, and adults too! They say, 'Is it Jesus?' They keep asking, 'Who's that? Is it Jesus?' The thing rushes away, and then they go to sleep. But they shout out a lot. But you can't get it and hold it down.

It is like the wind. Like the wind. People are always crying out.—*And you have seen it too?*—I myself too! Last night, I was sleeping, and it had a big head, and big feet, and I couldn't cry out, I looked out of the entrance, it was very dark, and I called—'Who's that?' because I was so startled, it went *saoow, saoow.* 'Is that Jesus? Jesus?' But it wasn't there. I sang a church song, slept a little, and sang again, in case something came in the hut again. Then when I sang, it went away. I slept a little; then the children called out from the other hut, 'Mother! Come, something is here, flapping, and now it's gone away. Did you see it?' 'Yes, we saw it but it went away.' We were very apprehensive. I said all right, keep quiet, it's over. It's always happening, you will see, and you will hear it.[26]

I myself had heard a child run outside screaming the previous night, part of the disturbance described. Martha told me that this sort of thing had not happened in Maiwut, but only in Karmi. There was something evil here: 'Something which flashes like a torch, they say, *dwak dwak dwak.*

---

[25] William Danga Ledko, Bonga, 3 Sept. 2000.
[26] Martha Nasim Ahmed, Karmi, 20 Sept. 1992.

It flaps like an owl, sometimes it lights up at night, *yar yar yar.*' I asked whether people might be afraid because so many died on the road, but Martha told me something in addition. Karmi was a place where many had died shortly before they themselves had arrived. There were skulls in the bush, human skulls, and armbones, which people had found over the road, beyond the clinic and towards the river. They had heard that the people living here before were all killed. Indeed this was one of the sites where a large number of highlanders from the north of Ethiopia had been resettled during the Mengistu regime, as a way of relieving the famines there. At the changeover of government, the local Anuak had massacred many of the people of this and other settlements. Martha mentioned that the Ethiopian officials had told the refugees not to wander on that side, where there were many bullets lying around, but to stay on the south side of the road, where there had been maize fields.

There has to be a complicated answer to the question as to what constitutes Christian faith in a context of great vulnerability as in a refugee settlement like Bonga. Barbara Harper heard later about the apparitions in Karmi from a group of Christian women, none of whom admitted to having seen the frightening *arum* themselves; those who saw them were 'the people who had gone to the dance'. It is no longer a matter of choice between the 'old' and the 'new', because these have themselves been realigned. Alongside the remarkable flourishing of the churches, even through the period when the main body of refugees had no formally ordained pastor, and even surviving the strange outbreak in Itang at Christmas 1990, we have to recognize the pull towards a counter-view within the world they shared. It is plain that we have to report a new dualism; of God/Jesus on the one hand, and devils on the other. Individuals have to locate themselves in this world, which might look like a battle ground to protagonists of whatever world religion; but it is an interlocking and encompassing world in itself for the people, who do not necessarily wish to fight an ideological battle in addition to all their other struggles. Where can people go for guidance? The inner capacity of people to perceive ground-truths through dreaming, as I have already indicated, is still central to the way they orient themselves in the present situation. From the modest evidence I have been able to gather, it is quite clear, in addition, that dreams are more than the creation or emanation of any individual consciousness as such. As Akira Okazaki's work has shown in relation to the Ingessana, dreams are historical as well as psychological phenomena, at least in the way they are reported and shared with listeners at the time, and later passed on to be recalled as almost 'prophetic' understandings.[27]

There are many examples of what we might see as 'reasonable' dreams about the trek, specifically of people having foreseen future flight. Barbara Harper was driving myself and a young SIM worker, Sarah di Pasquale (now Sarah Shannon), up to Addis Ababa in 1994 when we found ourselves discussing dreams. Barbara mentioned how Tukka, widow of Luyin (Obadiah), had told her of a dream her husband had had long ago. He had said to Tukka, 'Some time in the future, you are going to have to escape from Chali, and we'll all be going on the road, but I'm going to die on the road, and you and Dhithi [their son Martin Luther's wife], are going to get lost from the rest of the group. But you will find your way to Khartoum.'[28] Six years later, Barbara spontaneously mentioned Luyin's dream again to me, emphasizing that it had come to him years and years before the people fled, or at least that was how people now spoke about it. Barbara also mentioned that Michael Beya, by this time the main pastor of the Chali church in Bonga, also often reported dreams. 'Before the army came and attacked them, at Chali, he had a dream and he warned the people ahead. I *think* it was there. . . . But he ordered everybody to get up and flee, and sure enough, the army came right after them.'[29] The Uduk even became known for their dreams among some of the other Sudanese they met along the way. In Nor Deng, I heard from a Nuer SPLA officer about an Uduk lady who had a dream in Itang that they were not safe there.

Some reflections on the past acquire a dreamlike character in themselves, especially when 'prophetic' words or happenings are recalled from the past and related to the present. Comparisons between present dilemmas and traditions of the past are sometimes quite straightforward. Past aggression from armies and slave traders is a particularly prominent theme, referring mainly to the times of the notorious Sheikh Khogali Hassan of the Ethiopian border hills—the whole period summed up as the dreadful times of 'Kujul' (see Historical Introduction).

[27] See, for example, Akira Okazaki, 'The making and unmaking of consciousness: Nuba and Gamk strategies for survival in a Sudanese borderland', in Richard Werbner (ed.), *Postcolonial Subjectivities* (London: Zed Books, 2002).

[28] Barbara Harper, near Bonga, 30 Nov. 1994.

[29] Barbara Harper, near Bonga, 1 Sept. 2000.

For example, chief Soya Bam of Pam Be commented: 'When things were like this before in the old days there was a big chief in Pam Be, Bamagud; he gathered people together, when people were scattered in the grass; but now it is very, very difficult.' I asked if things today were like the days of Kujul. 'Yes, that's it; but don't you think this is worse than Kujul? This is worse. Bamagud, he went, and brought the government, and gathered people together.' I asked where was there a good government today who could do this? 'Where, yes indeed! There isn't one! The governments now just fight each other. It is only *arum* that can help people.'[30]

The blind lady Tocke also referred back spontaneously in Bonga one day to Bamagud, and the days of fleeing in the bush a century before, a time to which she traces the survival of her particular matrilineal line or birth-group, the Bitko. Her memories moved on from the circumstantial to the strangely prophetic. She saw, in her own way of remembering, warnings from Bamagud of the future coming of aeroplanes and motor vehicles, from which they would have to run. Her references to Ulu refer to the 1890s. The RAF was bombing the Nuer as early as the 1920s;[31] and I have noted that there were planes in Kurmuk in the 1930s (Figure 4b on p. 22)—not to forget the bombing of the Doro mission in Meban country by the Italians in 1941. But the first ones the Chali people saw close up were the mission planes, for which they cleared a landing place around 1950.

Tocke, your own mother is called Baske? And your people from long ago, would you like to tell me a story about them that you have heard?—I will tell you a story. Other people found us. . . .—Yes. We fled from Kujul in the past. Those mothers of ours who bore Baske, and an old uncle of ours called Basima, they were born from Ulu, long ago.—*You fled to Ulu?*—Yes, fleeing from the homeland, *pam* Bitko. We fled, and children were born in the bush. We Bitko. . . .—*Now you fled from Kujul up to Ulu, is that why you called one of your people 'Kujul'?*—Yes, Kujul. And then they bore that uncle Basima. . . . She ran with the baby in her arms. People said, her brothers said, 'Take this baby with you!' She was running. The blood was coming from her belly and she gave birth. She was going along, fleeing to Ulu, and she had the baby, and carried it with her. . . .

[30] Soya Bam, Karmi, 20 Sept. 1992.
[31] Douglas H. Johnson, *Nuer Prophets: A History of Prophecy from the Upper Nile in the Nineteenth and Twentieth Centuries* (Oxford: Clarendon Press, 1994), 192–5.

People went to Ulu in one big group together. Then there was one man who led the people home. And he was called, at that time long ago, that man was called Bamagud. He is the one who became the leader of the people who had gone to Ulu. That's the story people used to tell us.— . . . *Did he know Arabic, maybe, or* . . . —Yes, he knew Arabic, that's why he led the people home. Led them home, divided them up, across the whole of the homeland. Long ago. He divided people up, taking them in a whole big group and directing them here and there to fill up the homeland. This is our way, and that is your way, and this one over here. Like that. Sorting us out on the land.[32]

Tocke wished to talk to me seriously, because I could pass on what I had heard. 'If we talk to you like this, the children will later come to know these things. Because in the future I won't be here. We shall die here in this place!' Those of us around laughed and reassured her. 'Does *arum* keep us for ever? I might go and die right here in front of you. . . . Hunger killed so many, and I was left to survive, to reach Ethiopia here. . . . Arum helped me. Arum helped me. You'll see another time, it will come and cut my throat, *tabat*!' She pointed out, quite straightforwardly, that if something happened again and people had to flee away, 'How can I go with them, blind like this?' She regaled us for a while in the entertaining way she had with dramatic stories of stumbling around and grazing her hands and feet on the long road, making everybody laugh. Then she became quite serious again.

The time of Kujul? That was different. . . . This time, things have grown much worse; because of running around, around, we have been running all around, over the whole world maybe. Right over there; [indicating], right down there, [indicating another direction], people fled from Itang, to, er, that place we went to on the way to Nor, but I've forgotten its name, the place where they took us in a boat, the Dhamkin told us to go, you will die of hunger later, come on and follow people. We appeared at Jikau, and they sent us on to Nor. They took us to Nor, was it Nasir, yes, we crossed the river at Nasir. Then we were released from there, on the way to Gambela. We appeared at Itang, and then towards Gambela itself. We stayed in Gambela a short time, and people led us to live in Karmi . . .

Now the time of Kujul was not like this. We fled from here [that is, home at the time] to Ulu, and people stayed a year, they say, just one, and Bamagud led people home. People then stayed at home. In the Sudan. . . . Then those people gave birth to the children whose names we still know, they lived in the homeland and gave birth to us.

[32] Tocke, daughter of Baske, Bonga, 6 Nov. 1994.

We grew up, and they said, 'Ah, one day in the future after us, after we are taken by *arum*—after we have died: you must understand this well. Because you too, later on, if you are attacked by the Bunyan, you will have to flee to the bush.'

Tocke began to reminisce about things she had heard as a girl which now seemed to be coming true. She recalled Bamagud, at the village of a chief called Gandal, warning them about future danger from aeroplanes and motor vehicles. This is particularly interesting for us, as 'Gandal' according to my notes corresponds to the 'Farag Effendi', *wakil* to Bamagud, whose photograph appears in the Historical Introduction above as Figure 2b.

The old people used to speak to us like this. When we were very young. 'Watch out for the python behind you,' they said! You will see a thing called *teyara* [Arabic; 'aeroplane'], you will see a thing called a *torombili* [old-fashioned Arabic; 'motor car'].'—*Oh? they said this?*—Yes! they said this. That man called Bamagud, at the village of another chief I saw when I was very young, called Gandal, he told us this. We were just little. 'There is a thing that flies up there like a bird,' he said. 'It is called *teyara*. You will see in the future. And a thing called *torombili*.'

People prepared the way for it, they truly did, when we had grown up a bit, and we saw it. We saw it, and thought, 'Aah, yes, this thing they talked about has arrived'. It had really arrived. We saw it when we had grown up a little; and they had said, 'You will have to do your own running away from this thing in the future,' they said, 'after our own time, we who are telling you this.' 'You will flee,' they said, 'you will flee in the bush right over there.'

What they had said was true. . . . I absorbed it when I was young, kept it in my Stomach [that is, as permanent remembered knowledge] and I understood it. Because they had said this, truly, people will flee and give birth. . . . And you will flee with the children. These were the warnings given, and like written words on paper.[33]

Tocke had had virtually no contact with the churches through her lifetime. But her memories were interestingly matched by those of another old lady, Jisawud, more recently fallen blind, and widow of Luke Sana (half-brother of Luyin) who had been an elder of the Chali church for many years. We spoke in 2000. She was mother-in-law not only to Pastor Michael in Bonga, but also to the late Timothy Newar, who had been head of the SIC in Khartoum but had sadly died in 1996. She remembered the time before the coming of the missionaries, and

---

[33] Ibid.

recalled that the possibility of having to flee again was very much in the people's minds. She was a girl at the time of the Italian fighting on the border at the beginning of the Second World War (though this had not affected the '*kwanim pa*, who 'just stayed at home in their places').

Our mothers were the first ones who had to flee, at that time of Kujul. And after they fled, they came back home, and built a few houses scattered here and there. Then the government came, from the direction of Malakal, and said they should group together to live in one place. And the missionaries came and found them, and brought the word of Jesus and gathered them together, when they had been living scattered here and there to hide themselves from Kujul. That was in the early days of our mothers.

When we first began to grow up, we didn't know anything about the old days. But our mothers began to tell us stories, and say, 'One day, you may have to flee somewhere, as we did.' We always knew that we might have to flee again. This is what our mothers told us. And my own mother died, before I knew her. People fostered me. . . . Before, we used to live normally, people grew up, gave birth to children, and it was just recently that we fled.

They were warned when the plane first came to Chali; that it would return and attack people.[34]

Jisawud's perspective is from the very heart of the old Chali church community. But she presents a view of the current situation in the light of the past which is in accord with Tocke's testimony and would make complete sense to most others of the older generation. The encounter of the '*kwanim pa* with evangelical Christianity, and their experience of militant Islamic rule in the northern Sudan, may have introduced profoundly different alternatives in the formal 'cosmology' or religious world available to the people. The impact of old ideas about loss and suffering, and wandering in the bush, may have joined in strange ways with the concept of a fight against evil, and the conjunction may have led to weird new dreams, visions, and enactments. But through dreams and memories, both strong Christian believers and others can find meaningful ways of connecting present experience with the past, and somehow rationalizing the world by looking back to the successive experiences of previous generations, as transmitted to them; and to kinds of self-understanding which refer back to times long before the advent of the missionaries.

[34] Jisawud Moyye, Bonga, 2 Nov. 1994.

11

Reunions, Retrospectives, and Ironies

I loved a girl but she refused me
I spoke to her and she wouldn't reply
I asked her name but she wouldn't say

You should tell your heart I love you
I am wretched
You are the one I love
You must tell your heart I want you
I love you but what is your name?
I love you completely

> *Listen to this in our own home language, you*
> *   'Uduk' over there!*
> *It may sound to you like 'white people's talk', but this*
> *   song is by the lads from home.*
> *Don't say 'These are foreigners'!*
> *For we will meet again one day if God allows*
> *And we send you greetings now.*

I loved a girl but she refused me
I made her an offer but she turned me down
I loved a girl but she wouldn't have me

> *We're lost in the wilderness*
> *Like the children of Israel* [1]

The main theme of this study, the 'master narrative', is one of displacement, loss, separations. But running alongside, and sometimes counter to this, are the experiences of coming together, of returning 'home' even if that home is a temporary one, of assistance between friends and even strangers when things are tough. There are some extraordinary,

---

[1] Sung by Thoha Puna Kasha on the lyre, in Arabic, accompanied on the plastic jerry-can and sticks in *daluka* or *kaloshi* style. The middle section consists of spoken interjections in Uduk. Nor Deng, 7 Oct. 1991.

even heroic, efforts by people to rejoin each other or at least to keep in touch. In the early years of the displacement, Chali remained the key location, in theory, of 'home'; though, later, Bonga itself became in practice a kind of 'home'. A strong theme recurs through my notes and recordings of rejoining kith and kin, rescuing lost individuals, and keeping in touch by one means or another over the distances and political fault-lines. I have chosen a few striking cases among dozens to illustrate how people lost or strayed along the way are sometimes able to show up and join their relatives again; how children, especially, are lost at times of violence, but just occasionally can be rescued or find their way home; and how people who depart of their own choice to seek education or a career are positively expected to return eventually. It would be a mistake to assume that convergence and reconciliation are always the case, and a romantic delusion to imagine that a small population like the *'kwanim pa*, however much they may share through the vernacular tongue and all that goes with it, are always cosily disposed towards amity and coming together. The links of kith and kin are sometimes overridden by the wider lines of conflict, as I also illustrate below. Belonging to different political worlds, especially that of the Sudanese predatory state on the one hand and those trying to escape it on the other, for purely pragmatic reasons, can become permanent. But over time, the wider political choreography may change, and those who have been separated may be able to reflect together on some of these ironies, while yet others find themselves in yet new kinds of exile.

PERSONS LOST BY ACCIDENT, WHO TURN UP YEARS LATER

Yukke was my neighbour in the hamlet of Wakacesh where I used to visit in the 1960s. She was married to Hada, the senior *arum* specialist. In Nor Deng, her daughter Labke reminded me of those days.

You used to come to Hada's place before, didn't you? I was there with you in William's village. You used to stay there with Peyko, Shadrach.—*Yes, and I remember Yukke very well.*— ...We lived at Yukke's there, and you used to call me, saying 'Labke! Come over and take this sugar!' So I would come and collect the sugar. You would call 'Hada! Come over here, and Kutha!' Hada would come over.

But Hada, we buried him, in Langkwai.[2]

Yukke had in fact survived Langkwai, but on the escape from there she had very sore feet. With the infant of another daughter who had died in childbirth, she took the turning to Assosa town, rather than down through the mountains. Yukke remained in Assosa for many years, relatives thinking she was lost, probably dead. To my surprise one day in Bonga, I heard the news that she had been 'found' and brought 'home'. We met up for a brief conversation, but scarcely had time to fill in everything that had happened over the previous seventeen years.

Quite a number of small children were lost in the rush to escape from Assosa and back through the mountains. Three were found wandering near Geissan by Sudanese soldiers, two weeks after the main dispersal from the Assosa camp in early 1990, and they were taken to Damazin and eventually Khartoum.[3] The armed movements opposed to the then Ethiopian government were attacking the Assosa garrison, and local elements of the OLF among the Bertha opened fire on the fleeing remnants of the SPLA, and on the refugees too, as described in Chapter 4. Some infants rolled down the gullies and had to be abandoned.

It was assumed that they would all have died, but in one surprising case, a young man survived. It was in Bonga in mid-2000 that I heard a story of a young man who had tried to register, as an Uduk refugee, at the second camp, Sherkole, set up in 1997 near Assosa. However, there was a problem, because he did not speak the Uduk language, and his cheeks bore the parallel scars which are a typical custom of the local Bertha. The clerks, with their very bureaucratic ideas of 'ethnic identity', refused to allow him to register. He claimed that as a child, he had been lost on the hazardous journey through the hills in 1990, falling down a ravine with his baby sister. The two children had in fact been rescued and brought up by a Bertha family. The girl later became ill and died, while the boy went off and had various adventures in Ethiopia (including fighting with the army in the north). When the Sherkole camp was opened, he decided to leave his adopted family and rejoin his own people. The one proof he had of his original identity was the wooden back-board which Uduk children use to carry around their infant

---

[2] Labke, daughter of Yukke, Nor Deng, 28 July 1991.
[3] Letter from Akira Okazaki to me of 16 Mar. 1990 after meeting Timothy Newar; confirmed in letter from Nathan Paul, 15 Apr. 1990.

siblings. He had kept this. When he showed it to some of the Uduk in Sherkole, they recognized him as one of their own, and worked out that his actual mother—who thought her children lost for ever—was now in Bonga. As I left Bonga, plans were afoot to bring the young man there to be reunited with his mother.

CHILDREN SCATTERED DURING FIGHTING AT ITANG, 1992

A considerable number of Uduk children were scattered by cross-fire and lost at Itang during the violent incident in July 1992. Some were 'adopted' by Anuak families, and of these a few were either traced by the UN and reunited with their relatives in Bonga, or have shown up of their own accord. Others may well by now be thoroughly assimilated as Anuak. However, memories are not always completely erased in these circumstances. Dawud Hajar reminded us in conversation of how lost children were known to be adopted in the past, and that the relationship created in this way would be a long-lasting one of mutual alliance, called *abas*, 'blood-connection'.

This is something that we know from long ago, when people used to make *abas*, when people were given protection. We were *abas* with so many people, there were Meban, Bunyan, who were adopted by people, and now they have become *'kwanim pa*.

And now when we came and lived with Anuak and this happened, those Anuak were owners of the land, they gave us protection, and we have become *abas*. When we came down from Assosa, to Itang, we found them here, they were friendly to us, we used to eat together.... They were good to us, they know that we are here, they brought our kids and gave them to their mothers. That is making an important *abas* link. This is a very important matter. It is not something to be forgotten. We should hold on to this for ever. This has been done among the Uduk from long ago....

Titus Solomon, part of this conversation, mentioned how very glad he was that his brother Sidiq had come back from the Anuak people, because his elder brother had died on the way from Itang. Dawud Hajar continued to praise the Anuak, and David Musa added his own observations:

D.H.: Somebody with a good heart [lit. 'the Liver of a real human being'] will not keep a child. If it had been Nuer who had taken those children, we would not have got them back. When we went to Itang, they would not have led us to the right house. We would not have found them.

D.M.: They would have asked us to exchange cows for the children. For a girl, they would have asked for five cows . . . for looking after them.

D.H.: The Nuer have a bad custom, these Nuer who have been marrying our girls, haven't you seen what happens? He will marry a girl and not pay, and when she gives birth to a child, the Nuer will want to take the child by force. 'Those children are not yours! They belong to that woman, and her mother's brothers!' The only children you can keep are your sister's kids, so you can call them your own nephews and nieces. If your sister's child is taken, you will have no seeds. But we have a good relationship with the Anuak, and maybe our children will marry them, and they will marry ours. . . . Maybe this will happen in Bonga when we live together with the Anuak.[4]

WOMEN DISPERSED THROUGH MARRIAGE TO SPLA SOLDIERS

Throughout my visits to the various places where the Uduk had found temporary refuge, I heard of case after case of sisters or daughters who had married, or gone off with, SPLA fighters. This had happened not only in Langkwai, but also in Itang the first time round. Some had taken a sister with them. These women were now spread all over the southern Sudan, some even in the international camps of Kenya and Uganda, and according to the occasional news filtering out, a good number had children of their own but were now abandoned. From the point of view of their relatives, as 'matrilineal' as ever, whether or not the women were still married to their husbands, they and their children were regarded as fully part of the body of the '*kwanim pa*, who should be somehow rescued. I was asked several times if I could ask the UN to bring them 'home' to Bonga. The loss of grown daughters seemed to make the women even more heavily despairing, I would even use the word 'traumatized', than the loss of infants, something to which they have long been hardened.

In one case, a woman told me in 1992 of one daughter marrying a Dinka soldier in Langkwai, and when everyone left there she took a sister and another girl with her, along with two small children. Another

[4] Dawud Hajar and David Musa, Karmi, 7 Jan. 1993.

of her daughters also married a Dinka and came with them down to Itang, and then to Nasir, where he left her; she then came on with the people to Kigille, but married a Pur (Shyita) man there who took her off to Wadesa to buy food, and she was never heard of again. In another case the woman's sons by an earlier marriage got taken off by the SPLA. Yet another woman told me how Dinka soldiers took off two of her daughters by force to Dimma camp. She knew this from an Ethiopian girl who worked for the UNHCR and had seen them there. Another mother, Peke, was still very distressed in 1994 about losing touch with her daughter Roda, taken off in a different direction by her Dhamkin husband in 1991. It was when they had been through the water and the swamps and arrived at Jikau that she noticed Roda was missing. Peke agreed that her daughter had willingly married this Dhamkin husband, but she missed her deeply. She had heavy thoughts about it, anxiety, *fikra* (Arabic) at night.[5]

Martha Ahmed also had a daughter who was by this time in Kakuma camp in Kenya, having had some treatment for a bad leg. She had a Dinka husband and several children, and Martha had been actively pressing the Red Cross to enable contact. In fact Martha was given a photo of her daughter during one of my visits, a photo partly brought on foot by a returning boy soldier (see Gindi Talib's story below). Mary, sister of Martha, explained how the 'heavy' thoughts, *fikra*, about lost children could make people really ill. As mentioned in Chapter 5, a son of hers had been shot by Gaajak Nuer bandits for the sake of his gun, on the road from Itang, the first time.

The women, our women, whose children have gone away, they think a lot about their children. Those who've been led away, they think they are lost. They worry about it at night, they eat their food, and worry at night. That child of mine, where can I find him? We ask, where have they gone? That child who was taken off, where is he or she now? We don't know their place. Who can tell us? There you are—those are the worries we have at night. Is this child still alive, or has she died? These are the heavy ideas we have. Some people die of this worry, even though they're not ill. Because the children have been taken off again and again. Now it's as though the youngsters had been sold. So what is happening to them? We feel our children have been sold. No one tells us anything, and this makes us think that they may have died. Some women go on worrying, worrying,

---

[5] Peke, mother of Roda, Bonga, 27 Oct. 1994 (video).

worrying, for years. They eat, but they get thinner and thinner. They go on worrying and one day these ideas may kill them.[6]

There were occasionally those who followed their kin or tried to trace them across the southern Sudan, especially the brothers of women who had married Dinka or other southern soldiers. I heard one such story from some Uduk who were temporarily in Nairobi in 1995. A young girl called Mara Wobe was one of those who married a Dinka husband in Langkwai. He took her off from there, with a small child. However, her brother, Wobe Dongo, followed them, right into the war zones, along with the fighters of William Nyuon's group. They were thought to be in the refugee camp of Mogale in Uganda, together with a number of children. The husband had wanted to take the children to Bahr el Ghazal. 'But Wobe said, "We shall leave together with those people, wherever they want to take the children. If they want to take them to Bahr el Ghazal, we go together."' An older man explained further: 'He said that if they will take these small children to where they are going, we had better go with them and die with them, in the place they are going. Because I cannot leave these small children to go by themselves.... Yes, these were children of his actual sister.'[7]

There are stories too of the return of some dispersed women. For example, after the fighting in Torit (near Kapoeta in Eastern Equatoria) in 1992, five of the Uduk women there were 'taken over to the government side', and flown to Khartoum. These women were able to locate the other *'kwanim pa* there and accommodation was found with them in the informal 'suburb' of Mayo on the southern outskirts of the city. Friends and kin were then able to resettle them and their children back in Chali. However, one woman was left behind in Torit. I was told her story quite spontaneously by a young man normally based in Khartoum.

I want to talk about the young daughter of Jandhi, a daughter of Marti who was separated from the time of fighting in Torit.... She had married a Meban in Torit, and tried to find her way of following the others to Khartoum. She came alone. And what route she took, how she came from there we don't know. We got the message that she was coming.

She made it to Khartoum, but then she just stayed on her own, not knowing how to find the place of the *'kwanim pa*, or where she could meet the *'kwanim*

[6] Mary Ahmed, Karmi, 19 Sept. 1992.
[7] Group discussion, Nairobi, 19 Nov. 1995.

pa, though there were some in Mayo, and some in Soba, and some in Fitteihab. She just stayed there, waiting around for four days, with her child on her back, asking people and looking for the *'kwanim pa*.

And then a certain soldier saw her misery and said, 'You won't find your Uduk here in Khartoum, because it is a very big place, and we don't know the place they live, or where to take you.' But they gave her a little money, saying she could find a vehicle to look for *'kwanim pa* in Damazin. . . .

She took a bus, from the market place at Suk al-Shabi, and went to Damazin. She arrived in Damazin, and again spent a long time, with her child on her back, riding in a donkey-cart, and looking for the *'kwanim pa*. Seeking, seeking, seeking, with her things on her head. And then, when the sun was about to go down, some Meban fellows came along speaking in Meban. She heard the Meban language, stopped the cart, and asked them, 'Are you Meban?' and they said yes.

She then explained who she was, saying, 'I am an Uduk woman. I am looking for *'kwanim pa*. If you know any Uduk person living near here, maybe you could take me there. I need a rest because I am very tired, carrying my baby on my back for so long and my things on my head.' The Meban fellows took charge of her. Saying, 'All right. We'll go to that house, where there is a *wathim pa* living here in Damazin.' They took her to the house of Machinga, Machinga Beini, and knocked on the door. Those people came quickly . . . at last, she could stay, and rest awhile, and they looked after her.[8]

In talking about this story, the group suddenly realized that the woman's mother, Jandhi Balajau, had been one of the 'orphans', some of them twins rescued from infanticide and looked after at the mission in the old days.

ITANG: THE BOYS' DEPARTURE, AND OCCASIONAL 'RETURN'

The story of the 'Lost Boys' of the southern Sudan has become well known in the West. One party of these were Uduk, and while only a few of these have shown up in America, they were scattered over the southern Sudan and some made it back to their people in Khartoum or in Bonga. Many children had been encouraged to go from the southern Sudan, where there were very limited chances of education, to the Ethiopian refugee camps in the late 1980s. And many of these were genuinely stranded when the camps had to be evacuated in 1991.

[8] Nairobi, 19 Nov. 1995.

There was a special centre for 'unaccompanied minors' among the seven centres for the displaced created around Nasir that year, and of these, some ended up as child refugees in Kenya and some were eventually resettled. But the Uduk group had left Itang before the evacuation. Paul Joseph, a teacher with some earlier training from Khartoum, organized a group of these boys from Itang as early as January 1991 in order to 'go to school in Kenya'. They were caught up in the renewed hostilities of late 1991–2, following the split in the SPLA, as the Sudan government pressed its advantage and regained territory in the far south. Some of these boys were looked over by SPLA recruiters and found too young. I had heard about the expedition from Joseph Jabir, Paul's father, in Nor Deng in 1991; he assumed his son was now teaching in Kapoeta, and wanted me to pass on the news that they themselves were now living in Nasir (after having to leave Itang and go back to the Sudan).

It was three years later, in Bonga, that I met up with some of the youngsters who had made it back there to be with their people, after many adventures. One of them was Gindi Talib, a son of Omda Talib el Fil. After the group got to Kapoeta, they waited for some time hoping to start school. Then they were divided up, some sent to Torit, others to Kenya, and Gindi was effectively diverted into the SPLA, selected with about thirty-five others to take part in a planned assault on Juba. From there, retreating soldiers were then dislodged from Liria by air attack. A comrade of his, Jenen Shakka, was so young he was left behind in Kapoeta and never even given a gun to use, but made it back northwards on his own with some Nuer (apparently civilians) fleeing back to Nasir. I quote from his story below, but start with Gindi, the Omda's son, who found himself in the war against 'the Arabs'. Gindi was born in Chali and went to the government school there. He was very small when the troubles started in the mid-1980s, and the people left for Langkwai. By 1994, in his mid- or late teens, he spoke at length about his life since leaving Itang, though I quote only some key parts of our conversation here.

When we were living in Itang, they took us to school. They said we would go to school in Kenya. We left on 5 January. We went through Fugnido, and we met a commander there who said, 'Why have you brought these youngsters, what are they going to do?' . . . We said we wanted to learn to read and write in school. He said no, we should go back, and return later. . . . We went on, and arrived at Dimma. It was the same there. 'Why have these small kids been sent?' . . . *Who led you from Itang to Fugnido at first?*—A Dhamkin. . . . He was called Bol, but we didn't know his father's name. He led us, until we got to Boma. Then the commander in Boma asked us, 'What are you all coming here for? All you youngsters?'

After some discussion as to what should be done with them, they were taken to Kapoeta, and then to Kenya, and then back to Torit.

And then the problem broke out. People said, 'Prepare youselves, you are all going to Juba. This is your land.' There was no school at all. . . . They said, 'The Arabs are sitting in your place, now we have to go and fight.' People gave us guns, and we went off to fight. They took us to Nimule there, we went from there to fight at Juba, we fought and fought, and the Arabs were too much for us, and we came back to a place called Liria. We stayed for a time in Liria, and I ran away from there.

I asked Gindi who was leading them to attack Juba, was it John Garang or Willliam Nyuon or who? He replied that he was with Garang, and William Nyuon, and Salva Kiir (this was before Nyuon broke away). Some of his friends were killed at Liria.

I reached Pibor, and lived there.—*Were you alone, or did you come with others?*— We were four. Four Uduk boys. Yes we ran together from Liria. . . . We said we were Uduk boys, and they said, 'Your people aren't in Nasir any more, they have gone to Kigille, and Pagak.' I said thanks, and went on. . . . I got to Kigille, and found the people there. I had come from very far, and I stayed there, and they asked me about the Janoub [Arabic; 'the South']. . . . They wanted me to leave the gun, and stop being a soldier. I stayed just two months, and then they came and took me off to another place of fighting. . . .

We were three months on the road, four or five months. We went to fight at Juba . . . we went to Pibor, to Malakal. . . . Then to Nasir, four months there. Then they said 'Do you want to go to your mother, your relatives?' They said, 'Yes, they are in Ethiopia.' Yes, they said I should take my gun with me, to kill wild animals. So I went on, with my gun, and then when I crossed over the border to Ethiopia I left it behind. So I reached my people here. That's my story.

I asked him about various names of boys I already had a note of, who might have been in the same group. Many of them he did know, and to give a raw sense of the whole predicament, I quote just a part of the detail he gave me.

And Hassan Puda Tuda?—Yes! I know him, the others I don't, but he was one of us. Hassan Puda I know.—*Where did you know him, when? Was he in Liria or where?* I left him in Uganda there, in the area of Uganda.—*Nimule?*—Yes, somewhere near Nimule, when we were in Nimule we had a campaign into Uganda.—*And then Tera Shwamalo Ngala?* Yes, he was together with us.—*and Thula Ethan?*—Thula Ethan is there.—*You know him?*—Yes. They're all Uduk lads. *And Dilab Rigim?*—Yes, he was one of them.—*And Luha Shuma?*—Yes.— *Did you all go to Nimule?*—That Luha Shuma, when he was in Torit, he fell, from a mango tree. He went up to pick mangoes, and he fell, and they took him to Nimule.—*He fell from a mango tree?*—Yes, from up the tree.—*Did he die?*— No, he survived.—*Thank goodness! and Walit Ahmed Gideon Lidi?*—We were together with them at Juba.—*And was he in Liria, the fighting at Liria?*—Yes, we fought at Liria. . . . —*And a fellow called Hassan Tutha Bakhit?*—Hassan Tutha Bakhit?—*He wrote a letter, and wrote the names of others too, Yunis Hadi, and Beshir Mamuth?*—Those fellows maybe got separated off.

Some of the boys at Liria had somehow arrived in Khartoum, and Gindi had been delighted to see a picture of three of them, brought by Pastor Timothy Newar, head of the Sudan Interior Church, on his visit to Bonga.

They were in Liria with us in that fighting. When we were bombed by the aeroplane, that's what scattered us. The Dhamkin all ran from the plane, and a lot of the boys thought we should go with them, but we stayed there. Lots of them felt the same way, they were afraid of the plane, always being afraid of being killed by the plane, 'Let's go with them!' and they went to Nimule. But I left them, and ran away. . . . I found them in this picture: I thought they had been killed, I got separated; this is from God [*arum*]. I found them in the picture, and I was very happy . . . I have only just heard that they are living in Khartoum. . . . I wish I had a picture too, the fellows in Juba, they don't know where I am. They may think I have died.

Gindi had met up several times on his various journeys with a particular friend (who happened to be from the Bertha people originally from the hills to the east of the Uduk homeland).

I found him again here in Bonga. . . . We thought we'd never see each other again, and talk to each other. *Arum* must be with us, to have brought us together again. We fled and got separated, in the bush, and thought we'd never find *'kwanim pa* again. . . . 'How did you manage?' 'Oh, we were hungry, some died of hunger, we fled from the place of fighting . . . But this thing called "government" [*hakuma*], if we had it among the *'kwanim pa* . . . and if the boys could go to school in Gambela, we needn't go back.' I laughed . . . and said, 'But I'm not going back to the south, no, no, that's the way of the devil.'

When Gindi had arrived in Kigille he found his father, Omda Talib, who tried to persuade him that he should go back with him to Chali (now, in 1992, under government control again). But Gindi preferred to follow the rest of the people across the frontier.

So why didn't you go back to Chali with your father?—Me? I was hungry for the people here. I wanted to see everyone. To see them more. I told him in Kigille there: 'Are the Arabs not there, is there not still a conflict there? . . . All right, you can go to the government, to the Arabs there, but I'm going to Ethiopia.' He said, 'But what for? You should come to our country.' I said there's still a quarrel there and the Arabs are there. And I was very small when we left, so I don't really know the Sudan well. . . . We have just been wandering. My father said, 'You don't understand, these black people are confusing things among themselves, you need to come back to the Sudan. . . . Are you going to live in the bush like this, or are you going to live at home?' I said I would prefer the bush. . . . Anyway, the government itself seizes people at the garrisons and puts them in the army. . . . —*Thank you very much Gindi, I understand things better now. . . . And later, I will write things down, the history of these things.*[9]

Paul Joseph himself was at this time in Kakuma. And through the networks, Gindi had not only information about some of the Uduk women dispersed across the south, but actually brought as far as Kigille a photo for Martha Ahmed of her daughter and son from the Kakuma camp in Kenya. Someone else carried it from him over the border, and I saw how thrilled she was.

Young Jenen Shakka had not been sent to the front line. But his story was also very vivid, and very brave. They had arrived on 25 May at Kapoeta. They had carried food to eat on the way from Dimma camp; it was the high-energy food Unimix, known as 'fafa', labelled 'USA'. It had been 'given by the white people of the UN'. They spent Christmas (1991) in Kapoeta, and went to Torit for the next Christmas. There was no sign of schooling for them. In his group were just a few *'kwanim pa*, including a son of Martha, Walid Japa.

We were living there, and then the Arabs came and attacked the place and we fled.—*Did they come with vehicles, or planes or what?*—They came with vehicles. . . . we fled with the Nuer . . . they were fleeing, down in that direction, and we came to Nasir.—*You came to Nasir with these Nuer?*—Yes.—*Were they not soldiers?*—No, they were not soldiers. The soldiers were separate . . . yes, I came on foot. . . . Ayod was on this side, on the inside, I went through Waat. I fled through Waat.—*You didn't take Gindi's route, through Malakal!*—No, I didn't go

---

[9] Gindi Talib, Bonga, 27 Oct. 1994.

there. . . . —*Didn't the SPLA people give you guns to carry?*—No, they didn't give us guns. We stayed just without anything.

—*And when did you get to Nasir?*—The 25th April 1993. . . . I just found some Bunyan [here, northern Sudanese or Bertha] fellows, and I asked and they said some had gone to Maiwut, and some had gone to Itang . . . a fellow who was looking after refugees said I should go to Itang and wrote a letter for me. You will find the people in Itang . . . On the way to Itang, yes, it was a very bad place on the way. If you carried a blanket with you, you could be killed. . . . —*Gaajak?*—Yes, Gaajak. They attack you, if you carry a blanket they would kill you.—*Did you see this with your own eyes?*—Don't you know the marks on their heads? A person who is not marked, they don't want him to pass along their way. Their race [Arabic: *ginis*] is different.

So I left all my stuff and went without anything, just in my skin . . . They asked about me, I was going with a Nuer fellow, he spoke to them in their language. He explained this boy is not a Nuba,[10] and they asked, 'Is he a Nuer?' and why was my head not marked; and he said, 'This boy has been in school. That's why he's not marked.'—*He deceived the other, saying you were a Nuer?*—Yes, he said I wasn't marked because I had been in school . . . I came to Itang with these Nuer, and up to Karmi. The senior man who was leading me was going to bring me all the way to my place, but people stopped him with a stick and said only Uduk were allowed to go to Bonga. So he stayed there. 'You want to see your mother? This is why I have brought you through these bad places.'[11]

Jenen was advised not to go on by himself on foot but to wait for a vehicle; but all the cars going wanted money from him. He was finally helped by a Nuer who mentioned his problem to the Ethiopian 'in charge of people'— I suggested this might have been Makonnen Tesfaye (who had known and helped the people since the first time in Itang), and indeed it was. Thus, young Jenen was able to find his people again, in Bonga, and was already attending one of the informal schools under the trees.

By 1995, other young men were present as far away as western Equatoria with Commander Malik Agar, himself from the Ingessana people of the southern Blue Nile and now in change of this front in the war; and some, along with some women, were in Uganda. Uduk lads were also in the Nuba Hills with the SPLA. One of those I met, washed up in Nairobi with no papers at all, was later resettled in Australia. From him I got news of my old friend William Dhupa, who joined the Arrow

[10] There had recently been extra-judicial killings of Nuba in Nasir.
[11] Jenen Shakka, Bonga, 2 Nov. 1994.

Battalion, fought in both the first and second battles for Kurmuk, and had acquired a star (promoted lieutenant), but had been wounded in the leg in the Nuba Hills, and was now in Natinga, an SPLA military camp near the Kenyan border. He was remembered by his colleagues as a brave and good man. The following passages are from general discussions held in Nairobi in 1995, partly in English.

[First voice] Yes, William Dhupa, he is in Natinga. He has a broken leg. He can't do anything any more. He's just in Natinga with the women, and with the other lads who've broken legs.—*Can he walk?*—He can walk, but only with a stick.—*Is there any doctor to treat him?*—Ay! He's just living with it like that, there's no doctor.—*He hasn't gone to Lokichoggio?*—Not at all. If you need to go there, you have to have a doctor to write you a note to take with you. If you don't have a letter you can't go.—*Is his leg actually broken?*—The bone has split on one side, and healed, but not in the right way...

[Another voice] The problem is that there are great numbers of this young red army,[12] who fled, don't want to serve any more... these young boys, some of them are looking for education and they don't get it, and they cannot make it by themselves. And also there are some wounded, we call them wounded heroes. In March I brought twenty-seven, and left them in Natinga. In fact we have 700 wounded.—*Good heavens.*—Some have got no legs, some got no two legs, some have nothing totally, and nobody's taking good care of them. That's it.[13]

Thus young lads like these were swept into the war situation in the far south, in the mid-1990s, and inevitably drawn into the shifting alliances of the SPLA, just occasionally making it back on their own to their relatives in the Ethiopian refugee scheme at Bonga. Meanwhile other contacts were being facilitated, or hampered, behind the scenes by the wider political alignments of the time, not always visible to the people involved. For example, there were high-level visits to Bonga by representatives and leaders of the SIC in Khartoum, such as the late Pastor Timothy Newar whose visit overlapped with mine in 1994. This might seem reasonable as a gesture of church solidarity, but the arrangements for his visas on leaving and re-entering the Sudan made by the church would also have been in line with the government's other efforts to tempt the Blue Nile refugees back home. When the head of the SIC, son of the late Pastor Paul, visited from Khartoum there was a noticeable

---

[12] The 'red army' were the child soldiers.
[13] General discussion, Nairobi, 19 Nov. 1995.

ripple of resentment among some of ordinary refugees who understood perfectly well that it would not be safe to go home. There were also at least preliminary discussions over sending teachers from the Sudan side to Bonga, something that the international SIM people (firmly present in both Khartoum and Addis Ababa) believed would not cause problems with either government. Recall that Sudanese officials at the consulate in Gambela were visiting Karmi a couple of years earlier and making direct appeals to the people, in violation of international law. I believe these contacts continued up to 1995, as their vehicles were often seen at the swelling village market just outside the refugee site, where they were 'buying vegetables'.

MISSED ENCOUNTERS

Meanwhile, in Nairobi in 1995, I heard from the small group of Sudan Interior Church people from Khartoum on a visit to Nairobi that they were puzzled and disappointed as to why they could not find out anything about their people in the Kakuma camp, itself of course strongly identified with the SPLA. A certain pastor, who used to be General Secretary of this church in Khartoum, had gone to the USA for study in 1985. He then came straight to Kenya, to help care for refugees there. A veteran from the Khartoum group explained (in English), 'Now he is holding the responsibility to help, but it seems now that he doesn't want to meet us, because we tried many times to find him and to talk with him, and ask him, but he didn't come. Also those pastors who came recently from Sudan tried to meet him, but he didn't—he just say that "I will come, I will come," but he wouldn't come. We don't know what he's, he's afraid of, in meeting us.' I tried to get over the point that since this pastor was caring for those who had left the Sudan out of fear for their lives, neither he nor the UNHCR could start arranging meetings with visitors holding Sudanese passports. My friend still could not see the problem, since all he wanted was some information about kith and kin in Kakuma camp, where the pastor visited regularly. And at the same time, there were some young men around in Nairobi who seemed to have dropped out of the SPLA and were seeking to 'return' to Bonga, where of course they had never set foot. Others were keen to join the refugee resettlement schemes for the USA, Canada, and Australia.

Looking back at the whole crucial period following the 1989 Islamist coup in Khartoum and the weakening of the Ethiopian government from about the same date, we see how fragile and uncertain conditions of life were for those who had been linked with the SPLA. Khartoum had indirectly, and possibly directly, supported the ambitious bid by the Nasir commanders to supplant Garang's leadership of the SPLA.[14] They immediately took advantage of the split in the movement which escalated into brutal internecine war, and extensive military advances by Sudanese forces into large areas of the south. In this they had tacit and even open support from the new Ethiopian government. The loyalties of individuals from all communities were open to new suspicions, and none more so than those from communities literally on the front line of the civil war, where territories and places had changed hands several times already. However, after the rupture in the new friendship between Khartoum and Addis Ababa from 1995, the 'Nasir faction' of the SPLA was no longer a key player and Garang's movement was strengthening again. The usual conflict lines and loyalties were being more or less re-established, though the goals of many supporters of the SPLA were shifting towards 'separation of the south' in some form, as against the secular democratic reform of the Sudan as a whole; this in itself created further areas of ambiguity and non-transparent behaviour by politicians.

It was shortly after the end of the Khartoum–Addis Ababa honeymoon period, in 1996, that I had a chance to talk with my old friend Stephen Missa, soon after his retirement from the final teaching phase of his career with the army. His account of the crucial years of uncertainty shows very vividly how the state and its priorities can override what individuals would otherwise know about a situation; and how the otherwise natural personal networking of even well-placed individuals can be frustrated.

I conclude this chapter of reminiscences and retrospectives with his story, a story which turns upon the self-evident expectation that a person would be loyal to their own kith and kin in a war situation; but ironically, how this was denied to him, and to the people whose welfare was constitutionally his concern, by the strategic priorities of the state at that time. Stephen Missa's participation in the defence and administration

---

[14] Johnson, *Root Causes*, 96, 99.

of his country remained purely professional, rather than ideological, throughout. His loyalty was—perhaps like that of the late Omda Talib of Chali—to the abstract conception of *hakuma*, government, in the sense of the Sudanese nation-state in its historical continuity, rather than to any particular regime which might hold power at a given point in time. I have previously mentioned how Stephen had once been part of the Damazin area command and had in fact opened the first army post at Yabus (Chapter 1). He had first been posted to Nasir in 1981–2, where he had happened to meet up with David Musa who was stationed as a policeman there (with two Nuer 'wives'). This was before the real resurgence of war, but just at the time when rebel fighters who had never accepted the 1972 peace agreement began to infiltrate from the Ethiopian side of the border near Akobo. He had commanded a small force sent to confront these men, now dubbed 'Anyanya Two' after the old guerrilla movement.

After the coup of Omer el Beshir in 1989, and the sudden escalation of the civil war it provoked, including the revival of SPLA activity in the southern Blue Nile (see Chapters 1 and 3), Stephen unexpectedly became the first Commissioner to be appointed by the new regime to Sobat Province, neighbour to the Blue Nile. (They were appointing mostly military people to man the civilian administration, in order to clear up the incompetence and corruption of the former regime.) Sobat was one of three provinces in Upper Nile State at that time, theoretically subject to Malakal, the others being Unity (where the army was in charge at Bentiu and there was no civilian government) and Jonglei (entirely under the control of the SPLA). The HQ for Sobat was supposed to be at Nasir, also then under the SPLA. Stephen's appointment was made quite suddenly in December of that year, at a time we now know was sensitive because Khartoum was making overtures to the commanders in Nasir. He was rushed south with other new Commissioners when news reached Khartoum of the large uprising and violent reprisals just after Christmas at Jebelein on the White Nile, not too far from Renk (see Chapter 1).

With this introduction to his new posting, Stephen went on to Renk, and opened offices for Sobat Province there and in Malakal, where he and his staff started instituting administrative reforms, and clearing up corruption. Given the timing, and the number of things happening, it is not surprising that Stephen did not hear details of the sacking of the

Assosa camp in the first few days of January 1990, and the subsequent treks of the Blue Nile people from place to place. He learned later from others based in Khartoum that they were 'moving about in the bush, but we didn't know what bush'. He had no idea they had got to Itang by mid-1990, nor, very surprisingly in retrospect, that they had arrived, under SPLA direction, back in the Sudan at Nasir by mid-1991. It was only when the government had agreed, under pressure from OLS and the Nasir commanders, to allow a barge upstream to Nasir with relief food, that Ahmed el-Ghadi Jabir, a friendly official, told him that his people there were in need. Stephen thought at first he meant 'his own people' in the sense of ordinary citizens of his province.

He told me he was sending food to my people, in Nasir . . . I said, 'What do you mean about my people, I know that my people are in Ethiopia.' He said, 'No, the Uduk people are in Nasir.' I said, 'OK, this is my province. Let me go with this food,' but [he said] 'No, stay here, you will be arrested by the SPLA, they will kill you for being the Commissioner'. . . . And I asked him again, what do you mean by 'my people'? And he told me that they were '*Your people* from Blue Nile, Uduk, and they're in Nasir.' I told him, 'No, they are in Ethiopia.' He said, they *were* in Ethiopia, but now they are in Nasir. . . . 'It is dangerous for you as a Commissioner to go there, because the SPLA will arrest you and make a big row over this.'[15]

Stephen was thus sitting in Malakal when the first barge arrived in late July and went on up to Nasir. He was kept out of the arrangements, which were made by the Upper Nile Governor and the army commander. I myself witnessed the arrival of the barge and the welcome it received (Figure 12 above), having no more idea than the refugees that Stephen was the government Commissioner for our area. He had been told nothing by army intelligence, nor by Riak Machar, then courting (or being courted by) Khartoum. He learned about the departure of the barge from some Uduk lads with the Sudanese army posted at the head of the Jonglei Canal just south of Malakal. Five or six of them had come to greet him when they heard he was in Malakal, and mentioned they had seen it going up the Sobat with a load of grain. They had no more idea than Stephen that there were some 20,000 '*kwanim pa* among the stranded around Nasir. If they had, he agreed with me that they would

---

[15] Stephen Missa, UK, 14 Sept. 1996.

probably have gone off on foot to join them. Stephen himself never heard that the Uduk were specifically in the place called Nor Deng until he got back to Khartoum later on.

Ahmed el-Ghadi Jabir was a Dinka from Melut (near Renk); he was 'a good man who always stood up for southerners'. Sadly, he was killed in a plane crash with other high-ranking officials going to Bentiu to look into the possibility of opening offices there, so that the Commissioner could start work. Stephen mentioned too that he was the man who 'brought up the issue about the slavery in the Abyei area, which was taken up by two Sudanese professors', Drs Ushari Mahmud and Sulei-man Baldo.[16]

I was recently asked, by a lawyer in Canada, 'How many cultures are there in the Sudan?' This lawyer was concerned with an appeal which turned on the question as to whether cultural factors could influence an accused's demeanour in court. One could find some very large figures for the 'numbers of cultures' in countries like the Sudan, but at the same time this is the wrong question. No group lives on its own, especially since the advent of modern communications; in the case of the Sudan, I have suggested that interconnections between the centre and periphery of the Sudanese state can be demonstrated in a recognizably modern form since the mid-nineteenth century, and assumed for an even longer period.

In the first chapter, I reconstructed the story of Faragallah, the Uduk man who became a tax collector for the Ottoman Turkish regime in the Sudan. He was imprisoned towards the end of the Mahdist era, along with others who had perhaps served in the Turkish armies as a result of the laying waste of their own country. Many were released on the arrival of the British-led troops at Omdurman in 1898, and others like Faragallah only after the pacification of the Ethiopian border. He returned to become again a trusted local chief back home, and with the well-remembered Bamagud to rally as many of his scattered people as possible. This story is surely a curtain-raiser for the stories of men drawn into the institutions of state, or of those who would contest its legitimacy, in our times. The story of 'his people', too, is a powerful trailer for today's stories, of people from a rural society transformed by

---

[16] Ushari Ahmad Mahmud and Suleyman Ali B. Baldo, *Al Diein Massacre: Slavery in the Sudan* (Khartoum: n.p., 1987).

its position in the modern frontierlands of a predatory state: not only caught up in the powerful projects of that state, but divided between the relative security offered by the organs of state themselves and that offered in theory by the distant hills beyond the frontiers, where unexpected powers and predators may, unfortunately, also lurk.

Epilogue
Current and Future Agendas

Big birds are coming to eat us in Bonga
Overseas lady, send us a plane!

.   .   .   .   .   .

Wait for Wendy to bring the plane
Where are these big birds flying to?
They're coming to land on the refugee place
They're coming to eat us in Bonga!
And what are the Uduk to do?[1]

The enormous scale of war and displacement in the Sudan was becoming evident in the late 1980s. People were beginning to realize that this conflict was far more severe in its conduct and its consequences than the first civil war of 1955–72. On my visit to Khartoum in 1988, prompted by hearing of the torching of all the Uduk villages and the disappearance of the people, Mark Duffield (then Oxfam's representive in the country) warned me not to expect that things would ever return to 'normal' in rural areas like the southern Blue Nile. He compared the situation to the Highland Clearances. The old small-scale subsistence farming would never come back, many of the displaced would never return, and the landscape would be transformed for the purposes of large-scale modern agriculture.[2] Twenty years later, this looks to have been an acute comparison.

To what are the refugees to return? Despite, or even because of, the material assistance they have received, courtesy of the Ethiopian

---

[1] A few lines from a song by Dangaye, in satirical mode, recorded by James Shama in Bonga, 2002.
[2] Cf. Mark Duffield, *Sudan at the Crossroads: From Emergency Preparedness to Social Security* (Falmer: Institute of Development Studies, University of Sussex, May 1990).

government and the international community, they are alienated from their previous existence as locally committed subsistence cultivators without many expectations of the wider world. They feel in some ways stranded in Ethiopia and want to return 'home', but they know that 'home' will not be very like the place the older generation remember. There is an ironic tone in the song above, almost teasing, recognizing the ambiguity in my own intermittent role as spokesperson—they know my influence was and is very limited, but to whom can they look? The big birds—whether planes with unknown cargo, or vultures—are circling overhead. Some of the youngsters who have returned report their surprise that there is no big river near Chali. They have very high expectations of the new dispensation in the Sudan, while older people know that a return to the old days of their own youth is impossible. Too much has happened between 'then' and 'now'.

In order to see more clearly the longer-term span of change, instead of thinking of a simple contrast between 'then and now', however, we could usefully recall the way that the Uduk used to think of their changing settlement patterns. Hamlets were not regarded as permanent in the old days (i.e. the 1960s of my original 'ethnographic present'). They were built to last perhaps three to five years, after which the huts themselves would be disintegrating and the social make-up of the hamlet would be changing. The hamlet would then be rebuilt, not too far away, and this move would match the pattern of 'bush-fallow' cultivation. The old system was not exactly 'shifting' agriculture, as people did not move on for ever clearing fields in virgin forest, but they did leave their main sorghum fields after five years or so when the soil was exhausted, and clear new ones, returning to the old sites, now recovered, after a generation or so. There is a term for an old village site: *madu*. The old sites are remembered as places where old uncle so-and-so lived, or died, and the physical trajectory of this series of movements of one's home over decades is well remembered as the framework of past events and activities. The scale was always very local. But the concept of a *madu*, a former place where we lived and met up and buried people or danced, lends itself directly to the larger scale of recent displacements and reconstructions. The remembered stories of what happened when we were all in Langkwai, or Nor Deng, or Karmi, is something that I can share in too, having turned up in one or another such former home, places which 'exist' no longer in themselves. Terence Ranger once pointed out that my research, while never planned as 'history', has turned out to be rather like the sort of things that historians do: they too try to reconstruct the life that once existed in places that perhaps no longer 'exist'. The extra point is that most historians never have the chance to share anything of life in places that subsequently disappear, while the orientation of most anthropological fieldwork is very much to the 'present life' of places: anthropologists are understandably accused of neglecting the time-dimension of the localities and societies they describe, of perpetuating the 'ethnographic present'. Being able to present 'field data' collected over a long period of time, and in a succession of now empty—or totally transformed—places, gives me the opportunity to provide a different kind of study in this book, something I feel is a significant contribution to historical anthropology. A further point about the old Uduk idea of life as a passage through village sites which regularly become *madu*, or historical markers, is that you are conscious of your present living site as another temporary resting place, and you are easily able to anticipate further living places in the future.

As I complete this book in early 2007, though obviously there can be no 'completion' to a story of this kind which is not yet over, the current situation is full of uncertainties on either side of the central section of the Sudan–Ethiopian border. Expectations for the future are based on hope tinged with irony rather than hard reason, as perhaps in the song quoted above. I will give a brief outline of the scenario as it stands on each side, especially as it impinges on the interests of the Uduk refugees, and then conclude with some observations about the way that conditions of this kind in the 'real world' could have significant implications for the ideas and practices of anthropologists, more accustomed to tracing the principles of 'present order' in social life, rather than the patterns of displacement, movement, and anticipation.

THE COMPREHENSIVE PEACE AGREEMENT OF 2005, THE NEW BLUE NILE STATE, AND THE CONTINUING CRISIS IN DARFUR

The peace agreement which was signed in Kenya on 9 January 2005, after long years of argument, stalemate, and eventual negotiation between the Khartoum government and the Sudan People's Liberation Movement, is being slowly implemented. The agreement recognizes a division between the political authority of the newly formed Government of National Unity in Khartoum, and the Government of the Southern Sudan operating from Juba. Agreements between the north and the south over the sharing of power, wealth, and resources were reached, on the basis of a somewhat notional geographical boundary—that is, the line that separated the former three southern provinces from their northern counterparts at the time of independence in 1956. This line was partly the result of pure administrative convenience, and several adjustments had been made over the years of the Condominium period. It will be remembered that the Uduk and Koma areas had been allocated, along with the Meban settled area, to Upper Nile in 1938 as part of 'Southern Policy', but the Uduk and Koma (the Chali and Yabus *omodiyas*) were re-transferred back to the Blue Nile in 1953, just before independence (see Historical Introduction). During the decades of civil war from the mid-1980s on, the SPLA had considerable success in attracting recruits from the marginal regions between northern and southern provinces (as from further afield) and in the case of the Blue Nile were able to establish control over significant areas (see Part I). It took some tough bargaining on the part of the SPLM delegation at the peace talks, and intermittent pressure from the Kenyan chairman, General Lazarus Sum-beiywo, and the international observers, to convince Khartoum that special constitutional provisions were essential for the three main 'marginal areas' north of the old boundary line. In the case of the southern Blue Nile, the final agreement provided for a new Blue Nile State, with its capital at Damazin, and constitutional arrangements to secure balanced political representation in the state assembly, a rotation of governor and deputy governor posts as between the National Congress Party (dominant in Khartoum) and the SPLM. The first governor was an appointee of the former, and his successor in late 2007 is to be an SPLM appointee. The boundaries of the new regional state include not only those areas of the old Blue Nile occupied for many years by the SPLA, but also important agriculturally productive zones which were never captured along the Blue Nile river up and downstream of Damazin, and in the rain-fed plains to the west.

John Garang's death in July 2005, in a helicopter accident in the far south, was a shock to the whole country, and perhaps created particular apprehension in the marginal areas. As part of the funeral cortège, his body was briefly brought to rest at Kurmuk air strip, and also to Kauda in the Nuba Hills, as a token recognition of the role these areas had

Figure 24. Funeral respects paid to John Garang de Mabior, late leader of the SPLA, as his coffin touches down at Kurmuk on its long journey by air around the southern Sudan and transitional areas (Getty/Tony Karumba—AFP)

played in the long struggle (see Figure 24). As I complete this account, many of the former SPLA fighters local to the region are now absorbed into the Joint Integrated Forces based in Damazin under UN supervision (see Figure 25). The whole of the new state is to be brought under integrated administration, though in practice the old Kurmuk district is still patrolled and run by the SPLM. However, its representatives are playing a full role in the regional assembly in Damazin; and of the people whose stories run through this book, Sila Musa has come south from Khartoum while Martha Ahmed has moved back into the Sudan and a little north, both to take on the duties of assembly members (Figure 26).

There is a certain nervousness over the forthcoming referendum for the south, provided by the peace agreement and due in 2011, in which the people are to be asked whether they wish to remain part of a united country or separate permanently. For the Blue Nile State, and especially those in its own far south, there will be worrying implications, especially if the 1956 boundary between the old Blue Nile and Upper Nile Provinces is to become a new international frontier. There are other sources of anxiety too as provisions for religious and personal freedoms

Figure 25. Former SPLA soldiers from villages across the Chali area, now part of the Joint Integrated Forces in the Blue Nile State (Damazin; photo by Martin Ebet BuBa, February 2006)

Figure 26. Assembly members Dau Mohamed (from the Ingessana Hills) and Martha Nasim Ahmed (Damazin; photo by Akira Okazaki, February 2006)

come to be tested. The SIM (now 'Serving in Mission') is developing a number of educational projects, especially in the Kurmuk district, and these may find themselves in more sensitive circumstances than anyone would have wished.

The underlying reason for general concern about the implementation of the peace agreement is, however, one that concerns the whole nation. There is, as of early 2007, no indication that the war in Darfur, now embroiling parts of Chad, will be resolved in the near future. The Khartoum government, even in its modified post-2005 form, is not only maintaining its aggressive counter-insurgency projects against its own people in that region, but is treating international opinion with contempt and arrogantly expelling international envoys. One realizes with a distinctly surreal sense of shock that implementation of peace in the south requires the cooperation and goodwill of the same political leaders who are pursuing war in the west. Resources, too, which have been promised towards the rehabilitation of the new south are being drained away towards the desperate humanitarian needs in the west.

THE REPATRIATION FROM ETHIOPIA, THE NATIONAL, AND THE INTERNATIONAL DIASPORA

Following the peace agreement, plans were put in hand by the Sudan and Ethiopian governments and the UNHCR for the repatriation of international refugees from Ethiopia to the south and to the Blue Nile State. The first returnees from Bonga and Sherkole to the Kurmuk district arrived in April 2006 (Figure 27 shows the scene). Further movements were resumed after the rainy season, in November 2006. Bonga's population by this time was over 17,000, of whom about two-thirds had returned by mid-2007. There was anxiety at the start in Bonga when many people insisted that all should go together; there was fear about the vulnerability of small groups travelling en route, and also the safety of any minority which might have to wait an extra year. On the Sudanese side of the border, where so little has survived of previous settlements or infrastructure, official anxieties relate to the positioning of adequate relief supplies to tide the new arrivals over until they can secure their own harvests. Help is fortunately coming from those relatives and local

Figure 27. Return to Kurmuk of the first batch of refugees from Bonga (April 2006, photo Crowder—SIM Sudan. The banner reads (Uduk and English) 'The Lord will keep you from all harm he will watch over your life/The Lord will watch over your coming and going...'(Psalm 121, 7–8))

communities who have been settled in the cities and towns of the northern Sudan, some for a generation or more, but are themselves keen to return 'home', and assistance is available for other internally displaced persons. It goes without saying that this 'returnee' community, like so many others, especially in the transitional areas of both north and south, will have to find ways of accommodating the long years of separation, spatial, political, cultural, and even in some cases religious, which the civil war caused.

The UNHCR has always been committed to finding durable solutions to refugee questions all over the world: either safe return home, acceptable integration into the host country, or resettlement in a third country. The resettlement programme for Sudanese was very active in the 1990s, when the American economy in particular was strong. While there was a good deal of uncertainty at first in Bonga and Sherkole, a modest number of individuals and families did sign up. The first to leave for the USA went in 1998, and shortly after a few were resettled in

Figure 28. Grandchildren of the late Shadrach Peyko Dhunya with friends, Salt Lake City, Utah, August 2002

Australia and Canada. Most have gone to the United States, where several dozen families are scattered over almost as many different cities. Settling into America was and is a very fast-changing situation, and of course with the peace agreement, resettlement of this kind has come to an end. I have visited some of the younger members of families I once knew in the old homeland, now thousands of miles away (Figure 28 shows some of the grandchildren of my original research assistant, Shadrach Peyko Dhunya, late brother to Stephen Missa Dhunya, and their friends, growing up in Salt Lake City, Utah). There have, nevertheless, been visits back to Bonga (even before the peace agreement) and to Kurmuk and Damazin (since the agreement). Photographs, phone calls, and even emails are helping to keep the links alive, and relatives in Khartoum find they can get their news of goings-on in Bonga via the United States.

ANTHROPOLOGY AND A CHANGING CONCEPTION OF 'THE LOCAL'

No small language community, especially in the middle of a complex and historically turbulent continent, can be usefully represented in isolation. That is not how such communities think of themselves. I have always tried to write about the Uduk in a wider context and avoid essentializing their 'culture'. But I have also been struck by the resilience of vernacular ways of apprehending life, those practices, attitudes, values, and broad conceptions which seem to lie below the surface of a language, the level at which I have written of a cultural 'archive' characteristic not only of the Uduk and their fellow Koman language speakers but even of a wider region. Today's conditions of upheaval, dispersal, and extended exile have actually stimulated contacts and arguably the 'performance arts' of song and music. Comings and goings have created a widening spatial network of shared intimacy. The refugees in Bonga cannot be understood separately from others who have moved north instead of south, who have become part of mainstream Sudanese society instead of seeking refuge from it, in a remote place where distinctiveness can be expressed.

The field anthropologist used to have a relatively straightforward task in getting 'inside' a community, to 'see the native point of view' (though the image was no doubt always a simplification of the reality). But these days, and particularly in circumstances of displacement, it is more difficult to see things from the 'inside' point of view. One can travel more easily to visit the deprived and suffering communities of the world, and move right into whatever physical space they have. But if a visitor to a refugee camp has never seen how the people lived 'at home', or has no idea about where the rest of the people 'back home' have gone, how can he or she engage with the people's silent memories of these things, memories which still shape the world for them? Yet even with the opportunities for extended, if intermittent, contact that I have had, the 'inside' story of a changing situation can only be a set of privileged glimpses. The anthropologist can never attain the distance from events, and relative clarity of analysis, which the historian enjoys. Nor does one have the luxury of post hoc knowledge, of knowing how things turned out *after* the period under study. Being 'in the middle' of a succession of events with a still uncertain outcome makes it difficult to provide any clear analysis, for that would mean prediction. I do not know how things will turn out; whether the repatriation programme will be completed soon, whether the peace agreement will be fully implemented, whether a government will ever come to power in Khartoum whose legitimacy is widely accepted. I do not know what will be the consequences of a continuing high profile of the Uduk returnees as evangelical Christians in a province of the northern Sudan, whatever the safeguards on paper; nor can I guess at the consequences for the southern part of the Blue Nile State if the boundary with Upper Nile is to become an international frontier, as would be the case if the south should opt for secession in 2011.

Over the years since the big displacement of 1987, my role as anthropologist has rather changed. My second more or less orthodox ethnography on the Uduk, *The Listening Ebony*, came out about the same time (1988) and I have written very few of the usual style of anthropological articles on these people since then. I have however produced reports and papers with background information and recommendations for the aid agencies (discussed in Chapters 5, 7, and 8); and I have written a succession of essays and book chapters, as well as delivering a string of lectures and seminar papers, which attempt to develop some kind of anthropological argument out of the chaos. For example, an early effort demonstrated the role of civil war in reinforcing ethnic visibility of minorities like the Uduk, and another tried to contextualize the very different responses to my own similar consultancy recommendations when set in the confusion of the southern Sudan on the one hand and post-socialist Ethiopia on the other. Another piece aimed critically at the management-style discourse of the aid industry criticized their facile deployment of the concept of 'empowerment'—by putting people on committees in the refugee camps, people who had lost their homes, their land and livelihood, and most recently had their guns confiscated.[3] I then tried to use the classic anthropological model of 'rites of passage' in analysing what happens to whole communities, and to individuals, when they cross from one politically secure space to another—whether between warlords or across international frontiers where 'identity' has to be registered. I took up anthropological issues of culture, cognition, and memory in a piece about fear and violence, following the fairly severe skirmish in Karmi transit camp where I was present with a documentary team from Granada TV. To emphasize the continuity, and indeed resurgence, of cultural practice I published a piece on the circular dance, which had become popular again in the refugee camps, and explored the experiential power of this form of bodily expression comparatively in the world of oppressed communities, including the American slave plantations.[4] I have also published on the despair of border minorities who have nowhere to hide on modern frontiers, especially those that were for a time frontiers of the Cold War, as the Sudan–Ethiopian border was. And I have written on the rhetoric of competing radio stations in the very dramatic war years of the late 1980s. Let me mention finally a sort of autobiographical article in which I trace the unplanned way in which my own involvement with the Uduk, and the minorities of the border region generally, has punctuated most of my professional life, and the problems of writing about all this.[5]

---

[3] 'Civil war and ethnic visibility', in K. Fukui and J. Markakis (eds.), *Ethnicity and Conflict in the Horn of Africa* (London: James Currey, 1994); Uduk resettlement: dreams and realities', in Tim Allen (ed.), *In Search of Cool Ground* (London: James Currey, 1996); 'Empowering ambiguities', in Angela Cheater (ed.), *The Anthropology of Power* (London: Routledge, 1998).

[4] 'The names of fear: history, memory and the ethnography of feeling among Uduk refugees', *JRAI* NS 3 (1997); 'Reforming the circle', *Journal of African Cultural Studies*, 13/1 (2000), 140–52.

[5] 'No place to hide', in James et al. (eds.), *Remapping Ethiopia* (Oxford: James Currey, 2002); 'The multiple voices of Sudanese airspace', in R. Fardon and G. Furniss (eds.), *African Broadcast Cultures* (Oxford: James Currey, 2000); 'Beyond the first encounter', in P. Dresch, W. James, and D. Parkin (eds.), *Anthropologists in a Wider World* (Oxford: Berghahn, 2000).

My story is not only about the Uduk. It seems important to me now that I present events and responses, certainly in part through their eyes, which resonate with the experience of so many other local and relatively 'innocent' rural groups visited by the demands, the promises of freedom and glory, and the cruelties, of war games fuelled from afar. I have written about processes that have dissolved the old 'community' as it once was—the way that individuals became soldiers in the national army, or became guerrillas, in one or another faction of the SPLA. I have tried to write about the extraordinary way in which news circulates within the medium of a vernacular language like Uduk, across the lines of civil war or international frontiers; and the implications of this for the social life of a minority language-network. As this book shows, at most key points of the long series of crises which have defined the course of recent history in this region, there have been witnesses on more than one side of what was happening, and their experiences have later been shared with the wider network of vernacular speakers. Some of their accounts have found their way into my collection of tapes.

I believe I was one of the first anthropologists to use tape recordings of stories, interviews, songs, and conversation regularly in my 1960s field-work, subsequently adding a little cine filming and then video, and I have added to my collection of such material at every opportunity since. The tapes offer a sense of 'here and now' more direct than the written sources on which a scholar normally depends. Each spoken text or conversation—or song—has its own 'dramatic unity' of the moment, set within a locally shared sense of place and time, persons and powers. With each violent event, each displacement or radical political change, the shape of the 'present moment' behind such recorded conversations has changed. There are relatively few other sources bearing on the 'history' of what has been happening to the people whose fortunes I have tried to follow; written documentation does, by this time, include reports and evaluations by the humanitarian and aid agencies, and even some news reporting in the media, though as I have suggested the 'discourse' of these institutions can be a world apart. But even in the world of public language, I have found contemporary radio reports (from a variety of stations, some of which I recorded myself) more compelling than printed sources—and today the internet sites offer a further glimpse into the immediacy of the present, almost a moving present, as so little from that source lends itself to coherent history.

I have long assumed that the real point of doing historical anthropology is to engage, by *indirect techniques*, but in an experiental sense *as directly as possible*, with the reality of past moments, and what gives those moments their salience for real-world actors who are themselves 'creating history'.[6] Here I have found Collingwood's writings particularly inspiring. I have found his ideas about the relevance, for mainstream history, of what is going on in remote areas, along with his conception of the key role played by the scholar's imagination in re-enacting the realities of the past, very pertinent to the methods of anthropology. But how does one integrate the delicacy of such work, an imaginative engagement with the individual consciousness of specific and often local places and people, with the current mass violence of the global struggles that today are shaping even the most local experience? We have to remember that all these events have an 'inside' as well as an outside significance, to reiterate another of Collingwood's themes.

Collingwood's tracing of some remarkably long and flexible chains of cultural transmission, for example in the domains of folktales and of crafts, also offers much for the anthropologist.[7] He even drew attention to the way that cultural styles may persist through periods of imperial rule, specifically in the case of the ancient Britons as against the occupying Romans. New materials were used during the occupation, but older styles re-emerged afterwards. We might ponder here too the remarkable emotional attachment in Europe to the survival of the Celtic languages, not to mention Celtic music and dance—I have often imagined the 'Blue Nile Borderlands' as a sort of 'Celtic fringe' to the heartlands of Sudanese or Ethiopian civilization. As with France and the British Isles, something of an aura of 'ancient authenticity' attaches to the defining margins. The Roman period would have seen many displacements of people from peripheral British or Breton villages, including their co-option into trading networks and armies of all sorts. But there would have been convergences too, and reunions, and homecomings, no doubt all helping foster a climate in which the network of Celtic speakers and their variously shared cultural life in

---

[6] James, *The Ceremonial Animal: A New Portrait of Anthropology* (Oxford: Oxford University Press, 2003).

[7] R. G. Collingwood, *The Philosophy of Enchantment: Studies in Folktale, Cultural Criticism and Anthropology*, ed. David Boucher, Wendy James, and Philip Smallwood (Oxford: Clarendon Press, 2005).

an ironic way *might actually flourish*, along with a greater self-consciousness about their commonality in relation to Roman overrule as such.

In the Uduk case, and that of other minority language-communities on the fringes of the modern developments of the state in Sudan and Ethiopia, the span of history for which the scholar has any evidence is less than the four centuries of our Roman occupation. But we do have some evidence from the nineteenth century which already indicates that the local cultural repertoire of the minority peoples includes modes of conscious response to the invasion of outside powers. I have argued elsewhere that early nineteenth-century Gumuz in exile in old Abyssinia knew better what slavery is than can be found in whole bookshelves of scholarly analyses.[8] And I have argued here that there is a long history to the way the Uduk—like so many other peripheral groups—have been partially drawn into the Sudanese state, while also partially resisting its clutches. Recall that I was alerted to the particular significance of this by Dawud Lothdha in Bonga, who notified me with some pride of his ancestor Faragallah who had been a tax collector for the Turks. Memories of such service to the government, *hakuma*, is a part of the *internal* history of a 'frontier' society as I have presented this concept, and it is not incompatible with pride in one's original homeland and way of life.

African society and politics are commonly discussed in images of citizenry: the state and civil society; customary and national law, political parties, votes, democracy, and human rights. But what relevance can this framework have, in places such as state frontierlands, where there may be no effective rule of law to underpin any viable standing of the citizen? No state, and cetainly no branch of the international humanitarian industry, including the UNHCR whose mandate includes protection, has yet provided a lasting framework for personal security to the *'kwanim pa*. The notion that somewhere there ought to be good government, *hakuma*, is as strong, but in practice as elusive as ever. The future may well be a string of temporary living places, all to become *madu* in due course, abandoned sites but not forgotten by those who left in so many different directions; in fact well remembered as the trajectory of history itself, as places where once we lived, and celebrated life.

---

[8] James, 'Perceptions from an African slaving frontier', in L. Archer (ed.), *Slavery and Other Forms of Unfree Labour* (London: Routledge, 1988).

Appendix: Chronology of Events

Date	Sudan	Ethiopia	Kurmuk	Chali	Refugee camps	W. J. visits
1938				Chali transferred from Fung to Upper Nile; missionaries arrive		
1941			Bombed by Italians			
1943				Missionaries leave Missionaries return		
1953				Chali and Yabus transferred to BNP		
1955	Start of first civil war					
1956	Independence					
1964				Missionaries expelled		
1965–9	1969 Nimeiry comes to power					Intermittent field trips to Chali area over 4½ years
1972	AA Peace Agreement					
1974–5		Revolution, fall of Emperor and estab. of new socialist govt.				2 major field trips to W. Ethiopia

1983	Outbreak of second civil war	Support of SPLA	Astride Cold War frontier			Brief trip to Chali area
1985	Popular uprising; Nimeiry falls		SPLA appears in extreme southern BNP; Kurmuk town astride front line of civil war in Sudan			
1986	Sadiq regime creates pro-govt. militias			SPLA take Yabus; intended attack on Chali foiled	Most of Uduk flee to Tsore, near Assosa	
1987	General advances of SPLA		Taken by SPLA, and left	Sacked by govt. then taken by SPLA		
1989	Beshir coup pre-empts peace process	Armed resistance spreads	Nov., taken by SPLA again	Nov., taken by SPLA again and remainder flee to Assosa	Assosa receives further people	Visits to AA and Kenya
Jan. 1990		Assosa falls	Kurmuk abandoned by SPLA, returned to SG garrison	Chali returned to SG garrison	Refugees flee Assosa back to Sudan, have to trek far south	
June–July 1990					Surviving refugees arrive Itang	
May–June 1991		Govt. falls			Refugees obliged to cross border and camp in Nor Deng	
Mid–late 1991	Split in SPLA and internecine fighting; OLS attempts to extend relief	New Ethiopian govt. installed; more friendly to Khartoum		Some returnees arrive from Nasir		Two field trips to Nasir and Nor Deng for OLS

Date	Sudan	Ethiopia	Kurmuk	Chali	Refugee camps	W. J. visits
Early 1992					Cross river to 'New Chali'	
May–June 1992	Govt. of Sudan major offensive southwards; Blue Nile refugees permitted to leave Nasir for Kigille			More returnees, from Kigille etc.; in course of next few years some also return from Damazin, Khartoum	Allowed to move to places nearer border, Maiwut and Kigille; rains fail. Split in core community: Gindi faction leads dash back to Itang	
July 1992					Armed confrontation in Itang, refugees caught in cross-fire	
Aug. 1992					Second wave crosses border	
Sept. 1992						Visit to Karmi for UNHCR
Jan. 1993					Battle of Karmi	Visit to Karmi with Dis. World
Feb. 1993					Refugees transferred to Bonga	
1994						Visit to Bonga

Year					
1995	Consolidation of SPLA and renewed relationship with Ethiopia				for UNHCR Visit to Kenya
1996–7	Taken again by SPLA	Taken again by SPLA	Taken again by SPLA, and returnees have to flee	New camp at Sherkole	
1998				First applicants taken for resettlement USA	
2000					Visit to Bonga for ZOA
2002					Visit resettled people in USA Visit to Kenya, in context of peace talks
2003	Civil war erupts in Darfur				
2004					Visit to Kenya
2005	Comprehensive Peace Agreement signed with SPLA, 9 Jan. 2005	Becomes part of new Blue Nile State, part of northern Sudan	Becomes southernmost extension of Blue Nile State		Visit to Kenya for Rift Valley Inst.
2006	First official returnees arrive early April	First official returnees arrive early April	First official returnees arrive early April	First convoy of returnees leaves Bonga, 31 March 2006.	Second visit to resettled people in USA
2007	War continues in Dafur			Repatriation continues	

Bibiliography

JRAI   *Journal of the Royal Anthropological Institute*
SIR   *Sudan Intelligence Reports*
SNR   *Sudan Notes and Records*

ARCHIVES, OFFICIAL DOCUMENTS

Bodleian Library, Oxford, BBC Summary of World Broadcasts, Middle East Series.

'The Comprehensive Peace Agreement between the Government of the Republic of the Sudan and the Sudan People's Liberation Movement/Sudan People's Liberation Army' [CPA], Nairobi, 9 January 2005.

Nickerson, G. S., 'Dar Fung and Burun country', National Records Office (NRO), Khartoum, Dakhlia I, 112/17/102. An abbreviated version was printed as 'Report on Dar Fung', *SIR* 145, August 1906. Appendix B.

'Protocol between the Government of Sudan (GOS) and the Sudan People's Liberation Movement (SPLM) on the resolution of conflict in Southern Kordofan/Nuba Mountains and Blue Nile States', Naivasha, 26 May 2004 (incorporated in the CPA).

Roseires archives, Sudan, 'Hanbook [*sic*]: Southern Fung District, Blue Nile Province, August 1959'.

Sudan Intelligence Reports (*SIR*), NRO, Intel 6.

BOOKS, ARTICLES

Abbink, Jon G., 'Paradoxes of power and culture in an old periphery—Surma, 1974–98', in Wendy James, Donald Donham, Eisei Kurimoto, and Alessandro Triulzi (eds.), *Remapping Ethiopia: Socialism and After* (Oxford: James Currey, 2002), 155–72.

Abbute, Wolde-Selassie, *Gumuz and Highland Resettlers: Differing Strategies of Livelihood and Ethnic Relations in Metekel, Northwestern Ethiopia* (Münster: Lit Verlag, 2004).

Africa Confidential, 39/17 (28 Aug. 1998), 2.

African Rights, *Facing Genocide: The Nuba of Sudan* (London, July 1995).

—— *Food and Power in Sudan: A Critique of Humanitarianism* (London: African Rights, 1997).

Allen, Tim, *Trial Justice: The International Criminal Court and the Lord's Resistance Army* (London: Zed Books, 2006).

Baumann, Gerd, *National Integration and Local Integrity: The Miri of the Nuba Mountains in the Sudan* (Oxford: Clarendon Press, 1987).

Bender, M. Lionel, *The Ethiopian Nilo-Saharans* (Addis Ababa: Artistic Press, 1975).

Boddy, Janice, *Wombs and Alien Spirits: Women, Men and the* Zar *Cult in Northern Sudan* (Madison: Wisconsin University Press, 1989).

Bruce, James, *Travels to Discover the Source of the Nile, in the Years 1768–1773*, vol. iv (Edinburgh, 1790).

Clapham, Christopher, 'Controlling space in Ethiopia', in Wendy James, Donald Donham, Eisei Kurimoto, and Alessandro Triulzi (eds.), *Remapping Ethiopia: Socialism and After* (Oxford: James Currey, 2002), 9–30.

Collingwood, R. G., *The Philosophy of Enchantment: Studies in Folktale, Cultural Criticism and Anthropology*, ed. David Boucher, Wendy James, and Philip Smallwood (Oxford: Clarendon Press, 2005).

—— *The Principles of History: And Other Writings in Philosophy of History*, ed. W. H. Dray and W. J. van der Dussen (Oxford: Clarendon Press, 1999).

Comrie, Aimée, 'The politics of food aid in the Sudan–Ethiopian borderlands', in Andrzej Bolesta (ed.), *International Development and Assistance: Where Politics Meets Economy* (Warsaw: Leon Koźmiński Academy of Entrepreneurship and Management, 2004), 161–72.

De Waal, Alex, *Famine Crimes: Politics and the Disaster Relief Industry in Africa* (Oxford: James Currey, 1997).

—— and Flint, Julie, *Darfur: A Short History of a Long War* (London: Zed Books, 2005).

Donham, Donald L., *Marxist Modern: An Ethnographic History of the Ethiopian Revolution* (Berkeley and Los Angeles: University of California Press, 1999).

Duffield, Mark, *Sudan at the Crossroads: From Emergency Preparedness to Social Security* (Falmer: Institute of Development Studies, University of Sussex, May 1990).

—— *Global Governance and the New Wars: The Merging of Development and Security* (London: Zed Books, 2001).

Dunbar, Robin, Knight, Chris, and Power, Camilla (eds.), *The Evolution of Culture* (Edinburgh: Edinburgh University Press, 1999).

Ehret, Christopher, *A Historical-Comparative Reconstruction of Nilo-Saharan* (Cologne: Rüdiger Köppe Verlag, 2001).

Evans-Pritchard, Edward E., 'Ethnological observations in Dar Fung', *SNR* 15/1 (1932), 1–61.

Ferguson, R. Brian, and Whitehead, Neil L. (eds.), *War in the Tribal Zone: Expanding States and Indigenous Warfare*, 2nd edn. (Santa Fe, N. Mex.: School of American Research, 2000).

Fernandez, Victor M., 'Four thousand years in the Blue Nile: paths to inequality and ways of resistance', *Complutum*, 14 (2003), 409–25.

Feyissa, Dereje, 'The experience of Gambella regional state', in David Turton (ed.), *Ethnic Federalism: The Ethiopian Experience in Comparative Perspective* (Oxford: James Currey, 2006), 208–30.

Forsberg, Malcolm, *Land beyond the Nile* (New York: Harper, 1958).

Gwynn, C. W., 'Surveys on the proposed Sudan–Abyssinian frontier', *Geographical Journal*, 18/6 (1901), 562–73.

Hammond, Jenny, 'Garrison towns and the control of space in revolutionary Tigray', in Wendy James, Donald Donham, Eisei Kurimoto, and Alessandro Triulzi (eds.), *Remapping Ethiopia: Socialism and After* (Oxford: James Currey, 2002), 90–115.

—— *Fire from the Ashes: A Chronicle of the Revolution in Tigray, Ethiopia, 1975*–1991 (Lawrenceville, NJ: Red Sea Press, 1999).

Hammond, Laura C., *This Place will become Home: Refugee Repatriation to Ethiopia* (Ithaca, NY: Cornell, 2004).

Hannan, Lucy, 'Sudanese tribe hounded out', *The Guardian* (3 Aug. 1992), 7.

Hill, Richard (ed.), *On the Frontiers of Islam: The Sudan under Turco-Egyptian Rule 1822–1845* (Oxford: Clarendon Press, 1970).

Hutchinson, Sharon, *Nuer Dilemmas: Coping with Money, War and the State* (Berkeley and Los Angeles: University of California Press, 1996).

James, Wendy, 'The Funj mystique: approaches to a problem of Sudan history', in R. K. Jain (ed.), *Text and Context: The Social Anthropology of Tradition*, ASA Essays 2 (Philadelphia: ISHI, 1977), 95–133.

—— *'Kwanim Pa: The Making of the Uduk People. An Ethnographic Study of Survival in the Sudan-Ethiopian Borderlands* (Oxford: Clarendon Press, 1979).

—— 'Lifelines: exchange marriage among the Gumuz', in D. L. Donham and Wendy James (eds.), *The Southern Marches of Imperial Ethiopia: Essays in Social Anthropology and History* (Cambridge: Cambridge University Press, 1986; reissued in paperback with new preface, Oxford: James Currey, 2002).

—— *The Listening Ebony: Moral Knowledge, Religion and Power among the Uduk of Sudan* (Oxford: Clarendon Press, 1988; reissued with new preface 1999).

—— 'Uduk faith in a five-note scale: mission music and the spread of the Gospel', in W. James and D. H. Johnson (eds.), *Vernacular Christianity: Essays in the Social Anthropology of Religion Presented to Godfrey Lienhardt* (Oxford: JASO, 1988), 131–45.

—— 'Perceptions from an African slaving frontier', in Léonie Archer (ed.), *Slavery and Other Forms of Unfree Labour* (London: Routledge, 1988), 130–41.

—— 'Antelope as self-image among the Uduk', in Roy Willis (ed.), *Signifying Animals: Human Meaning in the Natural World* (London: Allen & Unwin, 1990), 196–203.

James, Wendy, 'Civil war and ethnic visibility: the Uduk on the Sudan–Ethiopia border', in K. Fukui and J. Markakis (eds.), *Ethnicity and Conflict in the Horn of Africa* (London: James Currey, 1994), 140–64.

—— 'Uduk resettlement: dreams and realities', in Tim Allen (ed.), *In Search of Cool Ground: War, Flight and Homecoming in Northeast Africa* (London: James Currey, 1996), 182–202.

—— 'The names of fear: history, memory and the ethnography of feeling among Uduk refugees', *JRAI* NS 3 (1997), 115–31.

—— 'Empowering ambiguities', in Angela Cheater (ed.), *The Anthropology of Power: Empowerment and Disempowerment in Changing Structures*, ASA Monographs 36 (London: Routledge, 1998), 13–27.

—— 'The multiple voices of Sudanese airspace', in Richard Fardon and Graham Furniss (eds.), *African Broadcast Cultures* (Oxford: James Currey, 2000), 198–215.

—— 'Reforming the circle: fragments of the social history of a vernacular African dance form', *Journal of African Cultural Studies* (Special Issue: Festschrift for T. O. Ranger, ed. J. Lonsdale), 13/1 (2000), 140–52.

—— 'Beyond the first encounter: transformations of "the field" in North East Africa', in P. Dresch, W. James, and D. Parkin (eds.), *Anthropologists in a Wider World: Essays on Field Research* (Oxford: Berghahn, 2000), 69–90.

—— 'No place to hide: flag-waving on the western Frontier', in James et al. (eds.), *Remapping Ethiopia*, 259–75.

—— *The Ceremonial Animal: A New Portrait of Anthropology* (Oxford: Oxford University Press, 2003).

—— Donham, Donald, Kurimoto, Eisei, and Triulzi, Alessandro (eds.), *Remapping Ethiopia: Socialism and After* (Oxford: James Currey, 2002).

—— and Mills, David (eds.), *The Qualities of Time: Anthropological Approaches* (Oxford: Berg, 2005).

Jedrej, M. Charles, *Ingessana: The Religious Institutions of a People of the Sudan–Ethiopian Borderland* (Leiden: Brill, 1995).

—— 'The Southern Funj of the Sudan as a frontier society, 1820–1980', *Comparative Studies in Society and History*, 46 (2004), 709–29.

—— and Shaw, Rosalind (eds.), *Dreaming, Religion and Society in Africa* (Leiden: Brill, 1992).

Johnson, Douglas H., 'Sudanese military slavery from the eighteenth to the twentieth century', in L. Archer (ed.), *Slavery and Other Forms of Unfree Labour* (London: Routledge, 1988), 142–56.

—— 'The structure of a legacy: military slavery in northeast Africa', in 'Ethnohistory and Africa', ed. E. Steinhart, *Ethnohistory*, special number, 36/1 (1989), 72–88.

Johnson, Douglas H., 'Recruitment and entrapment in private slave armies: the structure of the *zara'ib* in the Southern Sudan', in Elizabeth Savage (ed.), *The Human Commodity: Perspectives on the Trans-Saharan Slave Trade* (London: Frank Cass, 1992), 162–73.

—— *Nuer Prophets: A History of Prophecy from the Upper Nile in the Nineteenth and Twentieth Centuries* (Oxford: Clarendon Press, 1994).

—— 'Increasing the trauma of return: an assessment of the UN's emergency response to the evacuation of the Sudanese refugee camps in Ethiopia, 1991', in Tim Allen (ed.), *In Search of Cool Ground: Displacement and Homecoming in Northeast Africa* (London: James Currey, 1996), 171–81.

—— (ed.), 'Introduction', *Sudan, 1942–1950, British Documents on the End of Empire*, series B, vol. v, part 1 (London: Stationery Office, 1998).

—— 'On the Nilotic frontier: imperial Ethiopia in the southern Sudan, 1898–1936', in D. L. Donham and W. James (eds.), *The Southern Marches of Imperial Ethiopia: Essays in Social Anthropology and History* (1986; paperback edn. Oxford: James Currey, 2002), 219–45.

—— *The Root Causes of Sudan's Civil Wars*, updated edn. (Oxford: James Currey, 2006).

Jok, Jok Madut, *War and Slavery in Sudan* (Philadelphia: University of Pennsylvania Press, 2001).

Keen, David, *The Benefits of Famine: A Political Economy of Famine and Relief in South-Western Sudan, 1983–1989* (Princeton: Princeton University Press, 1994).

—— *Conflict and Collusion in Sierra Leone* (Oxford: James Currey, 2005).

Kurimoto, Eisei, 'Fear and anger: female versus male narratives among the Anywaa', in Wendy James, Donald Donham, Eisei Kurimoto, and Alessandro Triulzi (eds.), *Remapping Ethiopia: Socialism and After* (Oxford: James Currey, 2002), 219–38.

Leopold, Mark, *Inside West Nile: Violence, History and Representation on an African Frontier* (Oxford: James Currey, 2005).

Mahmud, Ushari Ahmad, and Baldo, Suleyman Ali B., *Al Diein Massacre: Slavery in the Sudan* (Khartoum: n.p., 1987).

Makris, G. P., *Changing Masters: Spirit Possession and Identity Construction among Slave Descendants and Other Subordinates in the Sudan* (Evanston, Ill.: Northwestern University Press, 2000).

Malwal, Bona, 'In Kurmuk the thoughts are all about defeating the NIF regime', *Sudan Democratic Gazette*, 8/88 (Sept. 1997), 8–9.

Manger, Leif, 'The Nuba Mountains: battlegrounds of identities, cultural traditions and territories', in Maj-Britt Johannsen and Niels Kastfelt (eds.), *Sudanese Society in the Context of Civil War* (Copenhagen: North/South Priority Research Area, University of Copenhagen, 2001), 49–90.

Manger, Leif, *From the Mountains to the Plains: The Integration of Lafofa Nuba into Sudanese Society* (Uppsala: Scandinavian Institute of African Studies, 1994).

Nautrup, Birthe L., 'Sudan in the context of civil war: marginalization and Islamization among the Hadendowa', in Maj-Britt Johannsen and Niels Kastfelt (eds.), *Sudanese Society in the Context of Civil War* (Copenhagen: North/South Priority Research Area, University of Copenhagen, 2001), 91–112.

Okazaki, Akira, 'The making and unmaking of consciousness: Nuba and Gamk strategies for survival in a Sudanese borderland', in Richard Werbner (ed.), *Postcolonial Subjectivities* (London: Zed Books, 2002), ch. 3.

Pirrie, A. M., 'Report on the Burun country', *SIR* 155 (June 1907), appendix A, 4–6.

Prunier, Gérard, *Darfur: The Ambiguous Genocide* (London: Hurst, 2005).

Richards, Paul (ed.), *No Peace, No War: An Anthropology of Contemporary Armed Conflicts* (Oxford: James Currey, 2005).

Sanderson, Lilian Passmore, and Sanderson, Neville, *Education, Religion and Politics in Southern Sudan 1899–1964* (London: Ithaca Press, 1981).

Schuver, Juan Maria, *Juan Maria Schuver's Travels in North East Africa, 1880–83*, ed. W. James, G. Baumann, and D. H. Johnson (London: The Hakluyt Society, 1996).

Scott-Villiers, Alastair and Patta, and Dodge, C. P., 'Repatriation of Sudanese refugees from Ethiopia: a case study in manipulation of civilians during civil conflict', *Refuge*, 14/1 (1994), 19–25.

Scroggins, Deborah, *Emma's War: Love, Betrayal and Death in the Sudan* (London: Harper Collins, 2002).

Sudan Democratic Gazette, 11/121 (July 2000), 7.

Thelwall, Robin (ed.), *Aspects of Language in the Sudan* (Coleraine: New University of Ulster, 1978).

Trémaux, Pierre, *Voyage au Soudan oriental et dans l'Afrique septentrionale, atlas de vues pittoresques* (Paris, 1852–8).

Triulzi, Alessandro, 'Nekemte and Addis Abeba: dilemmas of provincial rule', in D. L. Donham and W. James (eds.), *The Southern Marches of Imperial Ethiopia: Essays in Social Anthropology and History*, paperback edn. (Oxford: James Currey, 2002), 51–68.

Turton, David, 'Migrants and refugees: a Mursi case study', in Tim Allen (ed.), *In Search of Cool Ground: Displacement and Homecoming in Northeast Africa* (London: James Currey, 1996), 96–110.

—— (ed.), *Ethnic Federalism: The Ethiopian Experience in Comparative Perspective* (Oxford: James Currey, 2006).

Willis, Justin, ' "The Nyamang are hard to touch": mission evangelism and tradition in the Nuba Mountains, Sudan, 1933–1952', *Journal of Religion in Africa*, 33 (2003), 32–62.

Willis, Justin, 'Violence, authority, and the state in the Nuba Mountains of Condominium Sudan', *Historical Journal*, 46 (2003), 89–114.

Wilson, Thomas M., and Donnan, Hastings (eds.), *Border Identities: Nation and State at International Frontiers* (Cambridge: Cambridge University Press, 1998).

Young, John, 'Along Ethiopia's western frontier: Gambella and Benishangul in transition', *Journal of Modern African Studies*, 37/2 (1999), 321–46.

THESES

De Blois, Jody. 'The promised land: refugee experiences of the Uduk in Ethiopia', Thesis Report for Cultural Anthropology, University of Utrecht, Eijsenga, April 2001.

Di Pasquale, Sarah, 'A study of the Uduk church in Bonga, Ethiopia', SIM Independent Study Report, 1995.

Falge, Christiane, 'The global Nuer: modes of transnational livelihoods', doctoral dissertation, Max Planck Institute for Social Anthropology, Halle, 2006.

Hammond, Jenny, 'The social construction of revolutionary change in northern Ethiopia, 1975–97', D.Phil. thesis, Oxford, 2001.

Hastrup, Anders, 'Displacing Darfur: purity and danger in Sudan's latest civil war', MA dissertation, Department of Cross-Cultural and Regional Studies, Modern Middle Eastern Studies, University of Copenhagen, 2006.

Lussier, Dominique C. P., 'A study of moral inequality among the Kunama speaking people of Western Eritrea', D.Phil. thesis, Oxford, 2000.

Mekonnen, Berihun Mebratie, 'The past in the present: the dynamics of identity and otherness among the Gumuz of Ethiopia', doctoral thesis, Norwegian University of Science and Technology, 2004.

Mkutu, Kennedy, 'Pastoralist conflict, governance and small arms in North Rift, north east Africa', doctoral thesis, Department of Peace Studies, University of Bradford, 2004.

Theis, Joachim, 'Zerstorung und Wiederherstellung eines Volkes: Geschichte und Ethnographie des Koma (Gokwom) im Sudan-Äthiopischen Grenzgebeit', doctoral dissertation, Free University of Berlin, 1990.

Van Uffelen, Jan Gerrit, 'Return after flight: exploring the decision making process of Sudanese war-displaced people by employing an extended version of the theory of reasoned action', Ph.D. thesis, Wageningen University, 2006.

Vermeulen, Ellen, 'Beyond emergency aid: possibilities of partial self-sufficiency among the Sudanese refugees in western Ethiopia', MA thesis in Development Studies, Catholic University of Nijmegen, 1998.

REPORTS

Ahmed, Abd al-Ghaffar M., 'Visiting Kurmuk: crossing to the SPLA/M controlled area, March 15–16, 2006' (May 2006).

Hutchinson, Sharon, 'Potential development projects for the Sobat valley region: a set of proposals prepared for Save the Children Fund (UK)', SCF/UK, London, 1992.

James, Wendy, 'Background report and guidelines for future planning: Nor Deng centre for Sudanese returnees, Nasir' (Nairobi, UN, WFP/Operation Lifeline Sudan, Southern Sector, Aug. 1991).

—— 'Vulnerable groups in the Nasir region: update on Nor Deng (Blue Nile returnees) and resettlement proposal' (Nairobi, WFP/OLS Southern Sector, 15 Oct. 1991).

—— 'Uduk asylum seekers in Gambela, 1992: community report and options for resettlement' (Addis Ababa, UNHCR, 31 October 1992).

—— 'The Bonga scheme: progress to 1994 and outlook for 1995. A report for UNHCR on assistance to Sudanese (Uduk) refugees in western Ethiopia' (Addis Ababa, UNHCR, 25 Jan. 1995).

—— 'Community services for Sudanese refugees in western Ethiopia: working proposals for Bonga and Sherkole' (Addis Ababa, ZOA Refugee Care, the Netherlands, 2000).

Lobo, Marie, 'Community services mission to the camps in western Ethiopia' (16–30 July 2000, Draft Executive Summary, UNHCR Regional Services Centre, Nairobi o/m in Ethiopia).

Multi-Donor Technical Mission, 'Report on mission to western region Sudanese refugee camps', (Addis Ababa: Feb. 1991).

Spriggs, Derek (SIM Project Coordinator) and Awet, John (SIC Project Co-ordinator), 'SIC Resettlement Programme 1993', Khartoum.

UNHCR, 'Community Services in UNHCR: an Introduction', Geneva, 1996.

UNICEF, 'The return to southern Sudan of the Sudanese refugees from Itang camp, Gambela, Ethiopia' (Nairobi, UNICEF/Operation Lifeline Sudan, 31 Aug. 1991).

ZOA Refugee Care, 'Beekeeping', Vocational Skills Programme, 1999, Translated into Uduk as 'Kup gwo mmothipa dham ki bore/', 2000.

FILMS

Famine Fatigue: ou le pouvoir de l'image, a co-production of La Sept/Point du Jour in association with Temps Présent (TSR), 1991. Directed by Patrice Barrat.

Orphans of Passage, Disappearing World: War. Granada TV, directed by Bruce MacDonald, 1993.

RECOMMENDED WEBSITES

Gurtong Peace Trust: **www.gurtong.org**
The Sudan Open Archive: **www.sudanarchive.net**
Voices from the Blue Nile: **www.voicesfromthebluenile.org**

Index